OBJECTS AND OTHER SUBJECTS

Studies in Natural Language and Linguistic Theory

VOLUME 52

The titles published in this series are listed at the end of this volume.

OBJECTS AND OTHER SUBJECTS

Grammatical Functions,
Functional Categories and Configurationality

edited by

WILLIAM D. DAVIES

University of Iowa, Iowa City

and

STANLEY DUBINSKY

University of South Carolina, Columbia

KLUWER ACADEMIC PUBLISHERS

DORDRECHT / BOSTON / LONDON

A C.I.P. Catalogue record for this book is available from the Library of Congress.

ISBN 1-4020-0064-2

Published by Kluwer Academic Publishers,
P.O. Box 17, 3300 AA Dordrecht, The Netherlands.

Sold and distributed in North, Central and South America
by Kluwer Academic Publishers,
101 Philip Drive, Norwell, MA 02061, U.S.A.

In all other countries, sold and distributed
by Kluwer Academic Publishers,
P.O. Box 322, 3300 AH Dordrecht, The Netherlands.

Printed on acid-free paper

Printed in the Netherlands.

DEDICATION

For David Perlmutter and Paul Postal

While they might not agree with many of the answers in this volume, were it not for their groundbreaking work, many of the questions might never have been asked.

TABLE OF CONTENTS

LIST OF CONTRIBUTORS ix

FORWORD xi

ACKNOWLEDGEMENTS xv

PART I: OVERVIEW

    1. WILLIAM D. DAVIES AND STANLEY DUBINSKY / Remarks on
       Grammatical Functions in Transformational Syntax 1

    2. MARK C. BAKER / Phrase Structure as a Representation of "Primitive"
       Grammatical Relations 21

    3. FREDERICK J. NEWMEYER / Grammatical Functions, Thematic
       Roles, and Phrase Structure: Their Underlying Disunity 53

    4. ALEX ALSINA / Is Case Another Name for Grammatical Function?
       Evidence from Object Asymmetries 77

PART II: OBJECTS

    5. HOWARD LASNIK / Subjects, Objects, and the EPP 103

    6. LISA deMENA TRAVIS / Derived Objects in Malagasy 123

PART III: SUBJECTS

    7. JAMES McCLOSKEY / The Distribution of Subject Properties in
       Irish 157

    8. GRANT GOODALL / The EPP in Spanish 193

    9. DIANE MASSAM / On Predication and the Status of Subjects in
       Niuean 225

    10. WILLIAM D. DAVIES AND STANLEY DUBINSKY / Functional
        Architecture and the Distribution of Subject Properties 247

REFERENCES 281

AUTHOR INDEX 297

SUBJECT INDEX 301

LIST OF CONTRIBUTORS

Alex Alsina
Department de Traducció i Filologia
Universitat Pompeu Fabra
La Rambla, 30-32
08002 Barcelona, SPAIN
alex.alsina@trad.upf.es

Mark Baker
Linguistics Department
Rutgers University
18 Seminary Place
New Brunswick NJ 08901, USA
mabaker@ruccs.rutgers.edu

William D. Davies
Linguistics Department
University of Iowa
Iowa City, IA 52242, USA
william-davies@uiowa.edu

Stanley Dubinsky
Linguistics Program
University of South Carolina
Columbia, SC 29208, USA
dubinsky@sc.edu

Grant Goodall
Department of Languages and Linguistics
The University of Texas at El Paso
500 W. University Avenue
El Paso, TX 79968, USA
ggoodall@utep.edu

Howard Lasnik
Department of Linguistics
University of Connecticut
341 Mansfield Road
Storrs, CT 06269, USA
lasnik@sp.uconn.edu

Diane Massam
Department of Linguistics
University of Toronto
130 St. George Street
Toronto, ON, M5S 3H1, CANADA
dmassam@chass.utoronto.ca

Jim McCloskey
Department of Linguistics
University of California, Santa Cruz
Santa Cruz, CA 95064, USA
mcclosk@ling.ucsc.edu

Frederick J. Newmeyer
Department of Linguistics
University of Washington
Seattle, WA 98195, USA
fjn@u.washington.edu

Lisa deMena Travis
Department of Linguistics
McGill University
1085 Dr. Penfield Avenue
Montreal, QC H3A 1A7, CANADA
ltravi@po-box.mcgill.ca

FORWORD

The initial idea for this volume began with discussions with Brian Joseph and Geoffrey Huck about a book that would explore the place of grammatical relations/functions in Principles and Parameters Theory and Minimalism. It was clear to both of them that (i) grammatical functions played a much more essential role in these theories than was generally acknowledged, and (ii) those new to the discipline very often had no appreciation for the origins and significance of such notions.

We briefly considered the possibility of writing a monograph surveying the recent developments in this area of syntactic theory, but we realized that there was a rich body of relevant work being done on this topic. It seemed that many working in P&P and Minimalism were unaware of the very significant work being pursued in this area, and of its relationship to earlier work and work in other paradigms. Thus was born the idea for a workshop that would bring together leading scholars in syntax to explore the place of grammatical functions (GFs) in transformational theories of syntax. This idea evolved into a three day workshop (supported by an NSF grant and by the USC College of Liberal Arts), held in July 1999 at the LSA Linguistic Institute in Urbana-Champaign (UI-UC). The workshop included presentations and commentary from: Alex Alsina (Universitat Pompeu Fabra, Barcelona), Mark Baker (Rutgers University), Richard Campbell (Oakland U / Microsoft Research), William Davies (University of Iowa), Stanley Dubinsky (University of South Carolina), Samuel Epstein (University of Michigan), Patrick Farrell (UC, Davis), Grant Goodall (University of Texas, El Paso), Howard Lasnik (Connecticut University), James McCloskey (University of California, Santa Cruz), Frederick Newmeyer (University of Washington), Norvin Richards (MIT), Daniel Seely (Eastern Michigan University), and Lisa Travis (McGill University).

The workshop took place 25 years after Perlmutter and Postal gave their lectures on Relational Grammar at the LSA Summer Institute. Their course on RG remains one of the most widely attended Institute courses on record and, perhaps, given the 15-20 years of vigorous research activity that it spawned, one of the more influential Institute courses ever given. Taking as its starting point the view that grammatical functions are primitive notions of the theory, work done in RG was a startling generative departure from the Standard Theory view, and attempted to explain a wide variety of clause-level phenomena in a wide variety of languages. In the time since that course, the role of grammatical functions has undergone some shifts in transformational syntax. These shifts have been in part in reaction to some of the discoveries in relationally-based theories and in part due to theory-internal developments. The 25th anniversary of the Amherst lectures seemed like an appropriate time to examine the current status of grammatical functions in transformational syntax.

Some 100 institute participants attended the public presentations and discussion of the 1999 workshop, and these included scholars representing an exceptionally broad range of theoretical perspectives. One of the NSF reviewers suggested that Davies and Dubinsky might learn a lot about current theoretical perspectives on grammatical functions, and indeed we did (as most likely did many others in attendance). Some of the questions that were addressed in the workshop presentations included:

- What are the number and status of subject positions?
- How many of these positions might be active in any one language?
- Can any properties of these positions be considered universal?
- What is the status and content of the EPP? Is the EPP active in all languages? Is the EPP manifested in the same way in all languages in which it is active? Should the EPP be abandoned altogether?
- What is the status of objects? Are subjects and objects to be distinguished or are they more similar than has been suspected? Do all languages make the use of the full range of objects and object positions?
- In what ways are the abstract configurational representations of the transformational theory representations of grammatical functions?
- All in all what is the status of grammatical functions in current transformational theory and what are the acceptable levels of variation from language to language that allow these notions to be viable and interesting before they should be abandoned simply as epiphenomenal mnemonic terms?

During and following the workshop, it became clear that a number of the presentations had converged in very interesting ways, and merited being brought together in print. After receiving encouragement for this venture from several quarters and enlisting the enthusiastic participation of several key contributors, we set about the task of pulling this volume together.

We are proud of the product of the efforts of the workshop participants and contributors, a volume that we hope will be of value both in assessing recent progress in the field, and in framing important questions for future research. As this book neared completion, we found that it likely has a wider audience than we had originally planned. While we had originally conceived of this volume as a collection of papers on a special topic, it turns out that the book has potential as a reader for an advanced course in syntax (or a syntax seminar). In fact, both reviewers made just this point, suggesting that its value as a class text would be enhanced with the inclusion of additional background information about RG, LFG, and HPSG, setting the stage for the papers included here and providing some theory comparison. However, rather than changing the focus of the book and delaying production significantly, we have opted to describe how the book might be used in a course, based on a successful course in which we used the papers in this volume. The course, as we taught it, involved a comparison of RG and P&P theory, however it would have been quite plausible to frame the course using LFG or HPSG as a theoretical counterpoint to the P&P model. The syllabus of the course was structured as follows:

(1) *A review of VP-shells and to Agr projections.* This unit focused on chapters 9 and 10 of Radford's (1997) text.
   a. In covering the material on VP-shells (chapter 9), reference was made to Sportiche's (1988) article on the VP-internal subject hypothesis, to Larson's (1988) article on VP-shells, and to the ensuing debate (in Jackendoff 1990 and Larson 1990).

b. In covering the material on Agr Projections (chapter 10), we also examined Pollack's (1989) article in *Linguistic Inquiry* and Lasnik and Saito's (1991) *CLS* paper.

(2) *A survey of Relational Grammar theory.* This part of the course used Blake's (1990) handbook as a guide, and included chapters from the Studies in Relational Grammar volumes and other key articles.

    a. In introducing the theory, we examined Perlmutter and Postal's (1983b) chapter on proposed laws of basic clause structure, as well as Keenan and Comrie's (1977) article on the noun phrase accessibility hierarchy.

    b. We next looked at "clause internal revaluations" and read Permutter (1984a) on the inadequacy of monostratal theories of passive, along with Bell (1983) on advancements and ascensions in Cebuano, Chung (1976) on an object creating rule in Bahasa Indonesia, Dubinsky (1990) on Japanese direct to indirect object demotion, and Perlmutter (1984b) on inversion in Italian, Japanese, and Quechua.

    c. In covering the topic of reflexives and impersonals, we read Perlmutter and Postal's (1984) chapter on impersonal passives and Rosen's (1984) chapter on the interface between semantic roles and initial grammatical relations.

    d. The unit on multnode networks and clause union covered Aissen and Perlmutter's (1976) article on clause reduction in Spanish, Perlmutter and Postal's (1983a) chapter on the Relational Succession Law, Gibson and Raposo's (1986) article on clause union, Rosen's (1983) paper on universals of union, Davies and Rosen's (1988) article on multi-predicate union, and Dubinsky's (1997) application of multi-predicate union to Japanese passives.

    e. The phenomenon of antipassive was covered by reading Davies' (1984) chapter in *Studies in Relational Grammar 2* and Davies and Sam-Colop's (1990) article in *Language*.

(3) *Current research in the syntax of grammatical functions.* The second half of the course used this volume as a text, and also made reference to a number of other key chapters and articles dealing with grammatical relations from P&P perspectives. This other material included parts of Mark Baker's (1988a) book on incorporation, Bobaljik and Jonas' (1996) article on subject positions and TP, Cole and Hermon's (1981) article on subjecthood and islandhood, Guilfoyle, Hung, and Travis' (1992) article on SPEC of IP and SPEC of VP, Eric Haeberli's (2000) paper on the EPP and Case, sections from Teun Hoekstra's (1984) book on transitivity, Kyle Johnson's (1991) article on object positions, and James McCloskey's (1997) article on subject positions.

ACKNOWLEDGMENTS

For their help and counsel in the early conceptualization of the workshop on "The Role of Grammatical Functions in Transformational Syntax" and the inception of the process that led to this book, we would like to thank Mark Baker, Paul Chapin, and Alec Marantz. We also owe thanks to the speakers and attendees of this workshop, for their presentations and their discussion of these, which ultimately enriched this volume. We thank Liliane Haegeman and one anonymous reviewer of this volume for their helpful comments, both on the individual chapters and on the overall organization of the book. We also wish to acknowledge Jacqueline Bergsma, Anne van der Wagt, and Susan Zwartbol-Jones of Kluwer Academic Publishers for all their help in the editing process, as well as Theresa McGarry of the University of South Carolina Linguistics Program for her diligence and hard work editing the final typescript. We are indebted to the NSF (Grant #SBR 9817364), the College of Liberal Arts at the University of South Carolina, and the University of Iowa Arts and Humanities Initiative for support of the workshop and this volume.

We want to thank our families (Melissa and Elijah Dubinsky; Pat Weir, Billy Davies, and Kate Davies) for putting up with us, and for all their good vibes and support, during our absences and unexpected presences.

Finally, we would like to thank each other. We certainly had an awfully good time putting this all together.

WILLIAM D. DAVIES AND STANLEY DUBINSKY

REMARKS ON GRAMMATICAL FUNCTIONS IN TRANSFORMATIONAL SYNTAX

The broad topic for this volume is the role of grammatical functions in transformational syntax, that is, what role the notions subject and object play in the theory of grammar. There has been a long-standing debate in the field regarding the status of grammatical functions as theoretical primitives or defined notions. The Chomskyan school has consistently stated the position set out in Chomsky's 1965 *Aspects of the Theory of Syntax* that grammatical functions are secondary notions that are definable on the basis of phrase structure representations of sentences. Work in other syntactic frameworks (first in Relational Grammar starting in the 1970's and later in Lexical-Functional Grammar starting in the 1980's) challenged this position, demonstrating the efficacy of capturing cross-linguistic generalizations in terms of grammatical functions and questioning whether or not these generalizations were available in theories with defined grammatical functions.

Developments in Chomskyan theory involved more and more explicit reference to grammatical functions (particularly *subject*), and after the publication of Chomsky 1981 (*Lectures on Government and Binding*), the place of grammatical functions in work based on his theories evolved in distinct ways. Some authors challenged the basic claims of Relational Grammar, while others sought to incorporate into Government and Binding theory some of the insights that had crystalized in the RG and LFG literature. Further developments in Government and Binding theory in the 1980's and precursors to Chomsky's Minimalist Program in the late 1980's and early 1990's incorporated yet more references to grammatical functions, including the notion *object*.

It has been 25 years since the introduction of Relational Grammar theory by Perlmutter and Postal at the 1974 Linguistic Society of America Linguistics Institute, and many of the insights of linguists working in that theoretical framework have been incorporated in one way or another into the Chomskyan framework. And, with the advent of a more highly articulated phrase structure in the late 1980's and the 1990's and highly abstract configurational representations, there is the appearance that grammatical function-based notions permeate the formalism. However, explicit examination of the role of grammatical functions in the theory has been lacking. It is thus an appropriate time to re-examine the status of grammatical

William D. Davies and Stanley Dubinsky (eds.), Objects and other subjects:
Grammatical functions, functional categories, and configurationality, 1—19.
© 2001 *Kluwer Academic Publishers. Printed in the Netherlands.*

functions and determine whether they are interesting viable notions or should simply be abandoned as epiphenomenal mnemonic terms.

The collection of papers in this volume addresses the role of subject and object in the theory largely by making specific proposals about phenomena in a range of languages. Most conclude that the properties of objects and subjects can be attributed to functional or phrase structural properties and include novel proposals for the representation of these properties.

In this chapter, we outline some of the foundational developments in the role of grammatical functions in syntactic description and analysis, beginning with Chomsky 1965 (section 1). In section 2, we treat, in somewhat more detail, recent developments in the treatment of subjects and objects. Section three elaborates on points of convergence achieved by the chapters in this volume, and points the way to a typology of language architecture and to further research in the area.

1. A POINT OF DEPARTURE

The assumption that GFs such as subject and direct object are definable in terms of phrase structure configurations, rather than being primitives of the theory, is a position which was first articulated in Chomsky 1965. Therein, Chomsky clearly distinguished GFs from grammatical categories such as NP, asserting that "the notions in question have an entirely different status" (p. 68) and that the functional information is redundant and "can be exacted directly from the rewriting rules of the base, without any necessity for *ad hoc* extensions and elaborations...to provide specific mention of grammatical function" (p. 73). Thus, it is assumed in Chomsky 1965 that GFs are defined notions, defined in terms of phrase structure configurations and perhaps only relevant to deep structure.[1] The general definitions that Chomsky assumes for grammatical functions are as follows: (i) Subject-of = [NP,S], (ii) Predicate-of = [VP,S], (iii) Direct-Object-of = [NP,VP], and (iv) Main-Verb-of = [V,VP] (p. 71). Thus, by these definitions in a structure such as (1), *sincerity* is the subject and *the boy* is the direct object.

(1)

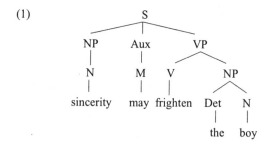

This position is reasserted in Chomsky 1981, in reaction to certain advances in the theories of Relational Grammar and the nascent Lexical Functional Grammar:

the less fully such notions as...grammatical relations... are reducible to primitives.., the greater the indeterminacy of grammars selected on the basis of primary linguistic data. There is, however, little reason to suppose that such indeterminacy exists beyond narrow bounds. Insofar as this is true, we should be skeptical about theories with a primitive basis containing concepts that cannot plausibly be assumed to enter into the determination of the primary linguistic data. (p. 16)

While it appears that little has changed within transformational syntax with respect to the status of GFs as theoretical primitives, in fact, the role of GFs has changed dramatically, albeit incrementally, in part in reaction to developments in nontransformational theories and in part due to theory-internal developments. GFs played no appreciable role in early Standard Theory treatments; however, the notion of subject was accorded a new and significant status in Chomsky 1973b, where reference is made in the Specified Subject Condition, "where by 'specified subject' we mean a subject NP that contains either lexical items or a pronoun that is not anaphoric" (p.239). In this paper the GF definitions (in particular subject, p.239) that Chomsky (1965) provided for the base component were extended to derived structures. Thus, in "Conditions on Transformations", the GF subject took on a significantly different role than it had previously had: it was a central concept in a key grammatical principle and it also had a wider application, relevant to derived phrase structures rather than simply base structures.

Concurrently and subsequently, new nontransformational paradigms arose in which GFs played a central role and were accorded the status of primitives. Beginning with Perlmutter and Postal 1972 and gaining significant status at the 1974 LSA Linguistic Institute (Perlmutter and Postal 1974), Relational Grammar (RG) sought to account for a wide range of cross-linguistic regularities in terms of GFs. In a spate of influential papers (Chung 1976, Permutter and Postal 1977, Perlmutter 1978, Postal 1977), basing its empirical results on a much wider range of languages than ever before, RG presented a serious challenge to the notion that GFs are derived notions by providing insightful universal and language-particular analyses utilizing GFs as core primitives of the grammar (and, correspondingly, that the configurational positions of phrases in a sentence are merely artifacts of how a particular language presents these primitives). Work in RG not only gave a central role to the GF subject but also to the GFs direct object, indirect object, and others, examining a number of clause-level and sentence-level structures which crucially referred to these GFs. Additionally, the late 1970s saw the rise of another relationally-based theory, Lexical Functional Grammar, as embodied in Bresnan 1978, 1980 and the papers in Bresnan 1982b. Like RG, LFG accorded GFs a central role in the analysis of universal and language-particular phenomena, and treated them as undefined primitives of the theory.

After the publication of Chomsky 1981, the place of grammatical relations in work based on his theories evolved in distinct ways. First, a few authors, such as Hoekstra (1984) and Marantz (1984), explicitly challenged the basic claims of RG theory. Others, such as Baker (1988) and Burzio (1986), attempted to build into GB some of the insights that had crystallized in RG and LFG literature. Baker's incorporation formalism was designed in large part to account for revaluations to object, which include the clause union/reduction phenomena treated extensively in

Aissen & Perlmutter 1976 and Gibson & Raposo 1986. Burzio, for his part, formalized an account of unaccusativity first presented in Perlmutter 1978.

At the same time, the publication of the GB theory in Chomsky 1981 and 1982 involved the further intrusion of GFs as undefined (or inconsistently defined) theoretical objects. In Chomsky 1981 (209-222), for example, the term SUBJECT is introduced into the calculation of "governing category". SUBJECT is used there to refer both to NPs occurring in the traditional, configurationally defined "subject position" (i.e. the immediate NP daughter of a clause or NP node), as well as to AGR (which is asserted to be the "nominal" content of INFL). On this formulation, the notion SUBJECT is no longer a purely configurationally defined relation, but one which identifies its referents variously on the basis of either configuration or labelling properties. With the articulation of the Extended Projection Principle (EPP), or more specifically the extended part of the EPP (Chomsky 1982:10), GFs came to play an even more critical role in the central assertions of the theory. Here it is stated that "the requirement that a clause have a subject is independent of the Projection Principle" and that this requirement is "a general principle governing D-structures, hence also governing structures derived from them". The "subject" of the EPP, however, is not the same as SUBJECT (since clauses of Romance languages are held to have "subject positions" in addition to the SUBJECT [i.e. AGR] which they would possess anyway). Putting this inconsistency aside, the EPP elevated the notion "subject" (albeit a configurationally defined notion) to the level of a UG determinant of core grammar (Chomsky 1982:13).

Since the mid-1980's, various developments in GB theory and what has evolved into Minimalism have further unsettled the traditional view of GFs in transformational syntax. One of these, the VP-INTERNAL SUBJECT HYPOTHESIS (see Kitagawa 1986 and Sportiche 1988 among others), resulted in the abandonment of a singular, configurationally defined "subject position", inasmuch as this hypothesis provides separately for deep (i.e. thematic) and surface (i.e. inflectional) subject positions. This notion that all subjects are derived led subsequently to a reexamination of the category INFL itself, and to proposals in which its various functional components are separated out into independently headed projections. The view (expressed first in Pollock 1989) that AGR and Tense reside in separate functional categories has opened the door for further discussion of the positions and properties of subjects, such as found in Guilfoyle, Hung, & Travis 1992, Bobaljik & Jonas 1996, McCloskey 1997.

At the same time that the notion "subject" has come under renewed scrutiny, there has arisen a corresponding interest in the traditional object functions of direct object (DO) and indirect object (IO). Drawing on the VP-internal subject hypothesis discussed above, Larson (1988) proposed a view of multiple object constructions in which the underlying positions of direct and indirect objects are comparable to that of subjects and direct objects. That is, just as the clausal subject occupies a D-structure spec,VP position superior to the complement, the direct object of a ditransitive verb is claimed to occupy a spec,VP (of a lower VP) and be superior to the indirect object complement in D-structure. This analogy is illustrated in (2), where VP_1 in (2a) should be compared to VP_2 in (2b).

(2)a.   Greer likes Speer.

b.   Greer sent a letter to Speer.

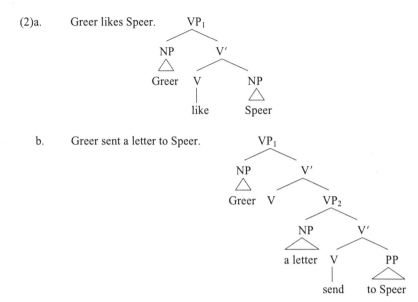

Larson's approach is developed further in Pesetsky 1995, where VPs having non-lexical heads (such as VP$_1$ in (2b)) are done away with and replaced by lexical projections (sometimes having phonologically null heads). The essence of these proposals was to divorce phrase structure from traditional constituency tests, in favor of representations in which thematic hierarchies map directly to a syntactic analog (much like the initial layer of structure in RG), a topic taken up by Baker in chapter 2.

While the D-structure representation of object GFs evolved in the manner shown above, the inflectional status of objects also underwent a metamorphosis. Following Pollock's (1989) proposal to separate the nominal (AGR) properties of inflection from Tense, Chomsky (1991) proposed separate AGR projections for subject and object (AgrS and AgrO). Under this proposal, both subjects **and** objects are derived categories, each coming to occupy the Spec of its respective functional category. This proposal had the consequence of doing away with the traditional configurational difference between subjects and objects (inasmuch as both are now claimed to occupy a Spec position), and replacing this with a difference that resides either in the labeling function (i.e. AgrS vs. AgrO) or in the configurational position of the Agr phrases relative to lexical projections (whether an AgrP selects or is selected by vP).

2. RECENT VIEWS ON GRAMMATICAL FUNCTIONS

2.1 On the subject of subjects

As noted above, the notion "subject" and its role in the grammar evolved considerably over the past three decades. While a configurational definition of subject remained intact and relatively unchanged from *Aspects* to *LGB* and into *Barriers* (the only change coinciding with the introduction of the CP/IP nomenclature), the role of subject became increasingly important. This is epitomized by the Extended Projection Principle of Chomsky 1982, which explicitly requires all clauses to have subjects, defined therein as [NP,S]. Since then, speculation has arisen regarding whether all languages obey the EPP and whether some languages satisfy the EPP in alternative ways. Additionally, developments in clausal architecture have radically reshaped the configurational definition of subject and, in fact, have cast doubt on whether a unitary notion of subject can be identified, as taken up in part III of this volume.

An early step in what McCloskey (1997) terms the "deconstruction" of a unitary subject was the introduction of the VP-internal subject hypothesis. This notion, that the subject originates in the VP and then in most (but not all) languages moves to spec,IP, entails the positing of two subject positions. Some of the most striking evidence for this hypothesis comes from Sportiche's (1988) analysis of quantifier float.

(3)a.   Tous les enfants ont   vu   ce   film.
         all   the children have seen this movie

   b.   Les enfants (*tous) ont   tous vu   (*tous) ce   film.
         the children   have all   seen   this movie

Sportiche adduces evidence for a VP-internal position for subjects in order to explain the fact that the quantifier *tous* 'all' in (3b) can appear between the auxiliary and main verbs, but not in other plausible positions (such as before the auxiliary verb or after the main verb). Sportiche suggests that for French (and the English analog), the NP complement of the quantifier may raise independently to spec,IP, leaving the quantifier stranded as shown in (4).

(4)   [$_{IP}$ [$_{NP}$ les enfants]$_1$ ont [$_{VP}$ [$_{QP}$ tous t$_1$] vu ce film]]

Of course, (3a) is derived by having the entire QP move from spec,VP to spec,IP. These facts, together with other considerations (e.g. adverb placement), provide evidence of a VP-internal position for the subject. Further evidence for a VP-internal subject position came from languages for which it was argued that the subject of the sentence never raises to spec,IP but remains in the VP at S-structure. Such proposals include Kuroda 1988 for Japanese and McCloskey 1991 for Irish.

The notion of two subject positions was developed further by Guilfoyle, Hung, and Travis (1992), who present an analysis of Austronesian languages that makes crucial use of the two subject positions, spec,VP and spec,IP. In their analysis, they extend the potential of a non-unitary notion of subject, and argue that the properties most often associated with a single argument and identified as "subject properties" can actually be split between two arguments in certain constructions in these languages. So, for example, in the Tagalog examples below (Guilfoyle, Hung, and Travis 1992:(25)) *babae* 'woman' possesses all subject properties in (5a), while the subject properties are split in (5b) between *babae* and *bigas* 'rice'.[2]

(5)a.   Mag-aalis   ng-bigas sa-sako   para sa-bata'   ang-babae.
          AT-take.out ACC-rice OBL-sack for   OBL-child TOP-woman
          'The woman will take rice out of the sack for the child.'

  b.   Aalisin   ng-babae   sa-sako   para sa-bata'   ang-bigas.
          TT-take.out GEN-woman OBL-sack for   OBL-child TOP-rice
          'The woman will take the rice out of the sack for the child.'

Under their analysis of (5a), the VP-internal subject *babae* moves from spec,VP to spec,IP (at the end of the clause), thus filling both subject positions. In (5b), *babae* remains in the spec,VP subject position, while the theme *bigas* moves to spec,IP. This is illustrated in (6)—n.b. t_2 is the trace of V movement.

(6)a.   [$_{IP}$ [$_{I'}$ mag-aalis$_2$ [$_{VP}$ t$_1$ t$_2$ ng-bigas sa-sako para-sa-bata']]
          ang-babae$_1$ $_{IP}$]

  b.   [$_{IP}$ [$_{I'}$ aalisin$_2$ [$_{VP}$ ng-babae   t$_2$ t$_1$ sa-sako para-sa-bata']]
          ang-bigas$_1$ $_{IP}$]

Under Guilfoyle, Hung, and Travis' analysis, typical Tagalog subject properties such as reflexive antecedence and being controlled are characteristic of the spec,VP position, while the properties of floating quantifiers and extraction accrue to spec,IP. When a single argument fills both positions (via movement), as is the case for *babae* in (5a), that argument exhibits all subject characteristics. In (5b), however, the deep subject *babae* originates in spec,VP and resides there at S-structure, while the object *bigas* moves out of the VP complement position coming to occupy the surface subject position spec,IP at S-structure. Accordingly, the subject properties in (5b) are split between these two arguments.

More recent accounts, particularly spurred on by the disassembling of INFL in Pollock 1989, have proposed yet other subject positions. In work on the Icelandic transitive expletive construction, Bobaljik and Jonas (1996) have argued that there is a subject position outside of VP but lower than spec,AgrSP (which replaced spec,IP as the identified S-structure subject position following Chomsky 1991). They identify this position as spec,TP. In the Icelandic construction, both spec,AgrSP and spec,TP are occupied by phonetic material. As McCloskey (1997) points out, with two subject positions in the inflectional layer, this either brings to three the number of identified subject positions or casts doubt on the VP-internal subject position. Additionally, Branigan (1996), Cardinaletti (1997), Kiss (1996), and Haegeman (1996) have proposed additional subject positions outside of the thematic and inflectional layers. For example, Branigan (1996) suggests that EPP features drive movement into spec,CP in verb-second languages. In such a proposal spec,CP thus becomes a GF position in those languages which have EPP-motivated movement to positions outside the inflectional layer.

Current theoretical proposals, calling for multiple "subject" positions and for the parcelling out of "subject" properties among them, are reminiscent of RG proposals of ten to twenty years earlier. The VP-internal subject position, assumed in most current work, has its analogue in the RG concept "initial subject". Analogous to current theoretical proposals for derived "subject positions" (in the inflectional layer of the clause), RG theory recognized the distinct status of "final subjects" in triggering agreement and feeding word order rules (among other things). For example, Bell (1976) proposed distinct grammatical properties for initial and final subjects in Cebuano, a proposal quite similar to that offered (in the current model) by Guilfoyle, Hung, and Travis for other Austronesian languages.

2.2 Objects and other objects

Unlike subject, the definition of the GF notion direct object was less troublesome to Chomsky's transformational theory at the outset. It was, by and large, assumed that direct objects of simple clauses (such as *her* in (7a)) are not derived. Subsequently, Chomsky's (1981) adoption of the Projection Principle entailed that no surface direct object can be derived from any other position. This helped provide justification for the exceptional case marking (ECM) analysis of accusative infinitival subjects, by which *him* in (7b) is a deep and surface subject despite its accusative case.[3]

(7)a.   James saw her.

b.   Garth wants [$_S$ him to leave]

Thus, the Projection Principle divided the class of apparent surface direct objects into true direct object complements (7a) and accusative infinitival subjects (7b). Under these assumptions, direct object is trivially defined as the NP sister of V.

This situation changed with the publication of Larson 1988, in which the position of a deep direct object was claimed to be dependent upon the valency of the verb. As shown in section 1 (example (2)), the direct object of a transitive verb is analyzed as the NP sister of V, while the direct object of a ditransitive verb is claimed to occupy spec,VP (of a lower VP). Thus, under a Larsonian approach to D-structure, object properties can no longer be attributed to a singular, configurational definition of the notion direct object.

While the Larson (and later, Pesetsky 1995) approach to lexical insertion did muddy the definition of deep-subject, it left intact the notion that direct objects are not derived (at least in contrast to the VP-internal subject hypothesis which held that subjects occupy distinct thematic and inflectional positions). However, following Pollock's (1989) division of INFL into distinct AGR and Tense components, Chomsky (1991) proposed an inflectional position for objects parallel to that of subjects. Based on work by Kayne (1989), Chomsky takes Pollock's AGR to be a "subject-agreement element" (AgrS), and suggests that there is an "object-agreement element (AgrO) ... [that has] VP as its complement". On this view, (7a) would have the following representation at LF.

(8) $[_{AgrSP}$ James$_1$ saw$_2$ $[_{TP}$ ... $[_{AgrOP}$ her$_3$ $[_{VP}$ t$_1$ t$_2$ t$_3$]]]]

As (8) illustrates, under the multiple Agr-projection hypothesis (as per Chomsky 1991) coupled with the VP-internal subject hypothesis, all subjects and all direct objects are derived (at least by LF).[4] Rounding out the picture, Bowers (1993) proposes a functional projection *PredP* which is instantiated inside the inflectional layer (IP) and outside the thematic layer (VP) and which mediates the relation between the subject and the VP. Unlike Larson's 1988 VP-shell analysis the instantiation of PredP is independent of the thematic requirements of the verb (which makes it distinct from the agentive vP proposed in Chomsky 1995, whose presence is triggered by the thematic structure of the verb). Thus, by 1993 we find proposals that collectively introduce functional projections corresponding to the three GFs (subject, direct object, predicate) that Chomsky rejected as being part of phrase structure in *Aspects*. Recent proposals (Franco 1993, Koizumi 1995, and Sportiche 1996) have gone further, and provided for a separate agreement element for indirect objects (AgrIO) which also projects a phrase.

Taken all together, these proposals lead to important questions about the place of functional projections in Universal Grammar. One can ask whether there is a universal stock of functional projections instantiated in every language or whether a universal repertoire of such projections forms an inventory out of which individual languages select a subset. Alongside this question is the issue of whether functional projections are instantiated in some fixed and universal hierarchy or whether the relative dominance of individual functional projections might vary parametrically from one language to another. Indeed these questions have been the subject of some discussion in the literature and the positions taken on these issues vary across a spectrum (see Iatridou 1990, Nash & Rouveret 1997, and Thráinsson 1996 for discussion). On one end of this spectrum is the more restrictive view that the set of functional categories and their relative dominance is fixed by UG. At the other is the suggestion that the inventory of functional projections and their relative dominance varies from language to language. As an example of the kind of debate that surrounds the instantiation of particular functional projections, one might compare Koizumi 1995 (which maintains that English has an AgrIO projection, in addition to AgrO) with Montrul 1998 (which assumes that AgrIO is specific to languages that have dative clitics, such as French and Spanish). In this volume (chapter 6), Travis claims that Malagasy has no derived objects (and presumably no equivalent of AgrO). There is even some question as to whether a particular functional projection is uniformly instantiated in all construction in a given language. As an example of this, Lasnik (chapter 5) proposes that AgrO is optional in English, leading to the possibility of both derived and underived objects.[5] There are various proposals regarding the relative dominance of functional projections (especially AgrS and T). Pollock 1989 posits TP above AgrP, while many subsequent analyses reverse this. The relative dominance of AgrS and T may in fact correlate with other aspects of language structure, such as word order. We find that proposals for V-initial languages converge on the view that T dominates AgrS (McCloskey, chapter 7; Massam, chapter 9). In chapter 10, we propose a language typology that reflects, among other things, the parametric variation of T/Agr dominance.

3. THE STATE OF FUNCTIONAL ART

In the ensuing discussion, we will point to a range of converging opinions on the status of subjects and objects cross-linguistically, as revealed in the chapters that follow. We will also indicate where the evidence either leads to divergent opinions about functional structure, or is simply inconclusive. Finally, we will sketch out what we believe to be an overarching set of functional parameters, which lead to a predictive typology of possible language classes and which may provide explanations for attested typological variation.

In what might be viewed as a relatively surprising result, two of the chapters in section one point to ways in which P&P theory has come to incorporate grammatical functions as primitives, albeit not always in the most straightforward manner and through rather different subparts of the theory. Baker (in chapter 2) suggests that phrase structure representations have evolved in such a way that at the thematic layer phrase structure is a representation of grammatical functions, where grammatical functions are encoded through configurational superiority. As these phrase structures are determined neither by traditional constituency tests nor by any language-particular properties, current Chomskyan theory essentially shares with explicitly relational theories the notion that grammatical relations are primitives. Taking a far different tack, Alsina (in chapter 4) investigates the application of the notions structural Case and inherent Case to distinguishing objects in multiple object constructions. He notes that various properties of objects in languages (e.g., pronoun incorporation, lexical binding) consistently accrue to structurally Case-marked objects as opposed to inherently Case-marked objects but that the thematic role of the argument targeted for inherent Case is not consistent between languages. On this basis, he suggests that the structural vs. inherent Case distinction has been used as another means of encoding distinctions between "object" GFs.

In chapter 2, Baker shows that configurational prominence can uniformly represent both intraclausal relational prominence and interclausal "embedding" prominence. Thus, the subject of a matrix clause has configurational prominence over its same-clause object and over its embedded clause subject. In an effort to achieve greater uniformity of representation, Baker suggests reducing all grammatical prominence (inter- and intra- clausal) to embedding prominence. He implements this through the adoption of a lexical decomposition strategy that requires at least one syntactic predicate for each subcategorized argument. By assuming, for instance, that a subject is in the specifier of a vP and that an object is in spec,VP, the intraclausal superiority of subject over object can be treated as arising out of an embedding asymmetry.

While lexical decomposition can clearly be used as a vehicle for mapping out relational prominence, Newmeyer (in chapter 3) points out that lexical semantic representations (LSR) cannot take the place of syntactic grammatical functions. He notes that there are important reasons for representing relational prominence syntactically, and reminds us that syntactically unaccusative structures can arise out of a varied set of lexical semantic representations (a point made early on in Rosen 1984). Since the set of possible argument structures is much smaller than the set of possible semantic representations, and since the mapping from semantic representations to argument structures is not fixed (as documented in Grimshaw 1979), there is still a need for an autonomous level of deep syntactic structure in which "grammatical functions, thematic roles, and constituent structure are not [necessarily] in alignment".

3.1 Subject attributes through the clause

There are a number of syntactic properties that are characteristic of a single nominal in English. These properties include being the controllee in control structures, bearing nominative case and triggering agreement on the verb, and obligatorily undergoing raising in appropriate contexts.

(9)a. Vanessa tried to phone Andrew.

b. *Andrew tried Vanessa to phone.

(10)a. Amy appears to be out of the office.

b. *Appears Amy to be out of the office.

Such properties have come to be known as "subject" properties inasmuch as they accrue to a single constituent referred to as the Subject in English. However, looking over a range of languages one finds that these properties can be distributed among distinct constituents in different languages. In order to understand the mechanism by which these properties are concentrated in a single constituent or divided among several, one must understand them to be reflexes of formally distinct syntactic attributes. Reviewing the list of properties just presented, we can ascribe controlleehood as arising from configurational or thematic salience, nominative case and agreement as arising from the interaction of an argument and a functional head or feature, and obligatory raising as being driven by an EPP (D) feature of the clause.

Taking these three syntactic attributes to be primitive, we find that in English the thematically/configurationally highest argument is the one which checks nominative case and triggers agreement and is also the same argument which responds to the D-feature in T. Accordingly, the full range of "subject" properties is mapped to a single argument in English. However, this is not the case cross-linguistically. In Spanish, for example, the three syntactic attributes just described are not necessarily localized in the same argument. As Goodall shows in Chapter 8, arguments other than the thematic subject may satisfy the EPP, checking off a D-feature in T.

(11)   A quién había visto la   madre de Juan?
        who   had   seen the mother of
        'Who had Juan's mother seen?'

According to Goodall, in (11), *a quién* checks off the D-feature as well as a Q-feature in T, satisfying the EPP. In languages such as Irish and Niuean, we find that the EPP feature does not interact with any argument. As McCloskey (Chapter 7) and Massam (Chapter 9) show, there is no EPP position in the clause. Consequently, thematic subjects only display a subset of the English "subject" properties described above (raising is optional in these languages). This is illustrated in (12) for Niuean (with data from Seiter 1983), where *tama* 'boy', the subject of the embedded clause, has raised to be subject of the matrix clause (12b).

(12)a. Kua kamata ke   hala he   tama e   akau.
        PERF begin SBJ cut ERG boy ABS tree
        'The boy has begun to cut down the tree.'

   b.   Kua kamata e   tama ke   hala e   akau.
        PERF begin ABS boy SBJ cut ABS tree
        'The boy has begun to cut down the tree.'

Finally, we find that a single one of these attributes may be associated with more than one argument. Massam proposes that in Niuean the subject and object of a transitive clause occupy multiple specifier positions of the same functional projection. Since they have the same configurational salience, they are equally able to undergo optional raising, as illustrated in (13), where the object of the embedded clause, *akau* 'tree', has raised to be subject of the matrix clause.

(13)   Kua kamata e   akau ke   hala he   tama.
        PERF begin ABS tree SBJ cut ERG boy
        'The tree was begun to be cut by the boy.'

Thus it is the many-to-one mapping from syntactic attributes to a single argument, which creates the illusion of a single set of "subject" properties in English (and other languages like it). The cross-linguistic evidence presented in this volume shows that the notion of subject is epiphenomenal rather than primitive.

It is also the case that the syntactic attributes which contribute to the epiphenomenon of subject are themselves parameterized rather than universal. For instance, we find that agreement heads (or features) can be obligatory or optional. Irish clauses do not require the presence of a nominal argument, thereby allowing for unaccusative predicates whose sole argument is prepositional.

(14)   Bhreáthaigh ar ab aimsir.   (McCloskey, ch. 7)
          became-fine on the weather
          'The weather became nice.'

In Niuean, on the other hand, the absolutive argument is obligatory.

Another parameterized syntactic attribute that plays a central role in the determination of clausal behavior is the EPP. We find, from cross-linguistic evidence, that the presence of an EPP feature appears to be universal. That is, the head of TP (or its equivalent) is always found to bear a category feature that induces movement into the inflectional layer of the clause. In this regard, though, languages vary according to whether this feature is D or V. In D-prominent languages, such as English, French, and Spanish, the EPP feature in T forces the appearance of a DP in spec,TP. In V-prominent languages, such as Bulgarian, Irish, and Niuean, the EPP feature induces the movement of V (or some projection of V) to T and yields (in most instances) V-initial word order. In V-prominent languages, EPP properties normally associated with the thematic subject are absent, since the EPP does not affect the distribution of any nominal element. Accordingly, in these languages, raising is optional as in (12), subject expletives are absent, and subject island effects are frequently missing. For instance, Bulgarian allows extraction from sentential subjects, as in (15) (Davies and Dubinsky, Chapter 10).

(15)   na kakvo$_1$ misliš   [če [da otide t$_1$] beše važno   za nego]
          to what   you.think that to go   was important for him
          'To what do you think that to go was important for him?'

The choice of V- or D- prominence also interacts with another parameter that determines the relative superiority of T (or the EPP feature) and Agr/Case. This parameter, as far as we can determine, is only active in D-prominent languages. Irish and Niuean, in addition to being V-prominent, also feature a T(-like) projection higher than Agr/Case. In contrast, English is D-prominent and has Agr above T. Spanish, while D-prominent like English, is like Irish in having T above Agr. This difference between Spanish and English results in certain key differences between these two languages. Unlike English, the thematic subject in Spanish need not occupy the preverbal position, since it only need check Agr/Case features lower in the clause. At the same time, unlike Irish, some DP element must check the D-feature in T higher up. This results in a obligatory "subject"-like position, which is sometimes filled by a nominal locative or by the trace of a moved *wh*-operator. The choice of EPP feature coupled with the relative height of T and Agr leads to a range of language types, as expressed in the following table.

	D-prominent EPP	**V-prominent EPP**
T/Agr	Spanish	Irish
Agr/T	English	——

3.2 Object properties

Lasnik (chapter 5) proposes that, while overt movement to check features is in general obligatory, AgrO in English is optionally present. Because of this, he argues, direct objects in English can be underived. As an illustration of this, he shows first that extraction from object NPs is ruled out when the object does raise to spec,AgrOP in order to bind a reflexive pronoun, as in (16).

(16)   ??Which senator did the special prosecutor question
         [two friends of __] during each other's trials.

When derivation is not motivated by binding requirements, the object may remain underived, thereby facilitating extraction, as in (17).

(17)   Which senator did the special prosecutor question
         [two friends of __] during the president's trial.

Lasnik concludes from this and other evidence that, at least for English, the AgrO can be distinguished from AgrS by its optionality. Similarly, Travis (chapter 6) proposes for Malagasy that the analog of the AgrO projection (AspP) is inert. She provides evidence that a number of constructions, previously assumed to involve derived objects, in fact involve derived subjects instead. She shows that Malagasy fails to have the equivalent of AgrO in its clause structure. Thus, both Lasnik and Travis agree that objects may be distinguished functionally from subjects, in at least some languages, in that the former may or must remain in their base-generated position within a basic transitive clause. This state of affairs is comparable to that of Niuean, for which Massam (chapter 9) claims that the Ergative argument is underived.

    In their account of objects, both Lasnik and Travis take the lower Agr/Asp projection to be intermediate between the two verbal projections (vP and VP), in keeping with recent proposals by Koizumi (1995). According to this view of clause structure the inflectional and thematic space cannot be divided into distinct layers, since an inflectional projection intervenes between two lexical ones, as in (18).

(18) $[_{AgrP} ... \text{Agr} [_{vP} ... v [_{AgrP} ... \text{Agr} [_{VP} ... V ...]]]]$

While this perspective erases a useful distinction between the inflectional and thematic space within the clause, it does simplify the representation of Agr. With this representation it is not necessary to distinguish between AgrS and AgrO, since the internal and external core arguments of the clause each have their own immediately dominating Agr projection. In examining Irish, McCloskey provides evidence that all inflectional projections are higher than vP so that there appears to be, at least in some languages, a strict separation of thematic and inflectional layers. At the same time, there also seems to be no clear consensus regarding the interpretability of functional heads and features. For Lasnik, agreement is mediated by the purely inflectional head Agr, while Travis suggests that the relevant projection is an Asp(ect) phrase. If Agr (and other similar features) are in fact borne by interpretable heads, then the motivation is reduced for drawing a clear division between inflectional and thematic layers of structure. At this point, though, the divergence of opinions on this point reduces the motivation for further speculation on this issue.

3.3 Functional parameters and typological variation

It is possible to identify a number of parameters of functional projections that account for some of the typological variation presented above. One such parameter is the nature of the EPP feature that resides in T. We suggested above (consistent with proposals by Massam & Smallwood 1997, Massam 2000b, and Rackowski & Travis 2000) that this can be characterized as V-prominence vs. D-prominence; that is, this feature on T will force either V-movement or D-movement. Languages such as English, French and Spanish are D-prominent, while languages such as Bulgarian, Irish, Malagasy, and Niuean are V-prominent.

A second, cross-cutting parameter is the relative height of the functional projections T and Agr. While we propose (in Chapter 10) that T always commands Agr projections (or features) in V-prominent languages, in D-prominent languages there is evidence of a split. In his proposal for Spanish, Goodall provides evidence that T is higher than Agr, showing that a non-nominative DP argument will satisfy the strong D-feature in T when the nominative thematic subject is postverbal. Conversely, in our account of English EPP effects, we provide evidence for the current view that one Agr projection is above T. In our account of English, the superiority of T over Agr (coupled with D-prominence) is shown to explain the concentration of "subject" properties in a single argument.

A final parameter of functional projections is the obligatory vs. optional nature of Agr heads or features. Starting with the assumption that there are two possible Agr heads or sets of features associated with transitive predicates—a high Agr feature (commonly referred to as AgrS) and a low Agr feature (AgrO)—the possibility exists for one or the other or both of these features to be optional in a language. For instance, Lasnik proposes that the lower Agr in English is only optionally instantiated. Putting a slightly different face on this, only the higher Agr feature in

English is obligatory. What this means is that ALL English clauses must have the higher Agr feature, that which has been associated with nominative Case and agreement. Thus, regardless of transitivity, there must always be a nominative argument in the clause. When the higher Agr feature is obligatory, the same Agr feature associated with the thematic subject of a transitive clause will need to also be checked by the single argument of an intransitive clause (whether unergative or unaccusative). This is schematized in (19).

> (19)a.   Transitive clause:
>   [Thematically-high-arg AgrX [Thematically-low-arg (AgrY) ...]]
>
>   b.   Intransitive clause:
>   [Single-argument AgrX ...]]

This state of affairs results in a case/agreement system traditionally characterized as nominative/accusative, in which AgrX is AgrS (or Nominative) and AgrY is AgrO (or Accusative). The need, in English, for a nominative argument in each clause might be seen as one side of the "coin" that motivated the Final 1 Law and other similar proposals (with the D-prominence of the EPP being the other side of that "coin").

In some ways, what Massam proposes for Niuean is the inverse of Lasnik's proposal for English. Citing the optionality of the Ergative argument and the obligatory nature of the Absolutive, Massam proposes an obligatory Absolutive feature in vP. In Massam's analysis then, the obligatory Agr feature is the configurationally lower one (in that it is checked by the lower of two arguments). In this circumstance, the same Agr feature associated with the thematic object of a transitive clause will need to also be checked by the single argument of an intransitive clause (whether unergative or unaccusative). It is this same Agr feature that is checked by the thematic subject of a transitive clause when the thematic object undergoes noun incorporation with the verb. This case system is schematized in (20).

> (20)a.   Transitive clause:
>   [Thematically-high-arg$_X$ [Thematically-low-arg$_Y$ AgrX AgrY ...]]
>
>   b.   Transitive NI clause:
>   [Thematically-high-arg AgrY [Thematically-low-arg ...]]
>
>   c.   Intransitive clause:
>   [Single-argument AgrY ...]]

The result of this is, of course, a case/agreement system characterized as ergative/absolutive, in which AgrX is Ergative and AgrY is Absolutive. The view adopted here unifies derivation of Accusative objects in English and Absolutives in Niuean, in that both reference the same (i.e. lower) Agr feature. The difference between them, then, has simply to do with optionality/obligatoriness of the relevant Agr features. This approach to case/agreement is similar to that developed by Bobaljik (1992), but consistent with proposals by Levin and Massam 1985 and Massam 1985. Characterized as the "absolutive-as-accusative" analysis, the agreement features of absolutive arguments are checked in spec,AgrO and those of ergative arguments are checked in spec,AgrS.[6] It should be clear from the discussion so far how distinct Agr realization requirements in these languages lead naturally to the traditional nominative/accusative and ergative/absolutive characterizations.

A third possible parameterization for agreement features is seen in McCloskey's analysis of Irish clause structure. Irish, like English and Niuean, instantiates two distinct Agr heads (or features), with the higher being characterized as Nominative (since it can mark intransitive arguments). However, according to McCloskey, both Agr heads are optional. The result of this is that some Irish clauses have only a single prepositional argument, and involve no checking of case/agreement (14). The optionality of Agr features, which can be distinguished as "high" and "low", gives rise to the following range of clause structure types.

	High Agr optional	High Agr obligatory
Low Agr optional	Irish	English (nominative/accusative)
Low Agr obligatory	Niuean (ergative/absolutive)	——

Irish, then, is a language which exhibits an extreme case of "subjectlessness". Irish contrasts most strongly with English, which has a D-oriented EPP, an obligatory (nominative) Agr feature, AND a requirement that both of these reference the same argument. It contrasts with Spanish, which has D-prominence in EPP and obligatory (nominative) Agr. And, it contrasts with Niuean, which has an obligatory (absolutive) Agr feature. A V-prominent EPP coupled with an optional (nominative) Agr feature leads Irish to exhibit no clausal requirements suggestive of having to have subjects.

4. CONCLUSION

This discussion leads us naturally to the question of where does this discussion leave us. On the one hand, individual grammatical functions (such as subject) appear not to be as much unanalyzable primitives as has been imagined in theories such as RG, LFG, and HPSG. On the other hand, subjects (or particular subject properties) are clearly distinct from objects (or their analogous object properties) in ways that are not fully understood and which suggest the existence of some primitive (possibly feature based) distinction. The papers that follow do not provide definitive answers to all the questions that are addressed in this volume, and in fact raise a number of additional questions about the status of grammatical functions in syntactic representations. They do, however, exhibit significant agreement on a number of issues, such that the resulting convergences clearly provide a path for future research in this area.

For example, the EPP, however it may ultimately be characterized, is clearly associated with subjects and not objects. It is also clear from some of the chapters in this volume that the derivation of subjects and objects out of the thematic layer into the inflectional layer of a clause is determined independently for each relation in the grammar of a given language. Thus, to the extent that objects are optionally derived in English, for example (Lasnik, chapter 5), their grammatical status is distinct from subjects in ways that have yet to be determined. The resulting situation appears to be as follows: (i) specific properties generally related to grammatical functions (such as agreement) have autonomous reflexes in the grammar and are often implemented here as distinct functional heads (e.g., Agr); (ii) at the same time, the relation between a particular property type (such as agreement) and its associated grammatical functions (such as subject and object) is not uniform across all grammatical functions. So, while (i) suggests that there is no discrete grammatical reflex for any particular grammatical function, (ii) suggests that there is more to the distinction between particular grammatical functions than "all and only" the functional properties that have been taken account of thus far. This then surely argues for further exploration into the underlying role of GFs as determinants of grammatical structure.

The sort of conclusion that the work in this volume points to was in many respects anticipated in Keenan's 1976b 'Towards a universal definition of "subject"'. In that paper, Keenan attempts to arrive at a definition of the notion subject by testing 30 some properties (some of which had been widely used as traditional diagnostics for identifying subjects) against data from a variety of languages. With respect to these properties he notes that no one of them is "both necessary and sufficient for an NP in any sentence in any L [language] to be the subject of that sentence." Keenan concludes that "'subject' does not represent a single dimension of linguistic reality. It is rather a cluster concept, or as we shall say, a multi-factor concept." Appealing to the metaphor of 'intelligence', which is recognized as "a combination of abilities", he draws an analogy between it and the properties that he attributes to the subject relation. He goes on to say, "Being a subject is...more like being intelligent than...like being a prime number." At the same time he suggests (hopefully) that "the concept of subject might coincide with...groupings of [these] properties, though in the worst of cases each [property]...would be an independent factor."

ENDNOTES

[1] Despite the fact that Chomsky uses the terms "logical subject" and "grammatical subject" in his discussion of grammatical functions, the structural definitions that he supplies for GFs are most directly applicable to deep structure configurations. As he notes (in note 32, pp. 220-221), the existence of sentences containing PP subjects or two initial NPs may necessitate a distinct set of GF definitions relevant to surface structure.

[2] In the glosses, AT stands for AGENT TOPIC and TT stands for THEME TOPIC. The other abbreviations are: TOP(IC), ACC(USATIVE), OBL(IQUE), and GEN(ITIVE).

[3] Of course, the assertion that *him* is a surface subject (8b) is of dubious status given the wealth of evidence to the contrary in Postal 1974, which has since been rerecognized as compelling beginning with Lasnik and Saito 1991.

[4] Empirical evidence for such a move is obvious in languages with overt object agreement (as in many languages of Africa and the Americas) as well as in participial agreement in Romance languages, as triggered by leftward movement of the object, as in the French example in (ib), as pointed out to us by Liliane Haegeman..

(i)a.　　Jean a détruit la preuve.
　　　　 'Jean has destroyed the evidence.'
　 b.　　Jean l'a détruite.
　　　　 'Jean has destroyed it.'

[5] The notion "derived", as it pertains to movement from lexical to inflectional positions, remains somewhat unclear as used in the current literature. One might take "derived object" to mean "any object that moves from a base position into an inflectional one". One might alternatively take it to mean "an object that moves from a base position into an inflectional one *before spell-out (i.e. overtly)*".

[6] An alternative view (as represented by Bittner 1988, Campana 1992, and Murasugi 1992) is what Campana characterizes as the "ergative-as-accusative" analysis, in which, under Minimalist assumptions, absolutive DPs have their features checked in spec,AgrS while ergative DPs have their features checked in spec,AgrO.

MARK C. BAKER

PHRASE STRUCTURE AS A REPRESENTATION OF "PRIMITIVE" GRAMMATICAL RELATIONS

One of the defining properties of the narrowly Chomskian approach to syntax[1] over the years has been its commitment to the idea that grammatical relations such as subject and object are not primitives of grammatical theory. Rather, these notions, inherited from traditional grammar, are to be understood in terms of more basic syntactic relationships, in particular phrase structure configurations. This view gives phrase structure a kind of primacy in Chomskian theory that it does not have in other frameworks. In this conceptually oriented paper, I want to reexamine this distinctive claim, reviewing the old controversy between Chomskian theory and Relational Grammar (RG) and related frameworks that that claim was part of. In the course of this, I will consider what the ongoing legacy of these debates is in the "post-RG" syntactic theories of the 2000s. This issue is roughly equivalent to the question of what the characteristic phrase structure representations of Chomskian theory actually mean within the network of assumptions that they are now embedded in. My basic claim is that the meaning of the old slogan has changed somewhat over time, as ideas about phrase structure have changed, in ways that have not been fully realized. In particular, the Chomskian notion of phrase structure has come partially unhinged from its origins as a representation of basic constituency facts. As a result, it is now fair to say that phrase structure is essentially a representation of grammatical function relationships, not fundamentally different in kind from the representations posited by the Relational Grammarians and others. However, I will argue that Chomskian phrase structure is a particularly *good* representation of grammatical relations. In particular, it is superior to relational nets or the f-structures of Lexical Functional Grammar (LFG) in that it captures certain basic properties of linguistic prominence that are not captured by these more general and flexible-looking representational schemes. Thus, while the meaning of the claim that grammatical relations are derived from phrase structure has shifted over time, that claim is still meaningful. Finally, I will ask *why* it is that phrase structure is such a successful representation, showing how this relates to lexical semantic work on the decomposition of verbs into more basic components.

William D. Davies and Stanley Dubinsky (eds.), Objects and other subjects:
Grammatical functions, functional categories, and configurationality, 21—51.
© 2001 *Kluwer Academic Publishers. Printed in the Netherlands.*

1. THE ORIGINS OF THE CHOMSKIAN VIEW

To put these issues into context, let us begin by reviewing how the claim that grammatical relations are expressed in phrase structure arose. In fact, it emerged rather naturally out of the sequence of topics that were investigated and came to be partially understood by generative grammar. However, my focus will be on the idealized conceptual order of the ideas, rather than trying to trace their actual historical order in detail. This conceptual order also reflects the way that Chomskian syntax is often presented to students in textbooks and syntax courses, and this may be of more current significance than the history itself.

The first step is motivating that there is such a thing as phrase structure for languages like English, showing how this phrase structure can be established using traditional constituency tests. For example, one of the less obvious features of English syntax is that there is a verb phrase that contains the verb and the direct object, together with some particles and PPs, but not the subject. (It is my informal experience that when introductory linguistics students are asked out of the blue which is more closely related to the verb, the subject or the object, they have no clear intuitions: 50% chose one and 50% the other prior to seeing any arguments.) However, one can show that the verb and the NP that follows it form a unit with a familiar battery of tests, including movement (1a), replacement with a pronoun (1b), deletion (1c), and coordination (1d).

(1)a.   Sue said she would eat the octopus, and [$_{VP}$ eat the octopus] she
         did - .

    b.   Sue will [$_{VP}$ eat the octopus], and John will [$_{VP}$ do so] too.

    c.   Sue will [$_{VP}$ eat the octopus], and John will [$_{VP}$ -] too.

    d.   Chris will [$_{VP}$ chop the vegetables] and [$_{VP}$ eat the octopus].

Once this notion of phrase structure is firmly in place, it is a rather trivial observation that subjects and objects always come in a fixed position in the phrase structure. In particular, the direct object is the only noun phrase that is contained in the VP but not in any smaller phrase. The subject is consistently contained in the clause but not inside the VP. Indirect objects in a sentence like *Chris gave the book to Pat* are uniquely contained in a prepositional phrase headed by *to*. And so on.[2] Since there is such a close relationship between the traditional grammatical functions and phrase structure positions, it seems unnecessary to refer to both in one's syntactic theory. Now, some representation of constituency is needed in the grammar anyway, to characterize which sets of words can be moved as a unit, or can be deleted, or can be replaced with a pronoun. Therefore, Chomsky (1965) eliminated subject and object with the following definitions in terms of phrase structure:

(2)a.   Subject is "NP immediately dominated by S" ([NP, S]).

  b.   Object is "NP immediately dominated by VP" ([NP, VP]).

  c.   Indirect object is "NP immediately dominated by PP headed by *to*" ([NP, PP]).

Logically speaking, the alternative reduction would have been to eliminate phrase structure in favor of grammatical relations. However, that makes little sense. For example, one wants to say that *as flat as a pancake* is a phrase in (3), even though it has little to do with the traditional grammatical relations.

(3)   Chris pounded the clay [as flat as a pancake].

Thus, phrase structure is more general and easier to motivate independently than grammatical relations. So if one can only keep one, it should be phrase structure. Basically, Chomsky's suggestion was an Occam's razor-style argument par excellance.

Next, investigation into other fancier phenomena reveals that there are many ways in which subjects, objects, and other phrases behave differently from one another. At the level of basic description, the operative generalizations can be stated in terms of grammatical relations. The following are familiar examples from the history of the field:

(4)a.   Only subjects can be controlled in nonfinite clauses.

  b.   The antecedent of a reflexive must be a subject.

  c.   The direct object becomes the subject of a passive verb.

  d.   Only the direct object can incorporate into the verb, etc., etc.

But using the equivalencies in (2), these statements can be rephrased in terms of phrase structure, as follows.

(5)a.   Only the highest NP in a nonfinite clause can be controlled.

  b.   The antecedent of a reflexive must be the NP immediately dominated by S.

  c.   The NP in VP moves to the Specifier of IP if the verb is passive.

  d.   Only the nominal that is the sister of the verb can incorporate into it, etc., etc.

In terms of the discussion so far, clearly nothing is lost by this translation. One might argue that nothing is gained by it either, except parsimony. But parsimony is something, the proper Chomskian would reply. For better or worse, the choice to develop one's principles of grammar around statements like those in (5)—or more basic statements from which these can be derived—accounts for the characteristic phrase-structure-centric cast of Chomskian theory. In this theory, establishing the structure is paramount to doing an analysis, and phrase structural relations such as "sisterhood", "government", "containment" and "c-command" usually figure prominently in the account.

2. THE RELATIONAL GRAMMAR CRITIQUE

A cogent and influential critique of this structurally oriented approach to syntactic theory was mounted in the 1970s and early 1980s. This critique was presented first and most prominently by the Relational Grammarians in articles like those in Perlmutter (1983c), but it was also adopted and extended by the papers in Bresnan (1982b) within Lexical Functional Grammar. It has also influenced other, less generatively-minded linguists to various degrees, sometimes consciously, and sometimes not. As a result, most other theories of grammar are much less concerned with establishing the phrase structure of a clause than narrowly Chomskian work is. Often, the matter of phrase structure does not even come up in these works.

The RG critique starts with the observation that traditional constituency tests like those in (1) for English often do not apply in other languages, or if they do they give quite different results. Indeed, the tests that reveal a VP constituent in English are actually somewhat rare crosslinguistically. There is nothing exactly like VP-fronting, or VP ellipsis, or VP conjunction in Warlpiri (Simpson 1991) or Malayalam (Mohanan 1982) or Mohawk, for example. The weak interpretation of these results would be that there is no evidence for a VP node in these languages. Typically, however, people took the stronger interpretation, that these observations showed that there was no VP in these languages. This conclusion was motivated by a tacit positivist-style assumption that any phrase that exists in a language should be detectable by this kind of evidence.

Now if languages differ in substantial ways in their phrase structures, this affects the feasibility of defining grammatical relations in terms of phrase structure, as in (2). For example, if there is no VP in Warlpiri or Malayalam or Mohawk, then one cannot distinguish the object from the subject in terms of elementary phrase structure configurations. There may simply be no phrase that contains the object but not the subject in these languages.

This could have turned out to be a positive result if the grammatical relations of these languages turned out to be substantially different from those of English. Thus, the next step is to look at grammatical phenomena other than simple constituency tests, to see if generalizations like those in (4) are valid crosslinguistically. Suppose, for example, that both the "subject" and the "object" in Warlpiri or Malayalam could be the antecedents of simple reflexives, and that both could be controlled by matrix clause constituents when in a nonfinite embedded clause. This would fit beautifully with the fact that these languages seem to have no VP, so both the subject and the object are immediate constituents of the clause. Phrase structure would vary across languages, and this would be a puzzle for strong views about Universal Grammar. But grammatical relations would also vary across languages, in a way that is correlated with the variations of phrase structure. This would be striking crosslinguistic evidence that phrase structure is central to syntactic theory.

However, this was not generally what was found (although see fn. 3 for some possible cases of this type). On the contrary, the Relational Grammarians found a rather impressive array of evidence that GR-related generalizations like (4) are more stable and robust across languages than basic constituency is. For example, Perlmutter and Postal (1977) focused on the passive, comparing (4c) to (5c). They showed that there are many languages in which it is not so attractive to think of passive as involving the movement of an NP from inside the VP to outside the VP as in (5c). In part, this is because it might be dubious whether there is a VP at all in the language in question. Also, on a more surface level, there are many languages in which passive sentences do not differ from active sentences in word order, but only in the case marking of noun phrases, or in the agreement inflections on the verb. For such languages, "movement" does not seem like a good way to think about the passive. (6) is one of Perlmutter and Postal's examples from Cebuano.

(6)a.　　Magluto' ang babaye ug bugas.　　ACTIVE
　　　　　cook-ACT NOM woman　rice
　　　　　'The woman will cook rice.'

  b.　　Luto'on　sa　babaye ang　bugas. PASSIVE
　　　　　Cook-PASS GEN woman　NOM rice
　　　　　'The rice will be cooked by the woman.'

However, if one thought of passive in terms of the traditional grammatical relations, then one could recognize a fundamental unity between (6b) and its English equivalent, a unity that has little to do with surface word order or constituency. In both languages the normal object becomes the subject, displacing the usual subject and creating an intransitive clause. Described in these terms, the passive is consistent across languages, whereas the observed differences are purely a matter of how the two languages encode subjects and objects. In English, the subject is realized as the first NP in the sentence (the NP dominated only by the clause), whereas in Cebuano it is realized as a postverbal NP preceded by the nominative case particle *ang*. Crucially, these differences are observable even in simple, active clauses. Thus, they are independent of the passive per se, and passive is better stated in a format that abstracts away from these matters. In other words, passive should be stated purely in terms of "primitive" grammatical functions. And it is not only passive that works like this, but a host of syntactic phenomena, including control, reflexivization, dative shift phenomena, incorporation, complex predicate forming processes, and so on.

With these empirical observations in hand, the Relational Grammarians and related approaches offered the following deduction. Grammatical relation phenomena are relatively consistent across languages. Phrase structure is not consistent across languages. Therefore, it is wrong to derive grammatical relation phenomena from phrase structure. Rather, they should be retained as elements of syntactic analysis in their own right, as "primitives" of syntactic theory. It is merely a coincidence that in English there happen to be one-to-one correspondences between structure and grammatical relations that make a reductive approach conceivable. When the theory is developed in this way, phrase structure is much less important than on the Chomskian approach and can be left to the periphery of the theory. The urgent task is to determine what the grammatical relations are in any given clause.

In practice, the Relational Grammarians rarely said much about phrase structure issues, beyond the basic facts that concerned the embedding of clauses and NPs. In particular, it paid little attention to the details of word order and its relationship to constituency. On this point, LFG illustrates the basic logic of the situation more clearly. LFG holds that every sentence has at least two representations that are quasi-independent of each other: a functional structure that is established by looking at GR-sensitive phenomena, and a constituent structure that is established by basic word order considerations. Phrase structure exists on this view—it is just not very interesting, not very relevant to other syntactic phenomena, and certainly not very stable across languages.

3. THE CHOMSKIAN REACTION

With this historical perspective in mind, the question of primary interest here is how has Chomskian theory responded in practice to the RG critique and the empirical facts that motivated it? How does Chomskian theory now compare to the theory before as a result of these issues being raised?

As is often the case on matters of high-level theoretical comparison, direct engagement over these issues was relatively light. Perhaps the most prominent direct responses to the RG critique were some passages of Chomsky (1981). In section 2.7, he questioned whether there was really a unified phenomenon of passive in the sense that Perlmutter and Postal (1977) assume. He claimed instead that there were simply various language specific constructions in various languages that happened to resemble the English passive to a greater or lesser degree. One of the interesting examples that he cites was the *yi-/bi-* alternation in Navajo, which does not fit comfortably under the usual passive rubric, but yet has some similarities to passive, both structurally and functionally (see Speas 1990 for more data and a Chomskian analysis). For example, (7b) is like a passive in that involves preposing and highlighting the thematic object, but it is unlike the passive in that the agent is not marked as oblique, nor can it be omitted in the context of an overt theme.

(7)a.   Ashkii at'ééd yiyiiłtsá.   ACTIVE
        Boy   girl   saw
        'The boy saw the girl.'

   b.   Ashkii at'ééd biiłstá.   PASSIVE?
        Boy   girl   saw
        'The boy was seen by the girl.'

Whether we call this a passive or not is an uninteresting terminological question, Chomsky suggests; it has the properties it does, whatever we call it. There is no universal passive to have a universal theory of, he argued, just particular passives to have particular theories of. Then in section 2.8, Chomsky proceeded to sketch a way of generalizing his theory to the passive in Japanese, which was at the time thought to be a nonconfigurational language, lacking a VP.

However, these relatively direct responses had fairly little impact on the subsequent development of the theory, in practice. The real influence of Relational Grammar came tacitly as various people tried to incorporate the impressive data and empirical generalizations that the Relational Grammarians discovered and described into their Chomskian theories (see, for example, Marantz (1984), Baker (1988), Speas (1990), among others). This proved interesting when it converged with considerations that arose internal to the Chomskian program itself as that program tried to pursue a finer-grained understanding of English and a greater degree of crosslinguistic generality in its own terms.

The key shift of perspective was learning to be distrustful of the traditional constituency tests. It is a crucial (partly tacit) assumption of the RG/LFG critique that these traditional constituency tests are reliable methods for establishing phrase structure relationships. They reason that since constituency tests are not available or give different results in other languages, phrase structure does not exist or is fundamentally different in other languages. But that conclusion does not necessarily follow. It could be that constituency tests give different results not because phrase structure is different, but because the internal workings of the tests themselves are different. In the ultimate scheme of things, there should be a substantive theory of VP preposing, a theory of ellipsis, and a theory of what can be a pro-form, as well as a theory of passivization and a theory of control. There is no a priori reason to think that these theories will be simple or trivial. Once we understand clefting better, there may be excellent reasons why (say) a VP can be clefted in some languages and constructions but not in others. In the earliest transformational syntax - often recapitulated in the earliest syntax teaching - the theories of movement, deletion, pronominalization, and conjunction are indeed rather trivial, offering a way to break into the system. If there were nothing else to say about them, then the simple claim that phrases move, delete, are replaced, and are combined as units might indeed lead to the stronger claim that all phrases should be recognizable in this way. But this is surely an oversimplification, mistaking the first draft of an understanding of these phenomena for a mature one. Thus, it is quite reasonable to concede to the Relational Grammar critique that traditional constituency tests are not reliable crosslinguistically without conceding that phrase structure itself is not present crosslinguistically. Now suppose that English-like phrase structure exists in a language like Malayalam even though it cannot be detected by English-like movements and deletions. Then the grammatical relations of subject and object can still be defined in terms of that phrase structure, and passive, control, and reflexive binding in Malayalam can be analyzed in terms of notions like c-command.

It is instructive to see how these concerns about constituency tests arose internal to Chomskian syntax itself, before considering further how they affect the comparison with RG and its allies. For various reasons, Chomskian theory in the 1980s and 1990s was led to enrich its stock of phrases beyond what was accepted previously. For example, it was argued that bare adjectival predicates form a "small clause" constituent with their NP subjects, at least in some contexts (Chomsky 1981, Stowell 1983). Later, Abney (1987) argued the determiner in English heads its own phrase, DP, distinct from the NP that is headed by the noun itself. As a third example, Larson (1988) argued that the two complements of a triadic verb in English constitute a phrase of their own, specifically a VP headed by a trace of the overt verb.

(8)a.   Mary considers [John overly proud of himself/*herself].

                                                                    Small Clauses

   b.   Mary bought [$_{DP}$ that [$_{NP}$ picture of John]].

                                                                    Functional heads

   c.   Mary gave [each worker t$_v$ his paycheck].

                                                                    Larsonian shells

But if one accepts these kinds of phrase structures, then one is clearly forced to acknowledge that not all phrases can be revealed by traditional phrase structure tests in any simple way. There is sporadic constituency evidence in favor of these innovations, but many of the traditional phrase structure tests do not apply to these new phrases. For example, many phrase types in English can be clefted, including DPs, PPs, APs, and CPs. However, one cannot cleft a small clause, the NP complement of a determiner, or a Larsonian shell:

(9)a.   *It's [John overly proud of himself] that Mary considers -- .

                                                                    Small Clauses

   b.   *It's [picture of John] that Mary bought that --.

                                                                    Functional heads

   c.   *It's [each worker t$_v$ his paycheck] that Mary gave --.

                                                                    Larsonian shells

If these phrase structure proposals are at all on the right track, then there are many phrases that are not readily detected by movement, even in highly configurational English. The same holds true for pronominalization and ellipsis: these phrases are not readily omitted or replaced by a pronoun.

(10)a.   *Mary considers [him smart], and Bill considers (it) too.

Small Clauses

    b.   *Mary thinks that [John is nice], and Bill wonders if (it).
        *Mary answered the third question correctly,
          and Bill answered the (it) too.

Functional heads

    c.   *Mary threw [John tv his jacket] and Bill handed (it).

Larsonian shells

Why does one get these patterns of facts, with some phrases being cleftable (or elidable, or pronominalizable) and others not? In many cases, this is still not well-understood, but it is assumed that there should be an explanation internal to the workings of (say) clefting. In some cases reasonable proposals have been put on the table. For example, (9a) and (9c) might be out because there is no source of Case checking for the NP at the beginning of the clefted constituent within that constituent; this could lead to a Case theory violation. On the other hand, (9b) might be out because the functional head D or C is not strong enough to license a trace as its complement, according to the Empty Category Principle or its descendents in more recent theory. Similarly, Loebeck (1995) among others proposes substantive syntactic conditions on which phrases can be elided and which cannot. In general, these gaps in the distribution of clefting and ellipsis are interesting syntactic puzzles, but they do not look especially mysterious or problematic for the overall framework. Rather, they should be amenable to the usual kind of syntactic inquiry.

These kinds of issues would need to be faced by Chomskian theory anyway in the course of pursuing its own agenda, even if there were no language other than configurational English. From this perspective, when the RG critique points out that second position clitics in Warlpiri (Simpson 1991) and clefting in Malayalam (Mohanan 1982) do not reveal a VP constituent, there is no particular surprise. One does not automatically assume that Warlpiri and Malayalam do not have a VP, but only that the structure of phrases in those languages somehow interacts with the nature of cliticization or clefting to have this effect. This could have as much to do with the nature of clefting in these languages as it does with phrase structure proper.

Now, if we no longer trust traditional constituency tests to reveal to us the basic phrase structure of a construction in a language in any straightforward way, how can that phrase structure be determined? There could be many ways, some easier to apply in one language and others easier to apply in another language. But if one is committed to the idea that phenomena like passive, control, and reflexives are structurally determined along the lines summarized in (5), then it is legitimate to infer from these phenomena the phrase structures that are needed to make them work properly. If clefting and cliticization and word order do not work smoothly from these structures, those are problems to be solved, but not necessarily reasons to hold back. In short, Chomskian syntax plunges ahead and assumes that the structures it needs to work properly are present.

Many particular examples of this characteristic approach could be cited. An early example is Chomsky's (1981) discussion of Japanese, in which he uses [NP, S] terminology that implies a certain kind of phrase structure for Japanese grammatical functions, even though these do not correspond to a directly observable "D-structure" or "S-structure." Hale's (1983) approach to Warlpiri is similar: he argues that a configurational "L-structure" exists for Warlpiri alongside the nonconfigurational "C-structure" that determines word order and clitic placement. This is similar to the "two independent levels" view of LFG, but with the significant difference that for Hale the representation of grammatical functions (his L-structure) has the formal properties of a phrase marker, over which predicates like c-command are defined.

Similarly, when I studied noun incorporation in languages like Mohawk in Baker (1988), I simply assumed that direct objects were the only NPs that were structural sisters of the verb, and used that as the basis for a structural explanation of why only direct objects can be incorporated. I then took the overall success of this account to be evidence that languages like Mohawk do in fact have phrase structures comparable to English, not worrying about how this fit with other issues about word order and constituency in the language (until later: see Baker (1991, 1996c)).

Another landmark in this changing attitude toward phrase structure is Larson's (1988) study of double object constructions in English. In these constructions, phrase structure does not seem to reveal any difference between the positions of *the Prime Minister* and *a letter* in a sentence like *I sent the Prime Minister a letter.* Both seem to be objects in the sense of being NPs immediately dominated by VP. However, Barss and Lasnik (1986) showed that there are differences between the two for most binding phenomena: the first object can bind the second but not vice versa. Barss and Lasnik look at this apparent conflict between phrase structure and binding theory and ask whether pure c-command is really the right condition on binding. However, Larson takes a markedly different approach: he takes it as established that c-command is the right condition on binding, and uses the binding facts to infer a novel phrase structure for English double object constructions. Thus, for him, GR-related phenomena are (almost) enough to establish phrase structure. In fact, Larson does make an effort to show that there is converging evidence for the structures he proposes from traditional phrase structure tests, such as conjunction. But his independent evidence is slender and debatable (see Jackendoff (1990) vs. Larson (1990)), and it is clear that this is not what is driving his account. Nor did anyone ever arrive at these phrase structures purely by traditional constituency tests.

Conceptually rather similar is the work on scrambling and word order in languages like Japanese and Hindi inspired by Saito (1985) and Hoji (1985), in which configurational structure is inferred indirectly and freedom of word order is derived from movement processes that fit within the internal logic of the system.

While many other examples could be given, the last one I will mention is Speas (1990), who considers nonconfigurationality in general, and Navajo in particular. She discusses the basis for inferring that a familiar phrase structure is present in languages in which it is not obvious. Among other things, she clearly makes the point that absence of evidence for configurational phrase structure is not evidence of absence of configurational phrase structure in the Chomskian ethos. She also proposes some analyses of nonconfigurationality as it is found in particular languages.

This work might strike the unsympathetic outside observer as a circular reaction to the RG critique: it assumes that phrase structure is fundamental, rather than grammatical relations, but in practice its evidence for phrase structure in many languages comes primarily from grammatical relation phenomena. But there is a more useful way to look at the comparison.

How did Relational Grammarians establish in practice that a certain NP was a subject at some level of a clause, and that another NP was an object? Since for them grammatical relations were primitive, there was no automatic way to decide this that was guaranteed to be reliable. One could not be certain, for example, that the subject would be in a particular position in the clause, or that it would have a certain theta role, or that it would bear a certain Case ending. Any of these facts might be relevant to identifying the subject in particular languages, depending on the basic linking rules of that language, but none of them was decisive a priori. Rather, in the best cases, the relational analysis of the clause was established by the convergence of a variety of kinds of evidence, as an inference to the best overall explanation.

How does this compare to the way that contemporary Chomskian approaches establish the phrase structure analysis of a clause? I see the two methodologies as fundamentally the same. Also for the Chomskian there is no single source of evidence that is guaranteed in advance to work. In particular, data from traditional constituency tests may well be relevant, but they are not a priori decisive until one knows how those tests work in the particular language under study. Like the relational analysis, the phrase structural analysis is established by the general pattern of evidence, as an inference to the best overall explanation. And that is as it should be in any theory. The best theory is not the one that brings everything into line with its one favorite fact, but the one that finds the greatest degree of harmony and convergence among all the facts.

If all this is so, then the fundamental difference between contemporary Chomskian theory and classical Relational Grammar is not exactly where one might think, based on casual exposure to the old slogans. Relational Grammar assumed that grammatical functions were universal, foundational to syntax, and could be identified in particular cases (only) by understanding the system as a whole. That was the practical content of their claim that grammatical relations were primitive. Chomskian theory does not differ markedly from RG in these respects. Therefore, I think it is reasonable to say that grammatical relations are, in the relevant sense, "primitive" in Chomskian theory too. The real difference between the two approaches is not so much in the status of grammatical relations as primitive or not, but rather in the kind of representational system that is used to represent grammatical relations. For the relational grammarians, the representation of choice was a relational network, whereas for Chomskian theory the proper representation of "primitive" grammatical relations is a phrase marker.

4. IS PHRASE STRUCTURE A GOOD REPRESENTATION FOR GRAMMATICAL RELATIONS?

This does not mean that the differences between RG style approaches and current Chomskian theory are small or insignificant. The fact that their main difference is in their representational schemes does not mean that they are mere notational variants. If we look at phrase structures not as replacing grammatical relations but as representing them, the next logical question is whether they constitute a good representation or not. Do the system's important formal properties accurately reflect the basic qualities of the thing being represented? If so, then it is a good representation. Or is it an arcane device, the basic topology of which has no theoretical relevance, interfering with the ability to capture generalizations rather than enhancing it? In that case, it is a bad representation system—a relic that preserves some of the idiosyncratic history of the field but is now more confusing and distracting than it is worth. Then it might be a good idea to get rid of it, replacing it with a "cleaned up" representation that was designed to present grammatical relations in language-neutral terms from the start, such as a relational network or an f-structure.

One can make a case that phrase structure does in fact happen to be a very good representational system for grammatical relations, better at capturing their basic nature than its competitors. To see how, compare the RG representation for a simple English sentence like *I persuaded John that Mary will cheat Bill*. These are compared in (11).

(11)a.   RG relational network

```
P       1    2              3(?)
                       _____
persuade I  John       P    1    2

                       cheat Mary Bill
```

b.   Chomskian phrase structure

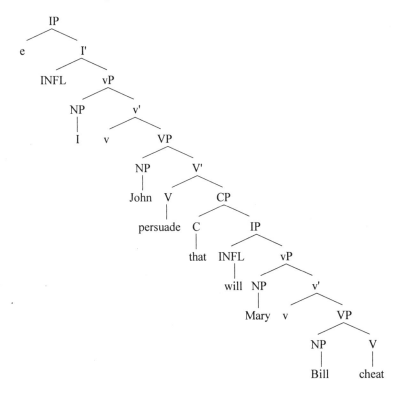

To a substantial extent, these two representations say the same things: that *Mary* is the subject of the embedded clause and *John* its object; that this embedded clause as a whole bears some grammatical relation (indirect object?) to the matrix verb; that *I* and *John* are the subject and object of the matrix clause, respectively. However, they express these relationships in representations that have different topologies. The relational net expresses subjecthood by writing a number 1 over the nominal that is on the same level as some P symbol that marks the predicate. The Chomskian phrase structure expresses subjecthood by (in this version) putting the nominal in the specifier of a v node that selects a verb phrase. To this degree, the two representations say the same things. But do they say them equally well?

There are some relatively minor differences worth pointing out immediately. The most obvious one is that the RG representation is (in this case) more succinct and easier to type. All things being equal, that is an advantage to the RG approach. (Although ease of typing and reading was not overall a major priority in the RG family of theories, as one can see by looking at the Arc-Pair grammar representations in Johnson and Postal 1980.) The RG representation also clearly abstracts away from language particular details such as word order and morphological marking. As part of this, it does not represent various elements of the clause that have no obvious significance for core grammatical relations phenomena, including the tense particles and complementizers. On the other hand, these "minor categories" are present in the Chomskian representation. Indeed, they are full partners in the representation, entering into the same basic structural relations of head, complement, and specifier as any other element. Which is the better choice here could be debated. Proponents of the relational net (or LFG's f-structure) could argue that these representations factor the linguistic information into modular parts, where the elements represented in the relational net have extensive interactions with each other but do not interact extensively with the linguistic elements not represented at this level. On the other hand, suppose that there is no clear modularity in this respect, but rather there are significant interactions between subjects and objects on the one hand and tense and complementizers on the other hand. This state of affairs would tell in favor of the Chomskian representation, which has all of these elements present in the same representation on the same terms. While there are things to be said in favor of both views, I suspect that the implicit claim of the Chomskian representation is more correct on this point. For example, it is clear that the nature of the Infl and Complementizer has important effects on how the subject is Case-marked, whether it is controlled or not, and even whether it can raise into the matrix clause, as shown by the familiar data in (12).

(12)a.   I predict that *she* will win.

    b.   I want *PRO* to win.

    c.   *I predict that *PRO* will win.

    d.   I am expected – to win.

    e.   *I am expected that – will win.

Thus, there do seem to be the kinds of interactions between the "minor" categories of C and Infl and grammatical function phenomena that justify including them in the same representation. If nothing else, there is a psychological/methodological advantage to this: if syntacticians are always required to write these minor categories into their representations, they do not have the luxury of forgetting that syntactic theory ultimately needs to account for their properties too.

But perhaps the most important property of the Chomskian mode of representation—and the one that I will focus on—is the distinctive way that it represents the *prominence* of one nominal over another. Languages are full of asymmetrical relationships, in which element A can be somehow dependent on element B but not vice versa. The most theory-neutral word for this phenomena that is more or less accepted by all generative approaches is "prominence": we say that B has prominence over A.

Now all the theories that accept the Relational Grammar critique (RG, LFG, HPSG, etc.) end up distinguishing two distinct kinds of prominence. First there is prominence internal to a single clause, the prominence that subjects have over objects and objects have over indirect objects. Keenan and Comrie's (1977) Accessibility Hiererachy was one important view of this kind. Relational Grammar spoke of the Relational Hierarchy; HPSG calls it the Obliqueness Hierarchy. It is also closely related to the Thematic Hierarchy used in LFG and many other approaches. Whatever the terminology, the relevant hierarchy expresses the kind of prominence that the matrix subject *I* has over the matrix object *John*, and that the embedded subject *Mary* has over the embedded object *Bill* in the sentence represented in (11). RG in particular built this hierarchy deeply into its terminology, calling subjects 1s, objects 2s, and indirect objects 3s. They also referred to it as an "advancement" when passive made an object into a subject or dative shift made an indirect object into a direct object. I will call this phenomenon "Relational Prominence", to coin a term that is relatively neutral among the variants.

These theories also have a second kind of prominence, which I will call "Embedding Prominence." This is a kind of prominence that comes as a result of embedding one clause (or other linguistically complex expression) inside another, which all theories do in one form or another to capture the basic recursiveness of natural language. This is the kind of prominence that the subject of a matrix clause has over the subject of the clausal complement in a sentence like (11), or that the object of a matrix clause has over the object of the clausal complement in such a sentence. Relational and Thematic Hierarchies say nothing about this kind of prominence by their basic nature. Both *I* and *Mary* are subjects in (11), and both bear an agent thematic role, albeit in different clauses. Therefore, the two cannot be distinguished by Relational/Thematic Hierarchies; they are not different in their Relational Prominence. Similarly, both *John* and *Bill* are direct objects bearing a theme/patient role in (11), so they too tie in terms of Relational Prominence. Any prominence that matrix clause constituents have over embedded clause constituents must be a different kind of prominence altogether. Again RG's terminology is instructive: the subject of an embedded clause could become the subject of a matrix clause as in the RG analysis of raising, but this was not represented by a change of number. Rather, it was a change in what the number was connected to; it was called an "ascension", not a "advancement". These two logically distinct kinds of prominence are summarized in (13).

(13)a.   *Relational Prominence*, of subjects over objects over indirect objects.
         1>2>3>…, and/or Agent>Theme>Goal>Oblique….
         (the prominence of *I* over *John*, *Mary* over *Bill* in (11))

   b.   *Embedding Prominence*, of elements in a matrix clause over elements in embedded clauses.
        (the prominence of *I* and *John* over *Mary* and *Bill* in (11).)

The logical distinctness of these two kinds of prominence is also illustrated by two kinds of "command" relationships that were proposed in the 1980s as alternatives to the Chomskian notion of c-command, introduced by Reinhart (1976, 1983). Bresnan (1982a) proposed a notion of f-command for certain kinds of control and anaphora, which was explicitly sensitive only to the embedding prominence in (13b). X f-commanded Y if Y was part of a clause that was embedded in the clause in which X bore its basic grammatical relation. There was no f-command asymmetry between the subject and object of the same clause. On the other hand, Grimshaw (1987) proposed a notion of a-command that was explicitly sensitive only to the relational prominence in (13a); no a-command relation held between phrases that were not co-arguments of a single head.

Against this background, it is a striking topological property of the Chomskian representation in (11b) that it represents the prominence of subjects over objects in exactly the same way as it represents the prominence of matrix subjects over embedded subjects. The Chomskian prominence predicate of choice is not the Relational Hierarchy, or f-command, but its distinctive notion of c-command. This is stated crucially in terms of phrase structure relationships as given in (14). (Here I emphasize the common conceptual core that all versions of c-command share, abstracting away from different proposals about exactly which phrases are crucial for c-command.)

(14)   X c-commands Y if the first phrase (of a certain kind) that properly contains X also contains Y.

This definition, together with the characteristic style of representation in (11) covers both relational prominence and embedding prominence in a uniform way. The subject *I* of the matrix clause c-commands the object *John* of that clause (relational prominence) according to this definition; it also bears the same relationship of c-command to the subject *Mary* of the embedded clause (embedding prominence). This makes the implicit claim that these two logically different kinds of prominence are really equivalent for natural language syntax. Indeed, I think this can be understood as *the* fundamental empirical claim that is being made by the Chomskian commitment to phrase structure representation in the post-RG era, when traditional constituency tests are given no analytical priority and phrase structure is understood abstractly as a representation of grammatical relations. This is summarized in (15).

(15)   Central claim of phrase structure: Relational prominence and embedding prominence are equivalent; they are the same with respect to syntax.

The Chomskian phrase structure is a uniquely revealing and truthful representation precisely to the extent that (15) is borne out by empirical research.

And borne out by empirical research it seems to be. Well over a decade since their original proposals, Bresnan's f-command and Grimshaw's a-command stand as minor historical curiosities, largely ignored even by their original proposers, compared to the continuing utility, power, and elegance of Reinhart's c-command. There are many linguistic phenomena in many languages that are in fact sensitive to relational prominence and embedding prominence in just the same way. I will give an illustrative sampling of this in very brief terms. All of the following examples have the same format. The (a) example shows that the subject has prominence over the object for some linguistic phenomenon. The (b) example shows that the relationship is asymmetrical, in that the object does not have equivalent prominence over the subject. The contrasts between (a) and (b) illustrate relational prominence. The (c) example shows that the matrix subject has the same kind of prominence over the subject of an embedded clause; the (d) example shows that the embedded subject does not have prominence over the matrix subject. Thus, (c) and (d) illustrate embedding prominence. The analogies (a):(b)::(c):(d) show the equivalence of the two kinds of prominence for syntax. As such, they support the interrelated ideas of c-command and phrase structure representation. (16) illustrates the equivalence of the two for bound variable anaphora in English—the question of whether a pronoun contained in a given noun phrase can be understood nonreferentially as a variable bound by a quantified noun phrase elsewhere in the sentence. This interpretation is possible only when the quantifier c-commands the pronoun (Reinhart 1983).

(16)a.   *Every boy* persuaded *his* mother that video games are good for you.

b.   **Her* son persuaded *every woman* that video games are good for you.

c.   *Every boy* persuaded the principal that *his* mother sang professionally.

d.   **Her* son persuaded the principal that *every woman* sang professionally.

(17) presents data about when a pronoun can be understood as having the same reference as a proper name elsewhere in the sentence. This is possible only if the pronoun does not c-command the proper name (Reihart 1983; known as Condition C in Chomsky 1981).

(17)a.   **He* persuaded *John's* mother that video games are good for you.

b.   *Her* son persuaded *Martha* that video games were good for you.

c.   **He* persuaded the principal that *John's* mother sang professionally.

d.   *Her* son persuaded the principal that *Martha* sang professionally.

(18) concerns the distribution of reciprocal anaphors in English, where the antecedent must c-command the anaphor, not vice versa (Chomsky 1981).

(18)a.   John and Mary persuaded each other's parents that video games are good.

b.   ??Each other's children persuaded Joe and Martha that video games are good.

c.   John and Mary persuaded the principal that each other's parents sing professionally.

d.   *Each other's children persuaded the principal that John and Mary sing professionally.

(19) gives data from multiple questions in English. Here the more prominent (c-commanding) *wh*-phrase must be the one that moves to clause initial position, while the less prominent (c-commanded) *wh*-phrase remains in its base position (Superiority, (Chomsky 1973a)).

(19)a.   Who persuaded whom that video games are good for you?

b.   *Who(m) did who persuade that video games are good for you?

c.   (?)Who said that who plays too many video games?

d.   *Who did who say plays too many video games?

(20) illustrates Negative Polarity Licensing, in which a contextually restricted item like *anyone* must be c-commanded by an item with inherent negative force like *nobody*.

(20)a.   Nobody persuaded anyone that video games are good for you.

b.   *Anyone persuaded nobody that video games are good for you.

c.   (?)Nobody persuaded the principal that anyone was sick.

d.   *Anyone persuaded the principal that nobody was sick.

Finally, (21) shows the same kind of parallelism between embedding prominence and relational prominence in the domain of NP movement. Underlying objects can become subjects on the surface if there is no thematic subject in the clause (RG's Unaccusative Advancement), but underlying subjects cannot become surface objects under the same conditions, as shown in (21a) vs. (21b). Similarly, embedded subjects can become matrix subjects when there is no thematic subject already there, but matrix subjects never become embedded subjects under comparable conditions, as shown by (21c) vs. (21d).

(21)a.   John fell t.

  b.   *t shouted John.

  c.   John seemed [t to win the race].

  d.   *t to say [that John seemed that it would rain].

In RG terms, advancements and ascensions seem to be a natural class, following the same principles, as opposed to retreats and descents.   Thus, relational prominence and embedding prominence are in fact equivalent for a large and varied set of natural language phenomena, just as the Chomskian mode of representation predicts.

Of course, there has not been much controversy over whether something like phrase structure exists *for English*.   With the RG critique in mind, it behooves us to see whether the equivalence of these two kinds of prominence is crosslinguistically robust, holding even in languages for which the importance of phrase structure has been questioned.   Unfortunately, the data on this point are still somewhat fragmentary: there are only a handful of typologically interesting non-Indo-European languages for which phenomena like disjoint reference and bound variable anaphora have been tested systematically.   However, the results we have suggest that this conclusion is indeed valid crosslinguistically.   For example, Lasnik (1989: ch. 9) shows that the same "condition C" pattern shown in (17) for English is found in far Eastern languages like Thai:

(22)a.   *Khaw chOOp cOOn.
            He   likes   John

  b.   (Not applicable; Condition B intervenes)

  c.   *Khaw khít   wáà cOOn chàlaàt.
            He   think that John is.smart.

  d.   cOOn khít   wáà khaw chàlaàt.
          John think that he   is.smart

The same is true in the African language Edo (Stewart, personal communication), and many others.   A more striking case comes from anaphors in Malayalam, which Mohanan (1982) argues to be a nonconfigurational language with no VP.   Still, it is true that the matrix subject in Malayalam can equally be the antecedent of a reflexive anaphor contained in the direct object or of one contained in the subject of the embedded clause.   However, the reverse relationships are impossible (see also Mohanan 1980).

(23)a.   Raajaawə [swantam bharyaye] nulli.
         King-NOM self's   wife-ACC pinched
         'The *king* pinched *his own* wife.'

   b.   *Raajaawine[swantam haarya]   nulli.
         King-ACC self's   wife-NOM pinched.
         '*His own* wife pinched the *king*.'

   c.   [Raajaawine[swantam bhaarya]   nulli   ennə] bhatane
         king-ACC self's   wife-NOM pinched that   Soldier-ACC
         mantri   wiswasippiccu.
         minister-NOM believe-made.
         'The *minister* convinced the soldier that *his own* wife pinched the king.'

   d.   (Not presented)

   The same pattern is found with *zibun* 'self' in Japanese, a language once thought to be nonconfigurational because of its extensive scrambling.
   This characteristic c-command pattern can even be found in Mohawk, a more radically nonconfigurational language on the surface. Mohawk does not have quantified NPs for independent reasons (Baker 1995), but according to Reinhart (1983) bound variable anaphora effects can be detected even with names as antecedents. If a pronoun is understood as a bound variable, it will give a "sloppy identity" reading in ellipsis contexts. Thus, (24a,c) in Mohawk show that matrix subjects are prominent over both direct objects and embedded subjects by this test, but objects are not prominent over the subject of the same clause ((24b)).

(24)a.   Sak   rao-tshenv erhar wa-ho-nut-e'   tanu' Tyer oni.
         Sak   his-pet   dog fact-he/him-feed-punc and Tyer too
         'Sak fed his pet dog , and Tyer did too.' (sloppy OK: Tyer fed Tyer's dog)

   b.   #Sak rao-tshenv erhar wa-ho-kari-'   tanu' Tyer oni.
         Sak   his-pet   dog fact-he/him-bite-punc and Tyer too
         'His pet dog bit Sak, and Tyer too.' (not sloppy: *Tyer's dog bit Tyer)

   c.   Uwari ako-ya'tuni wa'-uk-hrori-'   wa'te-w-atya'k-e' tanu' Sosan
         Mary her-doll   fact-she/me-tell-punc fact-it-break-punc and Susan
         oni.
         too
         'Mary told me that her doll broke, and Susuan did too.'
         (sloppy OK: Susan told me that Susan's doll broke.)

d.   (#)Rao-skare'   wa'-uk-hrori-'   tsi wa-hrv-hey-e'   ne Sak, tanu'
        his-girlfriend fact-she/me-tell-punc that fact-he-die-punc ne Sak and
        Tyer oni.
        Tyer too.
        'His girlfriend told me that Sak died, and Tyer too.'
        (sloppy predicted bad: *Tyer's girlfriend told me that Tyer died.)

Again the special topology of the Chomskian representation scheme is supported.[3]

Non-structural theories that distinguish relational prominence and embedding prominence typically also have to say something special about what happens when the two types of prominence conflict with one another. This issue can also be illustrated with the example in (11) *I persuaded John that Mary will cheat Bill.* In such a sentence, will *John*, the matrix object of *persuade* have prominence over *Mary* the embedded subject, or will the embedded subject have prominence over the matrix object? No answer emerges naturally from the nonstructural theory, precisely because the two types of prominence are independent. It could be that relational prominence is more important, so that all subjects will take precedence over all objects, regardless of the embedding relationships. Or it could be that embedding is more important, so that all matrix clause nominals take priority over all embedded nominals. Or maybe no prominence difference is defined in this situation. Or maybe prominence is unstable, varying from language to language or from sentence to sentence, depending on other factors. The nonstructural theories simply make no principled claim here.

In contrast, the Chomskian approach extends to this situation automatically, with favorable results.[4] Since relational prominence and embedding prominence are the same thing on this view, there is no special problem of comparing apples to oranges. It is all apples: c-command is well-defined in these situations, and should give the right results (as long as the phrase structures are correct). For example, the Chomskian approach clearly predicts that in a structure like (11b) the matrix object will have prominence over the embedded subject, not vice versa. This is because the first phrase that contains the matrix object—the VP—contains a phrase that properly contains the embedded subject—namely, the CP complement. Thus, the matrix object c-commands the embedded subject in this construction. This is correct, as show by the asymmetries in (25). (25a) illustrates bound variable anaphora; (25b) illustrates Condition C effects, (25c) the binding of reciprocal anaphors, (25d) Superiority, (25e) the licensing of negative polarity items, and (25f) NP movement.

(25)a.   John persuaded *every child* that *his* mother had baked cookies.
            *John persuaded *her* child that *every woman* had baked cookies.

   b.   *John persuaded *her* that *Mary's* mother had made cookies.
            John persuaded *Martha's* daughter that *she* had made cookies.

    c.   I persuaded *John and Mary* that *each other's* parents had called the police.
              *I persuaded *each other's* children that *Joe and Martha* had called the police.

    d.   (?)Who(m) did you persuade that who had called the police?
              *Who did you persuade whom had called the police?

    e.   ?John persuaded *nobody* that *anyone* had called the police.
              *John persuaded *anyone* that *nobody* had called the police.

    f.   John expected *Mary* [*t* to call the police].
              *John persuaded *t* [that *Mary* seems that it will rain].

In fact, the predictions here are more subtle than simply saying that embedding prominence is stronger than relational prominence across the board. If that were so, then one would also expect the matrix object to have prominence over noun phrases that are inside a clausal subject as well. However, c-command does not make this prediction: the first phrase that properly contains the matrix object would be the matrix VP, and this does not contain a clausal subject. Therefore, neither NP c-commands the other in this configuration, and the Chomskian approach predicts no asymmetry in prominence here. This is also correct: (26) shows that the matrix object does not have prominence over the subject of a clausal subject.

  (26)a.   *That *he* raised funds legally discredited *every politician*.

      b.   That *Mary* raised funds illegally discredited *her* in the eyes of the public.

      c.   ??That *each other's* parents called the police upset *John and Mary*.

      d.   *Who(m) did (the fact) that who raised funds illegally discredit?

      e.   *That *anyone* raised funds illegally discredited *nobody* in the party.

For example, if the quantified matrix object in (26a) had prominence over the embedded subject pronoun, one would expect that the pronoun could be interpreted as a bound variable, contrary to fact. Similarly, if the *wh*-phrase object in the base structure of (26d) had prominence over the embedded subject, then it should be possible for it to move to Spec, CP and license the other as a *wh*-phrase in situ, in accordance with Superiority; nevertheless (26d) is unacceptable. The other examples show similar results based on the other conditions sensitive to c-command.

In short, the Chomskian approach makes accurate predictions in this domain precisely because it collapses the two kinds of prominence into one in a certain way. Therefore, there are no conflicts between two different kinds of prominence of the kind that would require special regulations in other frameworks.   Thus, the technique of using phrase structure relationships to represent grammatical functions is a *good* representation system, both because it captures the fact that clause-internal prominence and cross-clausal prominence are equivalent for many relations and languages, and because it defines accurately how potential conflicts in prominence are resolved. This is the real empirical substance to the claim expressed somewhat misleadingly as "Grammatical functions are defined in terms of phrase structure relationships."

The Chomskian approach can also be compared to the nonconfigurational binding approach developed within HPSG by Pollard and Sag (1994). Pollard and Sag replace c-command with o-command, which they define recursively as follows:

(27)a.   Let Y and Z be synsem objects with distinct LOCAL values, Y referential.   Then Y locally o-commands Z just in case Y is less oblique than Z.

  b.   Y o-commands Z, if there is an X such that X contains Z, and Y locally o-commands X.

Their first step is to define local o-command, which is a straightforward version of the Relational Prominence idea: subjects are less oblique than objects, objects are less oblique than indirect objects, and so on.   Then (27b) works embedding prominence into the definition, by saying that X o-commands Y if it is less oblique than Y or if it is less oblique than something Y is embedded in.   In this way, o-command matches the empirical successes of c-command, while being compatible with a theory in which subject and object are not characterized in terms of phrase structure. This is the next best thing to the Chomskian approach. However, one can still argue that the Chomskian approach is conceptually better, because the HPSG condition in (27) is really just a thinly disguised disjunction. It regulates the way that relational prominence interacts with embedding prominence by brute force stipulation, and other kinds of interactions could have been described just as easily. The correct generalization about prominence emerges more organically and more necessarily out of the Chomskian system, arising from the nature of the representational system itself. That, in short, is the proof that this is a good system of representation.

5. *WHY* IS PHRASE STRUCTURE A GOOD REPRESENTATION FOR GRAMMATICAL RELATIONS?

However, it is still fair to ask why the Chomskian representation is so successful in this respect. Before accusing other theories of having veiled stipulations and arbitrary disjunctions, it is wise to take stock of one's own theory. Could it be that the Chomskian solution is also a cleverly disguised disjunction, built into the representation system where one might forget about it? *Why* should clause-internal relational prominence be equivalent to cross-clausal embedding prominence for many syntactic purposes? Is there really a substantive generalization being captured here? Or was it simply a lucky historical accident that Chomskian theory stumbled onto an attractive representation for grammatical functions by studying the quirks of constituent structure in English? I close this paper with some speculative remarks on this conceptual question.

Of course, it is desirable to say that this was not an accident, that English phrase structure turns out to be telling the truth for good reasons. What would those be? If one thinks about it, the purpose of a phrase structure representation is essentially to represent embedding prominence: X is a phrase in structure Y if and only if the words contained in X are a unit that is formed first and then combined with other material to form Y. (Here I use sequential derivational terminology, following Chomsky's (1995) conception of Merge, but this is not crucial.) In other words, X is embedded in Y. As already mentioned, this notion of embedding cannot be eliminated: any theory must somehow represent an embedding relation, given the recursive nature of natural languages. Thus, if embedding prominence clearly exists, and if there is only one kind of prominence in point of fact, then *clause-internal relational prominence must really be a type of embedding prominence.* This could be the deeper conceptual claim that would make the Chomskian phrase structure representation scheme more than a disguised stipulation.

In order to take this last step toward explanation, we must take a particular stand on certain details internal to the Chomskian approach, which I have remained neutral on so far. In particular, we must take a stand on exactly where the subject is generated. There have been at least three views about this in recent times, which are compared schematically in (28).

(28)a.   Chomsky 1986a

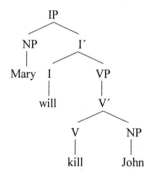

b.   Fukui and Speas 1986

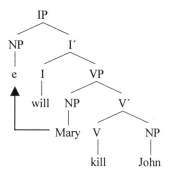

c.   Hale and Keyser 1993, Chomsky 1995

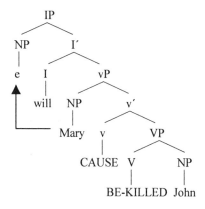

(28a) is the oldest view, familiar from Chomsky (1981, 1986a). It holds that the subject is generated outside of the VP, where it receives a special, designated external theta role from the V/VP. However, there is no real understanding on this view why the subject should be treated in this particular way —why most verbs should have one and only one argument that is designated as being external (see also Williams (1981), who takes this as an axiom). (28b) is one of the early versions of the so-called VP-internal subject hypothesis. This is the idea that there are no external arguments in the original sense, but rather the subject ends up outside the VP on the surface as a result of a raising operation, triggered by the need to get Case. This view as such also does not lead to a full understanding of the origins of relational prominence, since both NPs are arguments of the same verb. It is merely stipulated on this view that one NP is theta-marked within V-bar and the other within VP.

However, (26c)—currently the most commonly assumed version of the VP internal subject hypothesis—raises some new possibilities. It was proposed by Hale and Keyser (1993) in their effort explain theta-theory, and endorsed (with some modifications) by Chomsky (1995). Kratzer (1996) also proposes a similar idea, although she calls the higher head Voice. What is crucially different about this proposal is that the subject and the object are technically the arguments of two different verbal heads, both of which are in principle meaningful. This raises the possibility that the prominence relation between the subject and the object could be derived from the compositional relationship between the verbal heads that they are arguments of. If so, then relational prominence is truly reduced to a special case of embedding prominence.

The attractiveness of this approach comes from its ability to capitalize on a parallel between phrase structure and lexical semantics. From the standpoint of lexical semantics, many transitive verbs like *kill* are analyzed as accomplishments. These are taken to be internally complex: they consist of a process or activity component that is joined with a change of state component in such a way that the activity causes the change of state. This semantic complexity can be detected by certain characteristic patterns of entailment that these verbs enter into, familiar since the days of Generative Semantics. For example, the transitive accomplishment sentence *Mary opened the door* entails the intransitive change-of-state sentence *The door opened* (Dowty 1979, Parsons 1990). Even more strikingly, transitive accomplishment sentences with certain adverbs seem to have a scope ambiguity that suggests that the sentences are internally complex. Thus *Mary opened the door again* has a stronger reading, that Mary again caused the door to be open, and a weaker reading, that Mary merely caused it that the door was again open (see the above references, and also von Stechow (1995)). This lexical semantic research converges with the syntactic research that points toward (28c), suggesting that the lower verbal head in the structure stands for the resulting (change of) state and the higher verbal head stands for the causing activity. Now the theme argument *John* is naturally a part of the description of the resulting state; the state is characterized as a property (being dead, or better, having been killed) holding of the referent of *John*. Therefore it is natural for *John* to form a syntactic constituent with the lower verb. In contrast, the agent *Mary* does not play a role in describing the resulting state. The referent of *Mary* only plays a role in the activity that causes this state. Thus *Mary* naturally forms a syntactic constituent with the higher verbal head but not with the lower one. Put another way, the causing activity is a two-place relation that holds of a causing agent and a caused change of state. Thus, the corresponding head in the syntax is the head of a phrase that contains an NP expressing the causing agent and a VP expressing the caused change of state. The change of state in turn is made up of two elements: a thing and a property that (begins to) hold of that thing. Thus, the syntactic head corresponding to the property forms a phrase with an NP that denotes a thing, the theme. These are the natural embedding relationships, with the change of state being a constituent of the causing event, but not vice versa. Then the "relational prominence" of *Mary* over *John* in *Mary killed John* is really the same thing as the "embedding prominence" of *Mary* over *John* in a fully biclausal structure *Mary caused (it) that John died.* Both are rooted in the fundamental composition of atomic predicates with their arguments.[5]

This reasoning can be generalized to derive other instances of relational prominence from basic embedding relationships as well. For example, direct objects c-command NPs that are contained in *to*-phrases and other arguments expressed as PPs within the verb phrase. In RG terms, "2s" outrank "3s" on the Relational Hierarchy. In Baker (1996c, to appear), I explore a way of deriving this from a further decomposition of the verb, as shown in (29).

(29)

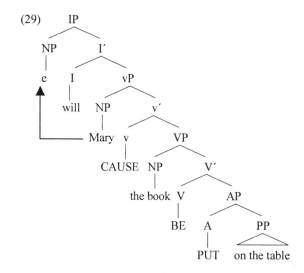

Here the accomplishment verb *put* is decomposed first into a causative element and an intransitive/inchoative element as before. Then this second element is further decomposed into an adjectival element PUT which denotes a pure property and a predicative element BE that creates a state out of the property by predicating it of an entity. (By this label, I do not mean to imply that the actual English verb *be* has precisely this function; see Baker (to appear) for details on the relationship of BE to copular particles in English and other languages.) This decomposition is motivated by various syntactic facts from the literature on unaccusativity and adjectival passives, facts that show that theme arguments are internal arguments of verbs but external arguments of derivationally related adjectives (Burzio 1986, Levin and Rappaport 1986, Cinque 1990). This is directly expressed in (29), in which the theme *the book* is outside the projection of the adjectival element PUT, but inside the projection of the operator that verbalizes that root. In contrast, phrases bearing theta roles other than theme can be the internal arguments of adjectives, as the locative phrase is in (29). This phrasal structure also represents the natural embedding relationships expected for compositional semantics, understood as follows. CAUSE is a verbal operator that takes two arguments, an NP (its agent)

and a VP (its resulting state) and creates an event. BE is a verbal operator that takes two arguments, an NP (the theme) and an AP (a property) and creates the state of the property holding of the theme. Finally, the A optionally takes a PP (which describes a goal, a source, or other kinds of path) and creates a property. Then, in the surface syntax of English PUT incorporates into BE, and PUT+BE incorporates into CAUSE to derive the complex verb, spelled out in the phonology as *put*.

The important point is that on this view one never has to stipulate any relational prominence between the two NP arguments of a single head. The issue doesn't arise, simply because none of the subatomic predicates takes more than one NP argument. They all take one NP argument plus possibly an internally complex verbal or adjectival argument. On this kind of view, relational prominence can be eliminated from the theory in favor of embedding prominence across the board.

Of course, in laying out this view I have focussed on the success stories and the easier cases. It is still an urgent open question how this program can be insightfully generalized to the full range of multi-argument verbs. To take a harder case, consider a stative transitive verb like *like*. This verb also takes both a subject and an object. Moreover, the usual syntactic evidence shows that the subject has prominence over the object, just as with other transitive verbs.

(30)a. *Every boy* likes *his* mother.   Bound variable anaphora
        **Her* son likes *every woman*.*

b.   **He* likes *John's* mother.   Condition C.
        John's mother likes *him*.

c.   *John and Mary* like *each other's* parents. Reciprocal anaphors
        ?Each other's parents like *John and Mary*.

d.   Who likes whom?   Superiority
        *Who(m) does who like?

e.   *Nobody* likes *anybody* around here.   Negative Polarity Licensing
        **Anybody* likes *nobody* around here.

f.   *John* is liked *t* by everyone.   NP movement

Indeed, stative verbs like *like* behave no differently from agentive accomplishment verbs like *kill* or *persuade* in these respects. Therefore, one would like to account for this prominence in the same way, by reducing it to c-command defined over embedding structures that are motivated by semantic compositionality. The problem is that there is not such good lexical semantic motivation for decomposing verbs like *like*. The same lexical semantics literature that uncovers internal complexity for accomplishment verbs typically claims that stative verbs are conceptually simple (see, for example, Dowty 1979). What we want is a structure like (31), where X and Y are meaningful elements such that X+Y equals *like*.

(31)

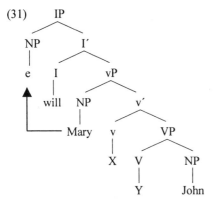

Conceivably, one could tough it out and say that *like* simply means "cause to be LIKED" just as *kill* means "cause to be KILLED (i.e. dead)." But this seems ad hoc. Also, there is no clear adverbial evidence for internal complexity in this case: *Mary will like John again* cannot mean "Mary will cause [John again be.liked]."

On the other hand, it is true that dyadic stative predicates such as *like* vary significantly how they are expressed across languages. Some languages use complex periphrastic expressions for them, such as "Anger is on me towards you" (Irish). This fact is peculiar if these predicates are semantically as simple as the literature says. Also, stative transitive verbs often have certain affinities to adjectives across languages. For example, they allow degree-like expressions that other transitive verbs do not. Thus, in English *I like Chris a lot* means "I like Chris to a large degree", whereas in *I walk the dog a lot*, *a lot* has a frequency reading (similar to *often*) not a degree reading. Thus, while I do not have a specific proposal to defend here, there is some cause for optimism that close investigation of these predicates crosslinguistically will point to a reasonable decomposition for them too—perhaps one involving an adjective and a verbalizing operator of some kind. Win or lose, this seems like an important next step for this research tradition to take.

6. CONCLUSION

In this paper, I have argued that the Chomskian approach to grammatical relations doesn't necessarily differ from Relational Grammar and other theories not oriented around phrase structure in quite the way that has traditionally been claimed. It should be conceded that grammatical relations cannot always be reduced to phrase structure relationships that can be established by independent syntactic tests. In that sense, grammatical relations are primitive. Nevertheless, it can still be claimed that phrase structure relationships are a particularly good representation of grammatical relations, because they express in an organic way the deep interrelationship between relational prominence and embedding prominence. These two kinds of prominence must be kept distinct in most other representation schemes, and this leads to missed generalizations and stipulations. Finally, I raised the question of whether there was a deeper grounding for Chomskian phrase structure representations so that the equivalence of relational prominence and embedding prominence would not be a bad theoretical pun but rather an explanatory reduction. In some cases, it looks like this deeper grounding can come from the compositionality of lexical semantics. However, more careful work needs to be done in this area before we can be sure that the project of reducing relational prominence to embedding prominence can be carried through with full generality.

NOTES

[1] By the "narrowly Chomskian approach to syntax" I mean the approach that Chomsky himself and those who follow him most closely have taken to syntax over the years, as contrasted to other generative approaches (which are Chomskian in a broader sense). I use this terminology because the official label of that approach has changed over the years that are relevant to this overview, from the Extended Standard Theory, to Government and Binding Theory, to Principles and Parameters, to the Minimalist Program. However, as far as I can see the basic notion of the relationship between grammatical relations and phrase structure has remained relatively constant through all these changes of label. Thus, I can abstract away from these evolutions in the framework, for the most part.

[2] For simplicity, in this article I put aside the complex question of what the grammatical relations are in a so-called double object construction like *Chris gave Pat the book*, about which much has been written in the literature on grammatical relations. Suffice it only to say that all of the classes of theories considered here have ways to generalize their basic premises to this case, for better or for worse.

[3] Of course, the world is a complicated place, and there is also evidence that might be interpreted as pointing the other way. For example, some syntactic relationships might be clause bounded as well as sensitive to c-command/prominence. For such relationships, the difference between c-command and relational prominence will be subtle at best. Negative polarity licensing in English might be a case in point, for speakers who find (20c) marginal. Reflexive anaphora is another in languages that do not permit examples like (18c). However, it is not particularly problematic for the Chomskian view that some linguistic relationships are subject to additional conditions. All that is necessary is that there be enough cases that run off pure c-command to show that it does not represent a spurious generalization.

More interestingly, Baker (1991, 1996c) shows that Condition C and wh-extraction in Mohawk seem to be sensitive to embedding prominence but not to relational prominence: these relations do not show subject-object asymmetries, but they do show differences between the constituents of a main clause and the constituents of an embedded clause. This looks a bit like f-command. However, in those works I argued that this is because Mohawk has a different kind of phrase structure, with overt subjects and objects (but not clauses) dislocated from their base positions. Similar facts hold in Warlpiri (Simpson 1991). These patterns can be interpreted as another kind of evidence in favor of phrase structure theories. As far as I know, these clause-internal binding asymmetries disappear only in languages like Mohawk and Warlpiri that are nonconfigurational, allowing extensive free word order and argument drop. Thus, there do seem to be correlations between some GR-sensitive behavior and surface word order properties. Such correlations are expected in structure-based theories, but not in theories that completely divorce things like binding theory from word order and constituency, expressing them at different levels of representation. This might show that there are limits to the RG critique, with different language types showing systematic differences in GR-behavior after all, although in a limited domain. See Baker (2000) for fuller discussion of these cases and their implications.

[4] This is particularly true if VP-shell structures in the sense of Larson 1988 are adopted (as in (11)), although some of the basic cases can be derived even without this innovation.

[5]   This view does *not* entail that *Mary killed John* is derived from a structure that is identical to *Mary caused John to die* in all respects, only that both structures involve similar embedding relationships that are interpreted compositionally. On the contrary, the embedded phrase in one case is a VP, and in the other it is at least an IP headed by *to*. Therefore, syntactic and semantic differences that are attributable to this difference in structure are expected.

FREDERICK J. NEWMEYER

GRAMMATICAL FUNCTIONS, THEMATIC ROLES, AND PHRASE STRUCTURE: THEIR UNDERLYING DISUNITY

1. INTRODUCTION

The purpose of this chapter is to argue against a position that nobody would have thought to adopt throughout most of the history of transformational syntax: the 'Deep Alignment Hypothesis' (DAH).[1] According to the DAH, grammatical functions (or relations), thematic roles, and configurational structure are in alignment at an underlying grammatical level. That is, a particular value for one implies a particular value for the others. Section 2 below traces the gradual development of the DAH over the past several decades. Section 3 critiques the hypothesis, arguing that the generalization that it embodies cannot be sustained. Section 4 is a brief conclusion.

2. THE DEVELOPMENT OF THE DEEP ALIGNMENT HYPOTHESIS

As transformational grammar progressed in the 1970s and early 1980s, the interdependency between grammatical functions and thematic roles became increasingly central to the theory (§2.1). Mark Baker's Uniformity of Theta Assignment Hypothesis (UTAH) and associated hypotheses led ultimately to the proposal that they are fully aligned at the deepest level of syntactic representation (§2.2).

2.1 Grammatical functions and thematic roles

In the earliest, i.e. pre-1970s, versions of transformational grammar, little appeal was made either to grammatical functions or to thematic roles. Chomsky in *Aspects of the Theory of Syntax* (Chomsky 1965) recognized the fact that notions such as 'Subject-of' and 'Direct-Object-of' had played a central role in traditional grammatical description, but that they had no independent theoretical status in transformational syntax. He suggested (p. 71) that they might be defined derivatively, based on phrase structure configuration. Hence, a 'subject' was a deep

William D. Davies and Stanley Dubinsky (eds.), Objects and other subjects:
Grammatical functions, functional categories, and configurationality, 53—75.
© *2001 Kluwer Academic Publishers. Printed in the Netherlands*

structure NP immediately dominated by S and a 'direct object' a deep structure NP immediately dominated by VP. However, in *Aspects* no grammatical process was posited that needed to make reference to either construct. Interestingly, he dismissed the idea that such relations had surface structure relevance and tentatively suggested (p. 221) that 'Topic-of' and 'Comment-of' were the surface analogues to 'Subject-of' and 'Predicate-of'.

Thematic roles were introduced into transformational grammar in Jeffrey Gruber's 1965 dissertation (Gruber 1976) and were exploited in the analysis of diverse syntactic phenomena in Fillmore (1968) and Jackendoff (1972). The relevant generalizations all held at derived, rather than deep, levels of structure. So Fillmore appealed to a hierarchy of θ-roles (or 'case-roles', as he called them) as a determining factor in the choice of surface structure subject and Jackendoff attempted to account for conditions on passivization and anaphor-antecedent relations in reflexivization in terms of a similar hierarchy.

A curious reversal occurred in the dozen or so years after 1970. Gradually, grammatical functions came to be seen as relevant to transformationally derived levels of structure, rather than D-structure, while thematic roles were appealed to in the explanation of 'deeper' processes. For example, the first appearance of grammatical functions in a theoretical statement was in Chomsky (1973a: 239), where they were built into a condition on the application of transformational rules:

(1)   No rule can involve, X, Y in the structure:
        $\dots [_\alpha \dots Z \dots - WYV \dots] \dots$
        where Z is the specified subject of WYV in α

In *Lectures on Government and Binding (LGB)*, their theoretical relevance was entirely surface-oriented. Here Chomsky introduced a novel grammatical function 'SUBJECT', defined as 'the subject of an infinitive, an NP or a small clause...' (Chomsky 1981: 209). 'SUBJECT' was employed in the definition of 'governing category' (p. 211):

(2) β is a *governing category for* α if and only if β is the minimal category containing α, the governor of α, and a SUBJECT accessible to α.

Since the notion 'governing category' was a crucial component of the binding theory and the binding theory was presumed to apply at S-structure, the grammatical relevance of the function 'SUBJECT' was at the surface.

The primary relevance of θ-roles, on the other hand, was at D-structure. In addition to playing a role in a multitude of lexical rules, specific θ-role labels entered — differently in different approaches — into the statement of the D-structure linking between thematic structure and phrase structure. By the late 1970s, no significance was attached to the θ-role borne by an element of S-structure.

The seeds of a possible alignment between grammatical functions, θ-roles, and configuration were sown early on in *LGB* thanks to two central principles of UG proposed there — the Projection Principle and the Theta-Criterion. The former can be thought of as a strengthened version of the Structure-Preserving Constraint (Emonds 1976). It requires that the subcategorization properties of lexical heads (e.g. verbs, nouns, adjectives, and prepositions) be represented at all three syntactic levels: D-structure, S-structure, and Logical Form. In other words, the Projection Principle entails that grammatical configurations (minor deletions and local movements exempted) remain unchanged throughout the derivation. A predicate that takes a subject, direct object, and an indirect object, say, at one stage in a derivation, must take them at all stages.

The Theta-Criterion demands a biunique relation between arguments and θ-roles:

> Each argument bears one and only one θ-role and each θ-role is assigned to one and only one argument. (Chomsky 1981: 36)

The Theta-Criterion thus prevents movement of an NP into a structural position to which a θ-role had already been assigned. In conjunction with a couple subsidiary assumptions, a consequence of the Theta-Criterion was that all thematic information relevant to the derivation had to be present at D-structure.

Chomsky's introduction of the Theta-Criterion was accompanied by surprisingly little discussion, most of which took place in a footnote (p. 139). He acknowledged the immediate roots of the principle in Freidin (1978)'s Functional Uniqueness Principle, but neglected to mention that a very similar condition was a centerpiece of Case Grammar (Fillmore 1968). Chomsky remarked that the Theta-Criterion, 'while not unnatural, is not obviously correct' (p. 139), noting that it was violated in Jackendoff (1972), where *John* in *John deliberately rolled down the hill* was assigned two θ-roles: Agent and Theme. Perhaps the major virtue of the Theta-Criterion, as things were viewed at the time, was an explanation of the apparent fact that the landing site of a movement rule is always to a position to which no θ-role is assigned (e. g., COMP and the subject of a passive or raising predicate). As first noted in Borer (1980), if movement were to take place to a position assigned a θ-role, then the combination of that θ-role and the one possessed by the moved element would lead to a Theta-Criterion violation.

The Projection Principle and the Theta-Criterion combined to reinforce the trend toward more 'abstract' analyses of grammatical phenomena that was initiated in Chomsky (1973a) and to invite even increased degrees of abstractness. For example, given the Projection Principle, traces of movement are required in order that the subcategorizational position of the moved element be represented structurally. Furthermore, given the subsidiary assumption that subcategorization is uniform across different uses of the same lexical item, the Projection Principle demands PRO subjects for infinitives. Since the verb *hope* has an embedded subject in (3a), it has to have one in (3b) as well:

(3)a.   John hopes [that he will be able to leave early].

b.   John hopes [PRO to be able to leave early].

Analogously, the Theta-Criterion demands a PRO subject for infinitives in order to prevent two different roles being assigned to the matrix subject. Note that in the following sentence, the subject argument of the higher verb is an Experiencer (or perhaps a Theme) and that of the lower an Agent. PRO is therefore necessary to avoid a Theta-Criterion violation:

(4)   Mary yearns [PRO to convince John that she is qualified].

Furthermore, the Theta-Criterion mandated a small clause analysis of certain predication structures. As pointed out in Williams (1994), in a sentence like (5a), *arrive* and *sad* assign different θ-roles to *John*. Therefore, given the Theta-Criterion, (5a) would have to be underlain by biclausal (5b):[2]

(5)a.   John left the room angry.

b.   John left the room [PRO angry].

2.2   *The UTAH and its consequences*

The next major step toward the triple alignment of grammatical functions, thematic roles, and constituent structure was taken in Baker (1988). The centerpiece of that book is the Uniformity of Theta Assignment Hypothesis (UTAH), formulated as follows:

> Identical thematic relationships between items are represented by identical structural relationships between those items at the level of D-structure. (Baker 1988: 46)

In other words, if Agents are encoded as deep subjects in one derivation, they are encoded as deep subjects in all derivations. Baker provided both conceptual and empirical motivation for the UTAH. Conceptually, he noted, the UTAH, in conjunction with the Projection Principle, 'constrain[s] the theory and make[s] it interesting' (p. 51). The Projection Principle, by itself, is compatible with base generation of whatever complex structure, leaving it with no 'empirical bite', as Baker put it. The UTAH, on the other hand,

> leads away from base generation in many cases. Yet unless the transformational component is limited by principles like the Projection Principle, it makes little difference what D-structure is assigned to a given form, because anything could happen en route to the interpreted levels of PF and LF. In this case, the UTAH would have little empirical content. However, in a theory which contains both, each provides a check against the undisciplined avoidance of the other. This is the kind of situation which can give rise to deep and true explanation. (Baker 1988: 51)

Baker derived his major empirical support for the UTAH from the incorporation structures that he analyzed in a multitude of languages. For example, many languages have a morphological causative with a biclausal causative as a thematic paraphrase. Consider the following pair from Chichewa:

(6)a. Mtsikana a-na-chit-its-a   kuti mtsuko   u-gw-e
       girl   SP-PAST-do-cause-ASP that waterpot PAST-fall-ASP
       'The girl made the waterpot fall'

   b. Mtsikana a-na-u-gw-ets-a   mtsuko
       girl   SP-PAST-OP-fall-CAUS-ASP waterpot
       'The girl made the waterpot fall'

The UTAH demands that these two sentences be derived from the same underlying structure, where (6b) is derived by movement of the verb –*gw*- 'fall':

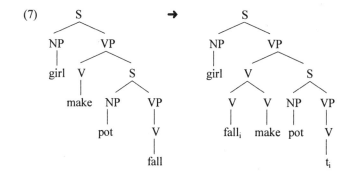

Baker argued that if we assume a movement analysis in such cases, we can appeal to the Empty Category Principle (ECP) and other constraints for an explanation of those situations in which incorporation fails.[3] In other words, a unique mapping of θ-roles onto grammatical structure was seen to be an essential component of the explanation of the cross-linguistic distribution of incorporation structures.

The year 1993 saw the birth of two research programs based on Baker's work, the central theme of each being the extension of the idea that seemingly monoclausal structures derive from complex embedding structures. One trend, represented by Hale and Keyser (1993), has carried out the syntactic derivation of such structures wholly within the lexicon. The UTAH, for Hale and Keyser, is instantiated at the most abstract level of lexical structure, the level of Lexical Relational Structure (LRS). Syntactic movement applies within the lexicon, deriving D-structure representations. Movement is posited to take place even in languages in which incorporation is not evident on the surface. For example, Hale and Keyser derived the predicate of sentence (8) as is illustrated in (9), in which the lower N (*shelf*) first incorporates with the P and then with the successive higher Vs:

(8)   She shelved her books.

(9)

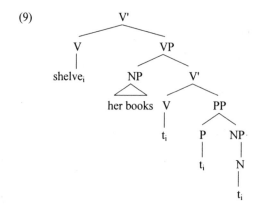

Hale and Keyser followed Baker in appealing to the ECP to explain why certain incorporation structures fail to occur. For example, (10) is underivable from its most plausible underlying structure, (11). The minimality condition on government for the ECP is violated, since the preposition is a closer potential governor of the trace than is the noun landing site:

(10)   *He shelved the books on.

(11)

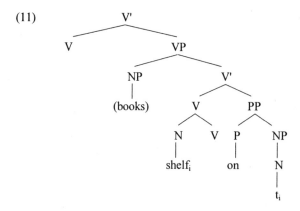

Most significantly for our interests, Hale and Keyser argued that an unexpected, but welcome, consequence of this complex embedding approach to denominal verbs and related constructions was the possibility of effecting an identity between positions in LRS and thematic roles. Thus if the highest V in (9), by virtue of its position in the tree and/or its taking VP as a complement, could uniformly be interpreted as 'causal', then the thematic role 'Agent' might turn out to be nothing more than the role borne by any external argument of a V in that position. Along the same lines, the external argument of the lower V would receive the role 'Theme' and the internal argument of the P the role 'Location'.

In a paper published the same year, Baker (1993) came to many of the same conclusions as Hale and Keyser, but maintained a strictly syntactic (as opposed to lexical) approach to the movements involved in the derivation of semantically complex predicates. Baker's approach

> ... assumes that there are notions like agent and patient, instrument, benefactive, and locative that are (in part) consistent and recognizable across peoples and cultures. *D-structure is then constructed directly from these categories* ... (Baker 1993: 32; emphasis added)

Note that this assumption takes us one step beyond the UTAH. If D-structure is to be constructed directly from Agents, Patients, and so on, then a D-structure like (9) for sentence (8) is mandated even in the absence of overt incorporation structures. Deriving (8) and the sentence *She put her books on the shelf* from markedly different D-structures would necessarily complicate the 'construction process' mapping thematic roles onto constituent structure. In other words, given the extended UTAH, it follows that that the subcategorizational properties of lexical items can be derived from their semantic properties, or given more current phraseology, that 'c-selection' can be derived from 's-selection'.

Baker's 1993 paper added a novel argument for the decomposition approach to semantically complex predicates (see also his chapter in this volume). He noted that there are two kinds of prominence relations that are important in syntax. One is intraclausal 'relational prominence' — that of subjects over direct objects, direct objects over indirect objects, and so on. The other is 'embedding prominence', that of the subject of a main clause over the subject of a dependent clause, for example. Historically, generative syntacticians have treated the two types of prominence very differently. But, Baker argues, if seemingly simple monoclausal structures are derived from more complex lexico-semantically derived structures, then relational prominence falls out as a subcase of embedding prominence.

Baker's approach was extended still further in Chomsky (1995). Chomsky argued for a complex embedding approach to *all* seemingly simple transitive structures. For example, he proposed to derive (13) from (12), where 'vP', 'v'' and 'v' are 'light' VPs, V's, and Vs respectively:

(12) He read the book.

(13)

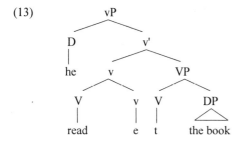

Such an analysis was dictated by the extended UTAH, as well as by a natural extension of the 'Larsonian shell' approach to structure (Larson 1988) and mechanisms internal to the Minimalist Program itself.[4]

The intimate association of roles and relations inherent in the models proposed in the mid 1990s by Hale and Keyser, Baker, and Chomsky was almost, but not quite, in keeping with a full-fledged DAH. One obstacle remained to its complete realization. The total alignment of thematic relations with grammatical functions had always seemed to be extremely problematic, given the evident many-to-few relation between them. After all, more than a dozen θ-roles have been proposed, while subject-of, direct-object-of, and indirect-object-of make up the stock of grammatical functions in the standard inventory. The inclusion of notions such as 'oblique', 'object of comparative', 'embedded subject', and so on as possible grammatical functions does little to engineer an alignment between them and θ-roles. Even if we confine our attention to (presumptively) underlying subjects of main clause transitives, this grammatical function may be represented by an Agent (14a), Patient (14b), Experiencer (14c), Recipient/Goal (14d), Comitative (14e), Locative/Theme (14f), Instrument (14g), and no doubt many other roles:

(14)a.   Mary killed John.

   b.   Mary underwent an unpleasant dental procedure.

   c.   Mary hates John.

   d.   John received a package from Mary.

   e.   Mary met Alice.

   f.   Mary contains billions of DNA molecules.

   g.   The crane loaded the truck.

How, then, could there possibly be a one-to-one relation between functions and roles? Dowty (1991) proposed a solution. He argued that the proliferation of θ-roles seen in the literature could be dispensed with in favor of two cluster-concepts called 'Proto-Agent' and 'Proto-Patient'. The particular role borne by a particular argument is determined by the number of entailments that the verb gives it. Dowty outlined these entailments as follows:

(27)   Contributing properties for the Agent Proto-Role:

   a.   volitional involvement in the event or state

   b.   sentience (and/or perception)

    c.   causing an event or change of state in another participant

    d.   movement (relative to the position of another participant)

    e.   exists independently of the event named by the verb

(28)   Contributing properties for the Patient Proto-Role:

    a.   undergoes change of state

    b.   incremental theme

    c.   causally affected by another participant

    d.   stationary relative to movement of another participant

    e.   does not exist independently of the event, or not at all
           (Dowty 1991: 572)

In Dowty's view, the argument whose predicate entails the greatest number of Proto-Agent properties will be lexicalized as the subject of the predicate; the argument having the greatest number of Proto-Patient entailments will be lexicalized as the direct object.

Baker (1997) saw the proto-role hypothesis as a way of getting the DAH to work. He wrote:

> However, an absolute version of the UTAH [i.e., the DAH — FJN] can still be maintained in the face of [examples such as (14a-g)] if one adopts Dowty's (1991) idea that the basic thematic roles are prototype concepts rather than categorically defined ones. On this view, it is possible to say that *John* in [(14d)], *the crane* in [(14g)], and *Mary* in [(14c)] are all (proto)-agents, and as such belong in the subject position. This is justified by the fact that each of these NPs shares certain semantic entailments with the prototypical agent *Mary* in [(14a)], although they do not all share the same ones. (Baker 1997: 109)

Nothing now seemed to stand in the way of effecting a deep alignment between grammatical function, (proto-)thematic role, and constituent structure. The DAH, as a consequence, has become a central ingredient of most theorizing within the Minimalist Program.

3. AGAINST THE DEEP ALIGNMENT HYPOTHESIS

The remainder of this chapter will present arguments against the DAH. Section 3.1 will suggest that a D-structure level must be posited at which grammatical functions do not line up with θ-roles. The following section 3.2 will question the linchpin of the DAH, namely, Dowty's proto-role approach. And §3.3 will rebut the idea that the semantic decomposition demanded by the DAH serves to reduce relational prominence to embedding prominence.

3.1   The independent need for D-structure

It will be argued here that there is a need for a level with the properties of classical D-structure, in which grammatical functions, thematic roles, and constituent structure are not in alignment. Such a consequence guts the DAH of its most appealing feature, namely, that it enables a 'minimalist' correspondence among these three seemingly disparate constructs.

In the theory defended in Levin and Rappaport Hovav 1995, each verb is associated with two lexical representations: a Lexical Semantic Representation (LSR) and an Argument Structure (AS; also called a 'Lexical Syntactic Representation'). At LSR, predicates are decomposed into syntactically relevant units of meaning. At this level we find structures parallel to those posited by Hale and Keyser for their level of 'Lexical Relational Structure' and by Baker for his underlying syntactic level. In other words, the DAH is realized at the level of LSR. Linking rules map LSR onto AS. The information in a verb's AS, together with the projection principle and the Theta-Criterion, determine the syntactic configuration that a verb is found in. In the words of Levin and Rappaport Hovav, 'the relation between argument structure and the D-structure syntactic representation [is] "trivial"' (p. 22).

Now let us consider the phenomenon of unaccusativity. Levin and Rappaport Hovav argue that it is 'syntactically represented but semantically determined' (p. 30). What they mean is that all unaccusatives have the same AS, in which there exists a sole internal argument and no external argument. Furthermore, unaccusativity is a property of semantically characterizable classes of predicates. That is, general linking rules relate the LSRs of unaccusative predicates to their AS representations. Significantly for our purposes, Baker endorses their analysis and comments that if they are correct, 'then the absolute UTAH [i.e., the DAH — FJN] is supported' (Baker 1997: 115).

The problem, however, is that there is a great disparity between the LSR of any given unaccusative predicate and its AS. In particular, several *different* LSRs are linked to the same unaccusative AS. For example, one class of unaccusative, that containing certain change of state verbs, has biclausal LSRs, as illustrated in the following LSR that Levin and Rappaport Hovav (1995: 83) propose for *break:*[5]

(15)   *break* [[x DO-SOMETHING] CAUSE [y BECOME *BROKEN*]]

On the other hand, verbs of existence and appearance such as *exist* and *appear*, which also have an unaccusative AS, have much simpler, monoclausal, LSRs.[6] Now, if the arguments for a particular LSR carry over, as it seems reasonable to assume, to arguments for a particular structure conforming to the DAH, then Baker would need operations corresponding to Levin and Rappaport Hovav's linking rules mapping the underlying syntactic representations for *break* and *exist* onto identical [__ NP] (i.e.

syntactically unaccusative) structures. And that would involve an implicit recognition that a shallower level like D-Structure is needed. The DAH would remain, in effect, holding of lexical relations, but not (deep) syntactic ones.

The idea, inherent to the DAH, that syntactic subcategorization can be derived from semantic role was central to Generative Semantics (Green 1974, McCawley 1976) and has been revived within Principles-and-Parameters approaches (Pesetsky 1982; Chomsky 1986b). There is little reason to believe it, however. Some of the more convincing rebuttals to Generative Semantics outlined in detail the difficulties with such a program (see especially Oehrle 1976; 1977; Wasow 1976). Wasow called attention to the intransitive verb *elapse*:

> My dictionary defines it as follows: '(of time) to slip by or pass away'; yet *slip by* may optionally take an object (*The hours slipped by them unnoticed*), whereas *elapse* may not (**The hours elapsed them unnoticed*). Or consider the difference between *dine*, *devour*, and *eat* with respect to transitivity; *dine* is intransitive, *devour* requires an object, and *eat* takes an optional object. Although the meanings of these words are subtly different, nothing in those differences predicts the difference with respect to transitivity (i.e., all seem to designate two-place predicates involving both some sort of food and a consumer of food). (Wasow 1976: 282)

Grimshaw (1979) documents a number of interesting mismatches between s-selection and c-selection. For example, she compares the verbs *ask* and *inquire*, both of which s-select a question:

(16)a.　　I asked what the time was.

　　b.　　I inquired what the time was.

Only *ask*, however, c-selects NP:

(17)a.　　I asked the time.

　　b.　　*I inquired the time.

The only attempt of which I am aware to subvert Grimshaw's conclusion, the appeal to Case theory in Pesetsky 1982, has been demonstrated to be inadequate in Rothstein 1992. It would appear, then, that the subcategorizational properties of heads need to be formulated at a level of D-structure, not at a level in which the DAH holds.

The nonsemantic basis for strict subcategorization holds even for those predicates instrumental in the formulation of the DAH. Consider *shelve*, for example:

> Hale and Keyser's proposal claims that the NP *shelf* satisfies the Location role in *We shelved the books*. However, *We shelved the books on the top shelf* has an overt Location, hence a double filling of the Location role. This of course violates UTAH, since it is impossible for two different NPs with the same θ-role to be in the same underlying syntactic position. In addition it violates the Theta-Criterion; it should be just as bad as, say, *He opened the door with a key with a skeleton key*. But it's perfect. (Jackendoff 1997: 232)

As has frequently been noted (see, for example, Pullum 1996), the complex embedding structures necessitated by the DAH bear a striking resemblance to the structures posited within the Generative Semantics framework. Generative semanticists too appealed to the semantic parallels between such pairs as *shelve the books* and *cause the books to be put on the shelf* in order to argue that at a deep level of syntactic representation they had to have the same structure. Literally scores of rebuttals appeared in the literature in the 1970s, arguing that such an idea is fundamentally deficient. These rebuttals were accepted by the community of generative syntacticians which evolved into the Principles-and-Parameters school, among whose practitioners include Chomsky, Hale, Keyser, and Baker. The question, then, is why if these rebuttals were forceful in the year 1970 they are not forceful 30 years later.[7]

It is worth citing the principal arguments from one of these earlier rebuttals, namely Fodor 1970. Fodor challenged the generative semantic derivation of *kill* and *cause to die* from the same underlying syntactic structure — a derivation adopted in its essentials by advocates of the DAH (see Baker in this volume). Fodor gave three reasons against such a derivation. First, he asked how, if *kill* is decomposed in the syntax, one might explain the ungrammaticality of (18):

(18)   *Mary killed John and it surprised me that he did so. (i.e. that he died)

If *John* is underlyingly the subject of a predicate with the semantics of *die* (or the unaccusative object of that predicate), then we should expect it to pass the '*do so* test', given that the following is grammatical:

(19)   Mary caused John to die, and it surprised me that he did so.

Second, Fodor suggested that a decomposition approach should predict, contrary to fact, that (20) is grammatical:

(20)   *Mary killed John on Sunday by stabbing him on Saturday.

Since (21) is grammatical, why shouldn't (20) be grammatical as well?:

(21)   Mary caused Bill to die on Sunday by stabbing him on Saturday.

Finally, Fodor asked why we get the following contrast:

(22)a.   Mary$_i$ caused John$_j$ to die by ___$_{ij}$ swallowing his tongue.

   b.   Mary$_i$ killed John$_j$ by ___$_{i*j}$ swallowing his tongue.

Again, we would expect the adjunct phrase to be able to modify both *Mary* and *John*, given that *John* is the underlying single argument of the intransitive (or unaccusative) *die.* Suffice it to say that none of these questions arise if *kill* is not lexically decomposed in the syntax.

It has been suggested (in Harley 1995 and by Lisa Travis, personal communication) that Fodor's arguments are not transferable to current work involving decomposition, since the structures posited by generative semanticists and those posited by Baker, et al. differ in a crucial way.[8] To be specific, generative semanticists posited an S node separating the parts of the decomposed predicate, while current work has a VP (or vP). If the processes that Fodor appealed to in order to subvert generative semantics were sensitive to sentential boundaries, but not 'lesser' ones, then one would not predict the grammaticality of (18) and (20), nor the ambiguity of (22b). One cannot, of course, dismiss such a possibility out of hand. Nor should one jump to accept it. Until the properties of 'light VPs' are better understood and elaborated, appeal to them to rescue the DAH from a version of Fodor's assault remains pure speculation.

To summarize, the decomposition structures demanded by the DAH do not render superfluous a level with the properties of D-structure. This level is needed in any event, thereby undermining any argument based on simplicity or elegance that might be advanced in favor of the DAH.

3.2   Problems with proto-thematic-roles

As was pointed out in §2.2, Baker appeals to Dowty's prototype approach to θ-roles in order to bring the number of such roles into alignment with the number of grammatical functions at a deep level of syntax. Unfortunately for this approach (and for the DAH), it is not difficult to find transitive verbs whose subjects and objects do not measure up to Dowty's thematic criteria for them. Baker (in this volume) recognizes the problem with *like.* But consider also such stative predicates as *receive, inherit, undergo,* and *sustain.* To illustrate, let us measure sentence (14d), repeated as (23), against Dowty's proto-Agent entailments:

(23)   John received a package from Mary.

(24)a.   VOLITION: *Mary*

b.   SENTIENCE/PERCEPTION: d.n.a.

c.   CAUSATION: *Mary*

d.   MOVEMENT: *the letter*

e.   INDEPENDENT EXISTENCE: *John, Mary*

John is a 'Proto-Agent' only by one-half of one test, while *Mary* passes two and one half. Hence, one would predict that *Mary*, not *John*, should be subject.

One might, on the other hand, choose to interpret Dowty's criteria as governing the *necessary* properties of the roles associated with each predicate, rather than focusing on individual sentences (such as (23)) in which that predicate occurs.[9] By this interpretation, the verb *receive* fares no better, as (25) illustrates.

(25)

Proto-Agt properties	[recipient]	[theme]	[source]
Volition	no	no	no
Sentience	no	no	no
Cause	no	no	no
Movement	no	yes	no
Independent existence	yes	yes	yes
Total	**1**	**2**	**1**

Proto-Pat properties	[recipient]	[theme]	[source]
Change of state	no	no	no
Incremental theme	no	no	no
Causally affected	yes?	yes	no
Relatively stationary	yes	no	no
No independ. existence	no	no	no
Total	**2**	**1**	**0**

If the assignments in (25) are correct, then for the verb *receive*, the theme should be the subject and the recipient should be the direct object, i.e., we should have sentences like **A package received John from Mary*. As far as subject properties are concerned, the theme necessarily moves and has an independent existence, while the only necessary property of the recipient is its independent existence. (Note that sentences like *The wall received a coat of paint* illustrate that the recipient need not be sentient.) As far as object properties are concerned, recipients are, I believe, always causally affected by another participant and stationary relative to the movement of another participant.[10]

Passive sentences (and most likely A-movements in general) pose a lethal problem for the attempt to link the DAH and the hypothesis of proto-thematic-roles. Consider the active-passive pair (26a-b). For the past two decades, or longer, it has been assumed that (26b) has a derivation schematically represented as (27) (though the intermediate trace in [Spec, VP] is a more recent innovation):

(26)a.   Mary ate the chicken.

     b.   The chicken was eaten by Mary.

(27)

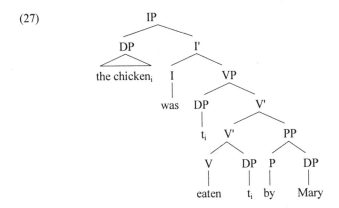

Such a derivation, however, seems to violate the UTAH even in its original (weaker) version. *Mary* has identical θ-roles in (26a) and (26b) and, therefore, by the UTAH, would have to be in identical D-structure positions in those two sentences.[11] But agent phrases of passives have not been analyzed as originating in deep subject ([Spec, IP]) position since before Emonds (1970) - and the Theta-Criterion, of course, explains *why* they cannot originate there. So we have a fundamental conflict between the UTAH and the Theta-Criterion. Worse, however, is the fact that (27) leads to the assignment of the wrong θ-roles, given a Dowtyan analysis. The argument with the most proto-Agent properties is not a deep subject; indeed the deep subject, being empty, has no thematic properties at all. That presents no problems for a semanticist like Dowty, who rejects null elements in syntactic derivations, but is highly problematic for the DAH. Even worse, the agent phrase can be omitted:

(28)   The chicken was eaten.

As Dowty makes clear in his paper, in sentences with only one DP argument, that argument is assigned the subject position by default. But in (26b), *the chicken* needs to be an underlying direct object.

One concludes from the failure of the prototype approach to thematic roles that we need a deep syntactic level in which the grammatical functions borne by NP arguments are not in a one-to-one relation with their thematic status.[12]

3.3   *Relational prominence and embedding prominence*

As noted in §2.2, Baker (1993, this volume) argues that relational prominence and embedding prominence reflect the same underlying generalization. Specifically, relational prominence is argued to be a type of embedding prominence, a result that can be derived, it is claimed, only if seemingly simple monoclausal structures are derived from more complex (lexico-semantically) decomposed structures. This section challenges that line of argumentation. It will suggest that Baker's identification of the two types of prominence is essentially correct. However, such an identification can be achieved without the semantic decomposition demanded by the DAH. In both cases, we simply have the prominence that is inherent in the asymmetrical c-command relation — a relation that governs many other types of grammatical asymmetries.

Baker demonstrates that a large set of syntactic generalizations holding within simple clauses are manifested in (uncontroversial) embedding structures. For example, consider bound variable anaphora (29a-d), Condition C effects (30a-d), antecedence of reciprocals (31a-d), and NP movement (32a-d). The (a) examples in each set show relational prominence of subjects over objects, while the (b) examples show that objects do not manifest the same prominence over subjects. The (c) examples show that a matrix subject has embedding prominence over an embedded subject, and the (d) examples show that embedded subjects do not have prominence over matrix subjects:

Bound variable anaphora:
(29)a.　　*Every boy* persuaded *his* mother that video games were good.

　　b.　　**Her* son persuaded *every woman* that video games were good.

　　c.　　*Every boy* persuaded the principal that *his* mother sang professionally.

　　d.　　**Her* son persuaded the principal that *every woman* sang professionally.

Condition C
(30)a.　　**He* persuaded *John's* mother that video games were good.

　　b.　　*Her* son persuaded *Martha* that video games were good.

　　c.　　**He* persuaded the principal that *John's* mother sang professionally.

　　d.　　*Her* son persuaded the principal that *Martha* sang professionally.

Antecedence of reciprocals
(31)a.　　John and Mary persuaded each other's parents that video games were good.

　　b.　　??Each other's children persuaded Joe and Martha that video games were good.

　　c.　　John and Mary persuaded the principal that each other's parents sang professionally.

    d.   *Each other's children persuaded the principal that John and Mary sang professionally.

NP-movement
(32)a.   John fell t.

    b.   *t shouted John.

    c.   John seemed to win the race.

    d.   *t said [that John seemed that it would rain]

Baker attempts to derive the ungrammaticality of the (b) sentences from that of the (d) sentences by arguing that for all practical purposes the former have the same structure as the latter. That is, the structural relation between the subject and object in (a-b) parallels that between the matrix subject and the embedded subject in (c-d). In other words, a consequence of decomposition is that the subjects and objects in the (a) and (b) sentences are arguments of different predicates. The relevant constraints, then, would treat the (a-b) relation identically to that of the (c-d) relation.

    Before proceeding further, it is worth pointing out that identifying the two types of prominence in the way desired by Baker is incompatible with conflation applying in the lexicon à la Hale and Keyser. In their approach, the (a-b) and (c-d) sentences would be structurally different throughout the syntactic derivation. Given that the generalizations governing the distribution of data in (29)-(32) are syntactic, rather than lexical, the Hale-Keyser approach has no formal mechanism available for deriving relational prominence from embedding prominence.

    Even in Baker's approach, in which conflation is purely syntactic, it is not clear that the semantically decomposed structures are sufficiently parallel to those in which sentential embedding uncontroversially exists in order for the prominence relations to be regarded as identical in the two types of structures. For example, he derives sentence (33) as illustrated in (34):

(33)   Mary will kill John.

(34)

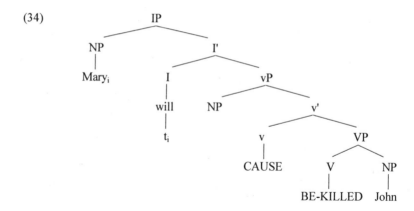

Tree (34), however, is not the structure of (35):

(35) Mary will cause John to be killed.

Sentence (35) has an internal INFL and therefore an internal IP. In order for the prominence relations in (33) to parallel those in (35), the VP separating CAUSE from BE-KILLED in (33) has to 'count' as the same as the IP separating *cause* and *be killed* in (35). But is that a reasonable assumption? Recall from §3.1 the suggestion that Fodor's arguments against deriving *kill* from *cause to die* do not apply to Baker's minimalist version of this derivation because Baker *does not* posit an internal IP. So, to escape the Fodorian refutation, VP and IP must have crucially *different* properties. Again, in the absence of a theory elucidating the behavior of the constituents of light VPs, we have no way of knowing whether prominence relations within them should or should not be expected to parallel prominence relations where a full IP occurs.

The principal objection, however, to decomposition as a means of unifying relational and embedding prominence is that it is unnecessary to take this step to get the desired result. In the two most frequently adopted approaches to phrase structure — the 'classic' view that allows ternary branching and the 'minimalist' approach that unites binary branching with Larsonian shells —the two types of prominence are already united by means of the asymmetrical c-command relation. In the former approach, which goes back at least to Rosenbaum (1967) and has been defended more recently in Jackendoff (1990), embedded sentences are sisters to V and any other complements to that V. Hence, any element internal to that embedded S will necessarily be asymmetrically c-commanded by any element in the higher sentence.[13] In the latter approach (see Larson 1988), in which subcategorized complements are nested, the geometry assumed demands that any element in a higher clause will asymmetrically c-command any element in a lower clause. Given the practically universal assumption that subject projections are higher than object projections, the asymmetrical c-command relation will be available via the specifier/complement relation. Hence, if we adopt one of these two approaches there is no reason to decompose simplex clauses, since asymmetrical prominence is an automatic consequence of asymmetrical c-command.

Only in an approach that assumes binary branching but rejects Larsonian shells would embedding prominence not fall out from asymmetrical c-command. However, few, if any, linguists take such a position, since Larson provided the strongest empirical argument *for* binary branching — it is necessary if binding principles are defined on c-command relations. Without Larsonian shells, therefore, binary branching is not a particularly compelling theoretical innovation (but see Kayne 1984, 1994).[14]

The most serious problem for the idea that capturing prominence relations demands semantic decomposition is it leads to the positing of decomposition where few would find it palatable. To begin, (36-38) below demonstrate the prominence of subject NPs over NPs in adjunct PPs:

Bound variable anaphora:
(36)a.   *Every boy* slept [in *his* own bed]

   b.   **He* slept [in *every boy's* bed]

Condition C:
(37)a.   *John* slept [in *his* bed]

   b.   **He* slept [in *John's* bed]

Antecedence of reciprocals:
(38)a.   *John and Mary* live in Chicago [near *each other's* children]

   b.   **Each other's* children live in Chicago [near *John and Mary*]

Presumably, then, following Baker, PP adjuncts of the intransitive verbs *sleep* and *live* have to be associated with some predicate *other than* those verbs and hence adjunct boundaries have to be structurally parallel to clausal boundaries. Otherwise, the structural relation between *every boy* and *his* in (36a) would not parallel that in (29c); the structural relation between *he* and *every boy's* in (36b) would not parallel that in (29d); and so on. But what predicate? One with a locative reading? If so, then what argument(s) would this predicate take that would allow the structure to be true to both the semantics and to the proto-thematic role hypothesis and at the same time not block coreference in the (a) sentences of (36-38)? The answers to these questions are by no means obvious.[15]

A parallel point could be made with respect to movements within clauses. Consider the fact that manner adverbs can be fronted within a clause, but sentence-adverbs cannot be lowered into the VP (with a preservation of the sentence-adverb reading):

Adverb movement

(39)a.   John cut the salami carefully

    b.   Carefully$_i$ John cut the salami t$_i$

(40)a.   Incredibly, John cut himself

    b.   *t$_i$ John [$_{VP}$cut himself incredibly$_i$]

Since asymmetrical NP movement within a clause, as in (32a-b), suggests to Baker that the subject and object are arguments of different predicates, by parity of reasoning, given (39-40), subjects and manner adverbs must be as well. Again, one wonders what those two predicates might be.

Head movements pose an even more serious challenge to the idea that all prominence relations reduce to embedding prominence, through the vehicle of semantic decomposition. So, within a CP, V may be raised to INFL, but INFL may not be lowered to V; INFL may be raised to COMP, but COMP may not be lowered to INFL:

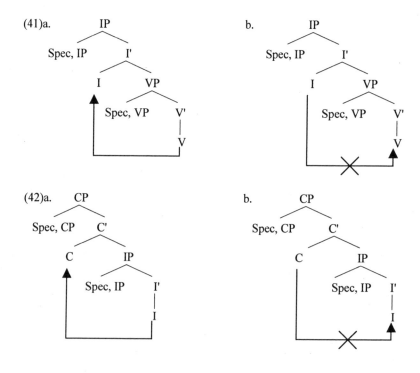

Such facts put advocates of semantic decomposition on the horns of a dilemma. On the one hand, they might attempt to be consistent and derive these asymmetrical movement possibilities by positing alternative structures to (41a-b) and (42a-b) that parallel those needed to capture the asymmetrical movement possibilities exhibited in (32a-d). One wonders what those structures would look like. On the other hand, they might opt out from a decomposition analysis and simply take the traditional position that the asymmetry of movement follows from asymmetry of c-command. But if so, then why wouldn't asymmetrical c-command suffice to explain (32a-d) as well?

In fact, cases of grammatical asymmetries resulting from one element displaying prominence over another are legion. For example, verbs select the complementizer of the subordinate clauses that they introduce, while complementizers never choose the verb of the higher clause; complementizers play a role in the choice of INFL within their clause, but not vice-versa; and it is the TNS feature of INFL that determines verbal morphology, not the other way around. With respect to sequence of tense phenomena, it is the tense of the higher clause that determines the 'tense shift' in the lower clause, it is not the lower tense that determines the higher. And deletion rules as well, exhibit prominence:

(43)a.   I'll sweep the floor only because Arthur will ____ too.

    b.   *I will ___ too, only because Arthur will sweep the floor.

In each of these cases, the prominence relation is a simple reflection of asymmetrical c-command. Given the wealth of grammatical generalizations that exhibit this structural relation, it is hardly surprising that it governs intraclausal relational prominence as well. There is no need to resort to semantic decomposition.

This section will conclude on a more speculative note. Insofar as it makes sense to think of one form of prominence being derivative of another form, it seems more plausible to regard embedding prominence as being derivative of relational prominence, rather than vice-versa. By several criteria, relational prominence is more basic. First, and trivially, every sentence has a main clause, but not all have (superficial) dependent clauses. Hence relational prominence is *always* overtly manifested, while embedding prominence is only *sometimes* manifested. The idea of embedding prominence driving relational prominence therefore has a cart before-the-horse feel to it. It is also worth pointing out that the text count of utterances with relative or complement clauses is vastly lower than those with main clauses alone (Biber 1989). If grammatical principles are derivative to some degree of facts about language use (a position characteristic of, but not unique to the 'functionalist' school — see also Hawkins 1994, Newmeyer 1998) — then the idea of a priority status for embedding prominence seems particularly problematic.

Second, it has long been known (see Ross 1973a) that subordinate clause phenomena form a proper subset of main clause phenomena. Again, why would grammar be designed so that principles governing the latter would be beholden to those governing the former? Third, there are learnability arguments for the centrality of main clauses (or main clauses plus the left edges of subordinate clauses). Lightfoot (1991) argues that all the child needs to construct his or her grammar are cues from the matrix S. Again, the centrality of embedding structures is called into question. And finally, linguistically-informed research in language evolution is virtually unanimous on the idea that subordinate clauses are a later development than simple clauses (see, for example, Bickerton 1990, Carstairs-McCarthy 1999). It seems odd that if the latter existed prior to the former, prominence relations within them would have had to 'wait' until the arrival of subordinate clauses.

In short, there appear to be no convincing argument for the semantic decomposition required by the DAH on the basis of the parallels between relational prominence and embedding prominence. Such a conclusion, therefore, further undermines the DAH.

4. CONCLUSION

Much current minimalist work assumes that grammatical functions, thematic roles, and configurational structure are in alignment, that is, a particular value for one implies a particular value for the others. It has been argued that such a view is untenable. The intuitions of earlier generations of formal syntacticians are correct — while the three constructs are not randomly associated, they cannot be linked in a one-to-one fashion.

NOTES

[1] I would like to thank Robert Chametsky, William Davies, Stanley Dubinsky, Heidi Harley, Julia Herschensohn, and Ray Jackendoff for their helpful comments on an earlier version of this paper. No doubt I will come to wish that I had followed their advice more closely.

[2] Chomsky was later to reformulate the Theta-Criterion as a property of chains, as follows:
Each argument α appears in chain containing a unique visible θ-position P, and each θ-position P is visible in a chain containing a unique argument α. (Chomsky 1986b: 97)
He wrote that 'this formulation of the Theta-Criterion permits a θ-position to receive multiple θ-roles, as in [(5a)]' (p. 97). I confess that I do not understand how this could be so.

[3] For example, the ECP prevents an incorporation which would lead to an embedded underlying subject becoming a derived oblique (*the girl fall-made on/to the pot) or one in which a verb in a sentential subject is incorporated ([that the pot fell] made the girl laugh →*the pot fall-made the girl laugh). In neither case is the trace of movement properly governed.

[4] Stanley Dubinsky has observed (p.c.) that Larsonian shells go hand-in-hand with a decomposition approach. While they do not necessarily involve extra (abstract) lexical heads (and their projections), they do involve extra (empty) heads (and their projections). The head of a shell is therefore neither lexical nor clearly functional. It is worth pointing out that Baker (1997: 123) assumes Larsonian shells and Larson (1988) the UTAH. For extensive discussion of this and related points, see Chametsky (2000).

[5] Levin and Rappaport Hovav note that the causer is often an Agent, but it need not be: natural forces such as earthquakes can fill the higher external argument position, for example.

[6] Unfortunately, Levin and Rappaport Hovav do not provide explicit LSRs for any verbs in this class.

[7] What would lead Chomsky to embrace an approach that he had once spurned? My (highly speculative!) answer is that it derives from his abandonment, in the course of the 1970s, of an independent level of semantic representation. That move created a dynamic encouraging the importation of purely semantic constructs, such as thematic roles, directly into the syntax. Hence the Theta-Criterion. And given the Theta-Criterion, the DAH and the decomposition that it entails follow as a matter of course (see §2.1 and 2.2).

[8] Harley (1995: §3.2.1.3) suggests that Fodor's arguments do not go through because the event structure of *kill* is not the same as that of *cause to die*. In the former, she argues, there is one event, in the latter, the causation is a separate event from the dying. The two-event structure of *cause to die* provides two possible domains for *do so* ellipsis, adjunction of time adverbials, and control of instrumental adverbials.

[9] Though Baker (1997) in his discussion of Dowty's hypothesis, does appear to adopt the latter interpretation.

[10] Dowty's theory countenances cases in which neither argument 'wins'. Thus, according to him, *fear* and *frighten* and other such pairs arise precisely because the arguments are so close in terms of their proto-Agent and proto-Patient entailments. It is not clear how a theory that works this way would fit into the DAH view that is being critiqued here.

[11] Baker, Johnson, and Roberts (1989), however, dispute this claim. In their analysis the UTAH is not violated, since passive morphology absorbs the external thematic role and the agent PP (when present) acts as a doubled clitic. Discussion and criticism of their approach would take us too far afield.

[12] For other critiques of the proto-role hypothesis, see Jackendoff (1996) and Croft (1998).

[13] If Jackendoff is correct, then, as he notes, linear precedence as well as c-command will be a relevant factor in determining relational prominence (on this point, see also Barss and Lasnik 1986 and Williams 1994).

[14] I thank William Davies and Stanley Dubinsky (p. c.) for the observations of this paragraph.

[15] William Davies and Stanley Dubinsky (p.c.) suggest that the approach advocated in Pesetsky (1995) would readily accommodate the presence of a locative predicate in (36-38). While such is indeed the case, it is important to point out that Pesetsky adopts a much weaker theory than the DAH. His 'Universal Alignment Hypothesis' does not demand that there be a biunique relationship between thematic roles and syntactic positions, but only that the linking patterns between the two be predictable. Thus Pesetsky is not required to posit decomposition in as many circumstances as is Baker and, in general, cannot derive relational prominence from embedding prominence. In fact, as I understand Pesetsky's approach, it is fully compatible with my hypothesis that prominence relations fall out from asymmetrical c-command.

ALEX ALSINA

IS CASE ANOTHER NAME FOR GRAMMATICAL FUNCTION? EVIDENCE FROM OBJECT ASYMMETRIES[*]

The facts of double object constructions in languages where objects are not distinguished by means of grammatical (or overt) case have been accounted for in a variety of ways often making crucial use of notions such as grammatical functions, grammatical relations, or Case, depending on the theoretical framework. Within GB,[1] one of the most successful approaches assumes that objects are distinguished by means of a contrast in terms of Case (Baker 1988a,b). According to this approach, an object has different syntactic properties depending on whether it has inherent or structural Case. The question that I want to raise is whether the term Case as used for this purpose is justified on cross-linguistic grounds. It could be that the term Case captures important properties common to languages both with and without grammatical case or it could be that it is just a way of avoiding the term "grammatical function" in a framework that claims not to have grammatical functions as primitive notions and that, by referring to two different concepts (namely, grammatical case and grammatical function), it complicates the formulation of a cross-linguistic theory of object asymmetries.

I will proceed as follows. First, I will show that the notion of grammatical function is captured in GB by means of Case and will argue that, despite claims to the contrary, it is not a derived notion, but a primitive notion, of the GB framework. In section two, I will present the facts of object asymmetries in languages such as Chichewa and show how the abstract Case distinctions are used to account for these facts. In section three, I will examine equivalent facts in a case-marking language (Catalan) and will propose the most reasonable correspondence between abstract Case and grammatical case in this language. In section four, I will show that there are serious problems with positing a single universal distinction in terms of Case for a cross-linguistic analysis of object asymmetries. Finally, I will conclude that the Case theory proposed for languages like Chichewa by Baker 1988a,b cannot be extended to languages with overt case and that, therefore, in languages without grammatical case, Case is not case, but simply another name for "grammatical function."

77
William D. Davies and Stanley Dubinsky (eds.), Objects and other subjects:
Grammatical functions, functional categories, and configurationality, 77—102.
© 2001 *Kluwer Academic Publishers. Printed in the Netherlands.*

1. ABSTRACT CASE AND GRAMMATICAL FUNCTIONS

In this section I will point out some differences and similarities between the use of abstract Case in some versions of GB and the use of grammatical functions in other frameworks. A standard claim has been that grammatical functions are primitive theoretical constructs in frameworks such as Relational Grammar, or RG, (as presented in Perlmutter and Postal 1983b, among others) and Lexical-Functional Grammar, or LFG, (as in Bresnan 1982b, among others) but are derived notions in GB. In RG and LFG, grammatical functions such as subject are said to be primitive because they cannot be derived from theoretical constructs whose purpose is not exclusively that of defining grammatical functions. This is true whether grammatical functions are treated as atomic notions, that is, not decomposable into smaller notions, as in many versions of these frameworks, where the notions "subject" or "object" are not taken to be made up of smaller elements, or are treated as the combination of features whose sole purpose is to define grammatical functions. For example, in the version of LFG found in Bresnan and Kanerva 1989, Bresnan and Moshi 1991, and Alsina and Mchombo 1993, grammatical functions can be regarded as composed of the features $[\pm r]$ and $[\pm o]$. These features have no other role but to define and classify grammatical functions. Therefore, even in these versions of LFG, grammatical functions should be seen as primitives of the theoretical framework, since the constructs from which grammatical functions are derived have no other purpose but to define and classify grammatical functions.

In contrast with RG and LFG, GB does not use grammatical function labels such as subject or object as primitive notions of the framework, since it is claimed that these labels merely describe specific phrase structure configurations. The term "subject," for example, describes the XP position in Spec of I'. None of the elements involved in the representation of the notion of subject in GB is designed exclusively for the definition of grammatical functions. The elements involved are X' Theory and syntactic categories such as I (for "Inflection") all of which have a variety of uses in the framework. This is a debatable point, although I will not dwell on it here, as we could perhaps argue that the functional category I has as its main function defining the grammatical function "subject." Among its other functions is that of being the position in which tensed auxiliaries can appear in English (the other position in which they can appear being C). However, since not all languages exhibit the special distribution of auxiliaries found in English, it appears that the association of I with tensed auxiliaries is a language-particular property of this category. It might then be argued that the only universal role of the category I is defining the notion of subject. (I has been replaced in this function by other categories in subsequent developments of the framework; in some versions, T or AgrS can be viewed as fulfilling the same role.)

However, the notion of grammatical function as used in frameworks like LFG is captured in GB not only by means of particular phrase structure configurations, but also by means of the notion of abstract Case. Different grammatical categories are assumed to assign different types of abstract Cases to the categories that they govern: I (at least, tensed I) assigns nominative Case and V can assign accusative Case. It is important to note that, although terms such as Case, nominative, and accusative are used, these terms do not refer to what is generally taken to be grammatical case. It is for the purpose of distinguishing abstract Case form grammatical case that the word "Case" is spelled with a capital when referring to abstract Case. Grammatical case (also called morphological case) describes a system of overt oppositions that serve to identify the grammatical function or the thematic role of the various dependants in a clause. In a language like Latin, nominative case identifies subjects of tensed clauses, among other uses, and accusative case marks the objects of certain verbs and prepositions, the subjects of certain infinitival clauses, etc. Despite the correlation that exists in languages like Latin between grammatical case and grammatical function, it is not possible to reduce grammatical functions to grammatical case. For example, not all languages have a system of grammatical case; yet, presumably all languages have different grammatical functions. Chichewa is an example of a language without grammatical case in which the distinction between grammatical functions such as subject and object is manifested in a variety of ways. And even in languages with a rich system of grammatical case, such as Icelandic, case and grammatical function need to be kept distinct. This is a point made by Holmberg and Platzack 1995:29ff, where a distinction is made between lexical Case and structural Case, which seems to correspond, at least roughly, to the distinction between grammatical case and grammatical function respectively.

The basic assumption in GB Case Theory is that all languages use abstract Case, even though not all languages have grammatical case. Since all NPs (at least, overt NPs) need abstract Case, as required by the Case Filter, and different features of abstract Case are assigned to different positions in phrase structure, abstract Case can be seen as a mechanism that licenses different grammatical functions. Thus, a subject of a tensed clause is not only an NP in Spec of I', but an NP with nominative Case, and an object is not only an NP in the complement position of a verb (or a preposition), but an NP with accusative Case. In this way, the representation of grammatical functions in GB can be viewed as being decomposed into two parts: phrase structure configuration and licensing by Case. These two facets of the representation of grammatical functions in GB are not redundant, because the phrase structure configuration of a particular grammatical function does not correspond to a unique Case feature. This is the situation, for example, with the grammatical function subject (Spec of I'), as it is assigned nominative Case in tensed clauses, but not in nonfinite clauses.

Abstract Case becomes crucial in distinguishing grammatical functions in the analysis of double object constructions. Many theories within GB, such as Baker 1988a,b, rely primarily on different Case features to capture the distinction between the two objects. The fundamental difference between a primary and a secondary object is captured as the difference between structural Case and inherent Case, two different types of Cases.[2] In such theories, even though there may be a variety of phrase structure configurations for objects, the two types of Cases are not automatically predictable on the basis of phrase structure.[3] Thus, the distinction between structural and inherent Case emerges as the relevant means of capturing the different behavior of the two objects in a double object construction.

The abstract Case distinction between structural and inherent Case, as used in Baker 1988a,b, is equivalent to other distinctions proposed in the literature involving the terminology of grammatical functions, instead of Case. On the assumption that abstract Case is distinct from grammatical case, the contrast between structural and inherent Case is a primitive distinction of the framework (not derived from more elementary concepts) whose purpose is to characterize two different grammatical functions, sometimes called primary and secondary object. In this light, then, the often cited claim that GB does not have primitive grammatical functions is not correct. At least in theories such as Baker 1988a,b, there are primitive grammatical functions, although the terminology used to refer to them (structurally Case-marked NP vs. inherently Case-marked NP) does not make this obvious.

A plausible definition of grammatical function in a framework-neutral fashion is that a particular grammatical function (GF) denotes a class of morphosyntactic positions (or expressions) that are in covariation (formal interdependence) or in complementary distribution and, for any given predicate, have the same mapping to semantic roles (including possibly the null mapping).[4] (See Bresnan and Moshi 1990:165-166 and Bresnan 2000:94 for similar characterizations of grammatical functions.) For example, in Chichewa, a particular thematic role may be expressed as an NP adjacent to the verb in the VP or as an object marker prefixed to the verb stem or as no overt expression provided it can be interpreted as a displaced (or wh-) constituent. We can see that these different expressions behave as a class, among other reasons, because they are in complementary distribution (at least, in part): for example, a given semantic role may be encoded alternatively either as an NP in the VP or as an object marker, but not as both at the same time. Also, if an operation on the verb (such as passivization) causes the resulting structure to lack one of these expressions, the structure will also lack the other expressions belonging to the same class. In LFG, this class of expressions is called *unrestricted object;* in GB, it is called *structurally Case-marked object.* These two terms are synonymous, since they denote the same reality, which is a class of expressions; therefore, they denote a grammatical function. The concept of structural Case in GB is a primitive notion and its sole purpose is to define a GF. Therefore, grammatical functions in GB are primitive notions of the framework, as they are made up of elements whose sole purpose is to define GFs.

What this paper examines is to what extent it is appropriate to try to account for object asymmetries in languages with grammatical case and in languages without grammatical case by positing one single set of theoretical distinctions. The conclusion is relevant both for theories in which these theoretical distinctions are called grammatical functions and for theories in which they are called different types of Case. As we have seen, grammatical functions and abstract Case are different names for the same concept.

2. CHICHEWA

The distinction between inherent and structural Case is appealed to in Baker 1988a,b in order to account for certain asymmetries among objects. These asymmetries follow from the theoretical differences between these two types of Cases. Inherent Case is assumed to be assigned to a particular thematic role, whereas structural Case is not tied to any particular thematic role. The assignment of structural Case requires adjacency, whereas inherent Case does not impose this restriction. Structural Case, but not inherent Case, is affected by certain operations such as passivization and object marking.

When a clause includes a beneficiary or goal object, as well as a theme or patient object, the former is assumed to be assigned structural Case, whereas the latter is assigned inherent Case. Although structural Case can be assigned to any thematic role, inherent Case can only be assigned to themes or patients (as well as to some other roles, which we will not be concerned with here). As a result of this, a beneficiary or goal object must be assigned structural Case, as it cannot be assigned inherent Case and all NPs must have Case. Chichewa is assumed to be a language in which verbs can assign at most one structural Case. Since structural Case is assigned to the beneficiary or goal object, the theme or patient object cannot also receive structural Case, and so must be assigned inherent Case.

Thus, we can explain the word order asymmetry shown in (1) between a beneficiary and a theme object cooccurring in a clause in Chichewa:[5]

(1)a. Nkhandwe zi-ku-mény-ér-a   aná   njo⁻vu.
       10 foxes 10 S-PR-hit-AP-FV 2 children 9 elephant
       'The foxes are hitting the elephant for the children.'

   b. *Nkhandwe zi-ku-mény-ér-a   njovu   aᵛna.
       10 foxes 10 S-PR-hit-AP-FV 9 elephant   2 children
       'The foxes are hitting the elephant for the children.'

Since the beneficiary NP is assigned structural Case, it must be adjacent to the verb, as in (1a). The theme NP, which is assigned inherent Case, need not be adjacent to the verb. The form in (1b) violates the adjacency requirement on the assignment of structural Case.

These two objects also differ in that only one of them, the beneficiary, can be expressed by means of an object marker:

(2)a. Nkhandwe zi-ku-wá-mény-er-á   njo⁻vu   (aᵛna).
       10 foxes 10 S-PR-2 O-hit-AP-FV 9 elephant 2 children
       'The foxes are hitting the elephant for them (the children).'

   b. *Nkhandwe zi-ku-í-mény-er-á   äna   (njo⁻vu).
       10 foxes 10 S-PR-9 O-hit-AP-FV 2 children 9 elephant
       'The foxes are hitting it for the children (the elephant).'

On the assumption that an object marker is a manifestation of the structural Case feature of the verb (Baker 1988b:371), we explain that the beneficiary argument, but not the theme argument, can be expressed by means of an object marker. The object marker uses up the single structural Case feature of the verb, making it impossible for the verb to take an NP that needs structural Case, such as the beneficiary NP in (2b). Instead, when an object marker is present, the verb can take an NP that is assigned inherent Case, such as the theme NP in (2a).[6]

A similar contrast between the beneficiary and the theme arguments occurs when the verb is passivized:

(3)a.　　　A^{v}na　　　a-ku-mény-ér-edw-á　　　njo⁻vu　　　(ndí nkha⁻ndwe).
　　　　　　2 children 2 S-PR-hit-AP-PAS-FV 9 elephant　by 10 foxes
　　　　　　'The elephant is being hit for the children (by the foxes).'

　　b.　　　*Njovu　　　i-ku-mény-ér-edw-á　　　äna　　　(ndí nkha⁻ndwe).
　　　　　　9 elephant　9 S-PR-hit-AP-PAS-FV　2 children　by 10 foxes
　　　　　　'The elephant is being hit for the children (by the foxes).'

Assuming that the passive morpheme removes the verb's structural Case, it follows that, in a language like Chichewa, the verb can only assign inherent Case. Thus, the beneficiary NP can move to the subject position, where it receives structural (nominative) Case, whereas the theme argument appears in object position with inherent Case, as in (3a). If the theme NP should appear in subject position, as in (3b), the beneficiary NP, in object position, would not be able to satisfy the Case Filter, as it cannot receive inherent Case from the verb and the verb has no other Case but inherent Case.

As we have seen, the distinction between inherent and structural Case can be used very successfully to account for syntactic asymmetries among objects in a language like Chichewa. At this point it should be noted that the role of this Case distinction in explaining object asymmetries is similar to other distinctions proposed in the literature. The Case distinction is equivalent to the distinction between Direct Object and Direct Object Chômeur found in classical RG treatments of double object constructions in languages like Chichewa. It is also equivalent to the distinction between primary and secondary object proposed by Dryer 1986 and to the distinction between unrestricted object and restricted object found in Bresnan and Moshi 1990 and Alsina and Mchombo 1993. We should ask ourselves whether there is an advantage in attributing this distinction to Case theory, a theory that also has to deal with systems of overt case-marking.

If the theory summarized here involving an abstract Case distinction can be extended in a natural way from languages without grammatical case to languages with grammatical case, then there is good reason to assume that the same principles underlie both types of languages and that the relevant notion involved is abstract Case. If, on the other hand, that theory cannot be extended in a natural way to languages with a system of grammatical case, it will be necessary to admit that overt case distinctions and the distinctions among objects in languages without grammatical case are of a completely different nature and should not be subsumed under the notion of abstract Case.

3. CATALAN

In this section, we will examine a language that makes a distinction among objects manifested in the overt marking of these objects. Unlike Chichewa, where objects are not marked in any way that can help identify their thematic roles, Catalan (like the other Romance languages and like many other languages) marks the objects of a double object construction differently depending on their thematic role. For example, the goal (or indirect object) is marked with dative case, manifested as the preposition *a* when the argument is expressed as an NP or by means of specific clitic forms when the argument is expressed as a pronominal clitic, whereas the theme (or direct object) is in the accusative case, normally unmarked on NPs and characterized by a different set of clitics. Example (4) illustrates the difference in case-marking between the two object NPs in Catalan - the accusative theme *l'amagatall* and the dative goal *a la rata.*

(4)   El gat ha ensenyat l' amagatall a la rata.
        the cat has shown   the hiding place DAT the rat
        'The cat showed the rat the hiding place.'

The first question to ask is whether both the theme and the goal complement in this clause are objects of the verb: given that one of them (the goal) is introduced by a preposition, it might appear reasonable to suggest that the goal argument is in fact not an object of the verb, but an object of the preposition, and that the prepositional phrase is an oblique complement of the verb. However, there is abundant evidence showing that the goal argument in an example like (4) is an object. Alsina 1996a:150-160 argues for the claim that the dative object in Catalan is an object and not an oblique complement, because it behaves like a direct object, and unlike an oblique, with respect to eight different phenomena, which we review in the following paragraph.

(1) Personal pronouns with an object function are obligatorily expressed as clitics, with optional doubling; this is true both of direct objects and of indirect objects. Oblique phrases containing personal pronouns, on the other hand, are only optionally expressed as clitics, *hi* or *en,* and then without the possibility of doubling by independent pronouns. (Similar facts are noted by Kayne 1975:171 for French.) **(2)** Pronominal clitics representing an object, direct or indirect alike, express person and number distinctions, whereas the oblique clitics *(hi* and *en)* do not. (In addition, third person direct object clitics also express gender distinctions.) Also, there is no formal distinction between direct and indirect object in first and second person clitic forms, which is an indication of the commonality between the two objects. For example, the first person singular clitic form is *em,* the corresponding plural form is *ens,* etc., and each one can represent both a direct and an indirect object. **(3)** The reflexive clitic signals a binding relation between the logical subject and an object, either direct or indirect, but never with an oblique argument. **(4)** In Catalan, object clitics, direct or indirect alike, can be modified by the "floating" quantifiers *tot* 'all', or *cadascun* 'each', but oblique clitics cannot. (The corresponding fact is noted by

Perlmutter 1984b301-302 for Italian; see also Kayne 1975 for French.) **(5)** As observed by Suñer 1988:427 for Spanish, objects, both accusative and dative, contrast with obliques with respect to pronominal coreference: a pronominal object must be disjoint in reference with the subject of its clause, while a pronominal oblique (i.e., a pronominal object of an oblique preposition) is free to refer to the subject of its clause. **(6)** As reported in Demonte 1987 for Spanish, a possessive pronoun contained in the accusative object can be bound by a quantified dative object, as well as by a quantified subject, but not by a quantified oblique. Likewise, a possessive pronoun contained in a dative object can be bound by a quantified accusative object, but not by a quantified oblique. **(7)** As noted in Rigau 1988:505ff, when the resumptive pronoun strategy is used in relative clauses in Catalan, strong (or emphatic) pronouns cannot be used as resumptive pronouns functioning as subjects or objects, both direct and indirect objects, although they can when functioning as the objects of prepositional obliques. **(8)** Like direct objects and subjects, indirect objects can be the target of secondary predication, whereas obliques cannot.

All of these facts show that the dative or indirect object behaves like the accusative or direct object and unlike prepositional obliques. Therefore, we can confidently conclude that the dative object is an object, like the accusative object.

Having established that a sentence such as (4) contains two objects, we need to decide which of the two should be assumed to have structural Case and which inherent Case. Given the assumption that inherent Case is tied to a particular thematic role, whereas structural Case is not, accusative case fits the description of structural Case better than dative does. For example, the single object of a monotransitive verb is generally (although not always) accusative and it may bear a variety of thematic roles; in contrast, goal and experiencer objects are typically dative, whether they occur with another object or as the single object. When an object does not bear a thematic role to the verb, as in raising to object (or ECM) constructions, the object is always accusative, as in *El (acc.) considero un amic* 'I consider him a friend'. The assumption that accusative is (generally) structural Case and dative is inherent Case is also made for Italian in Belletti and Rizzi 1988, for Spanish in Suñer 1988, and for German in Haegeman 1991:174-175.

This assumption is consistent with the claim that structural Case is assigned under adjacency, whereas inherent Case is not. The unmarked order of two objects following the verb in Catalan is for the accusative object to follow the verb immediately and precede the dative object, as illustrated by the contrast between (4) and (5).

(5) ?*El gat ha ensenyat a la rata l' amagatall.
  the cat has shown DAT the rat the hiding place
  'The cat showed the rat the hiding place.'

If accusative is structural Case and structural Case is assigned under adjacency, we have an explanation for the contrast between (4) and (5). In (4) the structurally Case-marked NP *l'amagatall* is adjacent to its Case-assigner, the verb, but in (5) it is not, as the dative object appears between the two. The dative object, not being subject to the adjacency requirement, on the assumption that dative is inherent Case, can appear separated from the verb, as in (4).

The contrast between the dative and the accusative object with respect to passivization can also be explained by appealing to the assumption that dative is inherent Case and accusative is structural Case. In the passive form in (6), the subject can only correspond to the accusative object of the active form, as in (6a), never to the dative object, as shown in (6b).

(6)a.   L' amagatall   ha estat ensenyat a   la rata.
        the hiding place has been shown   DAT the rat
        'The hiding place was shown to the rat.'

   b.   *A/Ø   la rata ha estat ensenyada l'   amagatall.
        DAT/Ø the rat has been shown   the hiding place
        'The rat was shown the hiding place.'

Given the standard assumption that the passive morpheme absorbs structural Case, a passive verb form cannot assign structural Case. If accusative case is structural Case, it follows that a passive verb form cannot take an accusative object. The NP that would be assigned accusative case in the active form must move to the Spec of IP in the passive structure so that it can receive Case. Since the passive morpheme does not absorb inherent Case, the object that is assigned inherent (i.e., dative) Case remains in the position where it is assigned Case.

The facts about passivization are a strong indication that Catalan is not open to an analysis in which verbs can assign two structural Cases. There are languages for which such an analysis has been proposed, for example, Kinyarwanda and Japanese according to Baker 1988a:177. A feature of such languages is that either object in a double object construction can be the passive subject, which does not occur in Catalan.

We have seen up to this point that both a language with grammatical case, such as Catalan, and a language without grammatical case, such as Chichewa, can be argued to use the distinction between structural and inherent Case. To the extent that this distinction has identical or similar consequences in the two languages, it reinforces the hypothesis that there is a universal theory of abstract Case. Under this view, grammatical case is one of the possible manifestations of abstract Case, but not the only one or a necessary one. A particular abstract Case assignment may or may not have a reflex in terms of overt case, depending on the language, but whatever other reflexes it has should be uniform across languages. This is what we see in both Catalan and Chichewa regarding linear order of objects and choice of subject in passivization. In both languages, the NP with structural Case is adjacent to the verb and, therefore, precedes the other object in the active form and is the only possible subject in the passive form.

4. PROBLEMS

In spite of what the previous sections have shown, there are problems in trying to derive the facts of double object constructions in both types of languages (with and without grammatical case) from a single set of assumptions about structural and inherent Case. These problems include: (a) differences regarding the correspondence between thematic roles and abstract Case, (b) differences regarding the ability of objects to be expressed by means of morphologically incorporated pronouns, (c) differences regarding the ability of the objects to be affected by lexical binding processes, and (d) differences regarding the ability of the putative inherently Case-marked object to appear as the sole object of the construction. If both languages are assumed to distinguish the two objects of a double object construction by means of the distinction between structural and inherent Case and if this Case distinction has a uniform effect cross-linguistically (except with respect to whether it is manifested overtly or not), we predict that both languages should exhibit the same asymmetries among objects. But the fact is that the two languages behave differently in all four respects mentioned above.

4.1 Thematic role differences

The restrictions concerning which thematic roles may or may not be assigned inherent Case are different in Catalan and Chichewa. In Chichewa, goals, beneficiaries, and agents (causees in causative constructions) must be assigned structural Case. In examples (1)-(3), this phenomenon is illustrated with a beneficiary object. We can tell that the beneficiary must be assigned structural Case because it has to be adjacent to the verb when expressed as an object NP, it may be expressed by means of an object marker, and it has to be the subject of a passive form. The same facts are found with the goal object of a verb like *pats-a* 'give', which indicates that it too must be assigned structural Case. The agent causee object in causative constructions in Chichewa shows the same behavior as goal and beneficiary objects with respect to word order, object marking, and passivization, as is shown in Alsina 1992. The following example illustrates this point with respect to word order:

(7)a.   Nuᵛngu   i-na-phík-íts-a   kadzidzi maûngu.
         9 porcupine 9 S-PS-cook-CST-FV 1a owl   6 pumpkins
         'The porcupine made the owl cook the pumpkins.'

   b.   *Nuᵛngu   i-na-phík-íts-a   maúngú   kadzi⁻dzi.
         9 porcupine 9 S-PS-cook-CST-FV 6 pumpkins 1a owl
         'The porcupine made the owl cook the pumpkins.'

The NP *kadzidzi* in (7) is the agent of the caused event, the cooking event. The assumption that this NP can only be assigned structural Case by the verb correctly accounts for the fact that it must appear adjacent to the verb, as in (7a), and cannot be separated from it by another NP, as in (7b). This assumption, coupled with the assumption that Chichewa verbs can assign at most one structural Case, explains that it is the causee (the agent of the caused event), and not the cooccurring object, that can be expressed by means of an object marker and can be the subject of the passive form.

In contrast with the analysis that we are driven to assume for Chichewa, the Catalan facts indicate that the appropriate analysis for Catalan is exactly the opposite. Examples (4)-(6) show that the goal object is marked with dative case. Having assumed that dative case is the morphological manifestation of inherent Case in Catalan, we have to conclude that the goal object is assigned inherent Case in Catalan. Beneficiary objects behave like goal objects in Catalan in that they too must be assigned dative case. The following example illustrates this point:

(8)a. Li   preparen   una bona acollida, a   la princesa.
       pro-3sg-dat prepare-3sg a   good welcome DAT the princess
       'They are preparing a good welcome for the princess.'

   b. No li   podràs   arreglar el cotxe, al   director.
       not pro-3sg-dat will-be-able-2sg to-fix   the car   DAT-the director
       'You will not be able to fix the car for the director.'

In addition, the agent of a caused event in a causative construction in Catalan is also expressed as a dative object when the construction includes an accusative object.

(9)a. Faran   signar el document a   tots els propietaris.
       will-make-3pl sign   the document DAT all   the owners
       'They will make all the owners sign the document.'

   b. No li   facis   pintar tota la   paret.
       not pro-3sg-dat make-2sg paint   all the wall
       'Don't make him paint all the wall.'

In (9a), *tots els propietaris* is the agent of *signar* 'sign' and it is a dative object, as can be seen by the case marker *a* and because it can be replaced by a dative clitic. In (9b), the agent of the caused event is represented by the dative clitic *li*, which clearly indicates that it is a dative object.

According to Chomsky (1986b:193-194), Case assignment is subject to the following *uniformity condition*: a verb that assigns inherent Case to an NP must also θ-mark that NP (also assumed by Baker (1988a:114, 1988b:366)). This condition does not explicitly require inherent Case to be tied to the same thematic role or set of thematic roles in all languages, but it does imply this if we couple it with the assumption that θ-marking is uniform cross-linguistically (as in Baker's (1988a) UTAH). If we assume that a specific θ-role cannot be assigned inherent Case because it is not θ-marked by the verb (as is claimed by Baker 1988a,b for goals and beneficiaries), then this θ-role should not be assigned inherent Case in any language. In addition, the θ-marking requirement on the assignment of inherent Case runs into problems with causatives in Catalan. If we make the standard assumption that the causative verb, *fer* in Catalan (*faran* in (9a) and *facis* in (9b)), θ-marks only one NP argument, the causer, it follows that the causee is θ-marked by the embedded verb, which assigns it the θ-role of agent, experiencer, etc., but does not receive Case from this verb, since the causee should be the structural subject of the embedded verb and a verb cannot assign Case to its subject. It seems necessary to assume that the causative verb assigns Case to the causee even though it does not θ-mark this argument, but the Case assigned to the causee is inherent (dative), in violation of the uniformity condition just stated.

In summary, objects whose thematic role is agent, beneficiary or goal must be assigned structural Case in Chichewa, whereas the same objects must be assigned inherent Case in Catalan, at least when they cooccur with an accusative object.

4.2 Differences regarding incorporated pronouns

One of the important differences between structural Case and inherent Case in Chichewa is that object markers absorb (or manifest) the verb's structural Case, but not its inherent Case. This is assumed in Baker 1988b:371 following Borer 1984 and others. That means that an argument that is assigned structural Case by the verb may be expressed by means of an object marker, but an argument that is assigned inherent Case may not. Given the assumption that the beneficiary must be assigned structural Case in Chichewa, while the theme or patient may be assigned either structural or inherent Case, the beneficiary receives the single structural Case of the verb and the theme is left with inherent Case. Thus, only the beneficiary object can be expressed by means of an object marker, as illustrated in (2).

This contrast between beneficiary and theme object is replicated in other double object constructions in Chichewa. A goal object or an agent object may be expressed by means of an object marker, like a beneficiary object, whereas the cooccurring object lacks this property. We can observe this contrast in a causative construction where the objects involved are an agent and a theme or patient

(10)a. Nu^{v}ngu   i-na-mú-phík-its-á   máûngu   (kadzi⁻dzi).
        9 porcupine 9 S-PS-1 O-cook-CST-FV 6 pumpkins 1a owl
        'The porcupine made it cook the pumpkins (the owl).'

   b. *Nu^{v}ngu   i-na-wá-phík-its-á   kádzi⁻dzi (maûngu).
        9 porcupine 9 S-PS-6 O-cook-CST-FV 1a owl   6 pumpkins
        'The porcupine made the owl cook them (the pumpkins).'

If we assume, as we did earlier, that the agent object must receive structural Case, it follows that it can be expressed by means of an object marker, as in (10a). Since the patient object cannot also be assigned structural Case, it receives inherent Case and so cannot be expressed by means of an object marker.

In Catalan, the linguistic form that corresponds most closely to object markers in Chichewa is what is known as pronominal clitics. There are some differences between object markers in the Bantu languages and pronominal clitics in Romance. For example, object markers in Chichewa are verbal prefixes occupying a specific slot in the verb form, between the tense marker and the verb root; in contrast, pronominal clitics in Catalan appear sometimes preceding the verb and sometimes following it, depending on the verbal morphology. However, they are very similar as far as their syntactic and semantic properties are concerned. They both have a pronominal interpretation, they are referentially dependent on a discourse topic, they are noncontrastive, they show formal agreement with their antecedent, etc. (see Bresnan and Mchombo 1987). Therefore, it is reasonable to consider object markers in Bantu and pronominal clitics in Romance to be the same kind of linguistic device, which we can call morphologically incorporated pronouns.

In Catalan, as in Chichewa, the structurally Case-marked object can be expressed by means of a morphologically incorporated pronoun. The object with structural Case, manifested as accusative case, in Catalan can be represented as a pronominal clitic, as in (11a), corresponding to (4), and in (11b), corresponding to (9a).

(11)a.　El　gat l'　　　　ha ensenyat a　la rata.
　　　the cat pro 3sg acc has shown　DAT the rat
　　　'The cat showed it to the rat.'

　　b.　El　　　faran　　　signar a　tots els propietaris.
　　　pro 3sg acc will-make-3pl sign　DAT all　the owners
　　　'They will make all the owners sign it.'

However, unlike what happens in Chichewa, the inherently Case-marked object in Catalan can also be expressed by means of a morphologically incorporated pronoun. Since structural and inherent Case are morphologically distinguished in Catalan as accusative and dative case respectively, the pronominal clitics that correspond to objects with inherent, or dative, Case are morphologically different from those that correspond to objects with structural, or accusative, Case. Thus, examples (12a) and (12b) correspond to (4) and (9a) with the inherently Case-marked object expressed by means of an incorporated pronominal.

(12)a.　El　gat li　　　　ha ensenyat l'　amagatall.
　　　the cat pro-3sg-dat has shown　the hiding place
　　　'The cat showed it the hiding place.'

　　b.　Els hi　faran　　　signar el　document.
　　　pro 3pl dat will-make-3pl sign　the document
　　　'They will make them sign the document.'

In (11), the pronominal clitic *l'* or *el* is the accusative object and, in (12), the pronominal clitics *li* and *els hi* are the dative object. In fact, both objects can simultaneously be expressed as pronominal clitics, as shown in (13):[7]

(13)a.   El gat l'   hi   ha ensenyat.
          the cat pro 3sg acc pro dat has shown
          'The cat showed it to it.'

   b.   Els hi   faran   signar.
          pro 3pl dat will-make-3pl sign
          'They will make them sign it.'

Thus, while Chichewa does not allow its inherently Case-marked objects to be expressed by means of morphologically incorporated pronouns, Catalan does. There is no apparent reason why this difference should exist. The two languages differ with respect to the presence or absence of grammatical case. The abstract Case distinction, present in both languages, is manifested as a grammatical case distinction in Catalan, but not in Chichewa. There is no explanation for why this superficial difference between the two languages should also have an effect in whether inherently Case-marked objects can be expressed as incorporated pronouns or not. Note, furthermore, that Catalan is a problem for the claim that incorporated pronominals are the manifestation of structural Case, as assumed by Baker 1988b and others.

4.3 Differences regarding lexical binding

Processes of lexical binding affect the argument structure of a verb by binding two of the thematic roles of the verb, with the result that one single grammatical function corresponds to the two bound arguments. The reciprocal morpheme in Chichewa involves such a process, as has been argued in Alsina 1993, 1999, 2001, Bresnan and Mchombo 1985, Dalrymple, Mchombo, and Peters 1994, Mchombo 1992, 1993. There is considerable evidence for this claim. For example, like other processes that affect argument structure, such as causativization, reciprocalization can feed other processes that affect argument structure and processes that change the syntactic category of the lexical item. In this respect, the reciprocal morpheme differs markedly from object markers (including the reflexive morpheme, which patterns like an object marker): a verb form containing the reciprocal morpheme can be causativized or nominalized, whereas a verb form containing an object marker cannot be either causativized or nominalized (see Alsina 2001). Such differences can be explained by assuming that object markers are the overt expression of an object function, but a reciprocal morpheme performs an operation on argument structure by which two thematic roles are expressed as one single grammatical function.

   As a result of this, a reciprocalized verb form in Chichewa has one object less than the same verb without the reciprocal morpheme. If we compare the double object construction in (1) with its reciprocalized counterpart in (14a), we observe that the latter has one object less than the former. Another important feature of the reciprocal morpheme is that it treats the two objects of a double object construction in an asymmetrical fashion: the beneficiary object can be affected by the process of lexical binding, as we see in (14a), but the theme or patient object cannot be affected by this process when a beneficiary object is present, as in (14b).

(14)a.   Nkha⁻ndwe zi-ku-mény-ér-an-a   njo⁻vu.
          10 foxes   10 S-PR-hit-AP-RCP-FV 9 elephant
          'The foxes are hitting the elephant for each other.'

    b.   *Nkhandwe zi-ku-mény-ér-an-a   aᵛna.
          10 foxes   10 S-PR-hit-AP-RCP-FV 2 children
          'The foxes are hitting each other for the children.'

Thus, the reciprocal morpheme reflects the same asymmetry among objects as object markers: in a construction with a theme object and a beneficiary object, the beneficiary can be affected by the reciprocal morpheme, but the theme object cannot. A theory that accounts for object asymmetries by appealing to a distinction between structural and inherent Case could account for the facts illustrated in (14) by assuming that the reciprocal morpheme absorbs the verb's structural Case (as is done in Baker 1988b:385, following a comparable analysis in Marantz 1984). Given the assumption that in Chichewa verbs can assign at most one structural Case, once the verb's structural Case has been removed by the reciprocal morpheme, the verb cannot take an object, such as a beneficiary object, that must be assigned structural Case, which explains the unacceptability of (14b). But such a verb can take an object, such as a theme or patient, that can be assigned either structural or inherent Case. (14a) is grammatical because the object is a theme and can, therefore, be assigned inherent Case.

Catalan also has a process of lexical binding: the so-called reflexive clitic, es/s'/se in the third person, involves a lexical binding process when it has a reflexive or reciprocal interpretation. Evidence that we are dealing with a process of lexical binding, and not with the overt expression of an argument, is found in Alsina 1993, 1996a (see also Grimshaw 1982 for the corresponding phenomenon in French and Marantz 1984 and Sells, Zaenen, and Zec 1987 for other languages). Although the reflexive clitic is morphologically the same type of element as other verbal clitics, it has different syntactic effects from those of other verbal clitics. For example, a nominalized infinitive cannot contain any verbal clitic except for the reflexive clitic (see Alsina 1996a).

If we take a verb in Catalan either of whose objects can be animate, we find that either of them can be affected by the reflexive clitic.

(15)a.   Les noies s'   han ensenyat les fotos.
          the girls REF have shown   the photos
          'The girls showed each other the photos.'

b.   Les noies s'   han ensenyat al   públic.
the girls REF have shown   DAT-the audience.
'The girls showed themselves (/each other) to the audience.'

Since the reflexive clitic in Catalan has essentially the same syntactic behavior as the reciprocal morpheme in Chichewa, we would expect them to be subject to the same syntactic constraints. (These two morphemes differ, though, in terms of their semantic properties: whereas the reciprocal morpheme in Chichewa only allows a reciprocal interpretation, the reflexive clitic in Catalan allows either a reciprocal or a reflexive interpretation. The choice between these two interpretations for the reflexive clitic in Catalan does not have any relevant syntactic consequences.) Thus, we would expect that only an object that needs structural Case could be affected by this process of lexical binding, just as in Chichewa. Since the theme of a verb like *ensenyar* 'show', which corresponds to the accusative object in an example like (4), is the argument that needs structural Case, we expect this argument to be able to be affected by the process of lexical binding of the reflexive clitic, as we see in (15b). But we would not expect the goal argument of this verb, which takes dative case (i.e., inherent Case) when expressed as an object, to be affected by this process. Yet, contrary to our expectation, the goal argument can be lexically bound by the reflexive clitic, as we see in (15a).

In order to explain the facts of the process of lexical binding in Catalan, we would have to assume that the morpheme responsible for this operation is not restricted to absorb only structural Case as in Chichewa, but absorbs either structural or inherent Case. Once again, Chichewa and Catalan differ in a way that is independent of their difference regarding the presence or absence of grammatical case distinctions. And, again, Catalan turns out to be the problem case for generalizing the assumption in Baker 1988b and others that lexical binding absorbs structural Case. The fact that Catalan, unlike Chichewa, has a morphological correlate of the distinction between structural and inherent Case does not provide an explanation for the difference with respect to lexical binding.

4.4 Differences regarding inherent Case as the sole Case

Chichewa and Catalan differ with respect to whether a verb taking one single object (i.e., internal argument) can assign it inherent Case. There is evidence that a verb in Chichewa assigns inherent Case to an object that cooccurs with an object that receives structural Case. This is the situation in double object constructions, which has been illustrated in the preceding paragraphs. The fact that one of the two objects in a double object construction lacks the ability to be expressed by means of an object marker or as the passive subject can be explained by assuming that this object has inherent Case. We can assume that the other object in a double object construction is assigned structural Case, because it can be expressed by means of an object marker, can appear as the passive subject, etc. For example, the asymmetries between the two objects illustrated in (1)-(3) indicate that the beneficiary is assigned structural Case, whereas the theme or patient is assigned inherent Case.

There is also evidence that a Chichewa verb can assign structural Case to the single object (i.e., internal argument) of the construction. For example, the single internal argument of a monadic verb such as *meny-a* 'hit', shown in (16a) with this argument expressed as an object NP, can be expressed by means of an object marker, as in (16b), and can be expressed as the subject of a passive form, as in (16c).

(16)a. Nkhandwe zi-ku-mény-á njo⁻vu.
   10 foxes 10 S-PR-hit-FV 9 elephant
   'The foxes are hitting the elephant.'

  b. Nkhandwe zi-ku-í-mëny-a (njo⁻vu).
   10 foxes 10 S-PR-9 O-hit-FV 9 elephant
   'The foxes are hitting it (the elephant).'

  c. Njovu i-ku-mény-ëdw-a (ndí nkha⁻ndwe).
   9 elephant 9 S-PR-hit-PAS-FV by 10 foxes
   'The elephant is being hit (by the foxes).'

The fact that the single internal argument in this construction can be expressed by means of an object marker, (16b), or as the passive subject, (16c), is evidence that this argument can be assigned structural Case. However, while there is no evidence that the single internal argument of a verb can be assigned inherent Case in Chichewa, there is no evidence either that it cannot be assigned inherent Case: we can assume either that the object NP in (16a) is necessarily assigned structural case or that it has an ambiguous analysis with either structural or inherent Case.

The possible morphosyntactic expressions of an inherently Case-marked object in Chichewa are a proper subset of the possible morphosyntactic expressions of a structurally Case-marked NP. If the single object of a verb in Chichewa appears as an NP following the verb, we cannot tell whether it is assigned inherent Case or structural Case, since both types of Case assignment are compatible with this morphosyntactic expression. There are some morphosyntactic expressions in Chichewa that are only compatible with the assignment of structural Case, such as object markers and passivization. But there are no morphosyntactic expressions in Chichewa that are only compatible with the assignment of inherent Case. Thus, the facts in Chichewa are equally consistent with the assumption that the single internal argument of a verb is assigned structural Case obligatorily as with the assumption that it is assigned either structural or inherent Case. In the latter case, any monotransitive construction would have an ambiguous analysis: in one analysis, the object is assigned structural Case and, in the other, it is assigned inherent Case. The Chichewa data underdetermine the choice of theory.

In order to narrow down the theoretical options, we should turn to languages similar to Chichewa as far as object asymmetries are concerned, but in which the assignment of inherent Case is unequivocally signaled by the morphosyntax. An instance of such a language would be Tzotzil, as described by Aissen 1983. In this language, in a clause with a goal object and a theme object, the verb agrees in person and number with the goal object and not with the theme object, and, when the verb is passivized, the goal, and not the theme, becomes the subject. It seems reasonable to assume that the phenomena of object agreement and passivization in Tzotzil are comparable to object marking and passivization in Chichewa, in the sense that both phenomena are sensitive to the distinction between structural and inherent Case: the verb agrees with the NP it assigns structural Case to and the passive morphology absorbs structural Case.

A relevant property of Tzotzil is that, whenever the clause contains two objects (or, more appropriately, two internal arguments) and in no other case, the verb includes the suffix -*be*. In the following examples, from Aissen 1983:280, 282, we see that a verb with one single object does not include this suffix, as in (17a), whereas the same verb taking two objects does include this suffix, as in (17b).

(17)a.   Ba y-ak'-∅   ?une.
          go E3-give-A3 PTS
          'He went to give it.'

    b.   Ti mi c-av-ak'-b-on   ?ep   tak'ine.
          if ASP-E2-give-BE-A1 much money
          'If you will give me a lot of money.'

    c.   Ti mi c-av-ak'-be-∅   ?ep   tak'ine.
          if ASP-E2-give-BE-A3 much money
          'If you will give him plenty of money.'
          [Not: 'If you will give me plenty of money.']

When the verb has a theme object as its sole internal argument, it agrees with it, as shown in (17a). When the verb takes a goal object, in addition to the theme object, it agrees with the goal object, and not with the theme object, as the contrast in (17b) and (17c) illustrates. As in Chichewa, the goal in a double object construction in Tzotzil would be assigned structural Case, whereas the theme object would be assigned inherent Case. Since the verb agrees with the NP it assigns structural Case to, it follows that it agrees with the goal object. The fact that the verb only agrees with one of its objects indicates that verbs in Tzotzil, as in Chichewa, can assign at most one structural Case. Passivization reveals the same asymmetry in Tzotzil, as shown in Aissen 1983:283: the goal argument of a verb like 'give' can be its passive subject, but never the theme argument. That follows from the assumption that the passive morphology absorbs structural Case from the verb, so that the NP that needs structural Case, in our example, the goal, cannot receive it from the verb and must move to the subject position to receive structural Case.

The suffix -*be* in Tzotzil appears on verbs that take a goal and a theme or patient objects, with meanings like 'give' or 'sell'; it also appears on verbs that take a beneficiary object, in addition to a theme or patient object, with verbs meaning 'kill', 'bring', etc.; and also on the causative verb *?ak'* in the Clause Union construction when and only when the complement clause is transitive. The fact that this suffix appears on the causative verb depending purely on the transitivity of the complement clause indicates that it is not an applicative affix. The most plausible analysis of this suffix is that it registers or marks the assignment of inherent Case. But in order to make this analysis work, we have to assume that inherent Case is a last resort option: a verb can only assign inherent Case when it has used up its structural Case. So, when the verb has one single object, it must assign structural Case to this object and, so, the suffix *-be* cannot appear on the verb. When the verb has two objects, the verb must assign structural Case to one of them and, since the verb can assign no more than one structural Case it must assign inherent Case to the remaining object so that it will not remain Caseless. In this situation, the suffix *-be* must appear on the verb, as it marks the assignment of inherent Case.[8] (The choice of which object is assigned inherent Case in Tzotzil is subject to essentially the same restrictions as in Chichewa.)

Thus, Tzotzil is identical to Chichewa regarding the type of object asymmetries that it exhibits. The main difference is that Tzotzil has an overt encoding of the assignment of inherent Case: the suffix *-be* indicates unambiguously that inherent Case is assigned by the verb in which it appears. That allows us to deduce that inherent Case is never assigned to the single object of a verb, since that suffix never appears on a monotransitive verb. This can be explained by assuming that inherent Case is assigned only as a last resort. Chamorro, a language like Chichewa and Tzotzil as far as object asymmetries are concerned, also signals the assignment of inherent Case: in this language, it is the NP with inherent Case that has a special marking and, as in Tzotzil, this marking only appears when the verb can be argued to have used up (or lack) its structural Case (see Gibson 1980 and Gibson and Raposo 1986). This being the situation in Tzotzil and Chamorro, as we have no evidence indicating that it is otherwise in Chichewa, we should assume that inherent Case is also a last resort option in Chichewa and, ideally, we should assume that this is a universal property.

In contrast with this, in Catalan there is direct evidence that inherent Case can be assigned to the single object of a monotransitive verb. Although it is reasonable to argue that the unmarked case feature for the single object of a verb is accusative case, therefore, structural Case, there are many intransitive verbs that take a dative object, that is, an inherently Case-marked object. The following examples illustrate clauses in Catalan whose single object is a dative object:

(18)a.   Ja   he   vist com somreies   a   la dependenta.
          emph. have-1sg seen how smiled-2sg DAT the shop attendant
          'I saw how you were smiling at the shop attendant.'

   b.   No li   menteixis, si vols   que t'   ajudi.
         not pro-3sg-dat lie-2sg   if want-2sg that you help-3sg
         'Don't lie to him, if you want him to help you.'

Verbs such as *somriure*, used in (18a), and *mentir*, in (18b), can be used either without any object or with a dative object, but cannot be used with an accusative object. We can, thus, conclude that such verbs lexically (or inherently) require their object to take dative case. Other verbs take an optional accusative object, in addition to a dative object, sometimes also optional. Some of these verbs would be *escriure* 'write', *pegar* 'hit', *respondre* 'reply', etc. It is important to note that, regardless of whether one or both of their objects are expressed, the case on the object depends on its thematic role and not on there being another object in the clause.

(19)a.   Encara no li   he   escrit (la carta).
         still   not pro-3sg-dat have-1sg written the letter
         'I haven't written (the letter) to him yet.'

    b.   Per què li   heu   pegat (una cleca)?
         why   pro-3sg-dat have-2pl hit   a   slap
         'Why did you hit her/give her a slap?'

These examples show that, with verbs such as *escriure* or *pegar,* the goal object is invariably a dative object, whether the theme object is expressed or not.

Given the assumption that, in Catalan, as in case-marking languages in general, dative case is inherent Case and accusative case is structural Case, we have to conclude that inherent Case can be assigned in Catalan to the single object of a verb. This shows yet another difference between languages like Chichewa and languages like Catalan: the single object of a verb cannot be assigned inherent Case in Chichewa, but it can in Catalan. In Chomsky's (1986b:193-204) discussion of inherent Case, there is no indication that inherent Case cannot be assigned to the single NP argument of a lexical item. In this respect, then, the situation in Chichewa would be unexpected.

5. CONSEQUENCES

The preceding section has brought out four differences between Catalan and Chichewa regarding structural and inherent Case. In the first place, the same thematic roles require a different Case assignment in these two languages: a verb meaning 'give' will assign structural Case to the goal and inherent Case to the theme in Chichewa, but will have the reverse assignment of Case in Catalan. In the second place, the two languages differ with respect to whether incorporated pronominals are sensitive to the distinction between the two types of Case: an incorporated pronominal may correspond only to an object with structural Case in Chichewa, but may correspond two both types of objects in Catalan. In the third place, lexical binding also treats inherently Case-marked arguments differently in the two languages: such arguments may be involved in a lexical binding relation in Catalan, but not in Chichewa. And in the fourth place, inherent Case is a last resort option in Chichewa, but not in Catalan: as a result, the single object of a verb may be assigned inherent Case in Catalan, but not in Chichewa.

What poses a problem for Case Theory is not so much that a particular property in Chichewa or Catalan contradicts some assumption standardly made within this theory, but that there are systematic differences in the behavior and distribution of the two types of Cases in the two languages. As a result, there cannot be a unified theory of Case that is cross-linguistically valid. Catalan raises a problem for the uniformity condition on the assignment of inherent Case, since causees may be assigned inherent (dative) Case without receiving a θ-role from the Case assigner. This language is also a problem for the assumptions that incorporated pronominals are a manifestation of structural Case and that lexical binding processes absorb structural Case. And Chichewa is a problem for the possibility of using inherent Case independently of the presence of structural Case. If each language were considered separately, any of these problems could be solved by modifying the relevant assumption accordingly. The problem becomes insoluble when we consider both languages: we cannot have a single universal principle about the distribution and properties of structural and inherent Case because we would not be able to accommodate the facts of both languages.

According to the theory presented here, all of the differences mentioned are independent of each other and independent of the obvious difference that distinguishes these two languages, namely, whether or not abstract Case is manifested as grammatical case. One of the fundamental ideas of Case Theory is that grammatical case is just one of the ways in which abstract Case can manifest itself. The presence or absence of grammatical case in a language, therefore, is just a superficial fact, which is not predicted to have any consequence in the syntax of the languages involved. Given this theory, the four differences between Chichewa and Catalan discussed in the previous section, in addition to the difference regarding the presence or absence of grammatical case, would have to be treated as an accidental clustering of properties. Each of these different properties would have to be treated as the result of a different setting of the corresponding parameter of variation. Following is a formulation of these different parameters of variation:

(20)   CASE-THEORETIC PARAMETERS:

1. An NP whose thematic role is agent, beneficiary or goal is assigned inherent Case.	(a) never (b) always
2. An inherently Case-marked argument may not correspond to an incorporated pronominal.	(a) ON (b) OFF
3. An inherently Case-marked argument may not be involved in lexical binding.	(a) ON (b) OFF
4. Inherent Case is a last resort option.	(a) ON (b) OFF

5. The distinction between structural and inherent Case is   (a) ON
manifested as an overt distinction between accusative and   (b) OFF
dative case respectively.

    Since these five parameters are formally independent of each other and have a
binary setting, we predict the existence of 32 (2^5) different languages, as far as these
parameters are concerned. Chichewa happens to have setting (a) for parameters 1, 2,
3, and 4 and setting (b) for parameter 5. Catalan has the opposite settings:[9] (b) for
parameters 1-4 and (a) for parameter 5. Crucially, there is no reason to expect that
the choice of one setting for a given parameter will restrict the setting for another
parameter. Given this view, the combinations of parameter settings found in Catalan
and Chichewa are just two out of 32 possible combinations of parameter settings.
What this implies is that the clustering of properties found in Catalan and Chichewa
is accidental, in that it is no more to be expected than any other combination of
properties. For example, for a theory with the parameters in (20), a language with
the same parameter settings as Chichewa except for parameter 1, with setting (b)
instead of setting (a), is as much to be expected as Chichewa. The problem is that
such a language is not known to exist. One of the predicted features of this language
is that example (2a) would be ill-formed, as the object marker refers to the beneficiary object, which would receive inherent Case, whereas example (2b), with the
theme object expressed by means of an object marker, would be grammatical, as the
theme would receive structural Case: exactly the opposite of Chichewa.
    The fact is that the clustering of properties found in Chichewa and Catalan can
be shown not to be accidental. Languages that exhibit the kinds of object
asymmetries discussed here consistently pattern either with Chichewa or with
Catalan. Specifically, if a language distinguishes its objects by means of
grammatical case, it will have the properties found in Catalan. One of the two case
features is more marked than the other (morphologically, in that it is more
consistently and distinctly marked, and thematically, in that it is assigned on the
basis of thematic roles or argument structure, etc.). The marked case feature is
conventionally known as dative and it is assigned to arguments whose thematic roles
are typically goals, beneficiaries, and experiencers and, depending on the language,
may include others such as possessors, agents in causative constructions, etc.
Examples of languages that distinguish their objects by means of grammatical case
are Latin, Turkish, Malayalam, Basque, Kannada, German, etc. Thus, parameter 1
consistently would take on setting (b) in these languages. If these languages have
incorporated pronominals, they correspond to both accusative and dative objects, as
would be required by setting (b) of Parameter 2. An example of a non-Indo-
European language whose incorporated pronominals correspond to both accusative
and dative objects is Basque (see Mejías-Bikandi 1990 and Davies and
Martínez-Arbelaiz 1995, among others). If a language with dative and accusative
case has a process of lexical binding, this process affects both arguments that get
dative case and arguments that get accusative Case. An example, again
non-Indoeuropean, of a such a language is Kannada, as shown in Mohanan and
Mohanan 1998. Finally, languages with dative and accusative case always have

some construction where a dative object appears as the sole object of the construction. We can see, then, that the clustering of properties found in Catalan should not be the result of setting five different parameters at random, but is cross-linguistically the only attested possibility for case-marking languages and our theory should be able to capture this cross-linguistic fact.

Leaving aside case-marking languages, languages without grammatical case fall into several subtypes, as has been shown in work by Baker 1988a, Bresnan and Moshi 1990, Alsina 1996b, among others. One of the major divisions separates asymmetrical languages from symmetrical languages, using Bresnan and Moshi's 1990 terminology. In Baker's Case Theory, the division corresponds to languages whose verbs can assign at most one structural Case (asymmetrical), such as Chichewa, and to languages whose verbs can assign more than one structural Case (symmetrical), such as Kichaga. Asymmetrical languages exhibit the kinds of object asymmetries found in Chichewa. Symmetrical languages don't, although they can have asymmetries in the ordering of object NPs and of object markers, as shown in Alsina 1996b, and possibly in other areas. What is cross-linguistically consistent is that, if a language lacks grammatical case and it has thematically conditioned object asymmetries, it will not allow inherent Case to be assigned to goals, beneficiaries, agents, etc., as required by setting (a) of parameter 1. In other words, the fact that a caseless language, i.e., a language with parameter 5 set to (b), has parameter 1 set to (a) cannot be an accident. Likewise, the fact that such a language has setting (a) for parameters 2, 3, and 4 cannot be assumed to be the result of a random setting of the parameters.

What this shows is that the facts of languages with grammatical case and the facts of languages without grammatical case cannot be explained by appealing to one single set of abstract distinctions responsible for object asymmetries. By committing ourselves to the idea that grammatical case distinctions are just one of the possible ways in which abstract Case distinctions are manifested and by assuming that object asymmetries in languages without grammatical case are also manifestations of abstract Case, we are making it impossible for us to have a restrictive cross-linguistic theory of object asymmetries. The first thing that needs to be recognized is a fundamental division between languages with grammatical case and languages without grammatical case. For languages with grammatical case, and only for such languages, it is appropriate to use the term "case." In such languages, some of the asymmetries among objects can be attributed to grammatical case distinctions. In languages without grammatical case, "case" is not an appropriate term to use to refer to the abstract distinction responsible for the kind of object asymmetries found in languages like Chichewa. If the abstract distinction found in these languages is assumed to be of a fundamentally different nature from case, there is no reason to expect parallel behaviors in languages with case and languages without case.[10]

The fact that, for example, an NP with inherent Case, to use the Case-Theoretic terminology, behaves very differently in a language with grammatical case and in a language without grammatical case is a problem for Case Theory, but is not a problem for a theory that recognizes the fundamentally different nature of object asymmetries in the two types of languages. To be more precise, it is not a problem, but an artifact of Case Theory. In order to claim that there can be such a thing as an NP with inherent Case in a language without grammatical case, we have to assume that there is a concept named abstract Case present in languages both with and without grammatical case that underlies the surface realization of arguments. If we reject this assumption and instead assume that case (or Case) is just grammatical case, there can be no such thing as an NP with inherent Case in a language without grammatical case.

What is the abstract distinction responsible for some of the object asymmetries in a language like Chichewa? Leaving aside Case-Theoretic approaches, most theories have assumed distinctions in terms of grammatical functions (or grammatical relations). Perlmutter and Postal 1983b, Aissen 1983, and others within the classical RG framework assume a distinction between Direct Object and Direct Object Chômeur. Dryer 1986 assumes a distinction between primary and secondary object. Bresnan and Moshi 1990, Alsina and Mchombo 1993, and others within the LFG framework assume the distinction between unrestricted object and restricted object. Since the Case-Theoretic distinction between structural and inherent Case for languages without grammatical case plays the same role as these other distinctions, we could say that the Case-Theoretic distinction is also a distinction in terms of grammatical function, with the peculiarity that the name "grammatical function" is replaced by the name "Case." As has been argued in this paper, this terminological replacement is not innocuous: the use of the term "Case" leads us to expect that the abstract distinction responsible for object asymmetries in languages like Chichewa is the same as the distinction responsible for object asymmetries in case-marking languages. As we have seen, this expectation is incorrect and we should therefore use different terms for the different concepts involved.

One could object to the assumption made in this paper that dative case is inherent Case and accusative case is structural Case in languages with grammatical case. We could, instead, say that both dative and accusative case are types of structural Case. If we adopted this position, the distinction between structural and inherent Case posited for languages like Chichewa would have no correlate in languages with grammatical case. In such a view, the abstract distinction responsible for object asymmetries in Chichewa would be different from the abstract distinction responsible for object asymmetries in Catalan: in one type of language, we would be talking of structural and inherent Case, whereas, in the other, we would be talking of dative and accusative Case (two kinds of structural Case). Although we would be using the term Case in both situations, we would still have to posit two different sets of abstract distinctions and we would have to explain why languages with grammatical case do not have the structural/inherent distinction for objects and why languages without grammatical case do not have the accusative/dative distinction. This alternative position accepts the idea that the distinction responsible for object asymmetries is a different one in the two types of languages considered, but chooses to give an illusion of theoretical unity by using the term "Case" for both.

A clarification is in order. Some frameworks that explicitly posit grammatical functions as notions not defined configurationally have evolved in recent years by introducing a level of argument structure, which is parallel to other syntactic levels such as the level that represents grammatical functions. The introduction of argument structure has implied filling this level with content, and some of its content is information that was previously assumed to be part of grammatical functions. In such a framework, where the work previously performed by grammatical functions is now factored out into argument structure and grammatical functions, we should ask ourselves whether the abstract distinction responsible for object asymmetries in languages like Chichewa should still be seen as part of grammatical functions, or is more appropriately treated as part of argument structure. I have argued elsewhere (Alsina 2001) that this distinction is part of argument structure. So, rather than calling it a distinction at the level of grammatical functions, we should consider it a distinction at the level of argument structure. This does not alter the conclusion that the terminology of Case Theory is not appropriate for capturing the distinction in question.[11]

NOTES

[*]   This paper has benefited from comments by the audience at the workshop on *The Role of Grammatical Functions in Transformational Syntax, July 10-11, 1999,* University of Illinois at Urbana-Champaign, by two anonymous reviewers, and by the editors of this volume William Davies and Stanley Dubinsky.

[1]   I use the term GB to refer to a class of theoretical frameworks that has been called "Government and Binding," "Principles and Parameters," and "Minimalist Program." Its main features are set down in work by Chomsky (1981, 1986b, 1993, 1995).

[2]   In the discussion that follows, I present one particular version of Case Theory, in other words, one particular theory that makes use of the terms "Case," "structural Case," "Inherent Case," etc. This is Baker's (1988a,b) theory, which has been successfully applied to explain the facts of object asymmetries in languages like Chichewa. There are many other theories that use those terms, including some that differ from Baker's (1988a,b) in that they attempt to unify structural and inherent Case, such as Lasnik 1995a, Collins and Thráinsson 1996, and Boeckx 2000, among others. I will not bring these theories into the discussion, as they have not been applied to the range of facts under consideration in this paper.

[3]   In Baker 1988a,b, what appears to be an NP in object position can be an NP complement of V, an NP complement of an empty P that projects a PP complement of V, or an NP subject of an ECM construction. The NP in any of these positions can be assigned structural Case, whereas inherent Case can only be assigned to the NP complement of V. The fact that the NP complement of V can be assigned either structural or inherent Case implies that the assignment of these two types of Cases is not absolutely predictable.

[4]   More precisely, if A and B are morphosyntactic positions and are in covariation or in complementary distribution and, for any given predicate, have the same mapping to semantic roles, we say that A and B are the same GF. This definition refers to *morphosyntactic positions,* which has to be understood as types of overt expressions, such as "accusative noun phrase," "noun phrase adjacent to the verb," "pronominal or agreement affix on the verb," etc. This characterization excludes "deep" grammatical relations: a d-structure direct object, for example, is not a type of overt expressions; no overt formal feature distinguishes a subject derived from (or coindexed with) a d-structure object position from a subject not so derived. Therefore, a d-structure direct object is not a GF as defined here.

[5]   The Chichewa data in this paper are taken from Alsina 1993. Transcription is according to the standard orthography, with the addition of hyphens in verb forms to separate morphemes and of tone markings as follows: as illustrated with the vowel 'a', long vowels may be low a⁻, high ä, rising aˇ, and falling â, and short vowels are either high á, or low, which is unmarked. Every noun in Chichewa belongs

to one of eighteen noun classes, denoted in the glosses by numbers. (See Bresnan and Kanerva 1989:41 for a table of the noun class prefixes in Chichewa.) The following abbreviations are used in the glosses:

AP:	applicative	O:	object marker	PS:	past
CST:	causative	PAS:	passive	RCP:	reciprocal
FV:	final vowel	PR:	present	S:	subject marker

[6]   The optional NP, given in parentheses in (2a), that agrees in noun class with the object marker is not an object NP, but an NP external to the VP, which can either precede or follow the VP and is freely ordered with the subject NP, when there is one, as has been shown by Bresnan and Mchombo 1987. It can be seen as a doubling NP, as in clitic doubling constructions, as suggested by Baker 1988b, or as a topic anaphorically linked to the object marker, as analyzed by Bresnan and Mchombo 1987.

[7]   The forms *li* and *els hi* of (12) are phonologically identical to the forms *l'hi* and *els hi* of (13) respectively, belonging to the dialect of Barcelona (see Bonet 1995 for details about clitic forms). We can tell that the latter correspond to both the accusative and the dative object, because, if, instead of a third person dative object clitic, we should use a first or second person object clitic, combined with an accusative clitic, the form would be distinct from the dative clitic alone: for example, with the first person clitic, *Em faran signar el document* `They will make me sign the document' vs. *Me'l faran signar* `They will make me sign it'.

[8]   In Aissen's 1983 analysis, developed within the framework of RG, the suffix *-be* is assumed to be a morphological reflex of the advancement of indirect object to direct object. This analysis is very similar to the one presented in the text in terms of empirical predictions. There are theoretical differences: in Aissen 1983, the advancement of indirect object is obligatory and restricted to clauses containing a direct object. The assumption that indirect object advancement is obligatory explains why goals, beneficiaries, and agent causees of transitive verbs never appear as anything but objects. The theory in the text does not require an equivalent assumption. Restricting indirect object advancement to clauses containing a direct object explains the fact that *-be* only appears on verbs with two objects (or internal arguments). This restriction achieves the same result as the assumption that inherent Case is a last resort option.

[9]   The formulation of parameter 1 is an oversimplification as regards its setting (b): the assignment of dative case in Catalan is not constrained only by thematic roles (see Alsina 1996a).

[10]   A reviewer observes that Catalan seems to be a symmetrical language with the restriction that the dative NP cannot fill the subject position in the passive. If 'symmetrical language' means a language whose verbs do not assign inherent Case and we assume that case-marking languages such as Catalan are symmetrical languages, then we have to conclude that dative is not inherent Case. That means that case-marking languages have a distinction between dative and accusative case (a distinction not found in caseless languages), whereas caseless languages of the asymmetrical type have a distinction between structural and inherent Case (a distinction not found in case-marking languages). Therefore, the abstract distinction needed for object asymmetries in caseless languages is different from the abstract distinction needed in case-marking languages, which is the conclusion this paper is arguing for. In other words, we cannot assume, as has been standard in the GB literature, that the distinction between structural and inherent Case, posited for caseless languages like Chichewa, is the abstract distinction found in languages such as Catalan. Thus, Catalan and Chichewa are very different as regards object asymmetries, but they are comparable (contrary to what the anonymous reviewer claims) and it is by comparing them that we can dispel the entrenched belief that the same set of distinctions in terms of abstract Case underlies both languages with morphological case and those without it.

[11]   Not all work within GB proposes to handle object asymmetries of the type found in Chichewa by means of Case-Theoretic distinctions. Alternative approaches within GB include Marantz 1993 and Woolford 1993, which space limitations prevent us from discussing here (but see Alsina 1996b for a critique of Woolford 1993).

HOWARD LASNIK

SUBJECTS, OBJECTS, AND THE EPP*

1. INTRODUCTION

It has been generally assumed that there is a major asymmetry between 'subject' and 'object' in English-type languages. In overt syntax, subject must raise out of its VP-internal position to the Spec of a functional head, while object remains inside the VP.[1] Over the last several years, however, substantial evidence has come to light indicating that object, like subject, raises out of its initial position, hence, that the asymmetry is only apparent. I will review this evidence, concluding that it is decisive. Subject raises to [Spec, Agr$_S$] and object to [Spec, Agr$_O$], driven by an EPP requirement of Agr. Nonetheless, I will show that a residue of the original asymmetry remains, as overt 'object shift' in English is, contrary to the situation with subjects, optional. I will suggest that that residual asymmetry is to be instantiated in terms of optionality of Agr$_O$ vs. obligatoriness of Agr$_S$. If Agr$_O$ is present, overt raising will be forced by its EPP requirement, and if an NP raises to satisfy that requirement, its Case will be checked. If Agr$_O$ is absent, there will be no overt raising; the nominal's Case will be checked by covert raising of its formal features to the V, or, alternatively, be licensed in situ by the Agree operation of Chomsky (1998).

2. BASIC EVIDENCE FOR OBJECT SHIFT IN ENGLISH

Lasnik and Saito (1991), reviving and extending some of the arguments of Postal (1974), propose that the exceptionally Case-marked subject of an infinitival clause moves into the higher clause. The arguments are to the effect that ECM subjects act as if they are higher than elements in the higher clause.[2] Some representative examples showing 'high' behavior for ECM subjects are as follows, illustrating, respectively, Condition A satisfaction, Weak Crossover mitigation, and Negative Polarity Item licensing:

(1)   The DA proved [two men to have been at the scene of the crime] during each other's trials

William D. Davies and Stanley Dubinsky (eds.), Objects and other subjects: Grammatical functions, functional categories, and configurationality, 103—121.
© 2001 *Kluwer Academic Publishers. Printed in the Netherlands.*

(2)   The DA proved [no suspect$_i$ to have been at the scene of the crime]
           during his$_i$ trial

(3)   The DA proved [noone to have been at the scene] during any of the
           trials

For the large majority of speakers I have interviewed, (1) – (3) contrast significantly
with corresponding examples with finite complements:

(4)   ?*The DA proved [that two men were at the scene of the crime]
           during each other's trials

(5)   ?*The DA proved [that no suspect$_i$ was at the scene of the crime]
           during his$_i$ trial

(6)   ?*The DA proved [that noone was guilty] during any of the trials

Under the standard assumption that c-command is involved in all of these
phenomena, and given that the adverbial clauses containing the items that need to be
licensed are all in the higher clause, the improved status of (1) – (3) vis-à-vis their
finite counterparts indicates that the ECM subjects must have raised into the higher
clause as well. If they remained in the lower clause, they could not c-command an
item in the higher clause. The Lasnik and Saito arguments were all of this general
character (and represent just one among several types of arguments presented by
Postal).

As observed by Postal and by Lasnik and Saito, in the kinds of paradigms just
considered, the behavior of ECM subjects is comparable to that of transitive objects.
The following examples parallel (1) – (3):

(7)   The DA accused two men during each other's trials

(8)   The DA discredited no suspect$_i$ during his$_i$ trial

(9)   The DA cross-examined none of the witnesses during any of the trials

For Postal, this kind of parallelism constituted evidence that the ECM subject raises
into object position. Lasnik and Saito examined this possibility but rejected it for
two reasons. First, the possibility of movement into a θ-position had been seriously
challenged since Chomsky (1981) (though the challenges were not entirely
conclusive, as also discussed by Lasnik and Saito, following McCawley (1988)).
Second, under reasonable (though not universally accepted) assumptions about
clause structure, even direct object is not high enough to c-command into an
adverbial adjunct. So, under those assumptions, even object raises. The null

hypothesis is that object and ECM subject raise to the same higher position (a non-θ-position, if Chomsky is correct).

3. 'HIGH' BEHAVIOR AND MOVEMENT: OVERT OR COVERT?

The clausal phrase structure proposed by Chomsky (1991) provides a possible target for the raising motivated by the above phenomena: [Spec, Agr_o], where Agr_o is a functional head just above VP. Chomsky suggested that such raising exists, but that it is covert, happening in the LF component. Given the word order of English, VO rather than OV, overt raising seemed impossible. However, there are long-standing reasons to think that covert raising does not affect binding possibilities. For example, Chomsky (1981), based on the following examples, argues that QR and LF wh-movement do not remedy Condition C violations.

(10)   Which book that John$_i$ read did he$_i$ like

(11)   *He$_i$ liked every book that John$_i$ read

(12)   *I don't remember who thinks that he$_i$ read which book that John$_i$ likes

Chomsky's point is that following QR, the LF of (11) would be structurally parallel to the S-structure (and LF) of (10), where *John* is outside the c-command domain of *he*. Thus, as in (10), there should be no Condition C effect, if LF is the level relevant to that condition. Similarly for (12) following LF wh-movement. The conclusion of Chomsky (1981) was that S-structure is crucial to at least one of the binding conditions.

Barss (1986) draws the same conclusion for Condition A, based on examples like the following:

(13)   John$_i$ wonders which picture of himself$_i$ Mary showed to Susan

(14)   *John$_i$ wonders who showed which picture of himself$_i$ to Susan

(13) shows that an anaphor within the embedded CP Spec can be licensed by an antecedent in the matrix subject position. Given this fact, the ungrammaticality of (14) is surprising if anaphors can be licensed by virtue of their LF positions, since it was standardly assumed at the time that in LF, the wh-phrase *which picture of himself* moves to the embedded CP Spec position, where it takes scope. Thus, at LF, the configurational relation between *himself* and its antecedent is virtually identical in (13) and (14). Hence, the ungrammaticality of (14) shows that anaphors must be licensed at a level prior to LF, e.g., S-structure (and possibly at LF as well; the example is moot on this point).

Under the minimalist assumption that there is no level of S-structure, there must be another way to capture these facts. At least these LF operations, QR and wh-movement, have no effect on binding possibilities. Therefore, the operations don't exist or they apply in such a way that binding possibilities don't change.[3] Lasnik and Saito (1991) and den Dikken (1995) draw the same conclusion about the 'expletive replacement' operation proposed by Chomsky (1986). As shown just below, in the existential analogues of (1) – (3) above, the 'associate' of the expletive doesn't display the 'high' behavior that is exhibited when that NP becomes the overt subject of the infinitival.

(15)   *The DA proved [there to have been two men at the scene of the crime] during each other's trials

(16)   *The DA proved [there to have been no suspect$_i$ at the scene of the crime] during his$_i$ trial

(17)   *The DA proved [there to have been noone at the scene] during any of the trials

The superficially peculiar agreement properties of existential sentences (apparent agreement with a non-subject: *There are/*is women in the room*) implicate some sort of movement operation affecting the associate (to get it near enough to Agr$_S$). But that movement operation must be very different from the one affecting direct objects and ECM subjects, since in the latter instances we do get high behavior.

4. THE NATURE OF OBJECT SHIFT IN ENGLISH

4.1 Overt Object Shift and the Split-VP Hypothesis

In several papers,[4] I have proposed that this near paradoxical state of affairs can be understood in terms of overt raising of object and ECM subject and overt raising of V to a still higher position. The movement of the associate of an expletive, on the other hand, is covert movement of formal features alone, hence does not create any of the relevant binding or licensing configurations.[5] The 'split-VP' hypothesis of Koizumi (1993) and Koizumi (1995), which I adopt in its essentials, provides the needed structure for the overt raising examples. The relevant portion of an ECM structure with raising is as follows:

(18)   She will prove Bob to be guilty

(19)

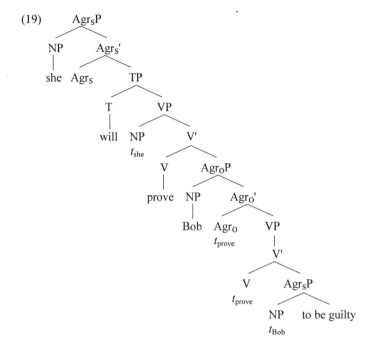

If the adverbials in (1) – (3) are attached in the vicinity of the lower matrix VP (perhaps right adjoined to that VP), the binding and licensing receive a natural account. Further, it is now natural to assume that the 'EPP' requirement driving raising to 'subject position' resides in Agr, hence is also responsible for raising to 'object position', under the plausible assumption of Chomsky (1991) that 'Agr$_S$' and 'Agr$_O$' are merely mnemonic, there really being just Agr, which can occur in various places in the structure. This result constitutes part of the promised asymmetry reduction.[6] An additional argument for overt raising of an object or an ECM subject has to do with the Pseudogapping ellipsis construction. This construction is exemplified in (20).[7]

(20)   Mary hired John, and Susan will ~~hire~~ Bill

Following Jayaseelan (1990), in Lasnik (1995d) I argue that the construction involves VP ellipsis, with the remnant having escaped from the ellipsis site via a movement operation. Departing from Jayaseelan, I argue that the movement operation is not Heavy NP Shift but rather raising to [Spec, Agr$_O$].[8] The structure of the second conjunct of (20) will be as follows, with the lower VP (in bold face) deleted.

(21)

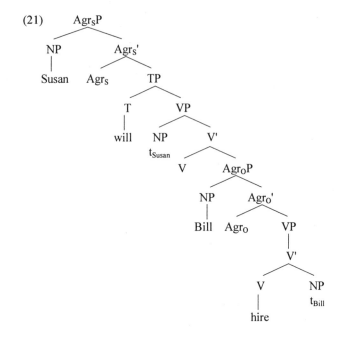

Note that it is hard to see how covert feature raising could create the observed ellipsis configuration. Thus, there is additional good reason for thinking we are dealing with overt movement. Now notice that an ECM subject also makes a good Pseudogapping remnant:

(22)   The DA proved Jones (to be) guilty and the Assistant DA will ~~prove~~ Smith ~~(to be) guilty~~

As in the binding and licensing paradigms seen earlier, objects and ECM subjects pattern together; both evidently undergo overt raising.

Even the complements of unaccusative verbs display the high behavior I am taking as indicative of object shift. Uriagereka (1988) observes that in the following example, the reciprocal can successfully take the associate as its antecedent, which is unexpected on the assumption that the position of complements is lower than that of adjuncts.

(23)   There arrived two knights on each other's horses

Uriagereka actually argues that LF expletive replacement, as in Chomsky (1986), is involved here. But, as noted above, there are very strong reasons for doubting that the LF movement of the associate of an expletive qua associate creates new binding possibilities, a point already made by Lasnik and Saito (1991). Given that, it is reasonable to conclude that in (23) *two knights* overtly raises to a position above the adjunct. Since we have already seen the same phenomenon with transitives, the account should be the same: the raising is to [Spec, Agr_O]. Pseudogapping provides further evidence, as pointed out by Roger Martin (personal communication). Martin observes that the associate of an expletive makes a reasonably acceptable Pseudogapping remnant:

(24)   ?There arrived an instructor but there didn't ~~arrive~~ a professor

On the account of Pseudogapping of Lasnik (1995d), briefly summarized above, *a professor* has overtly raised to [Spec, Agr_O].

4.2 Apparent Obligatoriness of Object Shift

Note that all of these phenomena just indicate that object shift is *possible*, available when necessary but not necessarily obligatory, a potential difference from subject shift. There is actually one phenomenon discussed by Postal (1974) and Lasnik and Saito (1991), but not yet discussed here, that argues that object shift *is* obligatory. Postal's statement of the argument is based on "a fundamental pronominalization constraint" due to Langacker (1969) which states that a pronoun cannot both precede and command its antecedent. There are a number of more recent formulations of this constraint, including the noncoreference rule of Lasnik (1976) and Binding Condition C of Chomsky (1981). Any of these formulations can correctly distinguish Postal's (25) from (26), but only if the embedded subject in (25) has necessarily raised into the higher clause.[9]

(25)   *Joan believes him_i to be a genius even more fervently than Bob_i does

(26)   Joan believes he_i is a genius even more fervently than Bob_i does

So far, then, the asymmetry seems to be successfully eliminated. English has overt object shift, and it is obligatory, parallel to subject shift. However, I now must turn to some reasons for thinking that object shift is not obligatory.

5. THE OPTIONALITY OF OBJECT SHIFT

5.1 Barrierhood of Subject vs. Object

The first argument that object shift does not always take place, is, in its essentials, due to Branigan (1992). It is based on the 'subject condition' effect, by which extraction out of a subject is much less acceptable than extraction out of an object:

(27)   ?*Who was [a picture of *t*] selected

(28)   Who did you select [a picture of t]

Branigan's point is that if object and subject both raise overtly, to [Spec, Agr_O] and [Spec, Agr_S] respectively, whatever constraint is responsible for subject condition effects cannot distinguish (27) from (28), since, given the cyclic principle, in both instances the island-creating movement to [Spec, Agr] would precede the wh-movement. In Lasnik (1995d), I offered a technical way to make the distinction, even if both subject and object raise. However, Takahashi (1994) provides the basis for a principled account of subject condition effects under which the crucial factor is, in fact, movement. Under plausible assumptions, Takahashi is able to deduce in approximately the following way that a moved item is an island: Movement creates a chain, which is, by hypothesis, a set of copies. Typically, all but the highest are ultimately deleted. But if extraction has taken place out of a high copy, it will no longer be identical to the lower ones it left behind. Reasonably, deletion 'under identity' will now fail. Assuming the deletion is necessary, the result is an ill-formed structure. Since (28) is fine, there is thus reason to believe that in that example the direct object is in situ. Of course, this does not entail that there is no object shift at all in English, just that it is not obligatory. And, as already noted in Lasnik (1995d), when the object is a Pseudogapping remnant, extraction from it is seriously degraded:

(29)   Bill selected a painting of John, and Susan should ~~select~~ a photograph of Mary

(30)   ?*Who will Bill select a painting of, and who will Susan ~~select~~ a photograph of

This fact is quite consistent with an approach to the subject condition along the lines of Takahashi's, given the argument above that a Pseudogapping remnant has necessarily undergone overt object shift.

There is a related prediction, which, though the judgments are subtle, seems to me basically correct. Recall the high binding behavior of objects shown in (7) – (9) above. I argued that such behavior implicates overt object shift. Extraction out of an object should thus be incompatible with high binding by the object, since high binding entails that the object has raised while extraction out of the object demands that the object *not* have raised. These contradictory requirements should lead to deviance. The following paradigms tend to bear that out.

(31)   The special prosecutor questioned two aides of a senator during each other's trials

(32)   ??Which senator did the special prosecutor question two aides of during each other's trials

That the deviance of (32) is due to the high binding can be seen by comparing (32) to a parallel example without an anaphor:

(33)   Which senator did the special prosecutor question two friends of during the president's trial

Negative polarity item licensing gives similar results, though, again, the judgments are delicate:[10]

(34)   The mathematician proved few theorems about Mersenne numbers during any of the lectures

(35)   ??Which numbers did the mathematician prove few theorems about during any of the lectures

(36)   Which numbers did the mathematician prove few theorems about during the conference lectures

These paradigms argue, contra Lasnik (1995d), that when an object has overtly raised (as evidenced by 'high' behavior) it *is* an island for extraction, and, therefore, since objects are not invariably islands, that such raising is optional.

5.2 Verb NP Particle/Verb Particle NP

The next argument is based on verb-particle constructions. Johnson (1991) persuasively argues that the order V-NP-prt arises from the raising of the NP from its base position, and the further raising of the V portion of the 'particle-verb'. Pairs like the following, then, indicate that the raising of the NP is optional:

(37)   Mary called up friends of John

(38)   ?Mary called friends of John up

Now notice that when the NP precedes the particle, extraction out of the NP is seriously degraded:

(39)   Who did Mary call up friends of

(40)   ?*Who did Mary call friends of up

Plausibly, (40) constitutes a violation of just the same type as the subject condition: a moved item is an island.

Kayne (1985) first discussed a very interesting verb-particle construction, later analyzed by Johnson (1991) in terms relevant to the present discussion. Johnson provides an insightful account of examples like (41) involving overt raising of the ECM subject *John*.[11]

(41)   Mary made John out to be a fool

Both Kayne and Johnson convincingly treat (41) as an infinitival counterpart of (42)

(42)   Mary made out that John is a fool

Now observe that the raising seen in (41) is optional. For most speakers, (43) is an acceptable alternative to (41).

(43)   Mary made out John to be a fool

Under the natural assumption, Johnson's, that the raising of *John* in (41) is object shift, we have yet another instance of optional object shift. Note, in passing, that the extraction test used just above cannot be used here or in any ECM constructions, since the ECM subject, even when it doesn't raise into the matrix clause, has already raised into embedded subject position. Thus extraction out of that subject is expected to be inhibited regardless, and that expectation is fulfilled:

(44)   ?*Who did Mary make friends of out to be fools

(45)   ?*Who did Mary make out friends of to be fools

Compare a standard ECM construction:

(46)   ?*Who did Mary consider friends of to be fools

Actually, (44) seems a bit worse than the other two examples, possibly related to the fact that prior to wh-movement, *friends of who* has undergone two instances of raising in that example, but just one in the others.

5.2 A Scope Ambiguity

An observation about scope that Zubizarreta (1982) attributes to Chomsky, and that is discussed again by Chomsky (1995), provides further evidence for the optionality of object shift with ECM subjects. Chomsky presents the following paradigm:

(47)a.   (it seems that) everyone isn't there yet

    b.   everyone seems [*t* not to be there yet]

Chomsky (p.327) argues as follows: "Negation can have wide scope over the Q in [47a]... but not in [47b]", concluding that "...reconstruction in the A-chain does not take place, so it appears." Suppose Chomsky is correct that with A-movement, there is no reconstruction capable of giving the configuration necessary for this scope effect, i.e., capable or replacing the raised quantifier back into the lower clause.[12] The question now arises as to the behavior of ECM constructions with respect to this scopal property. The *make-out* ECM construction behaves exactly as expected. When the word order makes it clear that a universal ECM subject has raised, that subject cannot be interpreted inside the scope of negation in the complement clause, as seen in (48).

(48)   The mathematician made every even number out not to be the sum of two primes

The only reading is the highly implausible one where the mathematician was engaged in the futile activity of trying to falsely convince someone that no even number is the sum of two primes (and not the far more plausible one where she is merely trying to convince someone that Goldbach's conjecture is false). Thus, even with strong pragmatic bias towards wide scope for the negation, it still isn't available, consistent with the raising analysis combined with Chomsky's claim. The alternative word order for (48), with *every even number* unraised, does allow narrow scope for the universal, for those speakers who accept the word order in the first place:

(49)   The mathematician made out every even number not to be the sum of two primes

(49) has the plausible reading missing in (48).

Now what of standard ECM constructions? Chomsky (1995) already implied that in that circumstance, a universal in subject position can take scope below complement clause negation, giving the following example:

(50)   I expected [everyone not to be there yet]

Chomsky does not explicitly claim that (50) is a standard ECM construction, but I assume that that is his intention. However, the situation is somewhat equivocal, since, as shown by Bresnan (1972), *expect* has multiple subcategorization frames (including one like *want*, which Lasnik and Saito (1991), essentially following Bresnan, argue does not involve raising into the higher clause).[13] Chomsky's observation stands, though, since even with unequivocal ECM verbs like *believe* and *prove*, my informants find narrow scope possible, even if somewhat disfavored, unlike the situation with raising to subject or with the *make*-NP-*out* construction. Some representative examples are as follows:

(51)   I believe everyone not to have arrived yet

(52)   I proved every Mersenne number not to be prime

Those same informants (along with everyone else, I believe) disallow narrow scope for the universal when it undergoes passive/raising to subject position:

(53)   Everyone is believed not to have arrived yet

(54)   Every Mersenne number was proved not to be prime

In (54), there is strong pragmatic bias towards narrow scope, but it is still not available. Only the wildly false wide scope reading exists. Since we have seen strong evidence for raising in ECM constructions, and for Chomsky's claim about lack of reconstruction with A-movement, the possibility of narrow scope for the universal in (51) and (52) again indicates that object shift is optional.

5.4 Quantifier Lowering?

There is another scope 'reconstruction' phenomenon that suggests the same conclusion. In Lasnik (1998b) and Lasnik (1998a), I point out that standard 'Quantifier Lowering' effects fail to obtain in a wide variety of cases. For example, (56) is the paraphrase for the 'lowered' reading of (55):

(55)   Someone is likely to solve the problem

(56)   It is likely that someone will solve the problem

But in numerous structurally parallel sentences, paraphrase of this sort fails. Consider the following example:

(57)   No large Mersenne number was proven to be prime

(57) cannot accurately be paraphrased by (58).

(58)   It was proven that no large Mersenne number is prime

Similar paraphrase failure occurs in the following pair:

(59)   Noone is certain to solve the problem

(60)   It is certain that noone will solve the problem

(59) describes a situation where the problem under discussion is of at least middling difficulty, and the potential problem solvers aren't omniscient. (60), on the other hand, is a sentence about either an impossible problem or a hopelessly inept group of solvers.

Significantly, though the judgments are subtle, the failure of 'Quantifier Lowering' seen in classic raising examples like (57) is also mirrored in the raising particle construction. Compare (61) with (62):

(61)   The DA made no defense witnesses out to be credible

(62)   The DA made out that no defense witnesses were credible

On pragmatic grounds, the only remotely plausible interpretation of (61) would be one synonymous with (62). But that interpretation is very difficult to obtain. Instead, the sentence has only the bizarre interpretation where the DA perhaps had the intention of trying to show that (some of) the defense witnesses were credible, but never acted on that intention. This is now as expected, if scope reconstruction (at least of certain types) is not available with A-movement, given the raising analysis of the *make*-NP-*out* construction. As also expected, (63) does have a reading like that of (62).

(63)   The DA made out no defense witnesses to be credible

Now notice that in a standard ECM configuration, the same complement can be interpreted with low scope for the negative expression:

(64)   The DA proved no defense witnesses to be credible

(64) does have a possible sensible reading, similar to that of (62). Given that such 'reconstructed' readings are not possible when there has been demonstrable overt raising, as in (61) or (65), one is led to the conclusion that there has been no such raising in (63).

(65)   No defense witnesses were proved to be credible by the DA

Finally, note that if the ECM subject has to be 'high' in order to license some element in the higher clause, then the lower reading for that ECM subject becomes impossible. The embedded clause in (66) cannot be interpreted as "No defense witnesses were credible", the way it can in (64).

(66)   The DA proved [no defense witnesses to be credible] during any of
         the trials

This provides further confirmation for the approach adopted here.

6. ARGUMENTS FOR OBLIGATORY OBJECT SHIFT,
AND POTENTIAL REPLIES

As opposed to these arguments for optionality, there are two arguments in the literature to the effect that object shift in English is obligatory. I turn to those now. The first was already mentioned, based on Postal's (25), repeated here:

(67)   *Joan believes him$_i$ to be a genius even more fervently than Bob$_i$ does

Optional raising cannot explain the Condition C effect found here; if the ECM subject can remain in the lower clause, it should avoid illicitly binding *Bob*, contrary to fact. But this phenomenon is, perhaps, not as problematic for the analyses presented above as it might first appear. After all, it is not uncommon for 'object shift' to be obligatory with pronouns even when it is optional with lexical NPs.[14] In fact, even in English, there is evidence for this state of affairs. Recall that in the *make-out* construction discussed above, many speakers allow the ECM subject to the right of *out* alongside the structure with that NP to the left:

(68)   Mary made John out to be a fool

(69)   Mary made out John to be a fool

If, as assumed above, an example like (68) exhibits overt raising, it is reasonable to conjecture that there has been no overt raising in (69). Significantly the analogue of (68) but with a pronoun as ECM subject is still good, but the analogue of (69) is bad, even for the many speakers who find (69) itself fully acceptable:

(70)   Mary made him out to be a fool

(71)   *Mary made out him to be a fool

This same pattern with a direct object has been familiar from the earliest days of generative grammar, as in this pair from Chomsky (1955):

(72)   The detective brought him in

(73)   *The detective brought in him

As proposed by Johnson (1991), these patterns are strongly indicative of some sort of obligatory movement with a pronoun. But this does not undermine the conclusion above that object shift in English is generally optional. The examples with pronouns presumably involve a cliticization process independent of typical object shift. Note, in this connection, that if the pronouns in the above examples are made 'strong' through focus, they can remain low:

(74)   Mary made out HIM to be a fool

(75)   The detective brought in HIM

Given this, one might expect that (67) can be salvaged by focusing *him*. But that expectation is unfulfilled:

(76)   *Joan believes HIM_i to be a genius even more fervently than Bob_i does

However, the impossibility of anaphoric connection here has nothing to do with Condition C. Rather, the focus itself undermines anaphora, as evidenced by the following pair, where neither raising nor Condition C is at issue:

(77)   After I talked to him_i, Bob_i left

(78)   *After I talked to HIM_i, Bob_i left

The second argument for obligatory object shift appears in Tanaka (1999). Tanaka claims that when a simple sentence contains both an interrogative direct object and an interrogative temporal expression, it is necessarily the former that undergoes wh-movement:

(79)   ?Whom did the DA accuse during which trial

(80)   ?*During which trial did the DA accuse whom

Tanaka observes that Superiority, as subsumed under the Minimal Link Condition, can account for this. That is, if at the point when wh-movement applies, the direct object is higher than the temporal adverb, then wh-movement of the adverb will be a longer move than wh-movement of the direct object would be. This tends to argue for obligatory object shift, since, under plausible assumptions about initial phrase structure, that would be needed to guarantee that direct object is higher than adverb.[15] However, it is not clear that Tanaka's generalization is correct.[16] For many speakers, the following two examples do not contrast, as reported by Bošković (1997):

(81)   What did John buy when

(82)   When did John buy what

On these judgments, we actually now have another argument for *optionality* of object shift.[17] (81) is derived if object shift takes place (again, if we assume with Tanaka and Bošković that the shifted object is higher than the adverb, an assumption that also played a crucial role in the account of the binding and licensing facts discussed earlier). (82) is derived if object shift does not take place (and if the base position of object is lower than that of adverb).

There is a related argument for obligatory object shift which I now turn to. While Bošković and Tanaka disagree about objects vs. temporal adverbs, they agree about ECM subjects vs. temporal adverbs, both claiming that when the two expressions are in competition, it is the ECM subject which must undergo wh-movement. Tanaka's examples are (83) - (84), and Bošković's are (85) - (86).

(83)   ?Whom did the DA prove to be innocent during which trial

(84)   ?*During which trial did the DA prove whom to be innocent

(85)   Whom did John prove to be guilty when

(86)   ?*When did John prove whom to be guilty

For (83) - (84), there might be the interfering factor I alluded to in note 16 above. (85) - (86), to the extent that they contrast with (81) – (82), do seem to argue for obligatory overt object shift of ECM subjects, Bošković's conclusion. However, the scope facts examined above argue that the movement is optional. I see no way to reconcile these two arguments, so I will merely note that I find the scope facts somewhat clearer than the contrast between (85) and (86). Perhaps significantly, the Superiority contrast seems considerably sharper in the *make*-NP-*out* ECM construction, where there is word order evidence that object shift has taken place:

(87)   Whom did the DA make out to be guilty when

(88)   ?*When did the DA make whom out to be guilty

Judgments really begin to fail at this point, but I think that with the *make out*-NP order, which, by hypothesis has no overt object shift, the Superiority effect is lessened:

(89)   ??When did the DA make out whom to be guilty

There is surely such a contrast in simpler verb-particle constructions:

(90)   ?*When did you call whom up

(91)   When did you call up whom

This is just as expected on the Johnson-style raising analysis.

7. THE REMAINING QUESTION

The last question I will consider is how the optionality of object shift can be stated. In Lasnik (1995d), I argued that the driving force for the overt movement of the NP is a strong 'EPP' feature in Agr_O. Following Chomsky (1991), I took Agr_O to be the same item as Agr_S, the labels merely mnemonic. Overt 'object shift' is then analyzable as the same phenomenon as the standard EPP. I assume that Case checking does not provide the driving force for the movement. Rather, it is just a side effect of EPP satisfaction;[18] there is no requirement that Case per se be checked overtly (though it must be checked eventually; it is a weak feature). One way to make the raising optional might be to abandon the idea that Agr_O is the same item as Agr_S, assuming, instead, that only the latter obligatorily has an EPP requirement. Agr_O would only optionally have the property. This is conceivable, but I am not yet ready to give up the uniformity of Agr. Some of the discussion in Chomsky (1995, p.350) hints at an alternative possibility (though not one that Chomsky himself winds up pursuing). Chomsky reasons that "If Agr has no strong feature, then PF considerations, at least, give no reason for it to be present at all, and LF considerations do not seem relevant." He thus suggests, in passing, that "Agr exists only when it has strong features."[19] Along these lines, suppose, then, that the optionality of raising is the optionality of Agr_O.[20] If Agr_O is present, overt raising will be forced by its EPP requirement, and if an NP raises to satisfy that requirement, its Case will be checked.[21] If Agr_O is absent, there will be no overt raising;[22] the nominal's Case will be checked by covert raising of its formal features to the V, or, alternatively, be licensed in situ by the Agree operation of Chomsky (1998).[23] This leaves us with the question of why Agr_S is obligatory while Agr_O is not, which is exactly the question of why the standard asymmetric EPP apparently holds. And at present, contrary to what I hoped when I began this investigation, I have no more to contribute to this question than anyone else does.

ENDNOTES

* I would like to acknowledge the helpful questions and suggestions of Daniel Seely, Rich Campbell, Stan Dubinsky, William Davies, two reviewers, and all the participants of my spring 1999 syntax seminar and of the 1999 LSA Linguistic Institute Workshop on The Role of Grammatical Functions in Transformational Syntax. This paper was completed while I was a Fellow at the Center for Advanced Study in the Behavioral Sciences. I am grateful for the financial support provided by the John D. and Catherine T. MacArthur Foundation, grant #95-32005-0.

[1] For the purposes of this paper, by 'object' I will mean the nominal expression that receives accusative Case.

[2] Postal presented scores of arguments over 400 pages of text. Here, I will just be concerned with a narrow range of the types Postal examined.

[3] The one, partial, exception to this that I am familiar with is the 'inverse linking' construction first discussed by May (1977). In sentences like (i), the pronoun can apparently be understood as bound by a quantifier that does not c-command it in overt syntax.

(i)   Someone from [every California city]$_i$ hates it$_i$

Note, though, that Condition A type binding still fails:

    (ii)   *Someone from [every California city]$_i$ hates itself$_i$

I do not understand why this should be, or, in fact, why (i) does not run afoul of the Weak Crossover constraint.

[4]   See Lasnik (1995b), Lasnik (1995c), and Lasnik (1995d).

[5]   I take the basic idea and consequences of feature movement from Chomsky (1995). However, Chomsky claims that the feature movement at issue, while not creating new scope possibilities, does create new binding possibilities. (15) – (17) above cast doubt on Chomsky's claim about binding. See Lasnik (1995b), Lasnik (1995c), and Lasnik (1997) for extensive discussion.

[6]   For two reasons, I take the EPP requirement to be independent of Case checking. First, I argued in Lasnik (1995d) that not just nominal expressions but also PPs move to [Spec, Agr$_O$]. Second, subject position of an ECM infinitive is not a Case checking position, yet movement to that position does take place, as will be amply documented below.

[7]   See Levin (1979) for extensive discussion and documentation of this construction.

[8]   Pseudogapping is possible with the first object in a double object construction as remnant. But the first object in a double object construction is resistant to undergoing HNPS:

    (i)   ?John gave Bill a lot of money, and Mary will ~~give~~ Susan ~~a lot of money~~

    (ii)   *John gave *t* a lot of money the fund for the preservation of VOS languages

Conversely, the <u>second</u> object is a poor Pseudogapping remnant, but freely undergoes HNPS:

    (iii)   *John gave Bill a lot of money, and Mary will ~~give Bill~~ a lot of advice

    (iv)   John gave Bill *t* yesterday more money than he had ever seen

[9]   There is a potential interfering factor in (25) (a Condition B effect with the pronoun in the elided VP), which Lasnik and Saito (1991) control for by giving the modification in (i), in which *Bob* does not c-command into the elided VP.

    (i)   *Joan believes him$_i$ to be a genius even more fervently than Bob$_i$'s mother does

[10]   Daniel Seely (personal communication) points out that (i) is somewhat better than the example in the text.

    (i)   Which actress do you think that Bill found no pictures of *t* during any of the searches

It is not clear why that should be. Seely also suggests another test, which, all else equal, seems to indicate that the proposal here is on the right track. He observes that if the anti-c-command constraint on parasitic gaps of Chomsky (1982) is valid, then high binding should be inconsistent with parasitic gap licensing. The relevant example is extremely complex, but to Seely's ear, and to mine, it is quite degraded, as predicted:

    (ii)   Which men$_i$ did the DA prove t_i to be there after each other$_i$'s lawyers had sued p.g.$_i$

[11]   Postal (1974) had a very similar argument for raising based on the *figure-out* construction, as in (i) (though, as Postal shows, possibilities for raising are very limited here).

    (i)   I figured it out to be more than 300 miles from here to Tulsa

[12] In fact, Chomsky argues that there is no A-movement reconstruction at all. See Lasnik (1999) for extensive discussion, including further arguments for lack of such reconstruction and consideration of arguments to the contrary.

[13] Like *believe*, and unlike *want*, *expect* allows passive-raising:

(i)   There is expected to be a storm

But unlike *believe*, and like *want*, *expect* allows a PRO subject of its complement:

(ii)   Mary expects [PRO to solve the problem]

[14] See Diesing (1996) and Johnson (1991) for discussion.

[15] Curiously, on Tanaka's assumptions about basic phrase structure (essentially those of Larson (1988)), nothing yet follows, since the base position of the object is already higher than the adverb.

[16] The relative heaviness of the two wh-phrases could be playing a role in Tanaka's examples. In fact, if we reverse the heaviness, (80) becomes perfect, as far as I can tell:

(i)   When did the DA accuse which defendant

[17] Bošković's account is actually somewhat different. For reasons of space, I will not go into it here.

[18] That is, Agr has no Case feature of its own. When T or V along with its Case feature merges with Agr, then a nominal expression that has raised to [Spec, Agr] will be in a Case checking configuration, even though the raising was driven by the EPP.

[19] I now do not actually view the EPP requirement as a matter of feature checking in the technical sense. Following Chomsky (1998), though in a somewhat different framework of assumptions, I take it that it is simply the requirement that a particular head have a specifier. See Lasnik (2001) for evidence in favor of this approach.

[20] See Kim (1997) for arguments that the position of a Pseudogapping remnant has a focus feature. Given the optionality of (the target of) raising that I have suggested, a fruitful line of inquiry would center on focus effects with raised objects and ECM subjects in general.

[21] As mentioned above, the obligatory raising of pronouns, I take to be an independent phenomenon, related to the clitic-like nature of unstressed object pronouns in English.

[22] Except for weak pronouns, which obligatorily cliticize to the verb, I assume.

[23] Though see Lasnik (In press) for arguments that feature movement cannot be entirely eliminated. Regardless of whether feature movement or Agree is adopted, there is an important question pointed out by a reviewer: Since V is capable of checking Case by itself in the absence of Agr_o, this possibility should also obtain in the presence of Agr_o. But then, given strictly cyclic derivation, under the long-standing assumption that A-movement is impossible for a nominal whose Case has been checked (see, for example, Chomsky 1986, p.199), raising to [Spec, Agr_o] should never be possible. For present purposes, I will adopt the 'derivation by phase' approach to the cycle of Chomsky (1999). Since the lower VP in the split VP (corresponding to Chomsky's V) is not a phase, checking can be delayed until the higher VP (Chomsky's v), the next phase.

LISA DEMENA TRAVIS

DERIVED OBJECTS IN MALAGASY

Austronesian languages have been used to raise questions about the status of the subject.[1] For example, Schachter (1976, 1996) shows that Tagalog (from the Western Malayo-Polynesian branch of Austronesian) divides its subject properties over two NPs (the Topic and the Actor) and suggests that it is inappropriate to talk about the grammatical relation of subject in such a language. With the introduction of VP internal subjects in the GB/MP framework (see e.g. Fukui & Speas 1986, Kitagawa 1986, Kuroda 1988, Koopman & Sportiche 1991), it has become possible to give this observation a structural correlation by placing the Actor in Spec, VP and the Topic in Spec, IP along the lines of Guilfoyle, Hung and Travis (1992) (GHT). In other words, with the assumption that all subjects are, in some sense, derived, we are able to separate the notion of the base-generated subject from the notion of the surface subject. Further, we might speculate that there are some languages that never make use of the derived subject position. In such a language (possibly a VSO language like Niuean – see Massam and Smallwood 1997, Massam 1998, this volume), the surface subject would remain in Spec, VP.

Even more recently, it has been proposed within the Minimalist framework that not only subjects but also objects move from a base-generated position to a derived position. If this is true, we can now ask questions about objects that formerly were only asked about subjects. For instance, is an object in its base-generated position or in a derived position in the overt syntax? Can both positions be filled simultaneously? The question I would like to address in this paper, does a given language – in this case Malagasy, another Western Malayo-Polynesian language – make use of its derived object position? If GHT are right, then Malagasy can fill both the base-generated subject position (Spec, VP) and the derived subject position (Spec, IP) simultaneously in the surface syntax. I will claim that Malagasy object phenomena are quite different and that Malagasy does not have more object-like positions than other languages, but rather has fewer. In more theoretical terms, I will argue that Malagasy has no derived objects. This means that Malagasy treats its objects like Niuean treats its subjects. What Niuean lacks in subject flexibility, Malagasy lacks in object flexibility.

An important theoretical issue can be addressed in the context of the generalizations given here which is the status of grammatical functions as primitives. In order even to describe the phenomena addressed in this paper, there is a need to have a notion of two subjects and two objects — one base-generated, one

William D. Davies and Stanley Dubinsky (eds.), Objects and other subjects:
Grammatical functions, functional categories, and configurationality, 123—155.
© *2001 Kluwer Academic Publishers. Printed in the Netherlands.*

derived — and each of these needs its own structural position so that both may be filled.

In the last part of the paper, I will speculate on the reason why a language such as Malagasy might lack derived objects suggesting that languages, or certain structural domains within languages, may be either argument checking or predicate checking.

1. DERIVED OBJECTS

Derived objects, while fairly new to the syntactic theory which developed into the Minimalist Program, have existed in earlier versions of Standard Theory (e.g. Rosenbaum 1967) and have a long tradition in Relational Grammar (RG) where many phenomena such as Raising to Object, Possessor Raising, and Applicatives have been subsumed under a rule of Ascension or Advancement to 2. In this section, using RG terminology, I introduce briefly three phenomena that have been characterized by derived objects — Raising to Object, Possessor Raising, and Applicatives — that will be further investigated in Malagasy. I will then show — using Possessor Raising as an example — how Baker (1988) incorporates these phenomena into GB theory without postulating object movement. Finally, I will introduce an additional object raising phenomenon, object shift, and show how the early Minimalist Program (Chomsky 1993) accounted for these moved objects, as well as the previously mentioned derived objects again using raised possessors to exemplify the mechanisms.

1.1 Derived objects in Relational Grammar: Ascension to 2

Raising to Object constructions where the thematic subject of a lower verb behaves like the grammatical object of a higher verb are the archetypal derived object constructions. A typical example of this is given in (1) below where *the children* is the thematic subject of the lower verb phrase *do their homework*.

Raising to Object (RtoO)
    (1)a.   We expect [that <u>the children</u> will do their homework.]

      b.   We expect [<u>the children</u>] [to do their homework.]

In Relational Grammar terms, the embedded 1 (subject) has become the matrix 2 (object).

In (2) below we see a case of Possessor Raising which again is arguably an example of a derived object. In the example presented here, agreement in Southern Tiwa suggests that the possessor of a direct object triggers the same type of agreement on the verb as does the indirect object in a double object construction.

Possessor Raising (PR)

(2)   Southern Tiwa (Allen et al. 1990:339)

a.   Ben-khwian-mu-ban
2SG:1SG\A-dog-see-PAST
'You (SG) saw my dog.'

b.   Ben-khwian-wia-ban
2SG:1SG\A-dog-give-PAST
'You (SG) gave me the dog.'

In Allen et al's analysis, the reason why the agreement in (2a) and (2b) are the same is that in both cases the subject 'you' is 2sg, the surface object is 1sg while the underlying object ('dog') is singular. Important for their paper is the fact that, in both cases, this agreement is triggered by a derived object. In the case of (2a), the final 2 is the possessor of the object. In the case of (2b), the final 2 was the original goal. This latter phenomenon where an oblique becomes an object is discussed next.

Applicatives have also received a derived object analysis, notably in the work of Chung (1976). In the example in (3) below, we see how the suffix *-kan* on the verb changes *Ali* from being an object of the preposition *kepada* in (3a) to being the object of the verb in (3b).

Applicatives

(3)   Indonesian (Chung 1983:219)

a.   Saja mem-bawa surat itu kepada Ali.
I   TRANS-bring letter DET to   Ali
'I brought the letter to Ali.'

b.   Saja mem-bawa-kan Ali surat itu.
I   TRANS-bring-to Ali letter DET
'I brought Ali the letter.'

In RtoO, Possessor Raising, and Applicatives, we have seen three environments where objects are created through a derivation of some sort. Clearly, not all languages exhibit these phenomena. In showing that a language does not have them, therefore, one hasn't necessarily shown that derived objects are ruled out in principle. What is surprising about Malagasy, however, is that it appears to have a form of all three, but each with a twist. In ECM constructions, the apparent raised object in fact remains within the lower clause. In Possessor Raising and Applicative constructions, the raised NP must become a subject rather than an object. It is for this reason that I will claim that Malagasy rules out derived objects in principle rather than simply lacking the appropriate environments which might make use of the derived object position.

Before turning to the Malagasy facts, however, I will show how derived object phenomena are treated in the Government Binding framework of Chomsky (1981), and its descendant framework, the Minimalist Program.

1.2 Derived objects in GB and the Minimalist Program

As mentioned above, the Minimalist Program even in its earliest form (Chomsky1993) has allowed derived objects. A step towards this, however, was introduced by Baker (1988) in his discussion of grammatical function changing rules. He gathered the three derived object phenomena mentioned above under the mechanism of incorporation. At the time of his work, however, the possibility of derived objects had not yet been introduced. Therefore, while these objects share with other objects the grammatical case relation with the verb, technically they do not share the structural position of other objects. As we shall see below, this relationship of case assignment was done via the Government Transparency Corollary (GTC).

1.2.1 Grammatical Function changing (Baker 1988)
Baker (1988) subsumes applicatives, possessor raising, and ECM under into one phenomenon by having all three sensitive to head-movement. What is common to all three constructions is that head movement occurs from a complement of the verb into the verb leaving an NP in need of case. Further, this head movement leaves the projection of the head transparent to government by the verb. Since the verb will now govern and assign case to the stranded NP, the NP will appear to be the object of the verb though, in fact, it will not have changed its hierarchical position in the tree.

We can see how this is done in the case of Possessor Raising shown below.[2] First an example is given from Oneida. Here the head of the object of the verb *nuhs* 'house' is incorporated into the verb leaving the possessor *John* stranded. Since the head of the object NP has moved out of the projection, the projection is transparent to government and case-assignment by the verb. The possessor is therefore assigned accusative case by the verb and therefore has the appearance of being the object of the verb.

Possessor Raising as N-incorporation
>   (4)   Oneida (Baker 1988:111)
>   Wa-hi-nuhs-ahni:nu: John
>   PAST-1SS/3M-house-buy John
>   'I bought John's house.'

(5)

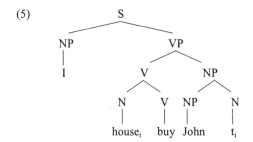

In Relational Grammar, Possessor Raising and ascension rules in general are restricted by the Relational Succession Law given below in (6) below.

(6)   Relational Succession Law (Perlmutter 1983a:35)

> An ascendee assumes within the clause ... into which it ascends the grammatical relation of its host NP (the NP ... out of which it ascends)

If an element is raised out of an object, then we expect it to become an object. In Baker's theory of incorporation, the apparent object creating rules are restricted by the Government Transparency Corollary given in (7).

(7)   Government Transparency Corollary (GTC, Baker 1988:64)

> A lexical category which has an item incorporated into it governs everything which the incorporated item governed in its original structural position.

The GTC is similar to the Relational Succession Law in that where the verb originally governs the host, it now governs the element stranded within the host. This means that if it assigned case to the host, it will now assign case to the NP within the host.

1.2.2 Object movement to AgrO

The notion of derived object is introduced early in the Minimalist Program. The reasons for proposing a derived object position were both conceptual and empirical. The conceptual reason had to do with the symmetry between structural case assigned to subject via a spec-head configuration with a functional category (thought at the time to be AgrS) and the structural case assigned to object via a spec-head configuration with a functional category (thought at the time to be AgrO). One of the main empirical reasons came from the phenomenon of object shift in Scandinavian languages (see Holmberg 1986). An example is given below of object shift in Icelandic where the specific object below can appear to the right of negation as in (8a) or to the left of negation as in (8b).

Specific Objects

    (8)   Icelandic (from Holmberg 1986:217)

      a.   Jon keypti ekki **bokina**
               Jon bought not   the.book
               'Jon didn't buy the book.'

      b.   Jon keypti **bokina** ekki
               Jon bought the.book not

Bobaljik and Jonas (1996) account for this variability in the positioning of the object through movement to a derived object position outside of the VP shown below in (9).

    (9)   AgrO   (adapted from Bobaljik and Jonas 1996)

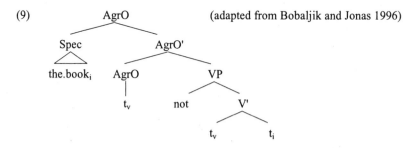

Once we introduce the possibility of having the structural object position as a Spec of a functional category which is filled through movement, all of the derived object constructions discussed above can be done through similar movement.[3] For example, Possessor Raising would be done in a similar manner with now the Possessor moving out of the object NP into the derived object position as shown in (10) below. For reasons too varied to go into here, I assume that the position of the derived object is within the VP, crucially below the position of the base-generated Agent in Spec, VP. Further, I assume the landing site is Spec of a projection of Aspect located between two VP shells.[4]

Possessor Raising

(10)

Note that in the example above, the logical object position and the derived object position are filled with lexical material simultaneously.

2. DERIVED OBJECTS IN MALAGASY

2.1 Background facts

Before turning to the problem of derived object in Malagasy, we must establish some preliminary facts concerning the syntax of this language. It is a Western Malayo-Polynesian (WMP) language, spoken in Madagascar. It is VOS and has fairly strict word order. Like many other WMP languages, it has a rich system of verbal morphology which allows arguments and non-arguments to appear in subject position. An example is given below in (11) where (11a) has Actor Topic (AT) morphology and the highest argument (here the Agent) is in the sentence-final subject position (subjects are given in bold). In (11b), the verb bears Theme Topic (TT) morphology and the Theme is in subject position. In (11c), the verb bears Circumstantial Topic (CT) morphology and the benefactive NP is in subject position. Note that in (11b) and (11c) the Agent, *ny lehilahy* 'the man', appears directly following the verb when it is not in the subject position.

(11)   Malagasy verbal morphology[5]

a.   Manasa   lamba ho an'ny   ankizy **ny lehilahy**.
       PRES.AT.wash clothes for ACC'DET children DET man
       'The man washes clothes for the children.'

b.   Sasan'   ny lehilahy ho an'ny   ankizy **ny lamba**.
       TT.wash' DET man   for ACC'DET children DET clothes
       'The clothes are washed by the man for the children.'

    c.   Anasan' ny lehilahy ny lamba **ny ankizy**.
           CT.wash' DET man   DET clothes DET children
           'The children are washed clothes for by the man.'

2.2 Raising to Object

One of the interesting things about the VOS order is that, being very different from English, it can often offer evidence for phenomena that might be obscured in an SVO language. The particular phenomenon that I have in mind here is the Raising to Object construction. This is particularly interesting in the context of work on derived objects. There has been a long and well-known debate on whether English, in fact, has actual movement in Raising to Object (RtoO) constructions. In most cases, if there were to be movement, it would be string vacuous as shown in (12) below.[6]

    (12)   The children believe the dog to be sleeping.

Certainly 'the dog' is the logical subject of the embedded clause and it receives case from the matrix verb. The question is whether this NP remains in the embedded subject position or whether it has moved to a matrix object position.

    In Malagasy, the issue appears to be simplified. As we can see in the pair of examples below, the subject of the embedded clause appears in sentence final position in the non-RtoO construction, but appears in (embedded) sentence initial position in the RtoO construction. (The non-RtoO embedded clause is also placed to the right of the matrix subject Rakoto while the RtoO embedded clause is placed to its left.)[7]

    (13)   Raising to Object in Malagasy
      a.   Nanantena Rakoto [fa   nianatra   tsara *ny ankizy*]
           PST.hope.AT Rakoto   COMP PST.AT.study good DET children
           'Rakoto hoped that the children studied well.'

      b.   Nanantena *ny ankizy* [ho nianatra   tsara] Rakoto
           PST.AT.hope the children PRT PST.AT.study good Rakoto
           'Rakoto hoped that the children studied well.'

Pearson (2001) argues we can see that the NP *ny ankizy* 'the children' is in object position in (113)b by looking at adverb placement facts. The data and the judgements that he provides are given below.

(14)   ? Nilaza   an-dRabe tamin-katezerana [ho mpangalatra]
          PST-NomP.say ACC-Rabe PST-with-anger   PRT thief
          Rasoa
          Rasoa
          'Rasoa said angrily of Rabe that (he was) a thief.'

On the basis of these data, we could say that Malagasy clearly has derived objects
while in English it is less clear. In spite of this, I will argue that Malagasy crucially
does not have derived objects while English does. I will return to the case of RtoO
constructions later after I have outlined my reasons for believing that Malagasy does
not allow derived objects.

    In the next two sections, I will suggest that Malagasy, while it has applicative-
like constructions and it appears to have possessor raising out of logical objects, in
each case the raised NP becomes the subject rather than the object.

2.3 Applicatives

As mentioned in section 1 above, in both the frameworks of Relational Grammar
and GB/MP, applicative constructions provide a place where arguably one would
expect to find derived objects. In Relational Grammar terms this would be
characterized as advancement from 3 to 2. As Baker (1988) shows, applicatives can
affect a range of arguments. He contends, however, that they are restricted to
benefactives, instrumentals, and (less commonly) locatives — all arguments of the
verb. Some of his examples are given in (15) below.

    (15)   Applicatives (Baker 1988:244)[8]
        a.   Benefactive (Chichewa)
              Mlimi a-ku-dul-ir-a nkandwe mitengo
              farmer cut-for   fox   trees
              'The farmer is cutting trees for the fox.'

        b.   Instrumental (Chichewa)
              Fisi   a-na-dul-ir-a mpeni chingwc
              hyena cut-with   knife   rope
              'The hyena cut the rope with a knife.'

        c.   Locative (Kinyarwanda)
              Umwaana y-a-taa-ye-mo amaazi igitabo
              child   throw-in   water book
              'The child threw the book into the water.'

    Kimaragang Dusun, a language closely related to Malagasy, also appears to have
an applicative construction as discussed by Kroeger (1990).[9]

(16)   Locative alternations in Kimaragung Dusun

      a.   0-po-suwang okuh   ditih   sada sid pata'an
             AT-OBJ_n-enter 1.SG.NOM this.ACC fish   LOC basket
             'I will put this fish in the basket.'

      b.   m-poN-suwang okuh   do pata'an do sada
             AT-OBJ_t-enter   1.SG.NOM ACC basket ACC fish
             'I will fill the basket with fish.'

Turning now to Malagasy, we see that it too has a way of promoting a locative to a term, but interestingly promotion is always to subject. In Malagasy this is done by the Circumstantial Topic morphology mentioned above. Below I give a range of examples that show just how productive this process is. It not only allows locatives to become subjects, but also benefactives, instrumentals, time, price, and manner. Further, while some of these promoted objects are clearly in the subject position (sentence finally), others must appear in a clefted position.[10]

(17)   Malagasy Circumstantial Topic
             (b-f from Rajemisa-Raolison: 112-113)

      a.   Benefactive
             Nividian'ny   lehilahy lamba   **ny ankizy**
             PST-CT-buy-DET man   clothing DET child
             'The man bought the clothing for the children.'

      b.   Instrumental
             Anapahany bozaka **ny antsinay**
             CT-cut-3SG grass   DET knife-1PL.EXC
             'He cuts the grass with our knife.'

      c.   Locative
             Itoeranay   **ity trano ity**
             CT-live-1PL.EXC this house this
             'We live in this house.'

      d.   Time[11]
             Rahampitso no   handehanantsika
             tomorrow   PRT FUT-CT-go-1PL.INC
             'It is tomorrow that we will go.'

      e.   Price
             Valopolo no   nividíananany   hena omaly
             eighty   PRT PST-CT-sell-3SG meat yesterday
             'It was for eighty that he sold the meat yesterday.'

    f.   Manner
        Amin-kafaliana lehibe no iarahabanay   anao, Tompokolahy
        with-joy   great PRT CT-greet-1PL.EXCL 2SG   sir
        'It is with great joy that we greet you, sir.'

GHT account for the ability for an oblique to become a subject via P-incorporation.[12] In Relational Grammar, we might expect advancement to 2 of the formerly oblique item. Given Baker's notion of P-incorporation, it should be that the V+P complex can govern and assign case to the stranded P-object making it act like an object. Given a derived object version of the applicative construction, it should be that the stranded P-object could move to a derived object position to receive case from the V+P complex.

Perhaps unexpectedly, then, what happens is that the stranded P-object becomes the subject rather than the object. In Relational Grammar terms, there is advancement from 3 to 1. GHT have no account for this, in fact.[13] What I suggest is that there is no derived object position for Malagasy, forcing all processes that would otherwise promote an NP to object, to promote this NP to subject.[14] In other words, where other languages would allow movement of the NP to a derived object position to check the necessary features of the NP, in Malagasy this option is not available and the first appropriate position would be the subject position. With this hypothesis in mind, we will look at other constructions where we might expect to find derived objects.

2.4 Possessor Raising

Another construction where we have seen derived objects is the Possessor Raising (PR) construction. An additional typical example of Possessor Raising is given below. The possessor *kalulu* 'hare' appears within the object NP in (18a) and in the object position in (18b).

(8)   Chichewa (from Baker 1988:11)
    a.   Fisi   a-na-dy-a   nsomba za kalulu.
        Hyena SP-PST-eat-ASP fish   of hare
        'The hyena ate the hare's fish.'

    b.   fisi   a-na-dy-er-a   kalulu nsomba.
        hyena SP-PST-eat-APPL-ASP hare   fish
        'The hyena ate the hare's fish.'

2.4.1 Background

Similar constructions appear in Malagasy but with an interesting twist. The simple picture of Possessor Raising in Malagasy shows that possessors may only raise from logical object hosts to grammatical subject landing sites. In order to see this, however, we will have to look at some very complicated constructions in Malagasy.

In the discussion, I will first give an overview of other descriptions of the Malagasy data. Then I will present another relevant construction, Agent Raising, and argue that only by looking at a subset of the Agent Raising structures can we get at the appropriate generalization.

Some of the original literature on Possessor Raising pointed out that Malagasy seems to allow raising only to subject position. Examples from Perlmutter and Postal (1983a) are given in (19) below, followed by their characterization of the language specific restriction on possessor raising needed to capture the Malagasy facts.[15]

(19)   Malagasy (Perlmutter and Postal 1983a:44)
  a.   Nantsoin-d Rakoto [ny anaran'ny olona]
         PST-TT-call Rakoto DET name'DET people
         'The names of the people were called by Rakoto.'

  b.   Nantsoin-d Rakoto anarana [ny   olona]
         PST-TT-call Rakoto name   DET people
         'The people were name-called by Rakoto.'

  c.   Niantso   ny anaran'ny olona Rakoto
         PST-AT-call DET name'DET people Rakoto
         'Rakoto called the names of the people.'

  d.   *Niantso   anarana ny olona Rakoto
         PST-AT-call name   DET people Rakoto

> To prevent such derivations [as in (19a)], the grammar must state that in Malagasy, *the host of Possessor Ascension must be a subject.* (italics in Perlmutter and Postal)

This restriction, however, does not accurately account for the all of the facts. Hung (1988) makes the observation that Possessor raising only occurs with adjectives, unaccusative verbs, and passives.[16]

(20)   Malagasy (a-d from Hung 1988)
  a.   [Marary] ny   zanako.
         PRES.sick DET child-1SG
         'My child is sick.'

  b.   [Marary   zanaka] aho.
         PRES.sick child   1SG

  c.   [Nianjera]   ny   tranon-dRabe.
         PST.AT.collapse DET house-Rabe
         'Rabe's house collapsed.'

d.   [Nianjera   trano] Rabe.[17]
      PST.AT.collapse house Rabe

e.   [Soloan-dRasoa] ny lamban'ny   zanany
      TT.change-Rasoa DET clothes-DET child-3SG
      'Her child's clothes were changed by Rasoa.'

f.   [Soloan-dRasoa   lamba] ny   zanany
      TT.change-Rasoa clothes DET child-3SG

A way of expressing this generalization is that Possessor Raising must obey two constraints - it must be launched by the logical object, but its landing site must be the subject position.[18] In other words, while other languages have possessor raising from the logical object position to the grammatical object position, Malagasy only allows possessor raising from the logical object position to the grammatical subject position.

This is the simplest picture to give of Malagasy, but in fact the data above need a bit more explanation since subsequent to Postal and Perlmutter's work and Hung's work, it has been proposed that there are cases where, apparently, there is possessor raising to object. I will begin by presenting these counterexamples to the generalization, but then I will suggest that these are not true cases of possessor raising but rather constructions where the possessor is, in fact, base-generated as an argument of the verb. I will then introduce the Agent Raising construction and argue that a subset of these are true raising constructions and in these we can see the true restrictions on raising at work.

First we will look at the examples where it appears that the possessor has raised into object position. Keenan and Ralalaoherivony (1998) (K&R) present an extensive study of Possessor Raising constructions in Malagasy. In this work, it is assumed that Possessor Raising is possible to object as well as subject positions. Below is a sampling of the examples that they give.

(21)   Possessor Raising to Object in Malagasy (K&R: 80)
  a.   [Manety   [ny volon-jana-ny]] Rabe
        AT.PRES.cut DET hair-child-3SG Rabe
        'Rabe cut the hair of his child.'

  b.   [Manety   [volo] [an-janany]]   Rabe
        AT.PRES.cut hair   ACC-child-3SG Rabe

  c.   [Manala   [ny fatoran'ny gadra]] Rabe
        AT.PRES.remove DET bond-DET   prisoner Rabe
        'Rabe removed the bonds of the prisoner.'

d.   [Manala   [fatorana] [ny gadra]] Rabe
      AT.PRES.remove bond   DET prisoner Rabe

If these are true cases of object raising, we can see that it is possible to have derived objects in Malagasy and the central thesis of this paper will be wrong. There are reasons, however, to believe that these constructions are base-generated as such. Many researchers who work on Possessor Raising constructions point out a possible confound in the data. For example, it is not clear whether (21d) is the result of promotion of a possessor to the object position or simply another possible base-generated structure. As has been pointed out, for example in Massam (1985), possessor raising structures may be syntactic or lexical, and it is possible to have both in the same language. In English we get the following examples.

(22)   English
  a.   Ilse kissed Perry's nose.

  b.   Ilse kissed Perry on the nose

  c.   *Ilse kissed Perry on Teddy's nose.[19]

We would not say that (22b) is a case of Possessor Raising even though, as (22c) shows, we can't have a distinct possessor. In the case of Malagasy, we can question the productivity of possessor raising. For example, in the following examples, we see that in these cases, the possessor cannot move out of the object unlike the examples we have see in (21).[20]

(23)a.   Mamaky   ny bokin-dRabe aho
          PRES.AT.read DET book-Rabe   1SG
          'I am reading Rabe's book.'

  b.   *Mamaky   boky an-dRabe aho
          PRES.AT.read book ACC.Rabe 1SG

  c.   Mividy   ny tranon-dRabe aho
          PRES.AT.buy DET house-Rabe   1SG
          'I am buying Rabe's house.'

  d.   *Mividy   trano an-dRabe aho
          PRES.AT.buy house ACC.Rabe 1SG

We can ask, then, if Malagasy has true possessor raising or simply allows something with possessor-like meaning to be generated as an argument of the verb. In the next section I will argue that Malagasy has both constructions and the only way to be sure to have the true raising case is to use a construction called Agent Phrase raising.

2.4.2 Agent Phrase Raising
In order to fully understand the restrictions on Possessor Raising, first we must understand a construction called Agent Phrase Raising. I begin by outlining the observations on Agent Phrase Raising presented in Keenan and Ralalaoherivony (1998). I will then show that even in some of these cases, one can argue that the raised possessor is base-generated as the argument of the main predicate. I will claim that only by looking at certain cases of Agent Phrase Raising can we be sure to have a true raising structure.

In Agent Phrase Raising, we get possessor raising from an unexpected position which looks like the Agent phrase (Spec, VP) of a relative clause which modifies the noun.[21] An example given by K&R is given below.

(24)   Agent Phrase Raising (Keenan and Ralalaoherivony 1998:86)
    a.   [vp Maro] [ny raharaha sahani**ko**]
              much   DET work   TT-confront-1SG
          'The work faced by me is great'

    b.   [vp Maro [raharaha sahanina]] **aho**
              much work   TT-confront 1SG

In (24a) the whole NP *ny raharaha sahaniko* 'the work faced by me' is the subject of the sentence. In (24b), the subject of the sentence, *aho* 'I', appears to be extracted from Spec, VP position of the clause (*sahaniko* 'confronted by me') modifying the noun *raharaha* 'work'. K&R assume that this is done by a type of reanalysis, or at least a possible alternative analysis of the data. They say the alternative analysis would have the "agent" as the possessor of the whole NP (note that the genitive form that a possessor takes is identical to the form of an Actor which has not become the subject). They show that the possessor of the NP can attach even to simple postnominal adjectives. Such an example is given in (25) below.

(25)   (adapted from Keenan and Ralalaoherivony 1998:87-88)
    a.   ny raharaha   'the work'

    b.   ny raharaha**ko**   'my work'

    c.   ny raharaha kely   'the small work'

    d.   ny raharaha keli**ko** 'my small work'

Taking their analysis, if the embedded agent/possessor can also be given the structure where it is, in fact, possessor the whole NP, then Possessor Raising can occur as before — a Possessor raises out of its NP.

Interesting for our concerns, K&R point out that Agent Phrase Raising is not possible from the object of a transitive verb, while it is possible from the single argument of an adjective or an unaccusative (K&R: 88).[22]

(26)a.   Nahita   ny vola   veriko/ notadiaviko   Rabe
          PST.AT.see DET money TT.lose.1SG/PST.TT.seek.1SG Rabe
          'Rabe found the money I lost/was seeking.'

     b.   *Nahita   vola very/notadiavina   ahy Rabe
           PST.AT.see money TT.lose/PST.TT.seek 1SG Rabe

     c.   Mamaky   ilay boky tiako   izy
           PRES.AT.read that book TT.love.1SG 3SG
           'He is reading that book that I love.'

     d.   *Mamaky   boky tiana   ahy izy
            PRES.AT.read book TT.love 1SG 3SG

(27)a.   Tsy tonga ny   vahiny nasaiko
          NEG arrive DET guest   PST.TT.invite.1SG
          'The guests that I invited have not arrived.'

     b.   Tsy tonga vahiny nasaina   aho
           NEG arrive guest PST.TT.invite 1SG
           'I am in the state of having the guests not show up.'

As the distinction between (26c) and (26d) on one hand and (27a) and (27b) on the
other shows, raising of the agent out of a relative clause is possible only when this
raising takes place to a subject position. While this observation helps support my
claim, there is a problem with this sort of reasoning. If Agent NP raising is not true
raising but rather simply a different argument structure, it is difficult to predict
which predicates might allow this. In other words, it is hard to know if (26b) and
(26d) are ungrammatical because they are ruled out in principle, or whether the
verbs *mahita* 'to see' and *mamaky* 'to read' simply do not allow this construction as
we have seen earlier in (23).

    In order to tease apart this issue, I will show that Agent NP Raising cases fall
into two distinct types — one which I will call true raising cases, the other I will call
pseudo-raising cases. In this latter group, the apparent possessor will be, in fact, an
argument of the matrix predicate. We will see that part of the distinction depends on
whether or not the main predicate is a verb or an adjective. If the predicate is an
adjective, then it will be a case of pseudo-raising. If the predicate is a verb, in some
cases it will be a true raising construction, in other cases a pseudo-raising
construction.[23] There are three ways in which the true raising construction can be
distinguished from the pseudo-raising construction: (i) the pseudo-raising
constructions often have an idiomatic interpretation while the true raising cases must
have a compositional meaning, (ii) the pseudo-raising constructions can be
causativized while true raising constructions cannot be causativized, (iii) in pseudo-
raising constructions, the relative clause is optional while with true raising it is not.
After some more examples of each type are given, the three criteria will be discussed

in turn below and I will conclude that only when the main predicate is a verb and the construction has compositional meaning is it a true case of raising.

(28)   Pseudo-Raising
          Adjective roots (stative): (like the *maro* 'many' in (24)) (from K&R:87)

   a.   Tsy lany   ny zavatra irin'ny   olombelona
          NEG exhausted DET things   TT.desire'DET humans
          'The things desired by humankind are unending.'

   b.   Tsy lany   zavatra irina   ny olombelona
          NEG exhausted things   TT.desire DET humans
          'Humankind has limitless need of things.'

   c.   Iray ny   lalana izorantsika
          one DET route CT.go.straight.on-1PL.INCL
          'The route we are taking directly is the same.'

   d.   Iray lalana izorana   isika
          one route CT.go.straight.on 1PL.INCL
          'We are taking the same route.'

   e.   Fohy/Kely ny andro niveloman-dRabe
          short/few DET days PST.CT.live'Rabe
          'The days during which Rabe lived were short/few.'

   f.   Fohy/Kely andro nivelomana Rabe
          short/few day   PST.CT.live Rabe
          'Rabe had a short life.'

(29)   True raising
          Verb roots (eventive): (like the *tonga* 'arrive' in (27)) (from fieldwork)

   a.   Tsy lasa   ny   vahiny nasaiko
          NEG leave DET guest   PST.TT.invite.1SG
          'The guests that I invited haven't left.'

   b.   Tsy lasa   vahiny nasaina   aho
          NEG leave guest   PST.TT.invite 1SG
          'The guests that I invited haven't left.'

   c.   Ho   avy ny mpianatra tiako
          FUT   come DET student   TT.like.1SG
          'The students that I like will come.'

d. Ho avy mpianatra tiana   aho
    FUT come student   TT.like 1SG
    'The students that I like will come.'

Idiosyncratic meaning: The first distinction between the two types of constructions comes from the less clear area of semantic shift. Keenan and Ralalaoherivony point out that many of the constructions which have the possessor as the subject are idiomatic in meaning and have a meaning that is not available to the non-raised structure where the possessor appears still within the NP. In fact, some of the apparently raised structures have no underlying counterpart as shown in (30).[24]

(30)a. Mafy toto   ity kirarao ity
         hard pounding this shoe this
         'These shoes can take a lot of abuse.'

   b.   *Mafy ny toton'ity   kirarao ity
          hard the pounding-of-this shoe   this

Both adjectives and unaccusative verbs can have idiomatic meanings and in these cases I would argue that the possessor has not raised out of the NP but is base-generated as an argument of the predicate. However, with unaccusative verbs, when the meaning is purely compositional as in (29b) and (29d) above, I would argue that the Agent has raised.[25] What is important for the other two criteria discussed below is that in just these cases where the meaning is compositional the construction cannot be causativized and the relative clause cannot be deleted.

Causativization: A second distinction between the true raising and the pseudo-raising constructions is found when they are causativized. If, as suggested by Keenan and Ralalaoherivony, Agent Phrase Raising cannot occur to an object position, then we would predict that that these constructions cannot be causativized. Causativization would make the subject into an object so what formerly showed up as raising to a subject position would now show up as raising to an object position. In fact, this would be the prediction of the present paper as well. The prediction does not hold of the adjectival constructions. Below we see an example where the non-raised construction is causativized in (31a) and in (31b) we see an example where the raised version of the construction has successfully been causativized.

(31)a. Mahamaro   ny raharaha sahaniko   ny fidiran'ny
         PRES.CAUS.much DET work   TT-confront-1SG DET return'DET
         mpianatra
         students
         'The return of the students causes there to be much work confronted by me.'

b.   Mahamaro   raharaha sahanina   ahy ny   fidiran'ny mpianatra
      PRES.CAUS.much work   TT-confront 1SG DET return'DET students
      'The return of the students causes me to have much work to be
      confronted.'

The verbal construction with compositional meaning, however, behaves
differently. In (32) below, we see that while the non-raised construction can be
causativized as in (32a), the raised construction cannot be as shown in (32b).

(32)a.   Mahatonga   ny vahiny nasaiko   ny   fampisehona
          PRES.CAUS.arrive DET guest   PST.TT.invite-1SG DET exposition
          'The exposition caused the guests invited by me to arrive.'

b.   *Mahatonga   vahiny nasaina   ahy ny   fampisehona
      PRES.CAUS.arrive guest PST.TT.invite 1SG DET exposition

Optionality of relative clause: Further, if K&R are correct in proposing that
Agent Raising comes about via a reinterpretation of the Agent of the relative clause
as the Possessor of the whole NP, the prediction would be that the relative clause
should be optional. This is, in fact, what we find in the adjective constructions as
shown in (33a) below. However, surprisingly, this is not the case with the verbal
counterparts with compositional meaning as shown in (33b).

(33)a.   [$_{VP}$ Maro raharaha (sahanina)] aho
              much work   TT-confront 1SG
          'I have much work.'

b.   [$_{VP}$ Tsy tonga vahiny *(nasaina)] aho
          NEG arrive guest   PST.TT.invite 1SG
          intended reading: My guests haven't arrived.

The fact that the relative clause in (33b) is not optional cannot be captured in the
reanalysis account. However, if this is truly a case of raising out of the embedded
structure, the embedded verb will be needed to assign a theta-role to the Agent.

With the most reliable cases of Possessor Raising restricted to these cases of
Agent NP raising, we can see that Possessor Raising — like applicatives — is
restricted to promoting NPs to subject position where in other languages it might
have promoted the NP to object position.[26] We have two instances, then, where we
expect raising to object but get only raising to subject. With this in mind, we return
to the Raising to Object construction discussed at the beginning of the paper in order
to determine whether or not true raising has occurred.

2.5 Another look at raising to object

If what has been said above is correct and Malagasy has no derived objects, we must re-evaluate RtoO constructions which appear to be a core case of derived objects. In fact, with a closer look, it is clear that raised objects in Malagasy behave very differently from raised objects in English. One of the problems of considering raised objects in English to have remained in their embedded subject position is that, with respect to binding, the object appears to act like a member of the matrix clause. As (34) shows, the embedded subject can be a reflexive bound by the matrix subject and may not be a pronoun bound by the matrix subject.

(34)a. The children$_i$ expect themselves$_i$ to receive lots of presents.
   b. *The children$_i$ expect them$_i$ to receive lots of presents.

Before going into the parallel facts in Malagasy, we have to recognize that binding in Malagasy is different from English in a variety of ways. It appears that binding is sensitive to D-structure positions as the data in (35) below show.[27]

(35)   Malagasy
   a.   Novonoiny   ny   tenany
        PST.TT.kill.his DET body.3SG
        'S/he killed himself/herself.'

   b.   *Novonoin'ny   tenany   izy
        PST.TT.kill'DET body.3SG 3SG
        'S/he killed himself/herself.'

   c.   Namono   ny tenany   izy
        PST.AT.kill DET body.3SG 3SG
        'He killed himself.'

   d.   *Namono   azy ny tenany
        PST.AT.kill 3SG DET body.3SG
        'Himself killed him.'

The grammaticality judgments above indicate that the Agent can bind the Theme and not vice versa, independent of the surface realizations of these arguments. There have been a variety of accounts for this (see e.g. Wechsler and Arka (1998) and Travis (1998)) and, as pointed out in these works, it cannot be dealt with simply by saying it applies at D-structure since it can be fed by rules such as passive in embedded contexts and raising to object as we will see immediately in (36b).

The RtoO data are given below. (36a) shows a simple RtoO example where the raised object is the logical subject of the embedded clause and (36b) is a case where passive in the lower clause has fed RtoO so that the raised object is the logical object of the embedded clause.[28]

(36)   Malagasy ECM
   a.   Mihevitra   an'iSoa   ho manaja   an'iBakoly Rakoto.
         PRES.AT.think ACC'Soa PRT PRES.AT.respect ACC'Bakoly Rakoto
         'lit: Rakoto thinks Soa to respect Bakoly.'

   b.   Mihevitra   an'iBakoly   ho hajain'iSoa   Rakoto.
         PRES.AT.think ACC'Bakoly PRT PRES.TT.respect'Soa Rakoto
         'lit: Rakoto thinks Bakoly to be respected by Soa.'

The crucial binding facts are given in (37). While, like English, the raised object may be a reflexive bound by the matrix subject, unlike English, it may also be a pronoun and retain the coindexation.[29]

(37)   Binding of ECM object in Malagasy
   a.   Mihevitra   ny tenany$_i$ ho manaja   an'iBakoly Rakoto$_i$.
         PRES.AT.think DET body.3P PRT PRES.AT.respect ACC'Bakoly Rakoto
         'lit: Rakoto$_i$ thinks himself$_i$ to respect Bakoly.'

   b.   Mihevitra   ny tenany$_i$ ho hajain'iSoa   Rakoto$_i$.
         PRES.AT.think DET body.3P PRT TT.respect'Soa Rakoto
         'lit: Rakoto$_i$ thinks himself$_i$ to be respected by Soa.'

(38)a.   Mihevitra   azy$_i$ ho manaja   an'iBakoly Rakoto$_i$.
         PRES.AT.think 3P.ACC PRT PRES.AT.respect ACC'Bakoly Rakoto
         'lit: Rakoto$_i$ thinks him$_i$ to respect Bakoly.'

   b.   Mihevitra   azy$_i$ ho hajain'iSoa   Rakoto$_i$
         PRES.AT.think 3P.ACC PRT TT.respect'Soa Rakoto
         'lit: Rakoto$_i$ thinks him$_i$ to be respected by Soa.'

Clearly this makes the raised object look very different from base-generated objects in Malagasy in spite of the adverb argument given by Pearson (2001: see (14)). Except for some idiosyncratic verbs, pronominal objects cannot be co-referential with their subjects.

(39)   *Manaja   azy$_i$ iSoa$_i$.
         PRES.AT.respect 3P.ACC Soa
         'Soa$_i$ respects him$_i$.'

Balinese data show that this binding fact cannot be linked to the other binding facts of Malagasy. In other words, it cannot be said that the fact that pronominal raised objects may be coindexed with the subject is related to the fact that Malagasy seems to allow binding to occur at D-structure. Balinese, in all other respects, has binding facts parallel to those in Malagasy. Comparable to (35) above, Balinese (an SVO language) shows the following pattern.

(40)   Balinese (from Wechsler and Arka (1998)):
  a.   Awakne tingalin=a   (W&A (41))
         self   OV.see=3SG
         '(S)he saw himself/herself.'

  b.   *Wayan tingalin=a   teken awakne   (W&A (42))
         Wayan OV.see=3SG PREP self
         'Wayan was seen by himself.'

  c.   Ia   ningalin awakne   (W&A (43))
         3SG AV.see   self
         '(S)he saw herself/himself.'

Like Malagasy, in a simple Balinese clause, the Agent can bind the Theme irrespective of its final syntactic realization. However, in RtoO constructions, Balinese is like English in that the raised object, if co-referential with the subject, must appear in the reflexive form. (41) shows a typical RtoO construction.

(41)   RtoO in Balinese
         Tiang nawang Nyoman Santosa mulih   (W&A (22b))
         1SG   AV.know (name)   go.home
         'I knew that Nyoman Santosa went home.'

In spite of the fact that binding in Balinese is quite different from binding in English in other ways, binding in Actor Voice RtoO constructions mirrors the English facts. The raised object must be in the reflexive form if it is coindexed with the matrix subject.

(42)   Binding in Balinese RtoO constructions
  a.   Ia$_i$ nawang awakne$_i$ lakar tangkep polisi   (W&A (110a))
         3SG AV.know self   FUT OV.arrest police
         'He$_i$ knew that the police would arrest self$_i$.'

  b.   *Ia$_i$ nawang ia$_i$ lakar tangkep polisi   (W&A (110c))
         3SG AV.know 3SG FUT OV.arrest police
         'He$_i$ knew that the police would arrest him$_i$.'

The binding fact found in the passivization of an RtoO construction, while perhaps surprising, is, in fact, consistent with the other facts of Malagasy. The pronominal form may remain even though it now is arguably not only in the same domain as its antecedent, but c-commands it. This is shown in (43). Again, Balinese acts like English rather than Malagasy as shown by (44).

(43)　Malagasy
　　　Heverin-dRakoto$_i$　　ho　hajain'iSoa　　izy$_i$
　　　PRES.TT.think-Rakoto PRT TT.respect'Soa 3SG
　　　'lit: He$_i$ is thought by Rakoto$_i$ to be respected by Soa.'

(44)　Balinese
　　　*Ia$_i$　tawang=a$_i$　　lakar tangkep polisi　　　(W&A (110d))
　　　3SG OV.know=3SG FUT　OV.arrest police
　　　'He$_i$ knew that the police would arrest him$_i$.'

Finally, the appearance of the reflexive in the RtoO construction in Malagasy most likely has very little to do with the construction itself. Below we can see that Malagasy (again unlike Balinese) allows subject reflexives in normal embedded tensed clauses. (This construction is given a * in P&R.)

(45)　Malagasy
　　　Mihevitra　　　Rakoto$_i$ fa　　hajain'iSoa　　ny　tenany$_i$
　　　PRES.AT.think Rakoto COMP TT.respect'Soa DET body.3P
　　　'lit: Rakoto$_i$ thinks that himself$_i$ is respected by Soa.'

(46)　Balinese　　　　　　　　　　　　　　　(Wechsler and Arka (109))
　　　Ia$_i$　tusing nawang apa　?*awakne$_i$ suba ngemaang I Nyoman
　　　3sg NEG　know　Q　　self　　PERF give　I Nyoman
　　　pipis-ne
　　　money- 3POSS
　　　'She$_i$ does not know whether she$_i$ has given I Nyoman his money.'

One could say that the difference between Malagasy and Balinese, among other things, is that in Malagasy, the raised object never becomes the object of the matrix verb while in Balinese it does.[30] This conclusion would fit in with the hypothesis being explored here that Malagasy does not have derived objects. Raising to Object, then, in Malagasy is not truly Raising to Object, just as Possessor Raising never truly raises a possessor to the object position, and applicative constructions only raise obliques into the subject position. [31]

3. POTENTIAL PROBLEMS

While there may be reasons to believe that Malagasy resists promotion to a derived object position, there are constructions beyond RtoO and the apparent Possessor Raising cases already discussed which suggest otherwise. I will explore two of these with the aim of showing, once again, that these are only apparent counter-examples. One set consists of apparent applicative constructions and the other has to do with specific objects.

3.1 Instruments and Material Themes

Paul (2000) and Pearson (1998) have done extensive research on another set of constructions that could be argued to show derived object characteristics. They show that both instrumentals and material themes can appear either as oblique arguments or as direct arguments of the verbs. Some examples are given below.

(47)   Instruments (Paul (2000): 35)
a.   Nandidy   ny hena tamin'ny   antsy Rasoa
         PST.AT.cut DET meat PST.with'DET knife Rasoa
         'Rasoa cut the meat with the knife.'

b.   Nandidy   antsy ny hena Rasoa
         PST.AT.cut knife DET meat Rasoa

(48)   Material Themes (Paul (2000): 34)
a.   Namafy   ny tany tamin'ny   voa Rasoa
         PST.AT.sow DET land PST.with'DET seed Rasoa
         'Rasoa sowed the land with seeds.'

b.   Namafy   voa ny tany Rasoa
         PST.AT.sow seed DET land Rasoa

Although the form of the verb does not change in either case, these appear to be instances where a P has been incorporated and/or an oblique has been promoted to the object position. Both Paul (2000) and Pearson (1998), however, argue for a base-generated structure for the (b) examples above and I will follow their lead. In both cases, the new object undergoes some change of location in the achievement of the event and Pearson calls these arguments displaced themes. He assumes that every verb that shows such an alternation has this displaced theme as the external argument of the predicate GO. Interestingly, not all instruments are able to undergo this alternation (from Paul (2000): 43).

(49)a.   Nihinana hena tamin'ny   antsy Rasoa.
         PST.AT.eat meat PST.with'DET knife Rasoa
         'Rasoa ate meat with the knife.'

b.   *Nihinana   antsy ny hena Rasoa.
         PST.AT.eat knife DET meat Rasoa

To explain this, Pearson distinguishes between instruments that are tools and those that are aids. Tools are more closely integrated into the event and as such can be generated as higher arguments.[39] Paul (2000) raises questions concerning this account but, like Pearson, feels that there is some semantic distinction that predicts which subset of instruments can appear here. What is crucial, for our purposes, is that it is only a subset of obliques that can appear in this position arguing against a syntactic movement analysis.

Another reason that these constructions are different (and distinct) is that in both cases this new object can be promoted to subject using a special form of the passive called the *a*-passive. If both instruments and material themes can appear in a special position due to their role in the event, it would make sense that there would be a special morphogical form to trigger movement (promotion) from this position.

(50)a. Adidy ny hena ny antsy.   instrument
         a.cut DET meat DET knife
         'The knife is used to cut the meat.'

   b.   Nafafin-dRasoa tany ny voa   material theme
         PST.a.sow-Rasoa land DET seed
         'The seed was used to sow land.'

Interestingly, the apparent derived objects of Possessor Raising and RtoO constructions do not consistently use the *a*-passive form for promotion to subject. We have seen a case of RtoO passive in (43) above where the passive (TT) form is *heverina* 'to be thought' and we have also seen a passive possessor raising construction in (20)e where the passive form is *soloana* 'be changed' — neither an *a*-passive form.

My conclusion here is that these constructions do not argue for a derived object position but rather point to an additional argument position within the VP which is higher than theme (see e.g. Matsuoka (1999) for similar claims). What is crucial is that it is not all cases of instruments that can be generated in this position. It is a subset of the instruments that fulfill other semantic requirements. If a language were to allow all instruments to appear in this position, I would take it rather to be closer to the case of Circumstantial Topic in Malagasy and true syntactic derivation.

3.2 Specific objects

In this last section I investigate the status of specific object in Malagasy.[33] The aim in doing this is to tie the data concerning derived objects in grammatical function changing operations to the data concerning specific objects. If object shift occurs to the same position as does promotion to 2 in RG terms, then we would expect that a language that blocks promotion to 2 will also not show object shift.

Objects in WMP languages have already come under investigation in various studies which explored the possibility that these languages are ergative. The reason why objects enter into the ergativity debate concerns their status in constructions where the highest argument is in the unmarked case — I will use the term NABS (Nominative/ABSolutive) from Massam (1991). If Malagasy were an ergative language, then when the highest argument is in subject position (i.e. Actor Topic (AT) constructions), the structure would not be transitive but instead anti-passive, i.e. the apparent object would in fact be an oblique. This claim has lead to various investigations of the objects in AT type constructions in WMP languages. Ones that I mention here, Maclachlan (1996) and Maclachlan and Nakamura (1997), note as others have done, that objects in Tagalog, a closely related language, must generally be non-specific.

(51)   Tagalog Specificity Effect
         (from Maclachlan and Nakamura 1997:310)
         Bumili   ng isda ang. lalaki
         bought-AT fish.ACC NABS man
         'The man bought (*the) fish.'

In (51) above, the object can only be interpreted as non-specific. As the example below shows, this has nothing to do with the morphology. If the *ng NP* is the non-promoted Actor in a Theme Topic construction, either the specific or non-specific reading is possible. Note further that the underlying object, now promoted to subject, must have the specific reading.

(52)   Binili   ng lalaki ang   isda
         bought-TT GEN man   NABS   fish
         'A/The man bought the fish.'

This observation relates directly to the question of whether a language has derived objects or not. One reason why the notion of derived objects has now become a mainstay in a MP type model is that it appears that objects may appear in two different places in a given language, often depending on how the object is to be interpreted. This is discussed in deHoop (1992) and Diesing (1995) among others but I will be using the discussion from Bobaljik (1995). He points out that the difference in where the object appears in some languages is tied to information structure — whether the object encodes new or old information. Two typical examples are given below, the first from Icelandic, the second from German.[34]

(53)   Icelandic (from Bobaljik 1995:127-128)

         context: Does he know Barriers?
         (Barriers = old information)

   a.   Hann les   **Barriers** alltaf
         he   reads **Barriers** always
         'He is always reading Barriers.'

b. #Hann les alltaf **Barriers**
   he reads always **Barriers**
   'He is always reading Barriers.'

(54) context: Does he know Chomsky's work?
    (Barriers = new information)

a. Hann les alltaf **Barriers**
   he   reads always **Barriers**
   'He is always reading Barriers.'

b. #Hann les **Barriers** alltaf
   he reads **Barriers** always
   'He is always reading Barriers.'

(55) Dutch (from Bobaljik 1995:126)
a. dat Jan Marie gisteren gekust heeft
   that Jan Marie yesterday kissed has
   'that Jan kissed Marie yesterday' [Marie = old information]

b. dat Jan gisteren Marie gekust heeft
   that Jan yesterday Marie kissed has
   'that Jan kissed Marie yesterday'
   [felicitous answer to: 'Who did Jan kiss yesterday?' = new
   information]

In each case above, we can see that the object encoding old information appears to the left of the adverb. The conclusion which has been drawn here is that there is a position to which an object must move if it is old information.

This is similar enough to the Tagalog data to suggest that it is part of the same phenomenon.[35] Taking the Tagalog data and the Germanic data with relevant conclusion together, we can posit, as is done in Maclachlan and Nakamura (1997), that Tagalog does not have the option of moving to a derived object position — at least in this construction. This suggests that Tagalog lacks one construction generally linked with derived objects. With this is mind we turn to Malagasy.

Unfortunately Malagasy does not show the same data set as Tagalog does. Objects in AT constructions in Malagasy can quite easily be specific.

(56) Malagasy Specific Objects
a. Nividy   ny trondro ny lehilahy
   PST-AT-buy DET fish DET man
   'The man bought the fish.'

    b.   ividy   trondro ny lehilahy
        PST-AT-buy fish   DET man
        'The man bought fish.'

Further, there are data much like the Germanic data above that argue that Malagasy does have the capacity to move specific objects to a different position.

    (57)a.   Tsy manasa   **lamba** *mihitsy* ve Rakoto?
             NEG PRES.AT.wash clothes at-all   Q   Rakoto

        b.   *Tsy manasa *mihitsy* **lamba** ve Rakoto?

        c.   Tsy manasa   *mihitsy* **ny** **lamba** ve Rakoto?
             NEG PRES.AT.wash at-all   DET clothes Q   Rakoto
             'Does Rakoto not wash clothes at all?'

As we can see in (57), non-specific NPs (NPs without determiners) must be adjacent to the V but specific NPs are free to move rightward.

While apparently problematic for the hypothesis being explored in this paper, the movement of specific objects in Malagasy also can be explained without recourse to a derived object position. As Bobaljik (1995) points out, there are a variety of ways that objects could appear outside of their normal position. He argues for two types of object movement — one he calls object shift, the other focus scrambling[36]. I will argue that the object movement in Malagasy is a case of focus scrambling rather that object shift. As Bobaljik writes (pg. 124, fn. 6):

> For me, "object shift" is movement of pronouns and full NPs to a fixed position to the left of the verb phrase. In the case of full NPs, this position is Spec, AgrO-P; and for pronouns some similar position ... This process ... is attested in all the Germanic languages save English. The term "focus scrambling" is reserved for a different process, quite marked in Dutch through freer in German and perhaps Yiddish.

Two characteristics of focus scrambling that distinguish it from object shift is its optionality and the range of positions that it can occur to. As shown by Rackowski (1998), specific objects have a range of possible positions with respect to adverbs in the language. The specific object may always appear adjacent to the verb and to the left of what would be a very low adverb in terms of Cinque (1999). The specific object, however, can also take a position between a variety of adverbs as the following data show (from Rackowski 1998).

    (58)   Tsy manasa x   tsara x tanteraka x foana x intsony x mihitsy
           NEG PRES-AT-wash well   completely always no.longer at.all
           x R akoto.
           Rakoto

    a. Tsy manasa **ny lamba** tsara tanteraka foana intsony mihitsy Rakoto

b. Tsy manasa tsara **ny lamba** tanteraka foana intsony mihitsy Rakoto

c. Tsy manasa tsara tanteraka **ny lamba** foana intsony mihitsy Rakoto, etc.

While perhaps an account could be created which would explain the variability in the positioning of the object, by viewing object movement as scrambling with a variety of landing sites, this variability is rather straightforward.

4. SPECULATIONS

While it is very preliminary to make broad generalizations based on a few facts from a few languages, one can form hypotheses that are clear enough to be falsifiable. And the stronger the claim, the more interesting the further work. Other work that I have been involved in, in particular Rackowski and Travis (2000), suggests that Malagasy derives its word order through predicate fronting. We hypothesized two types of languages, predicate fronting languages and argument fronting languages. Recasting this in theoretical terms, some languages need to check features of argument XPs while other languages need to check features on predicate XPs.[37] This may correlate with verb initial languages and SVO languages respectively. A very preliminary speculation would be that derived objects would be more apt to be found in subject first languages than in V-first languages. An interesting contrast arises in the case of Balinese and Malagasy, similar in many respects, but Balinese is SVO and Malagasy is VOS. And it is Balinese that seems to have true raising to object in RtoO constructions while in Malagasy seems to avoid promotion to object.

In order to test such a hypothesis, many more languages would require careful study. Kimaragang Dusun, for example, is a V-initial language which appears to have applicative constructions as in (16) above. Being V-initial, we might expect Kimaragang Dusun to be a predicate fronting language which, by hypothesis, should not have derived objects and therefore should not have true applicatives. Kroeger (1990) shows that the locative alternation in Kimaragang Dusun changes the affectedness pattern of the event (which argument is affected). For Baker (1996), a shift in affectedness indicated a difference in how the arguments were base-generated. If this conclusion is appropriate, Kimaragang Dusun does not have a true applicative construction.

Another language to investigate would be Kalagan, another V-initial language which I have argued elsewhere (Travis 1991, 1992) has derived objects. What is interesting about Kalagan is that there seem to be no derived subjects. For example, while Malagasy indicates movement of various elements to subject position through the morphology on the verb, Kalagan seems to indicate movement to an object position with the same morphology. This object position is, in fact, the same object position in Malagasy — appearing directly after the Agent and before all PPs. This is where non-specific objects occur in Malagasy, and it is where 'topics' occur in Kalagan.

(59)   Kalagan word order
   a.   Kumamang **aku** sa tubig na lata   kan Ma'   adti   balkon na
        AT-get   **I**   the water with the can for Father on the porch on
        lunis
        Monday
        'I'll get the water with the can for Dad on the porch on Monday.'

   b.   Kamangin aku **ya tubig** na lata   kan Ma'   adti balkon   na
        TT-get   I   **he water** with the can for Father on the porch on
        lunis
        Monday

   c.   Pagkamang aku **ya lata** sa tubig kan Ma'   adti balkon   na
        IT-get   I   **the can** the water for Father on the porch on
        lunis
        Monday

   d.   Kamangan aku **ya Ma'** sa tubig   na lata   adti balkon   na
        BT-get   I   **Father** the water with the can on the porch on
        lunis
        Monday

   e.   Kamangan aku **ya balkon** sa tubig na lata   kan Ma'   na
        LT-get   I   **the porch** the water with the can for Father on
        lunis
        Monday

We appear then to have a derived object position in a V-initial language. Further, unlike Kimaragang Dusun, appearance of an element in this position is not thematically restricted. However, while Kalagan is V-initial on the surface, it also does not make use of a derived subject position. Therefore, being V-initial does not preclude it from being SVO at some syntactic level. The claim here would be that the grammatical subject position is, in fact, pre-verbal, but movement to this position is covert.

While it may feel like hairs are being split very thin here, I believe that more can be learned about languages and about theory by generating new questions. In the end, the hypothesis that promoted these questions may be wrong, but the new data discovered in the process of the investigation can only help to further our knowledge and understanding.

NOTES

[1]   The content of this paper has benefitted from comments made by audiences at McGill and the Grammatical Functions Workshop at the University of Illinois and two anonymous reviewers. I am particularly grateful for input from Jonathan Bobaljik and William Davies. Native language input and observations from Saholy Hanitriniaina and Jeannot Fils Ranaivoson were invaluable. The usual

disclaimers apply. Funding for this research was provided by the Social Sciences and Humanities Council of Canada (410-98-0452).

2   For Baker's discussions of applicatives and ECM constructions, see Baker (1988) p. 231 and p. 488, fn. 4 respectively.

3   Lasnik (1999, this volume) has a similar analysis for Raising to Object constructions. Others such as Johnson 1991, Pesetsky 1989, Sportiche 1990, Travis 1991 also suggested that objects move in English.

4   I call this intermediate non-lexical category Asp(ect) following other work of mine (Travis 1991, 2000) but a similar VP internal functional category has been posited by Koizumi (1993) for similar reasons but which is called AgrO.

5   Following orthographic convention in Malagasy, I put in apostrophes to signal a specific morpho-phonological process of 'N-bonding' as described in Keenan (2000:32). Further, following convention within the linguistic literature, I use the terminology of Actor Topic, Theme Topic, etc. There is a long debate about whether these elements are or are not subjects (I assume that they are subjects). Since they have to be specific, they have often been called topics. See Kroeger (1992) for a discussion of topichood in Tagalog, a related language. Kroeger comes to the conclusion that these are not topics in the standard sense.

6   See Postal (1974) for arguments that these are raising constructions.

7   I gloss *ho* here as PRT (particle) even though it has been analysed as COMP in other work. By deciding that it is COMP, we are already settling on an analysis of these constructions that I want to avoid.

8   In these examples, I gloss with the same amount of detail as Baker (1988).

9   I will raise the possibility later that this is not, in fact, a true applicative.

10   We can tell that the word final constituent in (17)a-c (in bold in these examples) is the subject by the tests outlined in Keenan (1976a). In the examples (17)d-f, since clefting is generally sensitive to subjecthood, the clefted element is assumed to be a subject before clefting. Running the risk of overwhelming the reader, I nonetheless present some of the range of circumstantial constructions since it may be that the range of elements that can become subjects is important to the eventual analysis (see e.g. Paul 2000).

11   A cleft construction is forced in the case of time, price, and manner - as well as others for which I have not given examples. For an account of this, see Paul (2000).

12   But see Keenan (2000), and Paul (2000), for examples where it is not clear what P would have incorporated.

13   GHT do link the appearance of arguments to the overt morphology on the verb CT morphology arguably is comprised of three morphemes - one that indicates that P-incorporation has occurred, one that allows the verb to assign genitive case to the nonpromoted Actor, and one that assigns accusative case to the object. If accusative case must go to the base-generated object, then it could be said that the derived object has no choice but to move to the subject position to be case-marked. Baker (1988) however, shows that in applicative constructions, language specific strategies may be used to license the base-generated object. Malagasy does, in fact, have double object constructions (to be discussed below) showing that there are ways within the language to license two objects through accusative case assignment.

14   Paul (2000) argues that, since Malagasy shows the advancement of a wider range of arguments than normal applicatives, this is not a true case of applicative. In her account, the oblique becomes the subject because it will be the only element that can satisfy the EPP. If her account of the data is the appropriate one, this construction is not relevant for the matter at hand.

[15] Not all speakers agree on the ungrammaticality of (19)d which is what we might expect given the conclusions of this paper where raising to object depends on the lexical specifications of the verb. One of my consultants agrees that it is ungrammatical, the other finds it to be grammatical.

[16] Brackets are given to show more clearly what is contained in the VP. Keenan and Ralalaoherivony (1998) give several tests to confirm this bracketting.

[17] This case of possessor raising is not universally accepted by Malagasy speakers.

[18] If this characterization is correct, then the single argument of an adjective must be an internal argument. This would go against claims made by e.g. Baker (1996b) and Baker and Stewart (1997) — but as we will see shortly, it is not clear that adjectives allow true possessor raising.

[19] As pointed out to me by Tomokazu Takehisa (p.c.) sentences such as these are good if the possessed item can be interpreted as being inalienably possessed by the object – in other words if, for some reason, Teddy's nose has been attached to Perry's face.

[20] Accusative case marking in Malagasy is not a good indicator of objecthood. It only occurs on objects that are proper names or family relations, in both cases definite NPs. Since many of the constructions we are looking at require indefinite objects, we cannot use the presence/absence of accusative case as an indication of anything.

[21] Chamorro may have a similar construction as described by Chung (1998:266) and discussed in Travis (2000).

[22] One of my consultants does not like the version of this sentence with *veriko* 'lost' since he prefers not to have *-ko* attach to adjectives/roots.

[23] The distinction between adjectives and unaccusative verbs is interesting for two independent reasons. One is the distinction that Baker (1996b) and Baker and Stewart (1997) make between A roots and V roots. Another, more specific to Malagasy, is the often blurred line between adjectival roots and verb roots. For example, the root *latsaka* 'fallen' behaves like an adjective. This correlates with native speaker intuitions, but is surprising perhaps on translation grounds since it is used for the inchoative 'fall'. If this test turns out to be robust, it could be another way of distinguishing an otherwise fine line.

[24] More work needs to be done to determine the exact structure of both the pseudo-raising cases and the true raising cases.

[25] Admittedly, this is a very strange sort of movement for which I have no account.

[26] With respect to the Relational Succession Law given in (6), it is interesting to note that the host of the raised NP acts like an object in a number of ways though the Relational Succession Law predicts that it should behave like a 1-chomeur. Although it cannot bear accusative case since it must always be indefinite, it appears to the right of the non-promoted agent and to the left of VP adverbs.

[27] Malagasy reflexives are formed by using the word *tena* 'body'. In the cases I show, *tena* is given with a definite determiner and a possessive as in *ny tenany* 'the his/her body'. Since subject reflexives must always appear in this form due to the specificity restriction on subjects, I always choose this form even though objects can often appear in the bare form (*Namono (ny) tena(-ny) izy* 'He killed himself'). There are examples where the non-reflexive reading is possible ('He saw himself' vs. 'He saw his body') but I have tried to control for this so that I have only the reflexive readings. See Paul (2001), however, for a different view of reflexives in Malagasy. She argues that the true reflexive is *tena* and that *ny tenany* is always logophoric (as in Reinhart and Reuland (1993)).

[28] For more details on RtoO in Malagasy, see Paul and Rabaovololona (1998). Below we will see that RtoO in Malagasy is different from RtoO in English with respect to binding. There are other differences

as well. In Malagasy RtoO is quite productive — P&R give 52 verbs that allow it. Further, the embedded clause clearly has a tense specification that is independent of the matrix verb.

[29] While not crucial to this paper, it is interesting to note that in both (37) and (38), neither the pronoun nor the reflexive can be bound by the Agent of the lower clause *Soa*.

[30] Again, more work needs to be done to completely understand the nature of this construction. It is clear, however, that it is not just a matter of scrambling — or if it is scrambling, it must be to an A-position since in the structure where no movement has occurred, the embedded Agent (*Soa* in (45)) may also be the antecedent to the anaphor while this is not true of the structure with movement.

[31] This raises the question of what to do with the adverb data (see (14)).presented in Pearson (2001). The data are not clear are Pearson himself points out. The same example received from Paul and Rabaovololona (1998). Further work needs to be done on adverb placement however.

[32] Notice that the fact that only some instruments are allowed to appear in this construction distinguishes it from the cases that Marantz (1993) investigates.

[33] I thank Jonathan Bobaljik in particular for a discussion of the issues presented here.

[34] The discussion of the Germanic instantiation of these facts will be left quite cursory and admittedly, the correlation across the language families is only suggestive at this point.

[35] It is interesting to note that in both the Scandinavian cases (a subset of the Germanic cases) and the WMP case of Tagalog, at times this restriction is lifted. For example, in the Scandinavian cases, object shift is prevented when the finite verb has not moved to the V2 position (known as Holmberg's generalization). When object shift is blocked for independent reasons, the interpretation facts no longer hold. This is also true in Tagalog where, in cases where the object cannot, for independent reasons, become the subject, the specificity restriction is lifted. I mention this as an aside (pointed out to me by Jonathan Bobaljik) and one that would be interesting to pursue in further work.

[36] Bobaljik credits Neeleman (1990) for the term of 'focus scrambling'.

[37] In fact, a closer look at adverb placement in Malagasy suggests that Malagasy checks predicate features (has predicate movement) within the VP and the CP domain, but checks argument features (has argument movement) in the IP domain. This would explain why derived subjects but not derived objects are allowed. Further, there doesn't seem to be 'normal' wh-movement in Malagasy, just clefting.

JAMES MCCLOSKEY

THE DISTRIBUTION OF SUBJECT PROPERTIES IN IRISH

Virtually no one who has thought seriously about language and its structure has been able to avoid using the terms 'subject' and 'object'. This is a remarkable fact - that perceptive and knowledgeable observers have been willing to talk about 'subjects' and 'objects' in very disparate languages and feel reasonably confident that they knew what they were talking about. It is all the more remarkable, then, that in the intellectual tradition represented by the frameworks of 'Government and Binding', 'Principles and Parameters' and the 'Minimalist Program', the notions play no (recognized) role at all. That tradition has always insisted that talk of 'subjects' and 'objects' is either illicit or casual, and that reference to such terms is to be cashed out in terms of more primitive notions (phrase-structural measures of prominence, featural properties of heads, the theory of A-movement and so on).

The question that this volume and the workshop from which it derives[1] asks us to consider is whether or not this reductionist program has been carried out successfully. How can we measure the success of such a program? By asking, presumably, if descriptive success is compromised or enhanced by its adoption. My own assessment is that the program has been largely successful. Certainly, for the range of cases that I will be considering here, it seems fairly clear that the reductionist program provides some rather successful descriptions - descriptions, furthermore, which depend on core commitments of the program. To be more specific, I think that the kind of deconstruction of the unified notion of 'subject' that the program insists on has made available a more subtle and more successful understanding of the architecture of Irish clauses than was previously available.[2]

The purpose of the present paper is in the first place to try to show that this is so by examining Irish clauses in some detail, and in the second place to address a number of open issues within the larger framework in which these proposals have been framed.

1. CLAUSAL ORGANIZATION
AND THE UNDERSTANDING OF SUBJECTHOOD

It will be useful to begin by outlining a framework of assumptions. This will involve covering some familiar territory, but I want to go through the exercise all the same - partly to establish some useful background, and partly because it seems to me that some of the implications of the general framework have not been widely

William D. Davies and Stanley Dubinsky (eds.), Objects and other subjects:
Grammatical functions, functional categories, and configurationality, 157—192.
© 2001 *Kluwer Academic Publishers. Printed in the Netherlands.*

appreciated. This system of assumptions is not by any means universally accepted but it, or something like it, has driven a lot of recent work.

The understanding of 'subjecthood' (and of 'objecthood') offered in this conception is distributed and derivational. There is no 'subject position' and the various properties associated with 'the subject' are distributed across a range of distinct syntactic positions, some derivationally linked to one another, some not.[3] More particularly, 'subject' properties are associated with phrase structural heads and with positions in a local relation with those heads (θ-assignment by a lexical head, case and agreement associated with an inflectional head or heads, the obligatoriness property associated with the highest inflectional head, and so on).

The inventory and organization of the crucial heads is determined by the theory of clausal organization, which can be summarized in roughly the following terms.

A clause (TP) consists of a thematic domain (an XP within which all the semantic roles associated with a given choice of lexical head are realized) and an anchoring specification of tense and modality (compare Case Grammar (Fillmore 1968), see also Pollock 1997).

The relation between the anchoring element and the thematic domain is expressed syntactically by means of the standard phrase structural mechanisms. XP is the complement of (the complement of ...) the specification of tense/modality, itself a head T. For the case in which XP is headed by a verb, then, we have:

Bare nominal arguments (however they are understood syntactically: NP, DP, or KP) are syntactically 'needy', in that they require special licensing. A lot of what we think of as morphosyntax consists of these licensing relationships and there is a designated syntactic space - the space above VP and below C - which is reserved for these purposes. From this follows the prominence of bare nominal arguments (subjects and objects) with respect to other kinds of arguments and with respect to VP-level adverbial elements. Bare nominal arguments must raise out of the lexical domain to enter into local syntactic relations with the heads which are crucial for their morphosyntactic licensing (the heads which license nominative case, accusative case, subject agreement, object agreement and so on).[4]

Careful descriptive work has revealed the existence of at least three distinct licensing positions for bare nominal arguments in the space between C and V (Holmberg 1993, Holmberg and Nikanne 1994, Bobaljik and Jonas 1996, Zwart 1992).

(1)

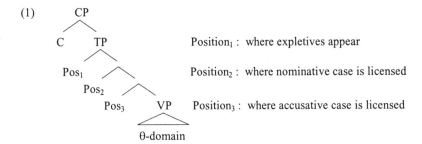

Position₁ : where expletives appear

Position₂ : where nominative case is licensed

Position₃ : where accusative case is licensed

All three positions are visibly occupied in a transitive expletive construction like the Icelandic example in (2):

(2)   það   borðuðu margir strákar bjúgur   ekki
         there ate   many boys   the-sausages NEG
         'Many boys did not eat the sausages.'   (Icelandic)

(3) shows how (2) relates to the schematic structure in (1):

(3)   EXP   V   DP   DP   NEG   VP
                [FIN] [NOM] [ACC]
         | | | |
         Pos₁   Pos₂   Pos₃   ∅

The finite verb occupies a position between Position One and Position Two; the expletive occupies Position One, the nominative subject occupies Position Two and the raised object in accusative case occupies Position Three.

Within this rough consensus, at least two important open issues can be identified:
(i) What is the position of origin of the subject?
(ii) How does the system ensure the right match between the inventory of bare nominal arguments within VP and the morphosyntactic mechanisms above VP which must license those arguments?

For the first question, the issue has been whether the position in which 'external arguments' (in the sense of Williams (1981)) are first licensed is relatively high or relatively low. Is this position entirely within the lexical layer (for present purposes, entirely within VP), or is it above the licensing-position of, for instance, objects.

For the second question, two kinds of answers have been offered. Chomsky (1995:Chapter Four, 1998, and 1999) suggests that the relevant licensing is accomplished by elements which need to be present 'anyway' - that is, heads which serve central semantic functions. The head which corresponds to the anchoring specification of tense and modality (T) is the element which licenses subject properties (i.e. T licenses both Position 1 and Position 2); the head which introduces the external argument is also the head which licenses object properties. That is, this head (Chomsky's 'v', Kratzer's (1994, 1996) 'Voice') licenses both external arguments and Position 3). (It follows from this general approach that there can be no principle restricting the number of specifier-positions to one.)

The second class of answers which has been offered to question (ii) involves the postulation of phrase structural projections whose sole purpose it is to license bare nominal arguments - the notorious AGR-projections so characteristic of syntactic analysis of the late 80's and early to mid 90's. On this view, each of Position 1, Position 2 and Position 3 would be the specifier of a distinct head. In one commonly accepted conception at least, Position Three is the specifier of an object agreement projection, Position Two is the specifier of the tense projection, and Position One is the specifier of a subject agreement projection.

On this view, the problem of matching the choice of VP-internal arguments with the choice of licensing mechanisms in the 'inflectional layer' (Rizzi (1997)) arises more urgently, since it must be ensured, for instance, that no object agreement projection is present if no bare nominal argument is selected as an internal argument

In what follows, I will have something fairly specific to say about question (i) (where external arguments originate). I will have little to say here about question (ii) though much of the material to be considered will be relevant for that discussion.

Before proceeding with all of that though, I would like to make a general observation that I think has not been sufficiently emphasized. This system in no way requires that clauses have subjects. If a particular set of lexical choices should lead to a situation in which there were no bare nominal arguments within VP, what would go wrong? Something would go wrong only if that set of choices interacted poorly with some forced choice in the inflectional layer - if some head whose presence was obligatory, for instance, bore a feature that required the presence of a DP - say in its specifier. But in the general scheme of things as laid out here, it is very unlikely that that could be a general requirement (one which would hold of every language). Inflectional heads are (on this view) the principal locus of inter-language variation. Whatever kind of feature it is, then, that requires the presence of DP within the inflectional layer in some languages should be subject to the same potential for variation as other aspects of the inflectional system.

Unadorned then, this general view of clausal organization predicts the existence of languages in which there will be no general requirement that clauses have 'subjects' (or indeed any DP-arguments). I think that this is a correct property of the system, and that Irish is, in fact, a language in which the subject-requirement (the EPP of Chomsky (1982)) is not imposed. The first part of this paper reviews and adds to the evidence that this is a reasonable way of looking at Irish clausal structure.

2. ABSENCE OF EPP EFFECTS

One of the more celebrated properties of Irish syntax is the rigid VSO order (more accurately [Verb (Subj) (Obj) (Complement) X]) characteristic of its finite clauses:

(4)a.   Thóg sí teach dófa   ar an Mhullach Dubh.
          raised she house for-them on the
          'She built a house for them in Mullaghduff.'

  b.   Do   fuair sé nuachtán Meiriceánach óna   dheartháir
          PAST got he newspaper American   from-his brother
          an lá cheana.
          the-other-day
          'He got an American paper from his brother the other day.'

In earlier work (McCloskey 1996a, 1996b), I argued for a particular way of understanding the basic facts of Irish finite clauses which involved two core assumptions:
    (i) V raises to T in finite clauses (and no further)
    (ii) EPP is inactive and Position 1 of (1) is as a consequence always empty[5]
    The ultimate effect of this combination of assumptions is illustrated in (6) for a simple example like (5):

(5)   D' ól sí deoch uisce
        PAST drink she drink water
        'She drank a drink of water.'

(6)

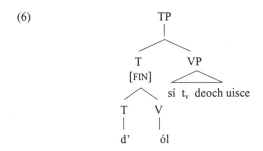

This treatment has a number of advantages. Most immediately, it provides a reasonably accurate account of the basic facts of order, constituency and ellipsis in Irish finite clauses (McCloskey 1991a, McCloskey 1996b, Duffield 1995, Carnie and Harley 1998) and places all these observations in a plausible typological context. The detailed discussion is in the references cited; I will not rehearse the arguments here, but rather sketch just one set of observations - for exemplification, and because they will be useful at a later point in the discussion.
    There is in Irish an ellipsis process which is used in the responsive function and in a variety of other contexts. In its most usual form, this process results in finite clauses which consist only of the finite verb (we will consider at a later point in the discussion some cases in which there is more material present than this). The assertion in (4a), for instance, could be followed naturally by the dialogue in (7):

(7)a.   A-r   thóg?
         INTERR-[PAST] raised
         'Did she?'

     b.   Creidim gu-r   thóg
         I-believe C-PAST raised.
         'I believe she did.'

     c.

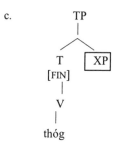

This ellipsis process mimics all the properties of VP-Ellipsis in English (McCloskey 1991a, Fiengo and May 1994). Given the proposal we are developing here, the process can be understood as ellipsis of the complement of T (the boxed XP of (7c)), with the finite verb 'surviving' the ellipsis because it has raised out of VP to T. (Compare Hebrew (Doron 1990, Sherman 1997, Doron 1999), Ndendeule (Ngonyani 1996), and possibly also Japanese, Chinese and Korean (Otani and Whitman 1991, Hoji 1998).)

On this view, Irish is unlike English in exactly two respects:
(i) since in English main verbs do not raise as they do in Irish, main verbs never survive VP-ellipsis in English.
(ii) since in Irish subjects do not raise as they do in English, subjects do not in general survive VP-ellipsis in Irish.

Irish, Hebrew and Ndendeule are alike with respect to the first property; Irish differs from Hebrew and Ndendeule only in the second property.

I will return to a more detailed examination of this process later in the paper. For now, it seems reasonable to conclude that the proposal about clausal organization sketched earlier allows us to understand this otherwise idiosyncratic process in Irish and to relate it in a reasonable way to the ellipsis processes in other languages which it so closely resembles.

All of these facts are open to other interpretations of course. If one believes, for instance, that the EPP holds universally, then one might propose that every VSO clause has the subject DP in a relatively low position (inside VP or in one of the lower inflectional positions associated with subject-properties) and that the specifier of TP is occupied by a null expletive pro (in effect taking every VSO clause to be a transitive expletive construction):

(8)

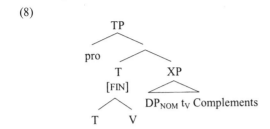

Languages of this general type do exist, I believe, and they show the range of properties that one might expect them to. Given what is currently understood of expletives, and their relation to nominative associates, two things might be expected given (8): (i) that the order [pro V DP X] would alternate with the order: [DP V t X], and (ii) that the nominative DP of (8) would show some trace of the definiteness restriction

There very likely are 'VSO languages' which show just these properties. It is possible, for instance, that the large number of VSO languages which exhibit a regular VSO - SVO alternation might be analyzable in these terms.[6] Irish, however, is not among these languages. SVO structures, as is well known, are completely impossible and there is no restriction on the range of DP's that may appear in the post-verbal subject position (a point we return to later).

On the face of it, then, the analysis schematized in (8) is not a particularly plausible alternative. What would be more interesting, though, would be to try to make a positive case - to try to show that the inactivity of the EPP is a parameter in the old sense Baker (1996b: 6-9) - a single switch whose setting one way or another determines an apparently diverse range of effects. I think that a case of this kind can be made, although much unclarity remains. In the following sections I argue that there are at least three properties of Irish clauses (beyond those already discussed) which can all be seen as reflecting a single parameter setting - the inactivity in the language of the EPP.

2.1 Subject-less Clauses

Irish has a large number of clause-types which, it has been argued (McCloskey 1996b), entirely lack 'subjects'. That is, these are clause-types which instantiate the possibility alluded to in the introductory section - clauses whose initial lexical array includes no bare nominal arguments and which as a consequence deploy none of the morphosyntactic mechanisms implicated in the morphosyntax of subjecthood. There are a number of sub-cases. One important one is the class of clauses built around unaccusative verbs - or more exactly the subclass of unaccusative verbs called 'salient unaccusatives' in McCloskey 1996b, a class which happens to have the property of selecting only PP and/or CP arguments.

(9)a.   Chuaigh de mo neart.
          went   of my strength
          'My strength waned.'

   b.   Bhreáthaigh ar an aimsir.
          became-fine on the weather
          'The weather became nice.'

An additional class of basically the same type is the class of impersonal passives derived from unaccusative verbs:

(10)a.   go bhfuil trialtha chó maith agat
          C is   proved so good by-you
          'that you have proved (to be) so good'

   b.   nuair a bhí tráite síos uaidh
          when C was ebbed down from-it
          'when the tide ebbed from around it'

(11)a.   nuair a bhí bogaithe ag an lá
          when C was softened by the day
          'when the day had become milder'

   b.   conus atá iompuighthe amach aige
          how is turned   out   by-him
          'how he has turned out'

In addition to these, there is a large class of lexicalized or semi-lexicalized expressions which show the same fundamental property:

(12)a.   Ná   fuil ort   fós?
          NEG INTERR C is on-you yet
          'Are you not dressed yet?'

   b.   Tá thiar orm (le   mo chuid oibre).
          is back on-me with my share work [GEN]
          'I am behind (with my work).'

(13)a.   Beidh daor ort.
          will-be dear on-you
          'You'll be sorry.'

   b.   Bhí linn!
          was with-us
          We had won!'

McCloskey (1996b) develops a set of arguments that in such clause-types no argument is promoted and further that they also lack null expletives. These are cases, it is argued, in which T is the only functional projection in the inflectional layer (those projections whose role it is to license bare DP-arguments are not projected since there are no DP-arguments to be licensed). Since furthermore EPP is inactive, no element appears in the specifier of T. That is, these are minimal clauses in a real sense - consisting only of a lexical projection and a T-projection.

2.2 Optionality of Raising

McCloskey (1986) documents that (Subject to Subject) Raising is systematically optional in Irish. The subject of the non-finite complement to a raising verb may appear either within the matrix clause (as in (14a)) or within the complement (as seen in (14b))[7.]

(14)a.   thaibhsigh súile na   deilbhe   di   a bheith iompaithe dearg
          appeared   eyes the[GEN] statue[GEN] to-her be[-FIN] turned   red
          'the eyes of the statue seemed to her to have turned red'   LG160

    b.   Thaibhsigh dó   na soilse a bheith níos boige
          appeared   to-him the lights be [-FIN] more soft [COMP]
          'The lights seemed to him to be softer.'   LG179

When the relevant DP's are pronominal, it can be seen that a DP raised to the matrix appears in nominative case (15a) but that it appears in a default accusative form when it remains in the complement clause (15b):

(15)a.   thaibhsigh siad   di   a bheith iompaithe dearg
          appeared   they[NOM] to-her be [-FIN] turned   red
          'they seemed to her to have turned red'

    b.   Thaibhsigh dó   iad   a bheith níos boige
          appeared   to-him them[ACC] be [-FIN] more soft [COMP]
          'They seemed to him to be softer.'

Further, the raised DP agrees with the matrix raising verb (16a), but when the DP 'chooses' to remain within the complement clause in the accusative case, the matrix raising verb appears in an invariant form known as the 'analytic' form, which encodes no agreement (16b):

(16)a.   Do   ráinís   an uair sin a bheith i gContae an Chláir.
          PAST chance[S2] that time be [-FIN] in County   Clare
          'You happened at that time to be in County Clare.'

b.   ráingig   an uair seo í   a bheith   i   gContae an Chláir
       chanced this-time   her be [-FIN] in County   Clare
       'She happened at this time to be in County Clare.'   PF109

Detailed argumentation can be found in McCloskey 1986 and I will not repeat those arguments here. I will concentrate rather on the following question - what aspects of Irish grammar make available the two options seen in (14) - (16)?

The option seen in (14b), (15b) and (16b) depends, in the first place, on the availability of a device for licensing accusative case in the subject position of a non-finite clause (as in Latin and Classical Greek).[8] The availability of this option will be a central part of explaining why raising is not obligatory, and of explaining why the un-raised subject has the form it has (accusative).

The availability of this device, though, cannot be the whole story. Three distinct factors (some having to do with properties of the raised nominal, some having to do with properties of the matrix clause) drive raising in an English case like (17):

(17)   She tends [$_{IP}$ t to go to bed early].

Raising of *she* in (17) satisfies case requirements of the raised pronoun. In addition it satisfies (i) agreement requirements and (ii) the EPP-requirement of the matrix clause. If EPP were active in Irish, (14b), (15b) and (16b) should be impossible. In the absence of raising, EPP would be unsatisfied in these examples and they should be ungrammatical. The grammaticality of (14a), (15a), and (16a) indicates the separation of EPP-requirements from Case and agreement requirements argued for in Chomsky 1998 and in Chomsky 1999. Raising in these cases is motivated by the case requirements of the raised DP (nominative and therefore unlicensable in the lower clause), and by agreement properties of the matrix finite verb complex (see McCloskey 1996b:270-273 for more detailed discussion).[9]

2.3 Existential Sentences

Consider now the structure of existential sentences in Irish. In their finite guise, they show the structure schematized in (18a) and exemplified in (18b) and in the two examples of (19).

(18)a.   [$_{TP}$ be [FIN] DP ann]

b.   Tá   taibhsí ann.
       be[PRES] ghosts in-it
       'There are ghosts.'

(19)a.   Bhí cuid mhór bidh   ann.
           was a lot   food [GEN] in-it
           'There was a lot of food.'

b.   Beidh   amadáin i gcónaí ann.
       be[FUT] fools   always in-it
       'There will always be fools.'

The element *ann* is a locative XP - originally, and probably still, a PP, meaning literally 'in it' but conventionally used to mean 'there':

(20)a.   Cuireadh   ann muid anuraidh.
          put [PAST-AUT] there us   last-year
          'We were sent there last year.'

   b.   Bhí sé ann.
          was he there
          'He was there.'

It is clear that *ann* is a predicate. The evidence is strong that *tá/a bheith* takes a small clause complement (Chung and McCloskey (1987)), in which case DP of (18a) is the subject of the small clause (raised, as we will see, to Position 2 of (1)), and *ann* is its predicate. *Ann*, furthermore, appears in predicate-position in the full range of small clause contexts documented in Chung and McCloskey (1987):

(21)   Is   fada [$_{SC}$ daoine ann a ghéilleann do phiseoga].
          COP[PRES] long   people in-it C yield[PRES] to superstitions
          'There have long been people who believe in superstitions.'

Existential *ann* appears in an additional position characteristic of predicative expressions - in the predicative copula construction, which has the schematic structure in (22) (Doherty 1996, Carnie 1995, Doherty 1997, DeGraff 1997, Legate 1997, Legate 1998):

(22)   [Tense   XP[PRED] (do+)DP]

(23a) illustrates the basic case. (23b) illustrates the use of *ann* as a predicative expression in the construction:

(23)a.   Is   as   Doire dó.
          COP[PRES] out-of Derry to-him
          'He's from Derry.'

   b.   Ní   ann dúinn a thuilleadh
          COP[NEG] in-it to-us any more
          'We don't exist any more.' AGMTS46

If all this is on the right track, the structure underlying existentials must include at least the substructure (24):

(24)   [sc DP [Pred ann]]

where *ann* is an existential predicate. That the predicate is semantically contentful (that *ann* is itself the element which corresponds to the existence predicate) can be seen from the fact that it can function as contrastive focus in the cleft construction:

(25)   Ba   ann a bhí   an saol neamh-bhuartha an t-am sin.
            COP [PAST] in-it C be [PAST] the life   untroubled   that time
            'It really is true that there was an untroubled life at that time.' RGB71

(25) is difficult to render in idiomatic English, but its pragmatic effect derives exactly from the normal understanding of focus constructions combined with the idea that the alternative set in (25) is the pair {'exist'/'not exist'}.

This partial analysis raises a number of difficult questions. The first has to do with the status of *ann*. We have seen that *ann* is a (semantically contentful) existential predicate. But it is also the kind of locative pro-form which is characteristic of existential syntax quite generally (Clark 1978, Lyons 1967, Lyons 1968, Freeze 1992) It seems important, in particular, to make a theoretical link among Irish *ann*, English *there* and French *y*. One possibility that suggests itself immediately is to follow a line of thought initiated in Moro 1989, Hoekstra and Mulder 1990, and Moro 1997, who propose that elements like existential *there* in English are predicates which raise to Spec,TP to satisfy the EPP. The fact that such raising fails to take place in Irish, on this view, would be a further reflection of the fact that the EPP is inactive in this language. This account has the advantage of making a direct link between the locative pro-forms of Irish and English, and of accounting for the different surface syntax found in the two languages in terms of an independently attested difference between them: the EPP is active in English, inactive in Irish.

This argument must be considered very tentative, since it rests on an understanding of elements like expletive *there* which is controversial and which may or may not turn out to be viable.[10]

What is clear though is the following. Existential constructions represent one of the constructions where one can most reliably expect to find impersonal constructions in a language - constructions involving an expletive element and an associated indefinite argument. In Irish, though, there is no sign either of an expletive element or of the expected definiteness restriction: Definites, proper names and pronouns appear freely in the pivot position:

(26)a.   Táimse   ann ó   roimh Abraham a bheith ann.
            be[PRES S1] in-it from before   be[-FIN] in-it
            'There was me before there was Abraham.'

b. Bhí an dara   cogadh domhanda ann   na blianta sin
    was the second war   global   in-it those years
    'There was the Second World War in those years,'   EB118

c. Tá   tú   ann.
    be[PRES] you in-it
    'You exist.'/'There's you.'   AFAP118

This property too will fall plausibly into place if Irish is a language in which the EPP is inactive.

3. INTERIM SUMMARY

The kinds of arguments I've been trying to marshal here are a little difficult to make, because they almost all involve the **absence** of some feature, configuration or construction (the absence of null expletives in particular). And there can be many reasons why a given one of them might be absent from a given language. Nevertheless, the observations gathered here have, I think, a certain cumulative force. All of these apparent idiosyncrasies of Irish grammar fall into place in a reasonably natural way if EPP is not an active force in the language.

4. PARTIAL RAISING

Say we assume, then, that Irish is a language in which the EPP is inactive and that what that means more particularly is that Position 1 of (1) is never activated.[11] Earlier versions of this general line of analysis (McCloskey 1991a, for instance), as well as the version alluded to in Chomsky 1993, assumed that the external argument (when present) did not raise out of the lexical domain at all. It has become steadily clearer, though, that this view cannot be right. **If** VP contains one or more bare DP-arguments, then the most prominent of them **is** subject to a raising requirement. It must raise to a position to the right of, and lower than, the position occupied by the finite verb (a position which I identify with Position 2 of (1)). This is evident from the following kinds of considerations:

4.1 Passive and Unaccusative Structures

In passive and unaccusative structures, raising of a DP internal argument to the 'nominative position' is obligatory in Irish just as it is in well-studied languages (see McCloskey (1996b) for detailed argumentation). For a 'salient unaccusative' like that in (27a), the evidence is very strong and very clear that the single argument (a PP) remains in complement position inside VP. But the evidence is equally strong and equally clear that when that single argument is a bare DP (as in (27b)), that argument has raised out of VP into 'subject position' (which for us must mean Position 2 rather than Position 1 of (1)).

(27)a.   Neartaigh   ar a ghlór.
         strengthened on his voice
         'His voice strengthened.'

    b.   Neartaigh   a ghlór.
         strengthened his voice
         'His voice strengthened.'

This contrast emerges in a number of ways, but most obviously in the periphrastic progressive aspect where it is evident that the PP-argument remains low (inside VP, I believe) but that the DP-argument has raised (to the standard post-verbal 'subject-position').[12]

(28)a.   Tá ag neartú   ar a ghlór.
         is strengthen[PROG] on his voice
         'His voice is strengthening.'

    b.   Tá a ghlór ag neartú.
         is his voice strengthen[PROG]
         'His voice is strengthening.'

The complex causative/inchoative alternation seen in (29) reveals a similar pattern. In the a-example, the CAUSE argument occupies the higher nominative position, but in the b-example, the subject of the lower predication occupies that position, as is shown clearly again, by the periphrastic form in (30).

(29)a.   Rinne sin leanná:n dínn.
         made that lovers   of-us
         'That made us lovers.'

    b.   Rinne leanná:n dínn.
         made lovers   of-us
         'We became lovers.'

(30)   go raibh cabaire breá ag déanamh díom
         C was   chatterer fine make[PROG] of-me
         'that I was becoming a fine chatterer'   FBF33

Exactly similar observations hold in the case of the perfective passive, where it is clear that a bare DP complement of the passive participle must raise in the routine and familiar way, as shown in (31):

(31)a.   Tá sé   críochnaithe againn
          Is it[NOM] finished   by-us
          'It has been finished by us.'

    b.   *Tá críochnaithe sé   againn.
          is finished   it[NOM] by-us
          'It has been finished by us.'

As in the case of the unaccusatives discussed earlier, PP-complements need not and must not undergo raising:

(32)a.   Tá labhartha agam leo.
          is spoken   by-me with-them
          'I have spoken to them.'

    b.   *Tá leo   labhartha agam.
          is with-them spoken   by-me

The pattern suggested so far, then, is that the post-verbal position (which we have identified tentatively with Position 2) is associated with the licensing of bare DP arguments and that its specifier position is categorically restricted in the way that this would suggest.[13]

4.2 Adverbial Distribution

There is a class of adverbial elements which can appear following the subject but preceding complements and adverbials. This class includes *riamh* (ever), *go fóill* (still, yet), *fós* (still, yet), *choíche* (ever), *i gcónaí* (always), *go minic* (often):

(33)a.   Ní   bhfuair aon bhean riamh roimhe greim láimhe   air.
          NEG took   any woman ever before-it grip hand [GEN] on-him
          'No woman had ever before taken his hand.'   CC17

    b.   Ní   chluinfeadh aon duine   choíche arís Ciarán ag gabháil
          NEG hear[COND] any person ever   again   making
          cheoil
          music[GEN]
          'Noone would ever again hear Ciaran making music.'

    c.   níor   bhuail aon fhear amháin fós liom   a bhfuil a   chuid
          NEG-PAST struck one man   one   yet with-me C is   his share
          éadaigh   ghlain   air.
          clothes[GEN] clean[GEN] on-him
          'I haven't yet met one single man who has his clean clothes on.'   AI6

The members of this class of adverbs are of course familiar from much recent work on constituent order in comparative perspective, and there is good reason to believe (on the basis of that typological evidence) that this class of adverbs attaches relatively high - no lower, in any case, than the edge of VP. If that interpretation is correct, then the fact that the post-verbal subject appears to the left of these adverbs indicates that it has raised out of VP.

There is in addition some evidence of a straightforward kind from within Irish that this class of adverbs attaches outside the Verb Phrase.[14] We have already had occasion to discuss the ellipsis process that produces so-called 'responsive' forms of the finite verb. The crucial examples are repeated in (34) (the three examples read as a dialogue):

(34)a. Thóg sí   teach dófa   ar an Mhullach Dubh.
        raised she house for-them on the
        'She built a house for them in Mullaghduff.'

     b. A-r   thóg?
         INTERR-PAST raised
         'Did she?'

     c. Creidim gu-r   thóg.
         I-believe C-[PAST] raised
         'I believe she did.'

As we have seen, this ellipsis process can be understood as elision of the complement of T (following raising of finite V to T). Now, exactly the same class of adverbs which may follow the subject can be stranded under this ellipsis process:

(35)a. An   bhfuair tú áit   chónaithe?
        INTERR got   you place living[GEN]
        'Did you find a place to live?'

     b. Ní   bhfuair go fóill.
         NEG got   yet
         'I didn't yet.'

(36)a. An   raibh tú riamh ar an Chlochán Liath?
        INTERR were you ever on the
        'Were you ever in Dunloe?'

     b. Bhí go minic. / Cha raibh go fóill.
         was often   NEG was   yet
         'I often was.'/'I wasn't yet.'

The adverbs of (35) and (36) must clearly be attached at some point higher than the attachment-point of the (elided) complement of T - perhaps adjoined to the complement of T, perhaps in some functional projection above that again. In this instance, at least, then, we can be sure that the adverbs of (33) must be above and outside the Verb Phrase.

Even if one assumes that the relevant class also has the possibility of attaching lower - inside the Verb Phrase, say - the point we wish to make can be made for a more restricted subclass of cases. Say one assumed a bifurcated Verb Phrase - vP for the external argument if there is one, VP for internal arguments. Say one assumed in addition that the relevant class of adverbs has the option of attaching to the lower category (VP). The fact that the crucial ordering possibility exists for unaccusatives still indicates that raising out of VP has applied in this subset of cases at least:

(37)a.   Fásann   na préataí   i gcónaí sa   lagán.
          grow[PRES] the potatoes always   in-the hollow
          'The potatoes always grow in the hollow.'

    b.   Níor   phréamaigh na crainn ariamh ar an oileán.
          NEG-PAST root   the trees   ever   on the island
          'The trees never took root on the island.'

    c.   Ní   tháinig   na daoine choíche 'na bhaile.
          NEG come[PAST] the people ever   home
          'The people never came home.'

4.3 Quantifier Stranding (Quantifier Float)

Confirmation of these conclusions comes from a consideration of Quantifier Float phenomena. Quantifier Float has not been systematically studied in Irish to date, and caution is therefore in order. Certain tentative and interim conclusions, however, seem reasonable. DP's which are built around the post-nominal quantifier *uilig* 'all' (see for instance (40a)) are of the type which we might expect, on the basis of typological considerations, to support quantifier float. This expectation is born out as is clear from examples like (39). The background here is that it is uncontroversial that Object Shift is obligatory in non-finite clauses (McCloskey and Sells 1988, Guilfoyle 1990, Duffield 1995, Carnie 1995, Harley 1995, and much subsequent work). Since verb-fronting applies only in finite clauses, this ultimately yields an SOVX order in non-finite clauses (abstracting away for the moment from some complex and interesting dialectal variations):

(38)   B'fhearr liom [$_{TP}$ iad   na páistí   a thabhairt 'na bhaile].
        I-would-prefer   them the children bring [-FIN] home
        'I would prefer for them to bring the children home.'

Consider now (39):[15]

(39)   Ar   cheart domh na véarsaí a rá   uilig duit?
        INTERR should to-me the verses   say [-FIN] all   for-you
        'Should I sing all the verses for you?'

The quantifier *uilig*, although construed with the fronted object *na véarsaí*, appears in exactly the position that one would have thought corresponded to the thematic position of the object. From this (and other observations we will consider shortly), it seems reasonable to conclude either that *uilig* appears in the origin-site of Object Shift, or else that it attaches to a phrase containing the trace of Object Shift. Under either interpretation, we have a diagnostic for A-movement. Consider in that light, examples like (40) and (41).

(40)a.   An   bhfuil   sibh   uilig sásta   anois?
         INTERR be[PRES] you[PL] all   satisfied now
         'Are you all satisfied now?'

    b.   An   bhfuil   sibh sásta   uilig anois?
         INTERR be[PRES] you satisfied all   now
         'Are you all satisfied now?'   SAB208

(41)a.   An   bhfuil   na préataí   uilig curtha agat?
         INTERR be[PRES] the potatoes all   sown by-you
         'Have you sown all the potatoes?'

    b.   An   bhfuil   na préataí   curtha uilig agat?
         INTERR be[PRES] the potatoes sown   all   by-you
         'Have you sown all the potatoes?'   SAB240

Here we are dealing with subjects in finite clauses, but parity of reasoning suggests that the occurrence of *uilig* which is separated from the DP with which it is construed also marks a lower 'subject-position' and therefore signals an application of A-movement. It follows, obviously, that the surface position of the post-verbal subject is not its position of origin.[16]

4.4 Semantic Properties of Subjects

There has grown up since the late 80's and early 90's a substantial body of work which examines the interpretive possibilities open to classes of DP, and which tries to make connections between the interpretive possibilities and the syntactic position occupied (at some relevant level of representation) by the DP. Diesing (1992) is one of the more authoritative and influential developments of this line of thought. What Diesing shows (simplifying a little) is that so-called 'strong' readings are characteristic of higher positioning and that so-called 'weak' readings are characteristic of lower positioning. For Diesing, the crucial boundary-point is the VP-boundary. DP's trapped within VP at the relevant level of representation are within the domain of existential closure and form part of the nuclear scope of larger structures of quantification. DP's which raise out of the VP make their semantic contribution in the restrictive clause of the quantification structure. The empirical consequences of these effects are the following:

(i) strong quantifiers may not remain within VP (hence may not be the pivot of an existential);
(ii) bare plurals in subject position (outside VP) have generic readings;
(iii) weak DP's in subject position have 'presuppositional' or 'partitive' interpretations. Weak DP's within VP (in the pivot of an existential for instance) show only 'cardinal' interpretations;
(iv) subjects of individual level predications have generic interpretations only.

With respect to these phenomena, Irish post-verbal subjects behave exactly, as far as I can tell, like English pre-verbal subjects. That is, bare plurals (when subjects of stage-level predications) may have either weak or strong interpretations. The strong (generic) interpretation is favored in (42) because the present tense in Irish tends to be gnomic:

(42)   Imreann   girseachaí leadóg.
         play[PRES] girls   tennis
         'Girls play tennis.'

The weak interpretation is favored in (43) because the combination of past tense and progressive aspect favors episodic interpretations:

(43)a.   Bhí   girseachaí ag imirt   leadóg sa   tsráid.
         be [PAST] girls   play [PROG] tennis in-the street
         'Girls were playing tennis in the street.'

   b.   bhí   cearca fraoich ag screadaigh áit   inteacht
         be[PAST] moor-hens   cry[PROG]   place some
         'Moor-hens were calling somewhere.'   EB143

Similarly in (44):

(44)   D'fhásadh   cruithneacht agus coirce sna   goirt.
         grow[PAST-HABIT] wheat   and corn in-the fields
         'Wheat and corn used to grow in the fields.'

Partitive readings of weak DP's are routinely available in subject position:

(45)   Labhair   cuid de na h-ionadaithe   ag an chruinniú.
            speak[PAST] some of the representatives at   the meeting
            'Some of the representatives spoke at the meeting.'

The readings available in (42) - (45) indicate, if this body of work is on the right track, that the 'subject' is outside whatever constituent it is (for Diesing VP) that determines the domain of existential closure. To the extent that this line of thought is reliable, we have additional reason to believe that the post-verbal subject in Irish is not inside VP.

5. SECOND INTERIM SUMMARY

The overall conclusion seems to be that in finite clauses the most prominent bare nominal argument (if there is one) must raise out of VP to a position lower than, and to the right of, T.

The point we are at, then, is that we take Irish to be a language in which the highest inflectional A-position (Position 1) is systematically unavailable. In this, Irish differs from most of the well-studied European languages. However, it resembles those languages which have transitive expletive constructions (like Icelandic for instance), in exploiting Position 2. This is the position to which the most prominent of the bare DP-arguments within VP must raise for licensing (external arguments in the case of transitives and unergatives; internal arguments in the case of unaccusatives and passives). For our analysis to go through here, it must be true of this position:

(i)   that it is restricted to phrases of category D (unlike Position 1 - the position, we have hypothesized, which the EPP cares about);
(ii) that its specifier be filled only by way of movement (there are no Position 2 expletives).

It is an interesting and important question how these properties can be guaranteed, but let us observe at this point that the analysis, if on the right track, provides evidence for the distributed view of subject properties with which we opened the paper. In the first place, we have seen evidence for the view that three of the properties often attributed to subjects - their obligatoriness, their distinctive morphosyntax and the characteristic range of semantic roles with which they are linked, are in fact associated with at least three distinct positions and the heads associated with those positions. We have also seen the typological peeling apart of some of the subject properties which was discussed in the opening sections of the paper. Irish is a language, we have argued, in which the obligatoriness property does not hold (if we are right, then this language has a broad range of truly subject-less clauses - all of those clauses, in fact, in which there happen not to be any bare DP arguments within VP). Even in Irish, though, with its restricted set of subject positions, it remains true that subjecthood is distributed across two positions - the position associated with θ-licensing and the position associated with morphosyntactic licensing of bare DP-arguments.

6. THE LOCUS OF SEMANTIC ROLE ASSIGNMENT

We have now seen some evidence for the basic correctness of the view of subjecthood outlined in the opening sections of the paper, and we have in addition seen some evidence for the more controversial view that the EPP is not a universal feature of natural language grammars - a position which is natural within the broader framework of assumptions within which we are working, but which has not been widely advocated (or even widely considered).

There is another controversial element within this broader setting which has been the focus of a good deal of discussion. This is the issue of what the lowest 'subject position' (the thematic position) is. Two influential points of view have emerged in this connection, which have rather different implications for larger questions about how clauses are organized.

The proliferation of categories within the inflectional layer has made it difficult to point to cases where one can say with confidence that the subject has remained within VP. Many effective and attractive analyses have been developed which depend crucially on the idea that under certain circumstances in certain languages, subjects may remain in some position lower than Position 1. What has proved much more difficult has been to assemble clear cases where one can be sure that the subject remains fully within the Verb Phrase, rather than being in some relatively low position within the inflectional layer.

This unclarity has combined with a revival of interest in some older concerns which were articulated clearly by Alec Marantz in the early 1980's. One of the properties of the Internal Subject Hypothesis is that it blurs in a fundamental way the distinction between internal arguments and the external argument (a distinction introduced by Williams (1981)). If all semantic role assignment is accomplished within lexical projections, then the structural difference between internal and external arguments is lessened.

The distinction remains important, though. Marantz (1984:23-31) in particular, argues that there is a fundamental difference in the way that semantic roles are assigned to internal arguments and the way in which they are assigned to external arguments. According to Marantz, complements are arguments of the verb and are assigned their semantic role by the verb alone. Subjects, on the other hand, are arguments of VP, and are assigned their role by the VP - which is, in turn, a composition of the verb with its internal arguments. Angelika Kratzer (1994, 1996) returned to these concerns and showed in particular that no currently known theory of argument structure can account for these observations, if it is assumed that the external argument is a direct argument of the verb. She proposed instead that there is a functional projection (which she calls 'Voice') which immediately dominates VP, and that it is this functional projection which is responsible for the assignment of roles associated with external arguments.[17]

The proposal found in Chomsky 1993, Chomsky 1995 (which adapts earlier ideas of Hale and Keyser 1993) is close in spirit to Kratzer's, since it also assumes a distinguished element (in this case a phonologically null verbal element to which lower verbs adjoin) which is responsible for the assignment of the roles characteristic of external arguments. For both Kratzer and Chomsky, the crucial element has VP as its complement, and internal arguments originate within VP. For both also, unaccusative structures simply lack the higher projection and include only (the lower) VP.

Both of these sets of proposals mark, in an important sense, a return to one of the earliest versions of the Internal Subject Hypothesis - that of Koopman and Sportiche (1991). Koopman and Sportiche held that the external argument is not actually internal to VP, but is rather adjoined to VP. The adjunction relation is the structural correlate of the predication relation which governs the realization of the external argument. The principal difference between this proposal and the more recent ones is the postulation of an empty head ('Voice' for Kratzer, 'v' for Chomsky) to regularize the phrase structural expression of the crucial semantic relation.

All of these proposals are conservative in the sense that they preserve the essential insight of the Internal Subject Hypothesis - namely that semantic role assignment for subjects takes place at a position lower than the position(s) in which morphosyntactic properties of subjects are licensed, and that the crucial position is in a very local syntactic relation with the projection (VP) in which internal arguments are realized.

But the postulation of a separate head responsible for the realization of external arguments has permitted the formulation of proposals which depart more radically from these assumptions. Since the head responsible for internal role assignment (V) is distinct from the head ('Voice' or 'v') responsible for external role assignment, it becomes possible to formulate theories in which the two heads are in a less local syntactic relation. Specifically, it becomes possible to propose that certain functional projections (Aspect, or the Object Agreement projection) intervene between the two. A variety of such theories has been proposed (see especially Travis (1991), Koizumi (1995), Harley (1995)). They seem to draw their plausibility from two sources. The first is that, as we have seen, it has proved unexpectedly difficult to point with confidence to cases where the external argument appears unequivocally within VP (in a position, say, below the target-position for Object Shift). If the subject originates below all the inflectional projections, why should it prove so difficult to document cases in which it remains in such a position? The second is that certain difficulties for the theory of locality of movement (the difficulty, in particular, of how the subject can cross the position of a shifted object) disappear if one assumes that the subject always originates in a position higher than that of the shifted object. One version of this set of ideas is schematized in (46) in which V_e is the element responsible for introducing the external argument, and V_i is the element responsible for introducing the internal argument(s) (correspondingly DP_e and DP_i represent the external and internal (DP) arguments respectively).

(46)

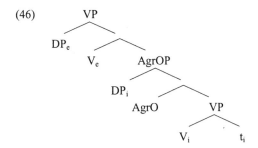

The hypothesis underlying theories of this general kind has come to be known as the Split VP Hypothesis.

Duffield (1995) and Carnie and Harley (1998: especially Chapter Four) both develop a version of these ideas and argue for it on the basis of Irish data specifically. In the version developed by Carnie and Harley (1998), it is assumed that the element which introduces external arguments is above an aspect projection, which is in turn above the projection in which shifted objects are licensed. This last projection, in turn, dominates VP - in which the verb and its internal arguments originate. That is, they assume a structure like (47):

(47)

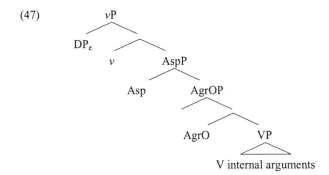

in which two functional projections intervene between the position in which external arguments are θ-licensed and the position(s) in which internal arguments are initially licensed.

The 'Asp' head of (47) is the locus where, for instance, the progressive particle (McCloskey 1983) *ag* originates. This particle (historically but not synchronically the preposition 'at') combines with the non-finite form of the verb to form progressive verbs which in turn then appear in a variety of syntactic contexts:

(48)   Bíonn   siad i gcónaí ag ól   tae.
         be[PRES-HABIT] they always   drink[PROG] tea
         'They are always drinking tea.'

V-raising to Asp in (47) produces complex progressive verb forms like *ag ól*.

I want to end this paper by considering some facts which suggest that the more conservative view, with its strict bifurcation between the thematic and the inflectional layer, is closer to being correct.[18]

6.1 Another Case Marking Strategy

The crucial evidence will involve a different way of marking subjects in Irish. Subjects of non-finite clauses and subjects of small clauses, may, under certain circumstances, be marked by the dative preposition *do*. This way of marking subjects has deep historical roots in the language; it occurs in every modern dialect and has been well described in traditional sources. It has not, though, figured much so far in generative work on the syntax of the language.

These facts will be of interest to us here for at least two reasons. They will in the first place provide us with a way of arguing about the point of origin of external arguments (the issue under contention in the debate about the Split VP Hypothesis). In addition, though, they raise their own questions about the nature of subjecthood. This is so because all informal descriptions of the phenomenon (including the one just given here) begin with the statement that the marking strategy in question is restricted to 'subjects'. If the broader point of view developed here is on the right track, then this reference too to 'subjecthood' must be theoretically eliminable.

The examples in (49) - (51) will give an initial sense of how this case-strategy works.

(49)   I ndiaidh dona Coláistí Ullmhúcháin   druidim
        after   to-the Colleges preparation[GEN] close[-FIN]
        'after the Training Colleges closed'

(50)   tar éis do lucht   na Parlaiminte   an caisleán a thógáil
        after   to people the Parliament[GEN] the castle   take[-FIN]
        'after the Parliamentarians took the castle'   STL233

(51)   Cén fáth domh an t-ábhar seo   a tharraingt chugam?
        why   to-me the subject DEMON draw[-FIN]   to-me
        'Why do I/should I/have I bring/brought this topic up?' CST56

In all cases, the dative preposition *do* marks the subject of a non-finite clause.

Notice that both subject and object precede the verb in the transitive structures of (49) - (51). A basic understanding of how non-finite clauses in the language work will be helpful at this point. Consider once again the schematic structure with which we opened our discussion:

(52)

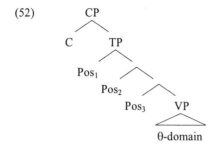

For non-finite clauses, the absence of tense markers, and the absence of verb-raising make it more difficult to determine what the syntax is than in the case of finite clauses. Nevertheless, we can summarize the large body of work on non-finite clauses in Irish by saying that subjects and objects (both normally accusative) occupy respectively Position 2 and Position 3 of (52) and that there is no raising of V to T. Position 1 is unutilized in non-finite clauses, just as in finite clauses (EPP effects are absent as in finite clauses). The ultimate result is the familiar pattern in which DP-complements appear to the left of V, but in which complements of other categories (CP, PP and so on), as well as most classes of adverbial, appear to its right. The other feature that needs to be mentioned is that (accusative) subjects are licensed freely in non-finite clauses independently of the external context. Transitive structures, as a consequence, look like (53):

(53)a.   i ndiaidh é   an t-airgead a thabhairt domh inné
         after   him the money   give[-FIN] to-me yesterday
         'after he had given me the money yesterday'

   b.   Bhí iontas mór air   [$_{TP}$ an t-athair mór é sin a rá]
         was wonder great on-him   the grandfather that say[-FIN]
         'He was very surprised that the grandfather would say such a thing.'

And intransitive structures look like (54). They are as expected; the subject is initial, the object is absent, and as a consequence, the preverbal particle - a marker of transitivity - is also absent:

(54)a.   Is cuimhneach liom [Ciarán labhairt   leat   mar sin]
         I-remember   Ciarán speak[-FIN] with-you like-that
         'I remember Ciaran speaking to you like that.'

   b.   Níor mhaith leat [mé creidbheáil   sa   rud]
         you-wouldn't-like me believe[-FIN] in-the thing
         'You wouldn't like me to believe in the thing.'

I will assume with most work in this area that the particle *a* is the head of the functional projection which licenses accusative case on an object (i.e. it is the head of which Position 3 is the specifier, sometimes called AgrO) and that V raises to right-adjoin to that head, producing complex prosodic words like *a thabhairt* in (53a), or *a rá* in (53b).

Notice that the account just sketched does not incorporate any version of the Split VP Hypothesis, in that it assumes that the thematic domain (VP of (52)) is contained wholly within the structures in which subject and object DP's (object DP's in particular) undergo morphosyntactic licensing.

With this much as background, let us go on to consider subjects marked by *do*.[19]

The examples in (55)-(57) illustrate the case-marking strategy for transitive structures:

(55)   bliain roimh di   bás   a fháil
       year   before to-her death get[-FIN]
       'a year before she died'   DO117

(56)   tar éis dó   an abhainn a chur   de
       after   to-him the river   put[-FIN] of-him
       'after he had put the river behind him'   FEB93

(57)   cad chuige duit   ceist   a chur   air sin?
       why   to-you question put[-FIN] on-that-one
       'Why did you ask that guy?'   LG93

(58)-(60) show the corresponding intransitive structures:

(58)   dhá uair a' chloig tar éis   don   tseirbhís tosú
       two-hours   after   to-the service   begin[-FIN]
       'two hours afer the service began'   SR92

(59)   an t-uabhar faoi ndeara   do Lúicifir titim   ó   na Flaithis
       the pride   the-cause-of to   fall[-FIN] from the Heavens
       'It was pride that caused Lucifer to fall from the Heavens.'   AG42

(60)   tar éis dó   filleadh   ar an gcathair seo
       after   to-him return[-FIN] on the city   DEMON
       'after he (had) returned to this city'   ODR272

This case-marking strategy is unrestricted in terms of the internal properties of IP (it appears, as we have seen, with both transitive and intransitive structures and the dative DP's in question may bear, as we shall see, a broad range of different semantic roles).[20]

The **external** distribution of clauses containing dative subjects, however, is very restricted. In most varieties, such clauses may appear only in adverbial and interrogative contexts (as seen in the examples already presented). Beyond that core distributional pattern, there is considerable variation - dialectal, idiolectal and register-based. Some speakers and some varieties permit clauses containing dative subjects in the complement position of a small subset of lexical heads:

(61)   ní   caoch a mheasann tú   dhom a bheith
         COP[NEG] blind c think   you to-me be[-FIN]
         'It's not blind that you think I am?'   GLL243

Similarly, some speakers and varieties (particularly Munster varieties) permit them in small clause complements of various types:

(62)   Ba   mhinic dhomsa im aonar
         COP [PAST] often   to-me   by-myself
         'I was often alone.'   CLIA86

(63)   is   annamh duit   mar so
         COP [PRES] rare   to-you like this
         'You are rarely like this.'   EDD24

(64)   Ní   fada dhom in bhur gcathair mhór
         COP[NEG] long to-me in your city   great
         'I haven't been long in your great city.'   EDD17

Putting these observations together, we see that dative subjects are licensed in initial position in non-finite clauses and in (some) small clauses. We have seen also that the larger structures in which dative subjects appear have a restricted distribution. Clauses with dative subjects are licensed primarily in adverbial and in interrogative clauses, but are also selected (in some varieties and idiolects) by certain verbs and adjectives.

What are we to make of this? Given the larger framework adopted, we are virtually required to assume that the dative subject appears in the specifier position of some head which bears a feature - call it [DAT] - whose function it is to license DP's prefixed with *do*.[21] [DAT] must be incompatible with a positive specification for finiteness - hence the restriction to non-finite and small clauses. Further, the feature must in turn be sensitive to the external environment in which it appears - being selected by certain instances of C. The core pattern is that only those instances of C associated with an adverbial or interrogative function select (a head bearing) [DAT]. More liberal varieties (those which allow (61) or (62) - (64) permit the selection of [DAT] by a broader variety of C elements. Thus the basic facts can be described.

What head bears the [DAT] feature? Given the apparent similarity in positioning between accusative and dative subjects of non-finite clauses, it would seem initially plausible to assume that they occupy the same position (Position 2 of (1)) as do accusative subjects such as are found in (53) and (54).

This view, however, is not obviously compatible with the selectional restrictions to which clauses containing dative subjects are subject. To account for that restricted distribution, it must be true that the [DAT] feature, or the head which bears the [DAT] feature, is accessible to selection by a higher external head. But Position 2 should not be accessible in this way (it is too deeply embedded). Given the structure in (1), only the head associated with Position 1 should be accessible to external selection (by C, for instance). That being so, we would expect that head position to be the one which bears the feature which licenses dative subjects:

(65)

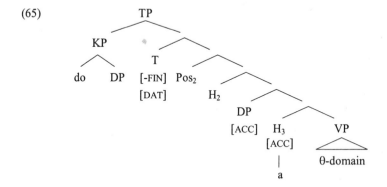

We are thus led to predict a difference in positioning between dative subjects and accusative subjects of non-finite clauses (since clauses containing accusative subjects seem to be absolutely free of lexical restrictions, as documented in some detail by McCloskey and Sells (1988)). Dative subjects should appear in a higher position than accusative subjects. This difference in position is in most cases undetectable, but it emerges in one crucial circumstance.

Negation in Irish is known to occupy a high position - to the left of and above the subject (Chung and McCloskey 1987, McCloskey 1984, McCloskey 1986, Guilfoyle 1990, Duffield 1995). In non-finite clauses (and in small clauses) negation takes the form of a marker *gan*:

(66)a.   B'fhearr liom   gan   iad   mé a fheiceáil.
          I-would-prefer [NEG] them me see[-FIN]
          'I would prefer for them not to see me.'

   b.   Cén fáth   gan   é a bheith   níos saoire?
          what reason [NEG] it be [-FIN] cheaper
          'Why isn't it cheaper?'

Dative subjects, however, **must** appear to the left of negation:

(67)a.   Conas d' aonaránach   gan   a bheith ag braistint aonarach?
            how   to solitary-person [NEG]   be [-FIN]   feel[PROG] solitary
            'How could a solitary person not feel solitary?'   AGMTS102

b.   ní   rabh iongantas dó   gan   mórán muinighin a bheith
      NEG was wonder   to-him [NEG] much trust   be[-FIN]
      aige as
      at-him out-of-him
      'It was no wonder that he had no confidence in him.'   BF199

(68)a.   *Conas gan d'aonaránach a bheith ag braistint aonarach

b.   *ní rabh iongantas gan dó mórán muinighin a bheith aige as

This observation suggests that the dative subjects we are concerned with appear in a higher position than do the more routine accusative subjects - in Position 1 rather than in Position 2, which is, we have assumed, the position in which accusative subjects appear.

Let's turn now to a more detailed consideration of how the licensing of dative subjects works in non-finite and small clauses.

The first thing that should be stressed is that DP's so marked are not thematically restricted in any way. These 'dative subjects' are not the kinds of dative subjects familiar from the literature on inversion and psych-predicates. Such subjects are restricted to bearing an EXPERIENCER role. But it should already be apparent from the examples cited, which show a range of different semantic roles associated with the 'dative' subject, that the dative subjects of Irish are not so restricted. It becomes more apparent still when we observe that 'derived subjects' (the single bare DP argument of a passive verb, for instance) may be dative, as shown in (69):

(69)   i ndiaidh don   fhéar a bheith bainte
        after   to-the hay   be[-FIN] saved
        'after the hay had been saved'   RR104

The dummy pronoun associated with extraposition structures (Stenson 1981, McCloskey 1996b, Noonan 1997) may also be dative-marked:

(70)   Is   fada dó   ráite ...
        COP[PRES] long to-it said
        'It has long been said that ...'   AG118

The conclusion seems to be that the mechanism which licenses dative subjects is not part of the system of **thematic** licensing in the language. We are dealing here with a species of structural case (not thematically restricted). That being so, in the general framework adopted here, it should be true that the relevant licensing mechanism is part of the morphosyntactic licensing system whose domain is the syntactic space between C and V.

Given these observations, and given the broader framework within which we are working, we are virtually forced to assume at this point that dative subjects undergo movement to reach their clause-initial position. To receive their semantic role they must originate low. But to be in a local relation with their licensing head (which is in turn accessible to selection by external heads), they must raise to the highest inflectional specifier position in TP. That the movement in question is A-movement is suggested by the fact that from their derived position, dative subjects may bind anaphors:

(71)   Tar éis dhóibh   beannú   da chéile
            after   to-them greet[-FIN] to-each-other
            'after they greet(ed) one another'

(72)   Tar éis dhóibh a chéile   a fheiscint
            after   to-them each-other see[-FIN]
            'after they see/had seen/will see each other'

If anaphoric elements like reciprocals require A-position antecedents, then from the grammaticality of (71) and (72), it follows either that the dative subject itself occupies an A-position or that it binds such an A-position (which in turn binds the anaphor).

Summarizing to date, we can bring the properties that we have observed together thus:

(i)   Dative subjects are licensed only in non-finite clauses (and in some varieties in certain small clauses).
(ii)   They are licensed in the 'subject position' of non-finite and small clauses.
(iii) In most varieties, they occur only in adverbial clauses and questions, but in more liberal varieties they may also occur in the non-finite complements of certain selecting heads.
(iv)   Within the (external) limits defined by (i) - (iii), this licensing device is completely productive (its legality does not depend on the verb of its own clause or on the semantic roles assigned by that verb).
(v)   Dative marked subjects are not thematically restricted.
(vi)   In all varieties and registers, a dative-marked subject may occupy a high 'subject-position' (above the position of shifted objects and above negation).

The analysis as developed so far may be summarized thus:

•   The particle *do* may be attached to any DP.
•   Its licensing position is Position 1 of (1). More specifically, the head of which Position 1 is the specifier must bear a feature [DAT] in order for the

'dative DP' to be licensed.

- DP prefixed by *do* raises from its θ-position to its licensing position. This movement is A-movement and is subject to the usual locality constraints on such movement, such that only the most prominent among the verb's bare DP-arguments may raise to the licensing position.
- C-elements also contribute to its licensing, but indirectly. Some, but not all, instances of C have the option of selecting an inflectional head bearing the feature [DAT] (compare *for-to* complements in English).

We have, at this point, I think, honorably cashed out the illicit references to 'subjecthood' with which our informal descriptions were larded.

6.2 Un-Raised Dative Subjects

What becomes interesting to note at this point, is that the dative subject in some varieties at least, has an additional position available to it.[22] Specifically, in conservative and formal varieties, dative nominals may in addition occupy a lower position - to the right of the shifted object and to the right of the infinitive. This alternative is illustrated in (73) - (77):

(73)   le lín úmpó   di   thar nais
         when turn[-FIN] to-her back
         'when she turned back'   SMB19

(74)   roimh theacht   domsa anso anocht
         before come[-FIN] to-me   here tonight
         'before I come/came here tonight'   LA61

(75)   i ndiaidh tosnú   dúinn ar maidin
         after   start[-FIN] to-us in-the-morning
         'after we started in the morning'

(76)   Le linn an airgid   a thabhairt di   dhó
         when the money give[-FIN] to-her to-him
         'when she gave him the money'   S65

(77)   Tar éis tig   a thógáil   dhóibh ar an mBuailtín
         after   house raise[-FIN] to-them
         'after they built a house in Ballyferriter'

The examples involving post-verbal positioning of the dative subject are felt to be formal and are not common in ordinary speech. They occur fairly freely, however, in published texts; they are well documented in traditional grammars (see Ó Cadhlaigh (1940) especially), and speakers, in my experience, have firm intuitions about what is possible and what is impossible. The pattern is most frequent, it seems, in Munster varieties but is also attested in other dialects, as shown by (78) which represents an Ulster variety.[23]

(78)   sa   bhliain i ndiaidh críochnú don   chéad chogadh domhanda
          in-the year   after   end[-FIN] to-the first   war   global
          'in the year after the first world war ended'   SSGD108

What are we to make of this possibility? What is striking about such examples is that the dative subject in this pattern occurs in exactly the position where we would expect the thematic position to be, given a theory in which the θ-domain in its entirety (including the position in which the external argument is realized) is below the inflectional layer. In particular, the dative subject marks a spot to the right of, and below, the Object Shift position (see Jonas 1996:170-171, McCloskey 2000) for similar evidence from Icelandic and a local variety of English respectively.) Since we have assumed V-raising to the head which licenses shifted objects (that is, to the position occupied by the transitivity marker a) the observed word order is as in (79):

(79)   [C [$_{TP}$ DP$_{Obj}$ a+V do-DP$_{Subj}$ ...]]

The interpretation that we need, given the assumptions made already, is that the relation between the licensing head bearing the [DAT] feature and the un-raised subject is that of 'covert movement' however understood - movement after spell-out, movement of features only, or a static AGREE relation governed by locality, the last clearly preferable on a number of grounds (Chomsky 1998, 1999).

It is important to stress that even in this circumstance (when the dative subject is un-raised) we crucially need to appeal to the presence and to the licensing ability of the higher inflectional head. This is because the same **external** distributional restrictions hold whether the dative subject appears in the lower or in the higher position. Those distributional restrictions on our account are determined by the [DAT] feature on the higher inflectional head and on the selectional relations that it enters into. To account for them in both cases then, it is crucial that the higher inflectional head (within the reach of selecting elements) be present whether the subject raises or not. At the level of technology, we can say that one of the markers of formal register in the more liberal varieties is that [DAT] is a 'weak' rather than a 'strong' feature.

From this account in terms of postponed movement (or equivalently for present purposes, featural movement or long agreement) we derive a prediction. On this account, there will be no level of representation on which the subject could be a possible binder for the shifted object. We therefore expect the kind of binding we saw in (71) and (72) to be impossible. This is clearly correct. The examples in (80) are well-formed because the dative DP in its thematic position c-commands the reciprocal in a less prominent argument position within VP:

(80)a.   Tar éis beannú   dhóibh dá chéile
         after   greet[-FIN] to-them to-each-other
         'after they greet one another'

     b.   D'éis an dá   theachtaireacht seo   a fháil   dúinn ó-n a chéile
         after   the two message   DEMON get[-FIN] to-us from each other
         'after we had received these two messages from each other'   U35

(81), however, is impossible. This is because the un-raised subject within VP does not c-command the raised object in Position 3:

    (81)   *Tar éis a chéile   a fheiscint dhóibh ar an mBuailtín
           after   each other see[-FIN]   to-them
           'after they had seen one another in Ballyferriter'

It is known independently of these concerns that postponed raising (or featural movement or long agreement) does not create new binding possibilities for anaphors. That is, the ungrammaticality of (81) can be understood in the same terms as English (82):

    (82)   *There seemed to each other/themselves to be many people eligible
           for the job.

Note that we can be fairly sure that precedence is not the relevant factor in the ungrammaticality of (81), since there is no general requirement that the binder of a reciprocal precede it. This can be seen with special clarity when the binder is a pronoun which undergoes 'Pronoun Postposing' (Chung and McCloskey (1987), Duffield (1995), Adger (1997), McCloskey (1999)). In such cases, the binder appears to the right of the reciprocal which it binds:

    (83)   Chuir   sí   i mullach a chéile   ar an urlár iad.
           put[PAST] she on-top-of each-other on the floor them
           'She piled them on top of one another on the floor.'

In addition, reciprocals within predicative phrases in the copula construction may be bound by subjects to their right (Doherty (1996)):

    (84)   Is   cosúil le-n a chéile   iad.
           COP[PRES] like   with each-other them
           'They are like each other.'

7. CONCLUSION

Drawing together the strands of this discussion, two conclusions seem plausible which are relevant for the larger issues we have been concerned with.

The first is that, in this instance also, the 'subjecthood' of the dative DP is best understood in distributed and derivational ways. At least two positions and two distinct heads are crucial in the licensing of such 'subjects' - a lower position, associated with the verb, in which a θ-role is licensed, and a higher position, associated with the head T, in which its structural case is   licensed. The two positions are derivationally related, and even when the presence of the higher one is obscured (because raising has not taken place), its presence is detectable in that clauses containing an un-raised subject are subject to just the same selection-based distributional restrictions as are clauses containing raised dative subjects.

The second conclusion is that we have here a new strand of evidence that the position of origin of external arguments is below the object shift position (the position in which accusative Case is licensed), as well as for the larger (architectural) conclusion that there is a more complete segregation between thematic and inflectional layers than is envisaged by the Split VP Hypothesis. The matter is hardly settled, but the Irish evidence is suggestive, I think, in that it is arguably a case where one can detect the lower thematic position directly and overtly. It is all the more suggestive in that the results thereby suggested are in harmony with similar observations from non-standard English (McCloskey (2000)) and from Icelandic (Jonas (1996)).

NOTES

[1]   This paper was prepared for the Workshop on Grammatical Relations in Transformational Grammar, held at the University of Illinois, Champaign-Urbana in July of 1999. My thanks to the conveners of the workshop - Stan Dubinsky and Bill Davies - and to the other participants for much help and guidance. I am grateful to two anonymous reviewers and to Peter Svenonius for comments on an earlier version of the paper. A very detailed and very penetrating set of comments by Noam Chomsky on a pre-final version was particularly valuable. I have not been able to respond to all the issues that arose in that correspondence within the limits of this revision.

[2]   The paper will focus on subject properties. But almost everything I will have to say applies equally to object properties, as far as I can tell.

[3]   In this, more modern conceptions differ from the 'Aspects' framework (Chomsky (1965), in which the notion 'subject' could at least be defined derivatively (the cluster of properties associated with subjecthood is associated with a single phrase structural position). Between 1965 and 1990, we witnessed, in effect, the death of the subject.

[4]   I restrict attention here to the IP-domain. As pointed out by a reviewer, however, it is distinctly possible that positions within the CP-layer also play a role in the licensing of subjects. This is particularly so in the context of the proposals of Rizzi (1997) in which the lowest head in the CP-layer encodes finiteness. Haegeman (1996) proposes that the specifier of this head is, under certain conditions, an A-position involved in the licensing of (non-contrastive) subjects. See also Haegeman 1992, Cardinaletti 1997 for relevant discussion. The existence of this possibility further strengthens the main point of the paper (since it involves a further 'distribution' of subject properties). I will set this possibility aside in discussing the Irish evidence, however, since it seems to me that the evidence remains strong that finite

verbs in Irish never raise into the C-layer and subjects remain to the right of the position of the finite verb (McCloskey 1996a, McCloskey 2001). That being so, the influence of elements in the CP-layer on the licensing of subject properties (at least as far as positional properties are concerned) will be limited. For nonfinite clauses, the situation might be different (see the discussion of section 6.1 below especially).

[5] We will have occasion to qualify this very general statement in the final section of the paper.

[6] For some relevant discussion of a closely-related language, see the discussion of 16th century forms of Welsh in Willis (1996: 6.3, pp213-219).

[7] Examples are frequently cited from published sources. When this is the case, it is indicated by means of a tag at the end of the translation line. For an explanation of these tags, see the Appendix ('Sources').

[8] Notice the promissory note: the reference to 'subject' here too must be discharged in some reasonable way. See Chung and McCloskey 1987, McCloskey and Sells 1988.

[9] Notice further that if expletives were available in the language (their existence motivated by the EPP), then (14b), (15b), and (16b) should be ungrammatical for the same reason as (i) in English and similar languages:

(i)   *There seems [somebody to be at the door].

Note in addition that the clause itself cannot be construed as occupying the EPP-position given the intervention of adverbial phrases and dative arguments in (14) - (16).

[10] A reviewer in particular points out that the utter impossibility of clefting *there* in English, in contrast with (25) in Irish, raises serious doubts about the idea that it might be in origin an existential predicate.

[11] We will have occasion to qualify the 'never' in this statement in the final section of the paper.

[12] Notice that the raising seen in (28b) cannot be triggered (in any straightforward way at least) by whatever functional structure is associated with progressive aspect, since no such raising is triggered in (28a), which presumably contains the same functional material as (28b).

[13] More detailed discussion and exemplification of all these patterns can be found in McCloskey (1996b).

[14] I will use the term 'Verb Phrase' as an informal cover-term to mean the maximal projection in which all the arguments of a given verb are realized - VP or vP.

[15] (39) was heard on a radio broadcast. See also Ó Curnáin 1996: vol. 2, p. 427.

[16] I assume that the participle in (41) raises to an Aspect projection. Similarly, the adjective in (40) has raised to the functional head from which the small clause is projected.

[17] Kratzer also assumes that the Voice projection is implicated in accusative case assignment, and thus arrives at a very direct structural interpretation of Burzio's Generalization, as indeed does Chomsky by a similar route. See also Déchaine 1993 (especially Chap. 2), Déchaine 1994 for distinct but related proposals.

[18] A condensed version of the argument is presented in McCloskey 1997. I take this opportunity to develop it in proper detail.

[19] Those familiar with this body of work will recognize that I am setting aside some intricate and important dialectal complexities here, in the interest of expositional ease. This simplification is not, as far as I can tell, dangerous. For more detail and discussion of all these matters, see McCloskey 1980, McCloskey and Sells 1988, Chung and McCloskey 1987, Guilfoyle 1990, Guilfoyle 1994, Noonan 1992,

Carnie 1995, Noonan 1994, Duffield 1995.

[20] This phenomenon should almost certainly be related to that of dative subjects found in some root infinitival clauses in Russian. On this, see Moore and Perlmutter 2000 and references cited there to much earlier work.

[21] It seems plausible to take *do* to be a head K which forms an extended projection, in Grimshaw's (1991) sense, with DP.

[22] I am grateful especially to Eibhlín Ní Mhurchú and to Bríd Ní Shúilleabháin for their patient help with the material of this section.

[23] Dónall Ó Baoill makes the interesting observation that in Ulster the option of lower positioning seems to be associated with a transitivity restriction - it is possible for intransitive but not for transitive clauses.

APPENDIX – SOURCES

Examples are frequently cited from published sources. When this is the case, it is indicated by a tag which consists of an abbreviation of the title of the publication, followed by a page-number. The abbreviations used have the interpretations specified below. For each text, the major dialect with which it is associated is also indicated.

AFAP:	*An Fear a Phléasc*, Mícheál Ó Conghaile, Galway	
AG:	*An Gabhar Sa Teampall*, Mícheál Ua Ciarmhaic, Kerry	
AGMTS:	*Ar Gach Maoilinn Tá Síocháin*, Pádraig Ó Cíobháin, Kerry	
AI:	*Allagar na hInise*, Tomás Ó Criomhthain, Kerry	
BF:	*Bruighean Feille*, Niall Ó Dónaill, Donegal	
CC:	*Cruithneacht agus Ceannabháin*, Tomás Bairéad, Galway	
CLIA:	*Cliathán na Sceilge*, Mícheál Ua Ciarmhaic, Kerry	
CST:	*An Chaint sa tSráidbhaile*, Breandán Ó hEithir, Galway	
DO:	*Dialann Oilithrigh*, Donchadh Ó Céileachair, Cork	
EB:	*Eadarbhaile*, translated by Seosamh Mac Grianna, Donegal	
EDD:	*Éist le Dubh Dorcha*, Seán Óg Caomhánach, Kerry	
FBF:	*Fiche Blian ag Fás*, Muiris Ó Súilleabháin, Kerry	
FEB:	*Fiolar an Eireabaill Bháin*, Seán Pheats Tom Ó Cearnaigh, Kerry	
GLL:	*An Gealas i Lár na Léithe*, Pádraig Ó Cíobháin, Kerry	
LA:	*Lá de na Laethanta*, Micí Sheáin Néill Ó Baoill, Donegal	
LG:	*Le Gealaigh*, Pádraig Ó Cíobháin, Kerry	
ODR2:	*Ó Donnbháin Rossa 2*, Seán Ó Lúing, Kerry	
PF:	*Paróiste an Fheirtéaraigh*, Tomás Mac Síthigh, Kerry	
RGB:	*Na Rosa go Bráthach*, Fionn Mac Cumhaill, Donegal	
RR:	*Róise Rua*, Pádraig Ua Cnáimhsí, Donegal	
S:	*Séadna*, An tAthair Peadar Ua Laoghaire, Cork	
SAB:	*Seanchas Annie Bhán*, Annie Nic Ghrianna, ed. Gordon W. MacLennan, Donegal	
SMB:	*Scéalta ón mBlascaod*, Peig Sayers, ed. Kenneth Jackson, Kerry	
SR:	*Sciúird chun na Rúise*, Pádraig Ó Fiannachta, Kerry	
SSGD:	*Stairsheanchas Ghaoth Dobhair*, Cáit Nic Ghiolla Bhríde, Kerry	
STL:	*Seanchas Thomáis Laighléis*, ed. Tomás de Bhaldraithe, Galway	
U:	*Unaga*, translated by Eoghan Ó Neachtain, Galway	

GRANT GOODALL

THE EPP IN SPANISH*

0. INTRODUCTION

One of the unsolved questions in current syntactic theory is why argument DPs that start out within the lexical layer of the clause (i.e., within vP or VP) must sometimes move overtly to a SPEC position within the inflectional layer. It is true that a relationship must be established between the DP and an inflectional head, in that the inflectional head must check a case feature on the DP and the DP must sometimes check phi-features on the inflectional head, but we know that this checking can be done even when there is no overt movement. Given the standard minimalist assumption that movement occurs only when necessary, we would then expect that the checking would always be done without overt movement. Since this does not appear to be true, we must say that certain features can only be checked through overt movement to the SPEC position of the head on which the feature appears (or, alternatively, through merger of an expletive in this position). Features that trigger this type of movement or merger are said to have the "EPP property" (Chomsky 1998).[1]

An obvious question which arises is why certain features have this property and others don't. One way to try to get closer to an answer to this question is to ascertain to what extent there is cross-linguistic variation in this regard. One could look, for example, at the patterns of raising out of the lexical layer which are attested, or at whether a feature which triggers overt movement in one language does so in all languages. It is this latter approach which will be the focus of this paper. The particular feature (or bundle of features) that I will examine is that found on T. In English, it is well known that T has a feature with the "EPP property," yielding the result that SPEC of T must be occupied, either by overt movement or by merger of an expletive.[2] This requirement imposed by a feature on T is often called simply "the EPP," and it is in this more narrow, traditional sense that I will use the term here (as opposed to the wider sense mentioned above in which it refers to any feature of any head which requires overt movement or merger). This EPP requirement has been widely discussed in the literature, but there is still remarkably little consensus on its cross-linguistic status. Chomsky (1998), for instance, presumes that it is universal, while McCloskey (1996b, this volume) proposes that it is not, based on evidence he provides that there is no EPP effect in Modern Irish. Alexiadou and Anagnostopoulou (1998), on the other hand, propose that it is

193

William D. Davies and Stanley Dubinsky (eds.), Objects and other subjects: Grammatical functions, functional categories, and configurationality, 193—223.
© 2001 *Kluwer Academic Publishers. Printed in the Netherlands.*

universal but may be satisfied in different ways. In non-null subject languages it is satisfied in the usual fashion, by agreement between SPEC of T and T, but in null subject languages it is satisfied by head movement of V to T, thus making phrasal movement or merger of an expletive in SPEC of T unnecessary. The EPP in the traditional, strict sense, then, only occurs in non-null subject languages in their analysis.

The language I will concentrate on here is Spanish, which is of particular interest with regard to the EPP for two main reasons.[3] First, it has a number of properties which would seem to indicate that it does not have an EPP requirement. Some of these are apparent at first glance and others require more analysis, but they point to the conclusion that SPEC of T does not need to be filled. Spanish would thus seem to provide straightforward evidence against the universality of the EPP. Second, since Spanish is a quintessential null-subject language, Alexiadou and Anagnostopoulou's typology predicts that it will not have the traditional EPP requirement, and in fact they use Spanish as evidence for their proposal. This type of link (such as they propose) between the presence/absence of the EPP and some independently needed property of the language is highly desirable, because it can provide the beginnings of an explanation for why some languages have the EPP and others don't, if that is indeed the case. If it should turn out that Spanish does have the EPP, however, this would seem to destroy any possible link between the absence of the EPP and the presence of null subjects. Thus there is a lot at stake in this apparently simple question of whether or not Spanish requires that its SPEC of T be filled.

One might think that determining whether Spanish has an EPP requirement would be a straightforward matter. V is assumed to occupy T, after all, so a DP immediately to the left of V could then be construed as evidence that there is an EPP, and the lack of such a DP could be taken as evidence showing the opposite. However, some independent properties of Spanish will make our job more difficult. For example, Spanish is a null subject language, so the lack of an overt DP to the left of V does not preclude the possibility of a null DP in that position. In addition, Spanish has very robust topicalization and focus-fronting processes, so it could be that a DP to the left of V is there by virtue of that type of movement, rather than by being attracted by an EPP feature. These processes involve A'-movement to the CP layer of the clause, but if there is no EPP and thus nothing in SPEC of T, they could have the effect of placing a DP immediately to the left of the V. Thus two major tasks in exploring the possibility of the EPP in Spanish will be determining whether there is a null DP in cases where SPEC of T appears to be unoccupied and whether preverbal DPs are there as a result of A'-movement or A-movement.

This paper will be organized as follows. In section 1, I will give an overview of some of the evidence from the literature that has led to the now predominant view that Spanish does not have an EPP requirement. In section 2, I will examine the status of preverbal subjects more closely and conclude that their surface position must result from EPP-induced movement. In section 3, I attempt to resolve this apparent contradiction by returning to the evidence from section 1 and showing how it can be accounted for insightfully under the assumption that there is an EPP. General conclusions will be drawn in section 4.

1. APPARENT EVIDENCE AGAINST THE EPP IN SPANISH

The first sign that might make us suspect that the EPP does not force movement to SPEC of T in Spanish is the fact that verb-initial word order is possible (see Ordoñez 1997 for discussion), as seen in (1).

(1)   Leyó Juan el libro.
        read   the book
        'Juan read the book.'

This is what we expect if phrases move to the left of the verb only by means of A'-movement, but it is surprising if T contains an EPP feature that attracts the closest DP to its SPEC. Assuming that V is located in T, we should then find this DP in preverbal position. The only way out is to say that there is a null expletive which satisfies the EPP feature, allowing the other DPs to remain VP-internal. This seems implausible, however, since the expletive should induce a definiteness effect, and (1) clearly shows that this does not obtain, as Alexiadou and Anagnostopoulou (1998) point out.

More subtle evidence in favor of an inactive EPP in Spanish comes from Uribe-Etxebarría 1992, who shows that quantified subjects in preverbal position have their scope frozen in place, while those in postverbal position do not. Thus in (2), *cada senador* 'every senator' has obligatorily narrow scope with regard to the *wh*-phrase *quién* in (a), while both narrow and wide scope are possible in (b).

(2)a.   A quién dices   que **cada senador** amaba?
        whom   say-2ps that each senator   loves

   b.   A quién dices   que amaba **cada senador**?
        whom   say-2ps that loves each senator
        'Who do you say that every senator loved?' (Uribe-Etxebarría 1992)

This is surprising if *cada senador* has moved leftward in (a) to satisfy an EPP feature, since such movement should not affect scope possibilities, as seen by the fact that *every senator* in the English translation may have either wide or narrow scope. Uribe-Etxebarría suggests that the facts in (2) are related to those in (3), first discussed by Lasnik and Uriagereka (1988).

(3)a.   Someone thinks that **every problem**, Mary solved.

   b.   Someone thinks that Mary solved **every problem**.

Lasnik and Uriagereka claim that *every problem* in (b) may have either narrow or (marginally) wide scope, but that when *every problem* is topicalized, as in (a), only the narrow scope reading is possible. The descriptive generalization that emerges is given in (4) (see Epstein 1992, Kayne 1998 for more recent discussion).

(4)   Overt A'-movement may not be followed by covert A'-movement of
            the same item.

(4) can then account for the lack of ambiguity in (3a), and it can do so in (2a) as
well, Uribe-Etxebarría suggests, if we make the crucial assumption that *cada
senador* has moved leftward by means of A'-movement.

        Ordóñez (1997) shows that this same account can be extended to facts
regarding *wh-in-situ* first discussed by Jaeggli (1987). Jaeggli showed that an
embedded subject *wh*-phrase may remain *in situ* when it is postverbal, but not
preverbal, as seen in (5).

(5)a.   *Qué dijiste   que **quién** compró el otro día?
            what say-2ps that who   bought the other day

   b.   Qué dijiste   que compró **quién** el otro día?
            what say-2ps that bought who   the other day
            'What did you say that who bought the other day?'

(4) allows us to account for (5a): *quién* must undergo covert movement so that it has
scope over the entire clause, but it cannot, if we assume that it has already
undergone A'-movement.

        A further reason for thinking that preverbal subjects are the result of A'-
movement and have not been attracted by an EPP-feature is that they are
incompatible with fronted focus phrases or fronted *wh*-phrases, as seen in (6) and
(7), respectively.[4]

(6)   ***EL LIBRO** Juan compró (no la revista).
            the book   bought not the magazine
            '**THE BOOK** Juan bought (not the magazine).'

   cf.   ✔**EL LIBRO** compró Juan (no la   revista).
            the book bought   not the magazine

(7)   ***Qué** Juan compró?
            what   bought
            '**What** did Juan buy?'

   cf.   ✔**Qué** compró Juan?
            what bought

This is surprising if the EPP is responsible for the preverbal position of the subject,
since we then expect that the subject would be in SPEC of T and that the focus
phrase or *wh*-phrase would be to its left within the CP layer. If, on the other hand,

the preverbal subject has undergone A'-movement, it is not difficult to imagine an analysis of (6) and (7) in which the movement of the subject to a preverbal position either competes for the same position as the focus phrase or *wh*-phrase (see, for example, Zubizarreta 1998) or otherwise results in two A'-processes interfering with each other (see, for example, Ordóñez 1997).

2. EVIDENCE IN FAVOR OF THE EPP IN SPANISH

We have now seen some good reasons for thinking that there is no requirement that SPEC of T be occupied in Spanish, i.e., that there is no standard EPP requirement. If this is true, it means that subjects appearing preverbally must be there as a result of A'-movement into the CP layer of the clause above TP. However, we shall now see evidence that seems to point in the opposite direction, suggesting that it is the EPP which triggers movement of the subject to a preverbal position.

2.1 Preverbal subjects do not have information status of topic or focus

A'-fronted elements in Spanish typically have a special information status that preverbal subjects do not share.[5] Fernández Soriano (1999), for instance, points out that in a neutral context, preverbal subjects are possible but other fronted elements are not. Thus (a) is a possible answer to the question in (8), but (b) is not.

(8)   ¿Qué pasó?
         what happened
         'What happened?'

   a.   Juan me regaló el anillo en el   parque.
            me gave   the ring in the park
         'Juan gave me the ring in the park.'

   b.   #En el   parque me regaló el   anillo.
            in the park   me gave   the ring
         'In the park he gave me the ring.'

If we assume that there is a relatively direct relationship between the information status of an element and its syntactic position, at least in the sense that phrases within the CP layer have a more specific informational role (e.g., topic or focus) and phrases within the inflectional level do not, this casts doubt on the idea that subjects are always fronted to the same position as topics such as *en el parque* 'in the park' in (b).[6]

There may also be differences in the reference possibilities of preverbal subjects when compared to other fronted elements. Cardinaletti (1997) claims that there are in Italian, and examples such as the following in Spanish seem to support this:[7]

(9)   Ayer   premiaron   una película acerca de Almodóvar.
            yesterday gave-prize-3pp a   film   about of
            'Yesterday they gave a prize to a film about Almodóvar.'

    (a)   **El director**, el   premio lo recibió en el teatro del   centro.
            the director the prize it received in the theater of-the downtown
            'The director, the prize he received at the downtown theater.'

    (b)   El premio, **el   director** lo recibió en el   teatro del   centro.
            the prize   the director it received in the theater of-the downtown
            'The prize, the director received at the downtown theater.'

The initial sentence in (9) brings up two possible directors: Almodóvar and the one
who made a film about Almodóvar. This sentence may be followed in the discourse
by either (a) or (b), both of which contain the DP *el director* 'the director.' We
would expect this DP to be able to refer to either of the possible directors, but in (a),
where it is syntactically a topic, it prefers to refer to the director of the film and not
to Almodóvar. In (b), on the other hand, the DP is a preverbal subject, and it is able
to refer equally well to either Almodóvar or the director of the film[8]. It is not known
why this difference should arise, but trying to account for it in a theory in which
topics and preverbal subjects are in the same position would seem to be much less
promising than doing so in a theory in which they occupy distinct positions. This in
turn lends support to the idea that subjects are fronted by a mechanism different
from that which fronts topics.[9]

2.2 Only one preverbal non-topic is allowed

Another distinctive property of preverbal subjects is that only one of them is
allowed. With a psych-verb such as *gustar*, for instance, either of the internal
arguments may be fronted, as seen in (10) and (11), but not both, as seen in (12).

    (10)   [A nadie]   le gusta esa música.
            to no one   pleases that music

    (11)   [Esa música] no   le gusta a nadie.
            that music   NEG pleases no one

    (12)   *[A nadie] [esa música] le gusta.
            to no one that music   pleases

We shall see in the next section that bare quantifiers like *nadie* 'no one' cannot be
topics, and the fact that *esa música* 'that music' is to the right of *nadie* in (12) means
that it cannot be a topic either. Thus in (12) neither of the fronted elements is a

topic, and the contrast between (10)/(11) and (12) shows that only one such non-topic, fronted element is possible. Multiple topics, on the other hand, are possible (see (9a), for instance), which again suggests that *nadie* in (10) and (12) is not a topic. This contrast between the obligatorily single preverbal subject and possibly multiple topics is consistent with the idea that subjects are fronted because of the (single) EPP feature while topics are fronted by means of A'-movement.

This analysis predicts that if the order of *a nadie* 'to no one' and *ésa música* 'that music' in (12) is reversed, then the sentence should be fine, and indeed this is the case:

(13)   Esa música, a   nadie le gusta.
         that music   to no one pleases

(13) is grammatical becaue *esa música* is able to be a topic (since unlike in (12), it is not to the right of a subject), leaving *a nadie* as the preverbal subject.

2.3 Preverbal subjects are not in topic position

There is also substantial syntactic evidence that preverbal subjects and topics do not occupy the same position in Spanish. First, it has often been noted that bare quantifiers are not able to be topics, as shown in (14) (see, e.g., Rizzi 1997).

(14)   *A nadie, Juan lo ha visto.
          no one   him has seen
         'No one, Juan has seen.'

Bare quantifiers are perfect as preverbal subjects, however, as in (15).[10]

(15)   Nadie   ha visto a Juan.
         nobody has seen
         'Nobody has seen Juan.'

If topics and preverbal subjects occupy the same position, it is difficult to see why this contrast would arise.[11] If, on the other hand, topics are in the CP layer and preverbal subjects are in SPEC of T, then the contrast between (14) and (15) is as expected, given the generalization in (4) (or the related account from Rizzi 1997 mentioned in footnote 11).

Second, Casielles (1997) has pointed out that bare nouns in Spanish are able to appear as postverbal subjects, as in (16a), but not as preverbal subjects, as in (16b).

(16)a.   Jugaban **niños** en el parque.
         played   children in the park

    b.   ***Niños**   jugaban en el parque.
            children played   in the park
            'Children were playing in the park.'

Crucially, bare nouns are able to be topics, as shown in (17), making it appear unlikely that preverbal subjects and topics occupy the same position.

  (17)   Yo a él **libros** no le   dejo.
           I   to him books no him-DAT lend
           'Books, I don't lend him.'

(17) in fact contains three topics (*yo* 'I', *a él* 'to him', and *libros* 'books'), but what matters here is that the bare noun *libros* is a topic. Casielles proposes that bare nouns are NP's, not DP's, and that only DP's are allowed in SPEC of T. This then gives us a plausible account of the ungrammaticality of (16b). (17), in contrast, is fine, because topics may be of any phrasal type.

    Third, it is well known that topics may be followed by a *wh*-phrase, as seen in (18).

  (18)   **Ese libro, cuándo** lo compraste?
           that book when   it bought-2ps
           'That book, when did you buy it?'

Within the system of Rizzi 1997, for instance, this is because the TopP projection may appear higher than the FocP projection which hosts the *wh*-phrase. If preverbal subjects are in SPEC of Top^0, they too should be able to appear to the left of a *wh*-phrase, and at first glance it appears that they can, as in (19).

  (19)   **Ese libro, cuándo** fue comprado?
           that book when   was bought
           'That book, when was it bought?'

However, the intonation and discourse context for (19) should make us wonder whether *ese libro* here is actually a topic. We can avoid this problem by using a subject which we know cannot be made into a topic, such as a bare quantifier, as seen in (20).

  (20)   ***Nadie, en qué clase** (no) estudió?
           no one in what class no   studied
           'No one, in which class did they study?'

      cf.   En qué clase no estudió nadie?
           in what class no studied no one
           'In which class did no one study?'

As (20) shows, a bare quantifier is incapable of appearing to the left of a *wh*-phrase, which again strongly suggests that preverbal subjects are not in topic position.

Another contrast between topics and preverbal subjects is that topics create an island for *wh*-movement out of an embedded clause, whereas preverbal subjects do not. This is seen in (21)-(22).[12]

(21)   ***A quién** crees   que **el premio** se   lo dieron?
        who   think-2ps that the prize   him-DAT it gave-3pp
        'Who do you think that the prize they gave to?'

(22)   **A quién** crees   que **Juan** le   dio el premio?
        who   think-2ps that   him-DAT gave the prize
        'Who do you think that Juan gave the prize to?'

If we assume that *wh*-movement is successive-cyclic, and that the *wh*-phrase must move to the left periphery of the embedded clause in order to be visible on the higher cycle (Chomsky 1998), we can then conclude that only the topic is in the left periphery and thus blocks movement of the *wh*-phrase. The preverbal subject, on the other hand, must be lower within the embedded clause and thus does not interfere with the movement of the *wh*-phrase to the left periphery.

A final piece of evidence concerns dialects in which preverbal subjects are possible in infinitival clauses.[13] In at least one such dialect, Northern Mexican Spanish, preliminary work indicates that although preverbal subjects are possible in this context, topics are not, as seen in the contrast between (23) and (24).

(23)   Para Juan lavar   las sábanas, tienen   que estar muy sucias.
        for   wash-INF the sheets   have-3pp that be   very dirty
        'For Juan to wash the sheets, they have to be very dirty.'

(24)   *Para las sábanas lavarlas   Juan, tienen   que estar muy sucias.
        for   the sheets wash-INF-them   have-3pp that be   very dirty
        'For the sheets, wash-INF-CL Juan, they have to be very dirty.'

Once again, this contrast is difficult to explain if topics and preverbal subjects occupy the same position, but it follows without stipulation if topics are in the CP layer and subjects are in SPEC of T. Notice that under Rizzi's (1997) analysis of the structure of CP, we expect *para* to occupy FIN^0, above the TP projection but below the position of topics. (23) and (24) are consistent with this view.

We have now seen evidence of various types that the topic and preverbal subject are in distinct positions. Significantly, the data in (18)-(24) point also to a more specific conclusion: that the preverbal subject is in a position lower than the topic. This followed from the fact that preverbal subjects, unlike topics, are not able to appear to the left of a *wh*-phrase and do not interfere with *wh*-extraction from an embedded clause, but are able to appear to the right of a complementizer in FIN^0.

2.4   Preverbal subjects are not in focus/wh- position

The facts we have seen so far would be consistent with the idea that preverbal subjects are in the same position as that of fronted focused phrases or *wh*-phrases (SPEC of FOC^0 in Rizzi 1997), which is generally below that of topics in Spanish. In this section, I will argue that this idea must be rejected and that the position of preverbal subjects is still lower than SPEC of FOC^0.

First, Torrego (1985) has shown that it is possible to extract a *wh*-phrase out of a *wh*-phrase which has itself been fronted, as seen in (25).

(25)   Este es el   poema del cual   no sé   [cuántas   traducciones ___]
          this is the poem of which no know-1ps how-many translations
          han   publicado.
          have-3pp published
          'This is the poem of which I don't know [how many translations ___]
          they have published.'

As we would expect, assuming that focused phrases occupy the same position as *wh*-phrases, the same is possible with a fronted focused phrase, as seen in (26).[14]

(26)   Este es el   poema del cual [TU   TRADUCCIÓN ___] publicaron
          this is the poem of which your translation   published-3pp
          pero no el   original)
          but not the original
          'This is the poem of which [YOUR TRANSLATION ____] they published
          (but not the original).'

Now if preverbal subjects occupy this same position, then wh-extraction should be possible out of them. But this is not the case, as seen in (27).[15]

(27)   *Este es el   poema del cual [tu traducción ___] ha ganado premios.
           this is the poem of which your translation   has won   prizes
          'This is the poem of which [your translation ___] has won prizes.'

So we conclude that preverbal subjects are not in SPEC of Foc^0.

A second argument concerns the fact that focused phrases and *wh*-phrases create islands for further *wh*-movement, as seen in (28) and (29).

(28)   **A quién** crees   que **EL CARRO** le   dieron (no la
           who   think-2ps that the car   him-DAT gave-3pp not the
          moto)?
          motorcycle
          '**Who** do you think that **THE CAR** they gave to (not the motorcycle)?'

(29)   *A quién quieres   saber   cuál   premio le   dieron?
        who   want-2ps know   which prize   him-DAT gave-3pp
        'Who do you want to know which prize they gave to?'

As mentioned earlier, one possible line of explanation here is that in order to undergo successive cyclic movement, the *wh*-phrase must move to the left periphery of the embedded clause so that it will be accessible to movement in the higher cycle. (28) and (29) are out because this left periphery is already occupied by a focused phrase and another *wh*-phrase, respectively. As we have already seen in (22), repeated here as (30), preverbal subjects do not create islands.

(30)   A quién crees   que Juan le   dio el premio?
        who   think-2ps that   him-DAT gave the prize
        'Who do you think that Juan gave the prize to?'

This very strongly suggests that preverbal subjects are in a position lower than SPEC of Foc^0.
        Finally, it is well known that movement of a *wh*-phrase (or focused phrase) licenses the appearance of a parasitic gap, as in (31).

(31)   Cuáles libros tiraste   [sin   haber   leído]?
        which books throw-out-2ps without have-INF read
        'Which books did you throw out [without having read]?'

A preverbal subject, on the other hand, does not license a parasitic gap, as seen in (32).

(32)   *Estos libros fueron tirados   [sin   haber   leído].
        these books were   thrown-out without have-INF read
        'These books were thrown out [without having read].'

This suggests that preverbal subjects, unlike *wh*-phrases, are not the result of A'-movement into the CP layer.[16]
        We are now able to conclude that preverbal subjects in Spanish are not located in the same position as *wh*-phrases and focused phrases.[17] Moreover, (28)-(30) indicate that preverbal subjects are in a position lower than these others.

3. ANOTHER LOOK AT EVIDENCE AGAINST THE EPP

At this point we have reached the following three conclusions: preverbal subjects are syntactically located in a position lower than the major phrasal elements in the CP layer (i.e., fronted topics, focused phrases and *wh*-phrases), only one preverbal subject is allowed, and preverbal subjects do not have the information status or reference possibilities of topics. We have seen that these conclusions cast doubt on the idea that a preverbal subject is a topic or is otherwise the result of A'-movement. They are perfectly consistent, on the other hand, with the idea that Spanish has an EPP requiring SPEC of T to be occupied.[18] SPEC of T is structurally lower than the SPEC positions within the CP layer, it is generally assumed that there is a single EPP feature which is only checked once, and SPEC of T is generally assumed to be devoid of the special interpretational properties of SPEC positions within the CP layer.

But how can these conclusions be reconciled with the data we saw in section 1 which suggested that there is no EPP in Spanish, or at least that phrasal movement into SPEC of T is not required? In this section we will examine each of the arguments from section 1 in turn and see what sort of analysis is available to us if we assume that there is an EPP requirement in Spanish.

3.1 Word order, expletives, and the definiteness effect

The first fact we have to face is that verb-initial orders are possible. Assuming that V is in T, an EPP feature would seem to require a DP to the left of the verb. There are two possible ways this problem could be handled. First, we could say that the EPP feature is simply optional in Spanish, and that the verb-initial order is what results when the feature is not present. The second and more interesting possibility is to say that the EPP feature is obligatory, so the verb-initial order must actually have a null element to the left of the verb.

Suppose that this second possibility is what we want to adopt. This immediately leads us to the second problem that we saw in section 1, which was that if there is a null expletive, we should observe a definiteness effect, whereas in fact none obtains. Zubizarreta (1998) suggests that this problem could be avoided if instead of an expletive, we have a null adverb or locative, which would not be expected to trigger the definiteness effect. As evidence for this, she shows that in Italian (based on work by Pinto (1994) and Adger (1996)), a non-focused postverbal subject is possible only where a null locative is plausible. That is to say, with verbs where a location seems intimately tied to the verb's meaning, even though it is not overtly expressed syntactically, a non-focused postverbal subject is possible, as seen in (33).

(33)a.   E arrivato Gigi.
           is arrived
           'Gigi has arrived.'

   b.   Ha telefonato Gigi.
           has telephoned
           'Gigi has telephoned.'

With verbs that do not seem to imply any locative argument, this non-focused postverbal subject is not possible. as seen in (34).

(34)a.   *Ha riso   Gigi.
          has laughed
          'Gigi has laughed.'

     b.   *Hanno starnutito tre   leoni.
          have   sneezed   three lions
          'Three lions have sneezed.'

These facts can be explained if we say that it is the null locative which satisfies the
EPP in (33). This null locative is the destination in (33a) and either the source or
destination in (33b). Since no locative argument is possible in (34), the EPP can
only be satisfied there by overt movement of the subject, which is then why the
postverbal subject is disallowed.

This neat explanation can only go through, of course, if we allow for the
possibility of null locatives, so the contrast between (33) and (34) thus constitutes
evidence for their existence. Given this, it is now at least possible that they exist in
Spanish as well, which could explain why there is no definiteness effect with
postverbal subjects. However, the equivalents of both (33) and (34) are possible in
Spanish, which would suggest, as Zubizarreta points out, that Spanish allows a
wider set of null adverbials than does Italian (perhaps including, for example, null
temporal adverbials).

If this is true, then evidence along the lines of (33) and (34) will be difficult to
find in Spanish, since some null adverbial will always be available to satisfy the
EPP, thus allowing the subject to remain in place. But what we should be able to
find are cases where adverbials do not need to be expressed overtly in Spanish, but
where they do in languages like English (assuming that English does not allow null
adverbials). Such cases seem to exist, as seen in (35).

(35)   (as sign in store)
     a.   Hay pan.
          'There is bread.'

     b.   #There is bread.

(35a) is very natural as a sign in a store, whereas (35b) would be quite odd in this
context. This can be explained if (a) allows for the possibility of a null adverbial, in
this context understood as "here" or "today," while (b) does not, which results in the
impression that (b) is a statement of general existence rather than one about a
particular place and time. Li (1990) notes a similar contrast between existentials in
Chinese and English:

(36)a.   Wo zhidao you gui.
          I   know have ghost
          'I know that there are ghosts.'

b.   I know that there are ghosts.

(36a) is pragmatically natural only when discussing a particular place or time, while
(36b) may be understood as a general statement of existence independent of any
particular place. Li attributes this contrast to the possibility of a null adverbial
subject in Chinese.[19]

If it is true that verb-initial clauses in Spanish contain a null adverbial which
satisfies the EPP, how can this be reconciled with the fact that overt adverbials in
English generally do not satisfy the EPP? One possibility, of course, is that the EPP
in Spanish is simply different from the EPP in English, in that the former may be
satisfied by a wider range of categories, but this is not a very appealing solution. A
more tempting possibility is to say that the EPP is the same in Spanish and English,
but that (some) locative and temporal adverbials in Spanish have a different
categorial status than their equivalents in English.   This actually has some
plausibility, in that it has been known for a long time that Spanish locatives and
temporals display a number of nominal characteristics. For instance, a number of
locatives require the preposition *de* 'of' in order to take an object:

(37)a.   encima de la mesa
          on   of the table
          'on top of the table'

   b.   detrás de la casa
          behind of the house
          'behind the house'

   c.   enfrente de la iglesia
          facing   of the church
          'facing the church'

Requiring a default preposition in order to take an object is a property of nouns (and
adjectives), but not of prepositions. Pavón Lucero (1999) points out as well that
these locatives, unlike ordinary prepositions, may themselves be the object of a
preposition when within a DP:

(38)a.   Se ha roto   [el jarrón de encima de la mesa]
          SE has broken the vase   of on   of the table

   b.   ??Se ha roto   [el jarrón de sobre la mesa]
           SE has broken the vase of on   the table
          'The vase on top of the table has broken.'

This suggests that *encima de la mesa* in (38a) is a DP (or NP), not a PP.

Another sign of nominal characteristics of some locatives is that basic locatives like *aquí* 'here' and *allí* 'there' can occupy argument positions ordinarily reserved for DP's, unlike their English counterparts:[20]

(39)a. Aquí me   da   miedo.
        here me-DAT gives fear

  b.   Allí no   me   gusta.
        there NEG me-DAT pleases

(40)a. *Here scares me. (cf. This place scares me.)

  b.   ?*I don't like there. (cf. I don't like that place.)

Even more suggestive is the fact that these locatives can trigger plural agreement, as in (41), and can raise, as in (42).

(41)   Aquí y alli me   gustan.
        here and there me-DAT please
        'I like here and there.'

(42)   Aquí parece darle   miedo.
        here seems give-INF-him fear
        'Here seems to scare him.'

As Davies and Dubinsky (this volume) point out, these are typical nominal properties. Crucially, these facts show that these locatives seems to have phi-features (allowing for agreement, as in (41)), and case-features (allowing for raising, as in (42)), i.e., just the features that may have the EPP property.

This area is clearly worthy of further exploration, but at this point we may conclude that it is at least plausible that certain locatives satisfy the EPP in Spanish, given that they behave like DP's in significant ways. If we assume that null locatives with these properties exist as well, it is then possible that it is this type of element that satisfies the EPP in cases where there is nothing overt in the preverbal position. The Spanish EPP under this view is the standard one; what makes the apparent verb-initial order possible is the existence of null locatives with DP properties.[21]

Thus the fact that Spanish allows clauses with an apparent verb-initial order in which there is no definiteness effect on the postverbal subject is not necessarily the clear evidence against an EPP requirement in this language that it appeared to be at first. As we have seen, there is some evidence for the existence of null locatives/temporals, and it is conceivable that it is these which satisfy the EPP in those cases in which the subject does not raise.

3.2 Quantifier scope

We now turn to the fact that quantified preverbal subjects in Spanish seem to have their scope frozen in place, as we saw earlier in (2), repeated here as (43).

(43)a.　A quién dices　que **cada senador** amaba?
　　　　 whom　 say-2ps that each senator　 loves

　 b.　A quién dices　que amaba **cada senador**?
　　　 whom　 say-2ps that loves　 each senator
　　　 'Who do you say that every senator loved?'

As we saw, (b) is ambiguous, whereas in (a) *cada senador* must have narrow scope. Uribe-Etxebarría (1992) argued that this freezing of the scope is a sign of A'-movement.　 This A'-movement property of the preverbal subject would be completely unexpected if Spanish has an EPP requirement, since EPP-induced movement of the subject to a preverbal position should exhibit only A-movement properties.

However, let us take a new look at this contrast between (43a) and (b) from the perspective of the theory of quantifiers of Hornstein 1999.　 Hornstein proposes that the freezing of scope in a particular position is not a property of A'-movement per se, but is characteristic of quantified DP's that are in positions of "informational demand." This follows from the following three assumptions: that within a copy theory of movement, all copies but one are deleted, that a copy which is in an informationally important position will need to be the one which survives, and that the position of the surviving copy is the one which determines scope.　 Now it is uncontroversial that there is some informational demand on the preverbal subject in Spanish, and indeed this is expected given the fact that there are (at least) two possible positions for the subject, just as we expect informational demand on shifted objects, in languages in which this is possible, since there is also another position in which objects can occur (see Chomsky 1999).[22] Thus independently of the type of movement involved, preverbal subjects are in a position of some informational demand, which in Hornstein's theory means that a quantified DP in that position will have its scope frozen.

So we are now able to explain the contrast in (43) while maintaining the idea that it is the EPP which forces the subject to move to a preverbal position.　 In fact, this account of (43) has an advantage over that proposed by Uribe-Etxebarría in terms of A'-movement.　 Many speakers have reported to me that they find the contrast between (43a) and (b) very weak, or even non-existent; that is, they at least marginally allow a wide-scope reading for *cada senador* in (43a) (see Gutiérrez-Rexach 1996 for discussion of some of the issues involved). This kind of variability in judgments is surprising if the contrast simply involves presence vs. absence of A'-movement, but makes more sense if what is at stake is the amount of informational demand on the preverbal subject position.　 As we have seen, there is some such demand, but we have also seen that preverbal subjects are allowed in discourse-neutral contexts, suggesting that the demand is not as great as in the case of topics or fronted focused phrases. This intermediate status of the informational demand on the preverbal subject position, combined with Hornstein's theory of scope, could then explain why the contrast in (43) is relatively weak.

3.3 Word order with fronted wh-/focused phrase

We now turn to the final argument that there is no EPP effect in Spanish, which involved clauses in which a *wh*-phrase or focused phrase has been fronted. If there is an EPP requirement, we would expect to find the *wh*/focused phrase within the CP layer followed by the preverbal subject in SPEC of T, but this is not what happens. Instead, we find that the subject is obligatorily postverbal in structures like this, as we saw in (6) and (7), repeated here as (44) and (45).

(44)   ***EL LIBRO** Juan compró (no la revista).
       the book   bought not the magazine
       '**THE BOOK** John bought (not the magazine).'

cf.   ✔**EL LIBRO** compró Juan (no la revista).
       the book bought   not the magazine

(45)   ***Qué** Juan compró?
       what   bought
       '**What** did Juan buy?'

cf.   ✔**Qué** compró Juan?
       what bought

As discussed earlier, if there is no EPP and preverbal subjects are the result of A'-movement, then it is at least conceivable that such movement would prevent fronting of the *wh*-/focused phrase.

There is one obvious way to try to preserve the EPP while still accounting for (44)-(45). If Spanish has obligatory T-to-C movement, we could then claim that the subject does occupy SPEC of T in the well-formed counterparts of (44)-(45), but that the verb has moved to a position to its left, just as occurs in *wh*-questions in English. This would indeed solve the problem of (44)-(45), but unfortunately, the thrust of the literature of the past several years is that T-to-C movement does not occur in environments like these in Spanish.

Let us now consider some of the evidence that has led to this conclusion. We will examine three main arguments against T-to-C movement in *wh*-questions in Spanish, involving properties of embedded clauses, auxiliaries, and adverb placement, before returning to the problem of how to account for (44)-(45).

First, in languages in which T-to-C raising does occur, it is at least very common for this raising to be blocked in embedded clauses, perhaps because the C position is filled with a null complementizer. This is illustrated for English in (46).

(46)a.   I don't know [what [John will buy]]

   b.   *I don't know [what will [John *t* buy]]

In Spanish, however, this sort of contrast between matrix and embedded clauses does not occur (even though complementizers are generally obligatory in tensed embedded clauses), as seen in (47).[23]

(47)a.   *No sé   qué Juan compró.
            no know-1ps what   bought

   b.   No sé   qué compró Juan.
            no know-1ps what bought
            'I don't know what Juan bought.'

As (47a) shows, the subject may not follow the *wh*-phrase in an embedded clause, contrary to what occurs in English (46a). This suggests that T-to-C movement is not what is responsible for the word order found in *wh*-clauses.

   Second, T-to-C movement typically affects the auxiliary, if there is one, leaving the main verb behind, as seen in English (48).

(48)a.   When **has** [John's mother *t* **danced**]?

   b.   *When **has danced** [John's mother *t*]?

But in Spanish, as Ordóñez (1997) points out, this is impossible, as seen in (49).

(49)a.   *A quién **había** la madre de Juan **visto**?
            who   had   the mother of   seen
            'Who had Juan's mother seen?'

   b.   A quién **había visto** la madre de Juan?
            who   had   seen the mother of
            'Who had Juan's mother seen?

It is tempting to say that (49a) is out because auxiliaries in Spanish may never be separated from the verb, but Ordóñez shows that at least in principle, the auxiliary and the verb are separable, as in (50), where something like T-to-C movement seems to have applied to the infinitive auxiliary.

(50)   De **haberlo** yo **sabido**, no te   habría dicho nada.
          of had-it   I   known   no you-DAT have   said nothing
          'Had I known, I would not have told you anything.'

Thus if Spanish truly had T-to-C raising in the context of a focused phrase or *wh*-phrase, then we would expect that the auxiliary alone would be able to raise, which (49a) shows to be impossible.

Finally, it has been argued by Goodall (1993) and Suñer (1994) that the placement of certain types of adverbs also provides evidence that T stays within TP in *wh*-questions (and presumably in focus constructions as well). This may be seen with adverbs such as *barely*, which are able to appear to the left of T, as seen in (51a). When *can* here raises to C, as in (51b), then of course *barely* can no longer appear to its left, as we would expect, and instead we get (51c).

(51)a.   You **barely** can see the screen from that seat.

    b.   *From which seat **barely** can you see the screen?

    c.   From which seat can you **barely** *t* see the screen?

In Spanish, the adverb *apenas* 'barely' seems to occupy the same position to the left of T (here occupied by the main verb *puedes*), as seen in (52a).

(52)a.   *Tú* **apenas** *puedes   ver la pantalla desde ese asiento.*
           you barely can-2ps see the screen   from   that seat
           'You can barely see the screen from that seat.'

    b.   *Desde cuál   asiento* **apenas** *puedes ver la pantalla?*
           from   which seat   barely can-2ps see the screen
           'From which seat can you barely see the screen?

But when there is *wh*-movement, as in (52b), then the adverb is able to remain in its preverbal position, suggesting that the verb has remained in T (and not raised up to C). This contrast between (51b) and (52b) would seem mysterious if both languages had obligatory T-to-C movement in *wh*-questions.

So we conclude that the inability of a preverbal subject to cooccur with a fronted *wh*-phrase or focused phrase cannot be explained by invoking T-to-C movement, and (44)-(45) thus continue to pose a serious problem for an account of Spanish which claims there is an active EPP.[24,25]

In order to begin solving this problem, let us consider why it might be that T-to-C movement occurs at all in some languages, and how it is that others seem to do without it. We will adopt the standard assumption that C may contain a feature that induces overt movement of a *wh*-/focused phrase to its SPEC, and let us assume as well, in the spirit of Rizzi 1996, that T may also contain such a feature. There are at least two types of motivation for this latter assumption. First, a number of languages exhibit special agreement morphology on the verb in clauses where a *wh*-phrase has been extracted (see, e.g., Chung 1982, Georgopoulos 1985, 1991, Finer 1998), suggesting that there is a *wh*-feature of some sort on one of the inflectional heads (i.e., within TP). Second, fronting of a nominative *wh*-phrase does not trigger T-to-C movement, as seen in (53).

(53)a.   Who ate the rice?

b.   *Who did eat the rice?   (OK only with emphatic reading)

This suggests that moving the *wh*-phrase to SPEC of T accomplishes the same thing that T-to-C raising ordinarily accomplishes, thus making the latter unnecessary in this case. This makes sense if there is a *wh*-feature on T: a nominative *wh*-phrase checks this feature when it is in SPEC of T, to which it is forced to move anyway by the EPP, but for other *wh*-phrases, which move to SPEC of C directly, T must raise to C in order for checking to occur.

The basic feature properties necessary to implement this idea are given in (54).[26]

(54)a.   ·   C has a Q feature (triggers overt movement)

b.   T has a Q feature (does not trigger overt movement)

c.   T is able to move to C[27]

Consider the derivation of a sentence like (53a). *Who* is attracted to SPEC of T, at which point its case feature is checked and it checks the phi-features and Q-feature on T. As the derivation continues, *who* also moves to SPEC of C.[28] Since T does not need to move to C for any reason, it does not. Now consider the derivation of a sentence with a non-subject *wh*-phrase, as in (55).

(55)   Who can John see?

The derivation proceeds normally as TP is built up: *John* moves to SPEC of T, where its case feature is checked and it checks the phi-features on T. The Q-feature on T is left unchecked for the time being. After C is merged, *who* will need to move to SPEC of C, attracted by the Q-feature on C. As for the remaining Q-feature on T, there are two possibilities: *who* could have checked it by moving to SPEC of T on its way to SPEC of C, or T could move to C first, thus allowing *who* to move directly to SPEC of C, where it would then be able to check the Q-features on both T and C. The second possibility requires only one instance of movement of the *wh*-phrase *who*, and perhaps because of this is the option that English chooses (although it also involves one instance of head movement).[29] In embedded clauses where this second possibility is not allowed (because T-to-C movement is not allowed), it may be the first possibility that is chosen.

I have now sketched an analysis of T-to-C movement according to which this process occurs as a way to facilitate checking of the Q-features on both T and C. I will assume that the Q features on T and C are universal and that T-to-C movement is simply one strategy available to allow both of these features to be checked. If it is true, as argued earlier, that Spanish does not have T-to-C movement, then it must use some other strategy to check these features. I propose that the strategy Spanish uses, in effect, is to move the *wh*-phrase first to SPEC of T and then to SPEC of C, checking each Q-feature in turn.[30] To accomplish this, Spanish has the properties in (56) (in place of those in (54) for English):

(56)a.   C has a Q feature (triggers overt movement)

   b.   T has a Q feature (triggers overt movement)

Consider first a clause containing a subject *wh*-phrase. This phrase is attracted first to SPEC of T, where it checks the phi-features and Q-feature on T, and then to SPEC of C, where it checks the Q-feature on SPEC of C, as shown in (57).

(57) $[_{CP}$ wh$_{SUBJ}$ $[_{TP}$ t $[_{vP}$ t ...

The result, then, is essentially the same as in English. When we have a non-subject *wh*-phrase, however, things will play out differently. This phrase will move to SPEC of T because of the Q-feature on T which forces overt movement. We would ordinarily expect the subject to be attracted to SPEC of T as well, by virtue of the EPP feature on the phi-features on T, but I will assume the descriptive generalization in (58).

(58)   Only one feature on a head may have an EPP-feature (force overt movement).

This generalization falls out straightforwardly if we assume, as was once standard, that movement to check a feature on head H must be to SPEC of H and that each head is limited to one such SPEC. This latter assumption in particular is no longer accepted uncritically (see Chomsky 1995 and 1999), with the result that it is no longer clear how to derive (58). Descriptively, however, (58) seems to be correct, and I will adopt it here. The effect of it for our purposes is that it will be impossible to have an EPP-feature on both the phi-features (or some particular phi-feature) and the Q-feature. I will assume that the result is that the EPP feature is only on the Q-feature, i.e., that only the Q-feature triggers overt movement.[31] This means, then, that although the *wh*-phrase moves overtly to SPEC of T, the subject has no reason to, so it remains in place, as shown in (59).[32]

(59) $[_{CP}$ wh$_{OBJ}$ $[_{TP}$ t $[_{vP}$ SUBJ $[_{VP}$ ... t

Given that the verb moves to T, this derives the obligatorily postverbal position of
the subject that we observed in (45) (and in (44) as well, assuming that the fronting
of focused phrases works in parallel fashion).

Notice that T-to-C movement does not occur here, because it does not need to.
Comparing (54) and (56), we see that the essential difference between English and
Spanish is that the Q-feature on T triggers overt movement in Spanish but not in
English. Once the former option is chosen, the need for T-to-C movement
disappears, because the Q-feature on T will always be checked by an element in its
SPEC. If the English-style option is chosen, then T-to-C movement becomes at
least a possibility, as we have seen, as one way to ensure that the Q-feature on T will
be checked.

Given this analysis of the fronting of wh-/focused phrases in Spanish, let us
now look more closely at the nature of the Q-feature on T, since this is the key
element in the analysis. One question about it which arises is what determines
whether or not it will appear on a given T. The answer seems to be that it appears
on the T of the clause over which the wh-/focused phrase has scope. For example, in
a sentence where a wh-phrase is extracted out of an embedded clause, Q is present
only on the T of the matrix clause. This is seen clearly in (60), where the subject is
obligatorily postverbal only in the matrix clause.[33]

(60)a.   Qué quiere Juan que María compre?
          what wants   that   buy

     b.   Qué quiere Juan que compre María?
          what wants   that buy

     c.   *Qué Juan quiere que María compre?
           what   wants that   buy

     d.   *Qué Juan quiere que compre María?
           what   wants that buy
          'What does Juan want María to buy?'

Within our analysis, it must be that T of the embedded clause contains the usual EPP
feature (i.e., no Q-feature). Notice that these facts parallel the behavior of T-to-C
movement in English, which also occurs only in the matrix clause in examples like
these. This is as we would expect, since T-to-C movement would have no reason to
occur if T does no contain a Q-feature.

We now predict that when the wh-phrase has scope only over the embedded
clause, as in an embedded question, the T of that embedded clause will have the Q
feature. This is borne out by the fact that the word order in embedded questions
parallels that of matrix questions:

(61)a. *Quiero   saber   qué María compró.
         want-1ps know-INF what   bought

    b.   Quiero   saber   qué compró María.
           want-1ps know-INF what bought
           'I want to know what María bought.'

(61a) is out because there is nothing to attract the embedded subject *María* to the preverbal position. Q on T has already attracted the *wh*-phrase *qué* there (on its way to SPEC of C), and given (58), T may have no other feature which triggers overt movement, so *María* must remain in place, as in (61b). In English, of course, embedded questions do not display T-to-C movement, but as mentioned earlier, this may be because such movement is independently prohibited in this environment, so a well-formed output is possible only if the *wh*-phrase checks the Q feature on T on its way to SPEC of C. Notice that this does not violate (58), because it is not the Q feature on T which triggers overt movement of the *wh*-phrase. The difference between Spanish (61a) and English (62), then, is that the Q feature on the embedded T in Spanish triggers overt movement, with the consequence that there will be no feature to trigger overt movement of the subject, whereas in English, the Q feature on the embedded T does not trigger overt movement.

(62)   I want to know what Mary bought.

The embedded T does trigger overt movement of the subject *Mary*, and the Q feature on C triggers overt movement of the *wh*-phrase.

    It appears that in relative clauses, *wh*-movement is triggered by a feature distinct from that of *wh*-questions (or perhaps occurs for reasons other than feature-checking altogether), so in this environment we do not expect to find a Q-feature on either C or T.[34] That this is correct is shown by the relative clause in (63).

(63)   el libro que María compró
          the book that   bought
          'the book which María bought'

Without a Q-feature on T, the usual EPP feature is able to force *María* to move to a preverbal position. Once again, this is also an environment in which T-to-C movement does not occur in English, as we would expect.

    Another question which arises is whether the Q-feature on T and the Q-feature on C always co-occur, as they have in all the examples we have seen so far. As we shall now see, the facts suggest that they do not. Specifically, it seems that the Q-feature on T is present only when true quantifier-variable binding is established within the clause, whereas the Q-feature on C is not sensitive to this. This may be seen in the fact that when the fronted *wh*-phrase contains quantifier-variable binding within it, the subject may be preverbal, as noted by Ordóñez (1997) (see also Rizzi 1997).

(64)   [A cuál de estas chicas] **tu   hermana** había visitado en Sicilia?
         which of these girls   your sister   had   visited in Sicily
         'Which of these girls had your sister visited in Sicily?'

This would appear to mean that the Q-feature is not present on T here. Another case of this comes from *wh*-questions with the equivalent of *why*. These have been widely observed to behave differently from other *wh*-questions in a number of languages, perhaps because they do not involve quantifier-variable binding of the usual sort (see Rizzi 1990, 1996). If this is true, then the fact that preverbal subjects are possible with *por qué* 'why' in Spanish is not a surprise:

(65)   Por qué **Juan** compró el libro.
         why   bought the book
         'Why did Juan buy the book?'

Thus the data in (64) and (65) suggest that it is possible to have the Q-feature on C without simultaneously having it on T, because the Q-feature on T is used only for true quantifier-variable binding. We would now also expect that T-to-C movement would be prohibited in the English equivalents of these environment, but as the English translations of (64) and (65) show, this does not appear to be true. I have no explanation for this.

   We are now at the point where we can reach conclusions about the relevance of fronted *wh*-/focused phrases to the question of the existence of the EPP in Spanish. As we saw at the outset of this section, a naive view of the EPP would lead us to expect that a fronted *wh*-/focused phrase would be followed by the subject in SPEC of T, but this is impossible in Spanish. We saw, however, that a closer look at T-to-C movement suggests that T has a feature that needs to be checked by the fronted *wh*-/focused phrase, and that if T-to-C movement does not occur, then the phrase will need to check it in SPEC of T. This in turn gave us an explanation for the inability of the subject to be fronted in this environment: the Q-feature on T forces overt movement in Spanish, and a single head can only have one feature with this property. Thus the traditional EPP is inactive in this environment, but it is inactive for a principled reason and in a way which sits comfortably with the view that that there is an EPP in Spanish. If this analysis is on the right track, we may then conclude that fronted *wh*-/focused phrases do not provide evidence for the view that Spanish does not have an EPP.

4. CONCLUSIONS

We have now seen that there is substantial evidence in favor of the EPP in Spanish, and that the major evidence against it can be reanalyzed to be made consistent with the EPP in what appears to be an insightful way. The most obvious conclusion that we can draw from this is that the typology proposed in Alexiadou and Anagnostopoulou 1998, in which only non-null subject languages observe the traditional EPP involving XP-movement to SPEC of T, does not look very promising at this point. Spanish is clearly a null subject language, yet what we have seen here suggests that it does have an EPP requirement.

This is not a particularly welcome result, since it may lead us to a scenario in which languages differ arbitrarily as to whether they have the EPP. This could be avoided if we say that the EPP is universal, which would be conceptually more pleasing, but this idea runs into the empirical problem that Alexiadou and Anagnostopoulou (1998) and McCloskey (1996b) provide what seems to be compelling evidence that Greek and Irish, respectively, do not have the EPP (at least, not in the traditional sense). Now Spanish may give us hope that what was once thought not to be an EPP language will turn out to be one upon closer inspection, but at present that is only a hope with regard to Greek and Irish.

It is tempting to say that Spanish shows that the EPP must be part of UG because the child would have no access to evidence for its existence, but this does not seem to be true. First, there is positive syntactic evidence for the EPP in the form of sentences like (22), repeated here as (66).

(66)   **A quién** crees   que **Juan** le   dio el premio?
        who   think-2ps   that   him-DAT gave the prize
        'Who do you think that Juan gave the prize to?'

The fact that the subject of the embedded clause does not block extraction should inform the child that this DP is in SPEC of T and not somewhere higher within the left periphery, since in that case it would block extraction. It is quite reasonable to assume that sentences such as (66) would be accessible to the child.

Further evidence for the child may come from the fact that preverbal subjects are possible in discourse-neutral contexts, as we saw in (8), repeated here as (67).

(67)   ¿Qué pasó?
            what happened
            'What happened?'

   a.   Juan me regaló el anillo en el   parque.
            me give   the ring in the park
            'Juan gave me the ring in the park.'

   b.   #En el   parque me regaló el   anillo.
            in the park   me gave   the ring
            'In the park he gave me the ring.'

If we make the assumption that phrases within the CP layer always have some pragmatically marked value (or very high information demand, in the sense of Hornstein 1999), then the fact that (67a) is possible in this context should suggest to the child that the preverbal subject is not within the CP layer.[35] Since this leaves SPEC of T as the only other plausible option, this should inform the child that there is an EPP requirement.

Thus, although the results of this paper may encourage us to look more seriously at the possibility of the EPP being universal, they are not incompatible with the possibility that languages vary with respect to the presence or absence of the EPP.

NOTES

* Earlier versions of this paper were presented at the 29th Linguistic Symposium on Romance Languages (University of Michigan), New Mexico State University, Arizona State University, the Workshop on Grammatical Functions in Transformational Grammar (University of Illinois), Universidad Nacional del Comahue, the 10th Colloquium on Generative Grammar (Universidad de Alcalá) and the 6th Encuentro Internacional de Lingüística en el Noroeste (Universidad de Sonora). I have benefited greatly from the comments and suggestions of the audiences at these places, and I am especially grateful to Mark Baker, Elena Benedicto, Heles Contreras, Lori Donath, Sam Epstein, Paula Kempchinsky, Pino Longobardi, Pascual Masullo, Cecilia Poletto, Dan Seely, Myriam Uribe-Etxebarría and the anonymous reviewers of this paper for their useful suggestions. Special thanks to Bill Davies and Stan Dubinsky for their many detailed comments on this paper and for their excellent work in organizing the earlier workshop upon which this volume is based.

[1] For possible ways of addressing these problems without use of the EPP, see Martin 1999 and Epstein and Seely 1999.

[2] I will not address here the question of which feature on T (out of Case, Person, Number, or perhaps others) is the one which has the EPP property.

[3] The term "Spanish" is of course an abstraction, and perhaps not a very useful one in this case. The data that I will present here are representative of most of mainland Latin American Spanish and at least some of Spain, but there are some significant differences between these varieties of Spanish and the many others not discussed here. The data presented here are the result of work with a large number of informants, most (but not all) of whom are from northern Mexico.

[4] I am using the term 'focus' to refer to constructions such as (6), in which the fronted phrase has no corresponding resumptive clitic and in which there is typically a contrastive reading. I will use the term 'topic' to refer to cases like (i), also known as 'Clitic Left-Dislocation'.

(i)   El libro, Juan lo compró.
            the book   it bought
            'The book, John bought.'

Here there is an obligatory resumptive clitic when the fronted topic is a definite object DP. There is no contrastive reading and no requirement that the subject be postverbal.
        Both (6) and (i) involve fronting of an object. When it is a subject which is fronted, the distinction between the focus and topic constructions becomes less obvious, since there is no resumptive clitic:

(ii)   Focus
            JUAN compró el libro (no María).
            'Juan bought the book (not María).'

(iii)   Topic
            Juan, compró el libro.
            'Juan, bought the book.'

Still, differing intonation patterns (roughly indicated by all-capitals in (ii) and by a comma in (iii)) and pragmatic contexts suggest that the distinction is nonetheless valid in the case of subjects.

[5]   A'-fronted elements also seem to have a special intonation pattern different from preverbal subjects, but I will not explore this area here.

[6]   See Goodall 2001 for further discussion of the idea that the CP layer is restricted to phrases such as topics and operators, and see Kempchinsky 2001 for analysis of the nature of PP preposing in Spanish.

[7]   Creating true minimal pairs that test for reference possibilities of subjects vs. topics without introducing unwanted pragmatic interference is very difficult. I am grateful to Giuseppe Longobardi and Stan Dubinsky for help in improving these examples, though they are not responsible for any remaining errors.

[8]   Notice that pragmatically, it is much more plausible for *el director* in (a) and (b) to refer to the director of the film and not to Almodóvar, given that one ordinarily gives prizes to directors of films, not to the people portrayed. It is thus all the more interesting that there is a contrast between (a) and (b), despite the strong pragmatic preference for only one of the readings.

[9]   By "subject" here I of course mean "non-topicalized subject." (9a) gives an example of a subject which has been topicalized, which is clear from the fact that it appears to the left of a topicalized direct object. Cases in which a subject appears immediately to the left of the verb, however, will generally be ambiguous in terms of the linear string between a topicalized and a non-topicalized structure, although the intonation and the pragmatic context do differentiate the two. Unless otherwise noted in what follows, what I refer to as "preverbal subjects" will be non-topicalized.

[10]   As would be expected, (15) remains grammatical when *Juan* is topicalized, making the sentence more parallel to (14):

> (i)   A Juan, nadie lo ha visto.

[11]   Ordóñez 1997 and Alexiadou and Anagnostopoulou 1998 are two recent attempts to explain this contrast while maintaining the idea that topics and preverbal subjects occupy the same position. Ordóñez suggests that the ungrammaticality of cases like (14) is due to an incompatibility between the accusative clitic and the negative quantifier. But this type of explanation seems ad hoc and uninsightful compared to Rizzi's (1997) proposal that quantifiers must bind a variable and that clitics don't count as variables. Notice that this phenomenon pertains not just to negative quantifiers:

> (i)   *Algo, lo dijiste.
>   'Something, you said it.'

In addition, it is bare quantifiers that resist topicalization, not negative expressions in general:

> (ii)   Nınguna de esas cosas, las tienes tú.
>   'None of those things, you have them.'

If (14) is out because of an incompatibility between the negative quantifier and the accusative clitic, it is not clear why (ii) is not out also. In Rizzi's (1997) account, on the other hand, (ii) is allowed because *ninguna* 'none' is able to bind a variable within the topic phrase.
        Alexiadou and Anagnostopoulou (1998) attempt to show that bare quantifiers are possible with a clitic when they are specific. This suggests that specific bare quantifiers don't bind variables, so they require a resumptive clitic. But this doesn't address the fact that in Spanish the same quantifiers with apparently the same interpretation show a contrast with respect to topic vs. subject position, as we have seen. It appears that the topic position never allows binding of a variable, while the subject position does.

[12]   There is some disagreement in the literature about the grammaticality of sentences like (21). Masullo (1992) finds them ungrammatical, while Ordóñez reports that they are grammatical. My own informants report that (21) is seriously degraded (in contrast to (22), which is perfect), so I will proceed on the assumption that (21) is in fact bad.

220   GRANT GOODALL

[13] Overt subjects are possible in infinitival clauses in some contexts in standard Spanish, but they are generally restricted to being postverbal (see Hernanz (1999) for an overview).

[14] The assumption that fronted *wh*-phrases and focused phrases occupy the same position works well as a first approximation and I will continue to adopt it here, but it may not hold up under closer examination. Barbosa (1999), for instance, presents a number of arguments from Italian (based on data from Rizzi 1997) that they occupy distinct positions. First, focused phrases can be followed by a topic, as in (i), but *wh*-phrases cannot, as in (ii):

(i)   QUESTO a Gianni gli dovrete dire.
            'THIS to Gianni we should say.'

(ii)   *Che cosa a Gianni gli dovremmo dire?
            'What to Gianni should we say?'

Second, a focused phrase can be followed by a subject, as in (iii), but a *wh*-phrase cannot, as in (iv).

(iii)   QUESTO Gianni ha detto (non quello che pensavi).
            'THIS Gianni said (not what you thought).'

(iv)   *Che cosa Gianni ha detto?
            'What has Gianni said?'

Third, a focused phrase may marginally be followed by a *wh*-phrase in embedded clauses, as in (v).

(v)   ?Mi domando A GIANNI che cosa abbiano detto (non a Piero).
            'I wonder TO GIANNI what they said (not to Piero).'

In addition, Lipták (2000) claims that in Hungarian, a focused phrase is possible in certain syntactic environments where a *wh*-phrase is not, suggesting that they occupy distinct positions. None of these facts from Italian and Hungarian appears to hold in Spanish, but focused phrases and *wh*-phrases do display differing behavior with regard to negation that may perhaps be attributable to distinct positions. As is well known, postverbal negative expressions generally require the presence of *no* to the left of the verb, while preverbal negative expressions prohibit it:

(vi)a.   *(No) ha venido nadie.

    b.   Nadie (*no) ha venido.
            'No one has come.'

However, when a negative object undergoes *wh*-movement, *no* is still required, but when it is focused, *no* is prohibited:

(vii)   [A ninguno de cuáles estudiantes] *(no) has visto?
            'Which students haven't you seen any of?'

(viii)   A NINGUNO (*no) has visto.
            'NO ONE have you seen.'

I won't attempt an analysis of this here, but it is conceivable that this contrast between (vii) and (viii) might be due to different positions for focused phrases and *wh*-phrases.

[15] (27) is ungrammatical under a neutral reading. As we would expect, though, it improves when *tu traducción* 'your translation' is focused, with appropriate intonation and a contrastive reading (parallel to (26)), since then the focused phrase is in SPEC of FOC^0, allowing for extraction.

[16]   The fact that (32) is perfect with a resumptive object clitic in the adjunct clause, as in (i),

(i)   Estos libros fueron tirados [sin haberlos leído].
              'These books were thrown out [without having read them].'

shows that the problem with (32) does not involve control of the PRO subject of the adjunct clause.

[17]   See Goodall 1993 for additional discussion of this point.

[18]   Though I won't explore this option further here, the evidence we have examined is perhaps also consistent with the idea that the preverbal subject is lower than fronted topics, focused phrases, and *wh*-phrases but still higher than SPEC of T, as is argued for Italian by Poletto (2000). Also worthy of further exploration are the possible implications for the analysis presented here of the idea that there are two distinct subject positions within the inflectional layer (see McCloskey 1997 for an overview and Cardinaletti 1997 for arguments from Romance).

[19]   One would then predict that like Spanish, Chinese would allow postverbal subjects without a definiteness effect. This prediction cannot be tested with unergative clauses, since in this case postverbal subjects are not allowed (perhaps because the verb does not raise high enough). With unaccusative clauses, on the other hand, postverbal subjects are possible, and a definiteness effect is observed:

(i)   Lai   le   yige ren.
              come ASP one man
              'A man came.'

(ii)   *Lai   le   tamen.
              come ASP they
              'They came.'

This is surprising if Chinese allows null adverbials, because such an adverbial should be a possible subject for (ii). Li suggests that these facts show that the definiteness effect should not be derived from properties of the expletive itself, under the assumption that the subject of (ii) is not necessarily an expletive.

[20]   As an anonymous reviewer points out, the more complex locatives *somewhere, nowhere, anywhere*, and *elsewhere* are able to occupy DP argument positions, as is the temporal *now*. This may be seen in cases such as the following:

(i)   I don't think **anywhere** had depressed me more, or made me want to live less.
              Guardian, Nov. 24, 2000 (p. 8, col. 6)

(ii)   If we have to go out, find **somewhere** near here that's nice and old.
              Independent, Weekend Review, Sept. 30, 2000 (p. 20, col. 3)

(iii)   **Now** appears to be the time to buy your package holiday for next summer.
              Times, Oct. 21, 2000 (Travel p. 4, col. 1)

At least with regard to the locatives, this is not surprising, since they resemble DP's in their internal structure.

[21]   There is evidence that temporal expressions also display some DP properties. Eguren (1999) shows, for instance, that temporals like *hoy* 'today' and *mañana* 'tomorrow' can be modified by temporal nominals such as days of the week and suggests that this is because of the nominal character of *hoy* and *mañana*:

(i)   hoy lunes
             today Monday

(ii)   mañana domingo
             tomorrow Sunday

It is interesting to note that this is impossible in English without a pause between the two words. In addition, Eguren shows that many temporal and locative expressions can take the diminutive suffix *-ito*, which is otherwise limited to nouns and adjectives:

(iii)   ahorita   'now'
             ayercito   'yesterday'
             aquicito   'here'

There is extensive dialectal variation with regard to this phenomenon, but most dialects seem to allow at least a few of these forms (see Eguren 1999 for a larger list).

[22] The concept of "informational demand" clearly deserves a fuller exploration than what I can provide here. Hornstein's basic idea, however, is that topic and focus positions are canonical examples of positions of high informational demand, while subject and object positions in a language like English are canonical examples of positions of no informational demand. What I am suggesting here is that the preverbal subject position in Spanish is of an intermediate status, with less informational demand than a topic but more than an English subject.

[23] This may not be true for all dialects, however. See Masullo 1992 and Baković 1998 for examples of dialects in which the pattern in (47) does not hold for all types of *wh*-words.

[24] For further discussion on the issue of T-to-C movement in Spanish and Romance, see Ordóñez 1997 and Barbosa 1999.

[25] Groos and Bok-Bennema (1986) and Zubizarreta (1998) pursue approaches in which the fronted *wh*-/focused phrase competes for the same position with the preverbal subject. These approaches are consistent with the idea that Spanish lacks T-to-C movement and bear some resemblance to the analysis to be proposed below. However, we have seen evidence that the preverbal subject is not in the same position as the fronted *wh*-/focused phrase, so we cannot maintain these approaches without modification.

[26] I will use "Q" as the feature label, in an attempt to be neutral between *wh*-phrases and focused phrases. As will be discussed below, it is probably an oversimplification to say that C and T have the same feature in any event, but I will maintain this oversimplification here for convenience.

[27] I am not using a feature on C here to motivate movement of T, because I just want T to move to C when it needs to in order to yield convergence. There is at present very little consensus on how head movement of this type works, or even if it exists, but it is not implausible that it is not motivated by the type of features that drive phrasal movement. See Chomsky 1999, Mahajan 2000, and Pesetsky and Torrego 2001 for a range of recent work on this topic.

[28] Notice that (54a) forces us to assume that subject *wh*-phrases move to SPEC of C (as in (53a)), yielding an instance of "vacuous movement." See Campos 1997 for arguments in favor of such an analysis from Spanish (and Grimshaw 1997 for a recent analysis which does not make use of this assumption).

[29] As mentioned in footnote 27, it may be that head movement is fundamentally different from phrasal movement and is thus not treated the same way by economy conditions.

[30] This follows in spirit the analysis that I proposed in Goodall 1993.

[31] This may follow from the principle that a specific property takes precedence over a more general one. The phi-features are more general in the sense that they are present in all tensed clauses, whereas the Q-feature is only a property of a few specific types of clauses.

[32] Since the Q-feature is what triggers movement of the *wh*-phrase to SPEC of T, this would seem to be an instance of A'-movement. Diesing (1990), I believe, was the first to propose that SPEC of T may be a possible landing site for A'-movement (see also Goodall 1992 and 1993).

[33] In some dialects this does not seem to be true, however. See Torrego 1982 and Baković 1998 for discussion.

[34] See, for example, the discussion in Rizzi 1997 showing that relative operators appear in SPEC of Force, in contrast to the SPEC of Focus position of *wh*-phrases in questions.

[35] This issue merits further exploration. As Mark Baker points out to me, there are languages (Mohawk, for example) in which there is good evidence that arguments that have undergone A'-movement to the left periphery do not seem to have any special informational demand. This might then mean that the child could not conclude from the information content of preverbal subjects that they must be in SPEC of T in Spanish.

DIANE MASSAM

ON PREDICATION AND THE STATUS OF SUBJECTS
IN NIUEAN*

0. INTRODUCTION

This paper explores the issue of subjecthood in an attempt to ascertain if the grammatical function subject has any application in Niuean, an Oceanic language of the Tongic subgroup (Pawley 1966, 1967). Various views of subjecthood will be discussed, and various asymmetries among arguments in Niuean will be examined. The claim will be that in Niuean there is no grammatical division of a sentence into subject and predicate, but rather into core predicate and arguments, with predicate fronting rather than subject externalization satisfying the Extended Projection Principle (EPP: Chomsky 1981, 1995). This predicts that there should be no grammatical subject in Niuean, and it is shown that this prediction is upheld. Among the verbal arguments, agent and patient behave identically for raising and deletion. One argument is distinguished as thematically highest for binding and control, and one case - absolutive - is distinguished as obligatory, but neither the highest argument, nor the one with absolutive case acts as grammatical (EPP) subject.

1. SUBJECTHOOD

It has become part of general knowledge that a sentence consists of a subject and a predicate. For example, Harper's English Grammar (Opdycke 1965:222) states that. "A sentence is a set of words complete in itself, containing subject and predicate." This insight is encoded in formal grammar in various ways, such as the Final 1 Law of Relational Grammar, the Extended Projection Principle (EPP) of Government and Binding theory and Minimalism, and in the concept of *pivot*, of Dixon (1979) and Foley and Van Valin (1984). Both the Final 1 Law and the EPP effectively state that a clause must have a subject.[1] In spite of the fact that subject is considered an essential notion in grammar, a clear definition of subject has been elusive. In most discussions, subject is identified as the NP which exhibits the largest subset of certain properties, such as bearing nominative case, having the ability to be raised or to float quantifiers, triggering agreement on the verb, having the ability to participate in inversion, and so on (egs. Harley 1995, Keenan 1976b, Kroeger 1992, Schachter 1996). Theoretically, subject has been defined along traditional lines in terms of a

225

*William D. Davies and Stanley Dubinsky (eds.), Objects and other subjects:
Grammatical functions, functional categories, and configurationality, 225—246.*
© 2001 Kluwer Academic Publishers. Printed in the Netherlands.

fundamental relation of predication which partitions a sentence into subject and predicate. Rothstein (1983) provides the following formulation of this view (see also Déchaine 1993).

(1) Predication (Rothstein 1983:19)

> A predicate is an open one-place syntactic function requiring saturation, or closure by an argument...The argument is subject... The paradigm case of predication is the simple declarative sentence, where the VP is predicated of an NP, for example [[John]$_{NP}$ [saw Mary]$_{VP}$] where the VP is predicated of the NP *John*.

In GB/Minimalism attempts are made to combine the two views of subjecthood above, by relating subject properties to a structural position created by predication. Through predication, one NP is external to the predicate, i.e. it is in the specifier of a functional projection above the verbal projection. Because of its superior structural position, this NP participates in operations that other NPs in the sentence do not participate in, such as raising and inversion.

In early generative research, the predication relation in a basic transitive clause was established at D-structure (eg. Williams 1980, 1981). With the VP-internal subject hypothesis however (eg. Fukui and Speas 1986, Kitagawa 1986, Koopman and Sportiche 1988, Kuroda 1988), it developed that even in a basic transitive sentence, the predication position for the subject was distinct from its thematic position so that predication belonged to a higher, grammatical domain of the tree. In this view, the grammatical subject is always created by extraction from the theta domain, usually of the highest argument, by a process known as externalization, which takes place due to an Extended Projection Principle (EPP) feature in INFL (Chomsky 1995). This analysis of basic clause structure creates two levels at which subjecthood can apply, one within the thematic domain, and one at the level of predication (eg. Dixon 1979, Guilfoyle, Hung, and Travis 1992, Kroeger 1992, Manning 1996). Soon thereafter, an additional functional projection was posited above V, namely the light verb (v). This reinforces the internal asymmetry (Marantz 1984) between the thematic subject and the thematic object. This is illustrated in (2).

(2)

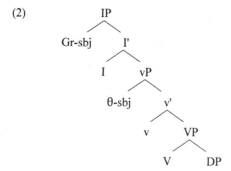

In Niuean it is not readily apparent that the characterization of sentence given in (1) can be upheld. There are two principal reasons for the difficulty. First, Niuean is a predicate first language, with [V/Agent/Patient/Other] word order. If the notion of predicate as defined in (1) above exists in Niuean, it is a discontinuous component of the language, since it wraps around a nominal phrase.[2] Second, Niuean has an ergative case marking system wherein the agent of a transitive clause receives a distinct case marker. As has been discussed extensively in the literature (egs. Anderson 1976, Biggs 1974, Dixon 1994), this means that it is difficult to pick out a single nominal phrase acting uniformly as subject across the sentences of the language. These properties can be seen below in (3a-d), which show the pre-nominal case marking for proper and common agents and patients/themes in transitive and intransitive clauses, as well as the predicate-initial nature of the language.[3]

(3)a.   Ne tohitohi a   Sione.
           Pst writing   Abs Sione
           'Sione was writing.'

   b.   Kua egaega e   kau kauvehe
           Perf rosy   Abs Pl   cheek
           'The cheeks are rosy.' (Sp.55)

   c.   Ko e tele e   Sione a   Sefa.
           Pres kick Erg Sione Abs Sefa.
           'Sione is kicking Sefa.' (S.73d:29)

   d.   Ne kai he pusi ia   e   moa.
           Pst eat Erg cat   that   Abs bird.
           'That cat ate the chicken.' (S.73a:29)

To understand the case system of Niuean it is essential to note that it cross-classifies for a proper/common distinction (where proper includes pronominals), as shown below.[4]

(4)   Niucan Case Marking

	ERG	ABS
Proper/Pronoun	e	a
Common	he	e

Even when one delves deeper into the grammar than word order and morphological case, a clear candidate for subjecthood does not emerge. Different linguists have reached different conclusions about which NP is subject, as we will see below. And in the view of Niuean developed in Massam and Smallwood (1997) and Massam (2000b, 2001), and for other languages in Davies and Dubinsky (this volume) there would seem to be no room for an EPP subject. In this analysis, it is the predicate which undergoes fronting to specifier of IP and this fronting satisfies the EPP requirement for the sentence, since Niuean is, in Davies and Dubinsky's terms, a V-prominent language. Since the EPP requirement is met by predicate fronting, there should be no further need to structurally distinguish an argument as subject (cf. McCloskey, this volume, who argues that the EPP feature is inactive in Irish).

In the rest of this paper I will first review the two views that have been advanced regarding Niuean subjecthood. I will then review the predicate fronting analysis mentioned above, summarizing its implications for subjecthood. I will then turn to an examination of what distinctions exist between nominals in Niuean, and will determine that the grammatical subject/non-subject distinction is not relevant in Niuean grammar, although some interesting distinctions are made between arguments at the thematic level. This conclusion is consistent with Schachter (1996) who argues that subject is not a relevant notion in Tagalog, and Dixon (1979, 1994) who argues that some languages can be without a pivot,[5] but it is also consistent with the claim discussed above that predication is a fundamental relation of sentencehood, and with the concept, also discussed above, that there are two levels at which subjecthood can be relevant.

2. SUBJECTS AND PREDICATES IN NIUEAN

2.1 Two Views of Niuean Subjects

In the study of ergativity it is common to use the terms A, S, and O, from Dixon (1968). *A* refers canonically to the agent of a transitive clause, *S* refers canonically to the single argument of an intransitive clause, and *O* refers canonically to the patient of a transitive clause. Of course non-agents can fill the A function, and non-patients can fill the O function, as in sentences like [Harriet likes Peter]. I will use these terms throughout this paper. A will refer to the ergative DP, O will refer to the absolutive DP in a transitive clause, and S will refer to the absolutive DP in an intransitive clause. Transitivity is defined by the presence or absence of an ergative DP.

In the literature on subjecthood in Niuean, there are two views. In one, argued for by Chung (1978), Chung and Seiter (1980), and Seiter (1980), and adopted by others, for example, Levin and Massam (1985, 1986), Niuean is viewed as a language which is syntactically accusative, though morphologically ergative. In this view, the subject of a transitive clause such as in (3c,d) is the ergative argument, and the subject of an intransitive clause such as (3a,b) is the absolutive argument. Thus, case does not reflect grammatical relations, and case marking aside, subject can be defined as in accusative languages. The Niuean subject is therefore A (canonically agent of a transitive clause) or S (single argument of an intransitive clause), and not O (canonically patient of a transitive clause), as it is in English. The arguments presented for this view are essentially that certain operations, such as control and binding, make reference to a class of NPs consisting of A and S, thus, the traditional subject.

The other view of subjecthood in Niuean is that of Biggs (1974) and Sperlich (1994). In this view Niuean is a language which is syntactically and morphologically ergative (though this is not the terminology these authors use). The subject, whether of a transitive or intransitive clause, is always the absolutive argument. Case does reflect grammatical relations, and subject is defined differently than it is in accusative languages, reflecting the differences in the case systems. In this view the subject is O or S and not A, unlike English. The arguments presented for this view centre on the observation that the absolutive NP (i.e. S or O) is obligatory in a sentence.

Thus, there is disagreement in the literature as to what constitutes the subject of the Niuean clause. In following sections we will present the arguments of each side. In other Oceanic languages also, there is similar debate as to which nominal phrase is the subject (egs. Cook 1991, Dukes 1998, Hooper 2000, Lynch 1972).[6] This debate is repeated throughout the Austronesian language family (egs. Austin 2000, Guilfoyle, Hung and Travis 1992, various papers in Li 1976, Schachter 1976, 1996, Travis and Williams 1983).

2.2 Niuean Predication

There has been no discussion of the Niuean grammatical predicate in the sense of (1), which is essentially the residue of the sentence once the subject is externalized. There is however, discussion of the Niuean predicate in a different sense of the term, as outlined below.

As noted above, Niuean is a predicate first language, often termed "VSO". This can be seen in the examples in (6). The word order is as shown below (TAM represents Tense/ Aspect/ Mood particles.)

(5)   Niuean Word Order
        TAM-(Neg)-Verb-(Adverbial Particles)-Argument(s)-(Obliques)

The slot after the TAM (which may be null), and after Negation (if present), is reserved for the verb, as shown. But, as is well known for Niuean as well as some other VSO languages (egs. Carnie 1995 for Irish, Lazard and Peltzer 1991 for Tahitian), it is not the case that only verbs can appear in this slot. This is seen by the following sentences, which show that nominal predicates and prepositional predicates (in brackets) can also appear in this slot.

(6)a.   Ai   [ko e   faiaoga] a   Mele
         Not Pred   teacher Abs   Mele
         'Mele's not a teacher.'

   b.   [Ko e tau kamuta] fakamua a   lautolu
         Pred Pl carpenter before   Abs   they
         'They were carpenters before this.' (S:136b:54)

c.   [Hå   he fale]   a   ia
      Pred in house   Abs   she
      'She is in the house.' (M:66)

It is thus more accurate to refer to Niuean as a predicate first language, rather than a VSO language, since the so-called "V" slot can in fact contain nominal or prepositional predicates and not only verbs. But, as observed in Massam (2000b) this introduces a new use of the word predicate, which is distinct from that in the quotes above. We distinguish the two uses by referring to the second type of predicate as "core predicate", including either the verb, or the nominal or prepositional phrase which substitutes for the verb in a non-verbal sentence. The concept of predicate in the English sense might be further specified with the term "residual predicate".

The notion core predicate, along with subject, is problematic in Niuean, because it seems that it can be either a lexical item (V) or a phrase (DP or PP). It is not at all clear why the predicate should vary like this. In other words, why is it not possible for the verb and its object to together form the core predicate, as in (7) just as the preposition and its argument together form the core predicate in (6c)?

(7)   *Ne [inu   e   kofe kona]   a   Mele.
        Pst   drink Abs   coffee bitter Abs   Mele
        ('Mele drank the bitter coffee.')

Massam (2001) shows that at times, even when the core predicate is verbal, it is in fact a phrase (VP) rather than the verb alone which appears in the core predicate slot.[7] These examples consist of so-called "Noun Incorporation" sentences, as in (8).

(8)a.   Ne [kai sipi mo   e   ika]   a   Sione
        Pst eat chip and Abs   fish   Abs   Sione
        'Sione ate fish and chips.'

  b.   Ne [inu   kofe kona] a   Mele
        Pst drink coffee bitter Abs Mele
        'Mele drank bitter coffee.'

The verbal predicate phrase (VP) occurs in the predicate slot precisely when the internal argument is an NP, rather than a DP, and hence cannot act as an independent argument of the sentence. This is supported by the fact that the so-called incorporated nominal cannot be preceded by any determiners, articles or case markers, hence it is arguably not a DP, but rather just an NP.[8] (7) shows that the incorporated nominal cannot be preceded by a case marker such as absolutive *e* (compare (7) with (8b)).

In most cases then, it is a phrase rather than a lexical item, that appears in the core predicate slot. It can be further posited that even in a simple non-incorporation sentence, the lexical verb does not appear alone in the predicate slot. Rather, in all

Niuean sentences, it is a phrase rather than a lexical item, which appears in the predicate slot. To advance this view, we hypothesize that in all non-incorporation sentences, the object has moved out of the VP via an obligatory object shift, so that the verb is the only phonological material remaining in the VP. This VP remnant movement, which is presented in detail in Massam (2000b, 2001) and also developed in Lee (2000), will be outlined in the following section.

3. THE NIUEAN CLAUSE

Given the view of predicate fronting presented above, we can present the derivations of basic Niuean clauses. Assuming a Minimalist framework, a Niuean transitive clause derivation would proceed as follows, with reference to the syntactic structure in (9).

(9)   <u>Niuean Transitive Clause</u> (eg. 3c,d)

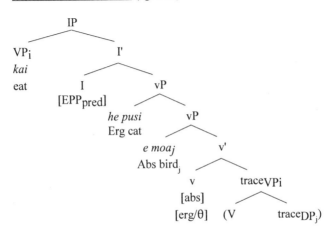

First the verb and the object DP are merged to form a VP. Since this VP and the DP within it later undergo move, they are shown as traces in (9). The verb and the object DP are shown in parentheses, since neither element in the VP is pronounced in the merge position, since the object shifts and then the VP remnant fronts to specifier of IP to check the EPP$_{Pred}$ feature, as outlined below. A light verb is then merged with this VP. This light verb is unlike the English light verb in that it contains two case feature bundles, the first, an absolutive case feature, and the second, a theta assigning feature with ergative case attached (Ura 1998, Woolford 1997). Since there are two separate case features, two arguments must appear in specifier positions of this head. The issue now becomes one of ordering of feature checking, a somewhat underdeveloped issue. I posit that the internal argument moves first to check absolutive case before the external argument is merged in. At this point, a Predication head, here called INFL,[9] merges with the vP. This head requires that the core predicate (here VP) raise to its specifier position in order to check an EPP$_{Pred}$ feature. Since the object DP has already vacated the VP in order to check absolutive case, only its trace is contained within VP, hence only its trace moves along with the core predicate VP to check the [Pred] feature.[10] TAM particles appear to the left of IP, in higher functional heads.

Note that it is unclear what principle would order absolutive checking before ergative checking. This is not the usual object shift ordering such as discussed in Chomsky (1995, 1998), where Merge (of subject) precedes Move (of object). But in Niuean, such ordering is essential (in the absence of tucking in - see note 10) in order to derive the right word order. We might consider that the strength of the absolutive case feature demands, not just the usual checking before the maximal projection is complete, but rather, premature checking, that is immediate checking before any other operation of merge or move. This degree of immediacy was discussed as a possible requirement of strong features - the derivation "cannot tolerate" a strong feature (Chomsky 1995:233). Chomsky then relaxed this requirement to allow a projection to complete itself before checking of strong features (Chomsky 1995:234). Possibly, there is variation on this point, so that some strong features require absolutely immediate checking, while others require checking before another projection is merged. One property of note here is that the merge of the ergative argument involves both theta assignment and case checking, thus it behaves as an inherently case marked element, while the merge of the absolutive argument is purely thematic, with the movement being required only for case checking. It might be possible to attribute the delay in the merge of the external argument to this inherent property.

The intransitive clause, shown in (10) below is similar except that here vP, being intransitive does not contain ergative case, nor an external theta role. Hence, the object simply raises to specifier of vP to check absolutive case.[11]

(10)   Niuean Intransitive Clause (eg. 3a,b)

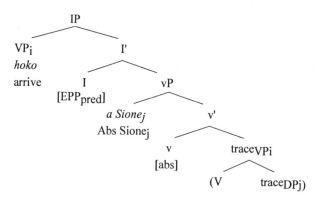

For completeness, in (11) I provide a derivation of a noun incorporating sentence.

(11)   <u>Niuean Noun Incorporation Clause</u> (eg. 8a,b)

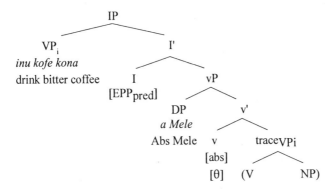

In (11), the light verb head cannot have its [abs] feature checked by the object, since this object is merely an NP, and has no case feature at all. Thus a transitive vP (one with an ergative case feature) is ruled out in this circumstance, since a transitive vP would then have an absolutive case feature which would not be able to be checked (assuming that absolutive case is an obligatory property of vP). Instead, the light verb is intransitive in that it has no ergative case (though it does have an external theta role). Thus, when the external argument merges into the specifier position, it checks absolutive case. When INFL attracts the core predicate to check its EPP [Pred] feature, the object NP (here *kofe kona* 'bitter coffee') fronts along with the verb, since it has not vacated the VP.

Based on this analysis of basic Niuean syntactic structure, an essential difference between Niuean and a language such as English emerges. Niuean requires predicates to undergo predicate fronting or externalization, and English requires subjects to undergo subject fronting or externalization. Both operations move phrases to the specifier of a predicational head (IP). We might expand from this to claim that the universal requirement for predication involves some sort of extraction from the pre-predicate domain, and that the requirement can be satisfied by extracting the highest argument from the pre-predication domain, or by extracting the core predicate from the pre-predication domain. If this view is correct, then while the notion of predication is universal, the notion subject is only relevant in languages of the English type (Massam and Smallwood 1997, Davies and Dubinsky this volume).

This view predicts that there is no grammatical EPP subject in Niuean. This in turn predicts that the superiority effects due to externalization should not be found in Niuean. Let us therefore revisit the issue of Niuean subjects.

4. ON THE EQUITY OF A,S,O

In the clause analysis in (9), the A and the O arguments are not in distinct specifiers, that is each does not have a distinct head for which it is the specifier. Therefore they are in the same minimal domain, defined as the smallest subset of elements which are contained in a maximal projection, excluding the head. (Chomsky 1995:178). According to Chomsky (1995), if two elements are in the same minimal domain, they are equidistant from a higher attracting head.

(12)   (Chomsky 1995:356)
          γ and β are equidistant from α if γ and β are in the same minimal domain.

We might expect, therefore, that the A and the O arguments in a structure such as (9) would show no superiority effects for movement. The structure in (9) resembles that proposed for language with overt object shift (Chomsky 1995). In most languages with object shift, however, it is not the case that either one or the other argument can undergo further movement to become EPP subject, in spite of the fact that they are equidistant from INFL, the target. This is ultimately due to the fact that only the subject has a case remaining (i.e. nominative) to be checked by INFL, the object having had its accusative case checked in specifier of vP.[12] In Niuean, though, both arguments have their cases checked in specifier of vP and there is no further case or EPP induced movement to specifier of IP, so the equidistance issue might seem to be moot. But there are situations where we can see that the two arguments are equidistant for further movement. In raising constructions we can see the lack of superiority effects in Niuean, since it is equally permitted to raise either the A, S, or O to the matrix clause.

In Niuean raising, an argument of a lower clause can raise to become the absolutive argument (S) of the matrix sentence.[13] I refer to this as "Raising to S". An example is given in (13). Note that I assume here that it is possible for a Niuean DP to check case twice in two different positions though only the case checked in the last position is realized phonologically (Bejar and Massam 1999).

(13)   Raising to S
     a.   To maeke [ke lagomatai he ekekafo e   tama e]
          Fut possible Sbjv help   Erg doctor Abs child this
          'The doctor could help this child.' (S.158:3a)
          (i.e. 'It is possible for the doctor to help this child.')

     b.   To maeke **e   ekekafo** [ke lagomatai e   tama e]
          Fut possible **Abs doctor**   Sbjv help   Abs child this
          'The doctor could help this child.' (S.158:4a)
          (i.e. 'The doctor is able to help this child.')

     c.   To maeke **e   tama e**   [ke lagomatai he ekekafo]
          Fut possible **Abs child this** Sbjv help   Erg doctor
          'This child could be helped by the doctor.' (S.158:5a)
          (i.e. 'This child is possible for the doctor to help.')

In (13a), a non-raised sentence is provided, where the embedded A is ergative and the embedded O is absolutive. In (13b), the embedded A argument, the agent, is raised to the matrix clause, appearing now with absolutive case, having become the S argument of the matrix clause. In (13c), the embedded O argument, the patient, is raised to the matrix clause to become the matrix S, as evidenced by word order (for other arguments that this is a raising operation, see Seiter 1980). These facts are discussed at length in Seiter (1980) and also in Massam (1985).[14]

The same holds for Raising to O, as seen in (14). In these cases an embedded S, A, or O is raised to act as a matrix O of a verb which also takes an ergative A argument.

(14) Raising to O
   a.   To   nakai toka e   au   [ke   kai he pusi e   ika]
        Fut not   let Erg I   Sbjv eat Erg cat Abs fish
        'I won't let that the cat eat the fish.' (S.196:76a)

   b.   To nakai toka e   au   **e   pusi** [ke   kai e   ika]
        Fut not   let Erg I   **Abs cat**   Sbjv eat Abs fish
        'I won't let the cat eat the fish.' (S.196:77a)

   c.   To   nakai toka e   au   **e   ika** [ke   kai he   pusi]
        Fut not   let Erg I   **Abs fish** Sbjv eat Erg cat
        'I won't let the fish be eaten by the cat' (S.196:78a)

In both (13) and (14) the argument moves from a specifer position of the embedded vP where it has checked either ergative or absolutive case, to the absolutive-checking specifier position of the matrix vP. This movement is presumably driven by the need of the matrix absolutive case to be checked. While many issues remain regarding Niuean raising, the data provided above show that A, S, and O arguments are treated identically for extraction in Niuean.

In fact, there are several other ways also in which A, S, and O arguments are equal in Niuean. Extraction of an argument for relativization, topicalization, question formation, and cleft leaves a null trace for A, S, and O as opposed to a pronoun copy used for extraction of obliques. (15a) shows the deletion of a relativized O, (15b) shows the deletion of a relativized A, and (15c) shows the pronominalization with the clitic *ai* of a relativized oblique.

(15)a.   mo   e   tagata   ne   moto e   koe (*a   ia)
         with Abs person [Pst punch Erg you Abs him
         'with the person who you punched' (S.12a.94)

   b.   ke he tama ka kai   (*e   ia) e   tau pateta
         to   child Fut eat Erg he Abs Pl   potato
         'to the child who's going to eat the potatoes' (S.12b.94)

c.   e   maga-aho ne kua makona ai   a   ia
      Abs piece-day [Pst Perf full   then Abs he]
      'the moment when he was full' (S.13.b:94)

Perhaps relatedly, 3rd person animate A, S, and O arguments (but not obliques - Seiter 1980) can be null if sufficiently identified by the discourse, as shown for an S argument in (16). And a floated quantifier, appearing as a clitic on the verbal complex can refer equally to an A, S, or O argument, as seen in (17a) for S, (17b) for A, and (17c) for O.

(16)   Ne   kitia e   au   a   Maka neafi.   Maololo lahi.
        Pst see Erg I   Abs Maka yesterday. strong   very.
        'I saw Maka yesterday. He's very well.' (S.130a.51)

(17)a.   O   oti [a   mautolu] he motokå
          Go,Pl all   Abs we,Pl, Excl in car
          'We're all going in the car.'

   b.   Kua   tele oti tuai [e   lautolu] a   au
         Perf kick all Perf Erg they   Abs me
         'They all kicked me.'

   c.   Ne kai oti e Sione [e   tau apala]
         Pst eat all Erg Sione Abs Pl   apple
         'Sione ate all the apples.'

It is easy to make the relevant generalizations about these facts, given the proposed structures in (9) and (10). Simply put, any argument in the specifier of vP can be null under extraction or under discourse identification, and can be referred to by a floated quantifier adverbial. As for the theoretical reasons for these properties, we can speculate that these direct arguments are thematically, and, given the invariant case properties of the transitive and intransitive light verb, grammatically recoverable, and hence can be null. And if quantifier domains are defined in terms of locality, then the last fact above falls in with the property of equidistance for extraction in that it relies on the A and O arguments being within the same minimal domain.

This lack of any distinction between A, S, and O arguments supports the claim that there is no externalization of one argument for EPP purposes in Niuean, as well as the claim that both arguments are in specifiers of the same functional head (given the definition of equidistance in (12)). It would seem that for purposes of locality and identification, the relevant distinction in Niuean is A, S, and O vs other.[15]

5. A,S VS. O: ACCUSATIVE ORGANIZATION

Although there appear to be no distinctions made between A, S, and O arguments for operations involving locality and null argumenthood, there are other operations which do make some distinctions. These divide into those which isolate A and S vs O, i.e. those which are used by Seiter (1980) to argue that Niuean is syntactically accusative, and those which isolate S and O vs. A, i.e. those used by Biggs and Sperlich to argue that Niuean is syntactically ergative (though they do not use this terminology). In the former group are binding, control and noun incorporation. In the next section we will discuss general issues regarding A and S referring rules, then we will proceed to examine binding, control and noun incorporation in Niuean. In section 6 we turn to the S,O vs A operations.

5.1 Thematic subjects

It is interesting indeed that the two main operations which isolate A and S vs O are binding and control, as these operations have been argued to make reference, not to grammatical subject, but instead to deep subject (Dixon 1979, 1994), or argument subject (Manning 1996), or VP-internal subject (Guilfoyle, Hung and Travis 1992) or thematic subject (Williams 1987, and relatedly, Travis 1998, Wechsler and Arka 1998).

As touched on above, many linguists have argued that the grammatical subject is not the only relevant NP for discussions of subjecthood. Instead, there are two grammatical domains in which some notion of subject is relevant. The first of these is the pre-predication, or thematic domain. If we use the term subject here, it refers to the argument with the highest thematic role assigned in the vP domain. The other notion of subject is relevant in the grammatical, or predication domain, and it refers to the argument which has been externalized for predication (EPP) reasons. Often, confusingly, these two notions refer to the same argument, as is the case for a sentence such as [Harriet saw Peter], where *Harriet* is both thematic and grammatical subject. But in other cases, they do not. For example, in a sentence such as [It appears that Harriet is sick], the expletive *it* is the matrix sentence grammatical subject, but not the thematic subject, which could be analyzed as non-existent, or as being the phrase *that Harriet is sick*, depending on whether internal subject is defined as the argument external to V', or as the highest argument in VP, which would include unaccusative objects. We adopt the more inclusive definition here.

Manning (1996) develops these ideas, building on work by others cited above. He argues that several of the classic subject referring processes are sensitive to the thematic subject (which, working loosely within Lexical Functional Grammar he terms the a-subject: "a" standing for argument structure), while others are sensitive to the grammatical subject (which he terms gr-subject). These processes are shown below.

(18)   Processes sensitive to a-structure: (Manning 1996)
         addressee of imperatives, control of DP-deletion in adverbial and
         complement clauses (equi NP deletion), incorporation, binding in
         reflexives…

(19)   Processes sensitive to gr-structure: (Manning 1996)
         relativization strategies, restrictions on topicalization, focussing and
         cleft formation, question formation, launching of quantifier float,
         raising restrictions, coreferential omission in co-ordination…

As discussed above, Seiter (1980) argues that in Niuean the subject is in fact the
A or S argument, as opposed to the O argument. He supports this claim by showing
that there are in fact, several processes in Niuean which operate with this
organization, i.e. which pick out either the A or S argument, as opposed to the O
argument. These are shown in (13) - see Seiter (1980) for discussion.[16]

(20)   Niuean operations which pick out A-S as opposed to O:
         (i) reflexivization/binding (A, S cannot be reflexive)

         (ii) complement control (only A, S can be controlled by the subject
         of a higher verb)

         (iii) incorporation (Only O can be incorporated, A, S cannot be)

Note that these operations are those which have been argued by Manning to refer
to the a-structure, or thematic, pre-predication domain. This means that prior to
predication externalization (which in Niuean involves VP fronting), the Niuean
sentence structure must allow A and S to form a natural class. Although the A
argument is merged in the specifier position of vP, and the S argument moves to the
specifier of vP (as does the O argument), A and S share in common that each is the
highest argument in the pre-predication domain. It seems therefore that the
arguments provided by Seiter (1980) for a A or S subject in Niuean do not argue for
an accusative organization of predication-level syntax. Rather, they argue that at the
thematic level, some Niuean processes single out the highest argument. This is the
case for other languages also, whether they are ergatively or accusatively case-
marked (Dixon 1994, Manning 1996).
    In the next section we will examine Niuean binding, some aspects of which
support the claim that it does not make reference to grammatical subject.

5.2 Niuean Binding

According to Seiter (1980), Niuean binding is relatively conventional. An A
argument may bind a O or oblique, and an S argument may bind an oblique. The
bound element is a pronoun followed by the emphatic particle *nî* as shown in (21).

(21)   Kitia he   tama fifine a   ia   nî   he fakaata
          see   Erg   child female Abs her Rfl in mirror
          'The girl sees herself in the mirror.' (S.214a:78)

In fact, possible binders are not limited to A and S, however, as the following example shows.[17] Here, an oblique NP binds another oblique. Hence the ability to bind an argument does not class A and S together as subject.

(22)   Ne fakatutala au mo Tule hagaao ki a   ia   nî
          Pst talk   I with Tule about to Pers him   Rfl
          'I spoke with Tule about himself.' (L:7)

On the other hand, according to Seiter (1980), an A, or S argument cannot be *nî* marked under co-reference with another nominal.

(23)   Kitia he tama fifine (*nî) a   ia   (nî) he fakaata.
          see   Erg child female Rfl Abs her   Rfl   in mirror
          'The girl sees herself in the mirror.' (S.217a:79)

Thus, binding can be said to unify A and S, vs O in a nominative/accusative pattern in their inability to host *nî*. This would lead us to posit that A is structurally superior to O, since c-command is usually a condition on binding.

But when we examine Niuean binding more closely it becomes clear that it is not as conventional as the above description suggests. First, the particle *nî* is optional in all cases, including the sentences above. Thus a sentence like (24) is ambiguous, as indicated.

(24)   Ne kamata ke   hifi e   Sione a   ia
          Pst begin   Sbjv shave Erg Sione Abs he
          'Sione began to shave himself.'
          "Sione began to shave him."

As discussed in Levin and Massam (1988), this means that Niuean is a language without a pronominal/anaphor distinction. Thus, Condition B of the Binding Theory (Chomsky 1981), namely "Pronouns must be free in their governing category" is not relevant in the language.

In addition to being optional, *nî* is ambiguous between a reflexive and an emphatic meaning, so that (25) is ambiguous, as indicated. *Nî* can also appear as a post-verbal clitic to emphasize the action of the verb, with a meaning 'just, only'. (25) contains an example of the verbal clitic use of *nî*, and indeed, it is often the case that *nî* will be found on both a verb and a nominal phrase in a clause.

(25)   Ita   nî   a   Pulevaka ki a   ia nî.
         angry Emph Abs Pulevaka to Pers he Rfl/Emph
         'Pulevaka's angry at himself.'
         'Pulevaka's angry at HIM.'

This also means that as a particle, *nî* does not always need to be bound. It is not even the case that when the *nî*-marked DP has a coreference interpretation it must be bound (i.e. c-commanded by a coreferential element). This is shown in (26), where *i a ia* 'he' is an oblique agent with a coreference interpretation, but is not c-commanded by its antecedent, which is a genitive DP contained in the S argument of the clause.

(26)   Mahele tuai e   lima ha Sione i   a   ia nî
         cut   Perf Abs hand of Sione Agt Pers him Rfl
         'Sione cut his own hand.' (S.215d.79)

Thus, strict c-command is not required for co-reference between a nominal and a pronoun marked with *nî*. It seems, then that Condition A of the Binding Theory "Reflexive pronouns must be bound in their governing category" is also not operative in Niuean.

In addition to there being no reflexive/pronoun distinction in Niuean, there are no reciprocal pronouns either. Reciprocity is marked by verbal morphology, as indicated in (27).

(27)   Ne fe-tele-aki   e   lautolu a   lautolu
         Pst Rcpr-kick-Rcpr Erg they   Abs they
         'They were kicking each other.'

Standard Binding Theory (as in Chomsky 1981) is thus not at work in Niuean. There is no class of anaphors vs. pronouns. (See also Dukes 1996 on Tongan.) In addition, c-command does not appear to be relevant. First, this is seen by example (26), where the *nî*-marked pronominal DP is not c-commanded by the antecedent. Second, the non-relevance of c-command might be seen in simple agent/patient reflexives, given that in the clause structure argued for above, there is arguably no c-command relation between agents and patients of regular transitive sentences. McGinnis (1998) shows that if two nominals are in specifier positions of the same head, there can be no coreference relation between them. She refers to this relation as Lethal Ambiguity.[18]

(28)   Lethal Ambiguity (McGinnis 1998:32)
         An anaphoric dependency cannot be established between two
         specifiers in the same checking domain.

Niuean appears to violate the Lethal Ambiguity constraint because A can antecede O even though, according to the proposed analysis, they are specifiers of the same head, the light verb. If Lethal Ambiguity effects are tied to the lack of c-command relations between the two specifiers, then it might be that Niuean appears to violate Lethal Ambiguity because c-command is not relevant for Niuean binding relations. Perhaps, rather than exhibiting a traditional binding relation dependant on c-command, in Niuean, any pronoun may optionally be construed as coreferential with a DP not thematically lower than itself, and if it is, it may optionally be marked with *nî*. If thematic hierarchy rather than c-command is relevant for *nî* marking, the apparent A and S natural class fact is explained.[19] The thematically highest argument in the sentence will be either the A or the S argument, hence it will never be marked with *nî*. This follows the Thematic Hierarchy Condition on Reflexives of Jackendoff (1972:148), as well as more recent proposals such as Wechsler and Arka (1998).

Clearly, more work remains to be done on the Niuean coreference system. But given its unconventional nature, combined with the general claims that binding makes reference to vP-internal roles, it seems that the A and S referring character of binding in this language noted by Seiter (1980) does not argue for the existence of a grammatical subject.

5.3 Control

The other operation which appears to pick out A and S vs O is control. Seiter (1980) states that control is possible only to the A or S argument of the embedded clause, and never to O.

Control, like binding, has been argued to make reference to internal roles. Williams (1987) argues that English binding and control make reference to theta-roles rather than to NPs. Guilfoyle, Hung, and Travis (1992) argue that the same operations make reference to VP-internal subjects in Tagalog. And control is one of Manning's a-structure referring operations, as noted above. Niuean control sentences are provided below. (29) shows that the controller is thematically determined. For the verb *loto* 'want', the controller is the experiencer, whereas for the verb *kotofa* 'choose', the controller is the patient. (29) also shows that the controlled element, which is obligatorily null, can be S or A. If the coreferential element is O, then it appears as a pronoun, as in (30).

(29)a.　Fia loto a　　ia　　ke　　tâ　　e　　fâloku
　　　　want　　Abs he　　Sbjv play Abs　flute
　　　　'He wants to play the flute.' (S.128a:136)

　　b.　Kotofa tuai e　　lautolu a　　au ke　　holoholo e　　tau kapiniu.
　　　　choose Perf Erg they　　Abs me Sbjv wash　　Abs Pl　dish
　　　　'They chose me to wash the dishes.' (S.128b:136)

(30)   Kua lali lahi   e   kapitiga haau ke   sake e au a   ia.
        Perf try really Abs friend   your Sbjv sack Erg I   Abs him
        'Your friend is really trying to get me to sack him.' (S.130a:137).

If control makes reference to the thematic structure, then it can simply target the highest thematic role of the embedded clause, as being the one with the most control over the action. This will result in an A and S pattern.

5.4 Noun Incorporation

Noun Incorporation, according to Massam (2001) results from the fronting of a VP in which the verb still has a complement, i.e. a complement that has not be moved to specifier of vP, as shown in (8) above. It is clear that NI will select only O's, and not A's, since A's never appear as a complement of V. As for an S argument, it can never appear as the incorporated noun in a noun incorporation structure, because if it remained in VP, there would be no other DP in an intransitive clause to check the obligatory absolutive case. This would cause the derivation to crash.

6. S,O VS. A GROUPING

We have examined operations which treat A, S, and O equivalently, and we have examined operations which treat A and S differently from O. None of these operations makes reference to a grammatical subject, although the latter group includes two operations, binding and control, which make reference to the thematically highest argument within vP. Since S,A can be grouped together thematically, there is no need to class them together as a structural subject. Remaining to study are the arguments for the treatment of S,O as a natural class. The principal argument provided by Biggs (1974) and Sperlich (1994) for an ergative structure, that is for the S,O vs. A definition of subject is that the ergative argument in Niuean sentences is optional, in that not all sentences contain an ergative NP, and in that if a verb exhibits transitivity alternations, it will be the ergative argument which is optionally expressed. (See also Hooper 2000 on Tokelauan.) This suggests that ergative case is very different from nominative case in English, and that it is in fact, more like accusative case. From this, Sperlich (and Dukes 2000 for Tongan) argues that the ergative argument is in fact an internal argument, like the by-phrase in English passive sentences (see also Marantz 1984, Woolford 1997), and that the absolutive argument is the true subject. Supporting the idea that the absolutive argument is the subject is that it appears with unmarked case. Biggs (1974) also defines subject as "what we are talking about", and invokes the argument that an important function such as subject should receive a uniform case marking.

The idea that the subject is the single required argument in all sentences is a common one, echoed by many who attempt to define the concept. It is clear that this test picks out the absolutive DP in Niuean. But we have argued that absolutive case is assigned internally to vP, which is supported by the [V/ergative/absolutive] word order, among other things. Thus, it cannot be argued that absolutive DP fulfills the function of EPP subject, that is, the subject that is extracted from within the thematic domain so as to partition the clause. Rather, we might see the absolutive DP as a sort of "inner" grammatical subject, following Roberge 2000 who presents a range of data which can be construed as exhibiting EPP effects within VP. Operations such as binding and control are late, thematically driven top-down operations, always isolating the highest theta role. Basic clausal architecture, on the other hand, works bottom-up. The verb merges first with its closest argument and if it is a DP (and not an NP as in noun incorporation structures), it will be attracted to specifier of the light verb to check absolutive case, which is always present on the light verb.[20] If the closest argument of the verb is an NP, which cannot check case, then some other argument must be merged into the specifier position to check absolutive case. So, ultimately, what is responsible for the obligatory nature of the absolutive argument is the feature composition of the light verb, which always contains an absolutive case feature.[21] And the secondary nature of the ergative case and argument (Bittner and Hale 1996) is tied to the optionality of the ergative case feature on the light verb, or rather, to whether a transitive or intransitive light verb is merged with VP. In this way ergative is indeed parallel to accusative case because each is the transitive case.

Differently from many other languages, "pivot" referring rules, i.e. rules that refer to grammatical asymmetries between arguments, rather than thematic asymmetries, are not found in Niuean. At the grammatical level, A, S and O appear to be equivalent. Moving down into the vP domain, Niuean is ambiguous with respect to "subject" identification, which has led to the different positions in the literature on this issue. As in other languages, control and binding make reference to argument hierarchy, and they are accordingly accusatively organized. What is more interesting is that the S,O vs. A character of the language, that is the ergatively organized aspect of the language, is also entirely internal to vP. Consider this in light of the claim in Manning (1996), which echoes common thinking in the field or ergativity studies (see also Dixon 1994), that all languages are accusatively organized at the level of a-structure. While this is true for Niuean in that the agent is merged in a higher position than the patient, it is not true that the external argument is obligatory, which is the case for an accusative system at the grammatical level. The primacy of absolutive case ensures that argument structure is ergatively arranged. However, it would still be unexpected that a language would be entirely organized on ergative grounds at the a-level (including binding and control), since operations which refer to highest argument (whether in terms of c-command or in terms of a thematic hierarchy) would not favour the absolutive argument over the ergative argument, since the latter is higher than the former. The possibility outlined in Sperlich (1994) remains open, however, namely the possibility of a language where the agent is expressed always as an oblique rather than as an inherently case marked external argument, thus appearing lower in the structure and in the thematic hierarchy than the absolutive argument.

7. CONCLUSION

This paper has examined the notions subject and predicate in Niuean. It was argued, based on previous work, that the notions as defined for English are irrelevant for Niuean, but that nonetheless Niuean exhibits a process of predication. Predication is not realized in Niuean as it is in English by the operation of subject externalization, but rather by a different operation of core predicate externalization. Thus, in both languages predication is a central grammatical organizing principle, but the externalization operations which satisfy predication are different in the two languages. Derivations were provided for transitive, intransitive and noun-incorporation structures in Niuean. If there is no externalization of an argument (subject) in Niuean, then it is predicted that no argument in Niuean should exhibit subject properties. In examining subject properties, we followed many other linguists in dividing them into two classes, namely internal or pre-predication subject properties and EPP or post-predication subject properties. It was seen that operations which refer to internal or thematic relations such as binding and control operate accusatively in Niuean, while operations which apply at the level of external or grammatical level do not make reference to any privileged DP. An additional complication in the language is that the light verb contains an obligatory absolutive case which creates an inner subject for the language, which is chosen along an ergative pattern, targeting the lowest argument in the clause. This has the effect that Niuean exhibits ambiguous ergative and accusative structure within vP, while exhibiting neither pattern at the level of grammatical or predication structure.

ENDNOTES

* An earlier version of this work was presented at the Fourth International Conference on Oceanic Languages, Niue Island, in July 1999. For help of various sorts, I would like to thank Bill Davies, Stan Dubinsky, and Wolfgang Sperlich, as well as Ken Cook, Fakahula Funaki, Robin Hooper, Sifa Ioane, Alana Johns, Harry Manamana, Elizabeth Pearce, Milan Rezac, Carolyn Smallwood, Pita Tanaki and anonymous reviewers. All errors are my own. Research funding for this work was provided by SSHRC (#410-97-0493).

[1] For Dixon (1979), a pivot is not necessary in a language, but the deep subject is universal. This fits well with the view of Niuean advanced in this paper.

[2] The predicate wraps around the ergative agent, if the agent is subject, and it wraps around the absolutive patient if the patient is subject. See below for discussion. Interestingly, it has been argued for another predicate initial language, Irish, that it has no EPP requirement (McCloskey 1996b, 1997, this volume). In addition, Davies and Dubinsky (this volume) argue that V-initial languages do not exhibit DP subjects.

[3] Examples are taken from a variety of sources, as indicated after each example. Data not identified for source is taken from my own consultation notes. The abbreviations used for data sources are: L=Lane 1978, M=McEwen 1970, S=Seiter 1980, Sp=Sperlich 1997. Where they were lacking, glosses have been added in this paper. In some cases, glosses have been changed for consistency. Orthography also has been changed in places to conform to Sperlich 1997. Abbreviations used in glosses are: Abs: absolutive, Agt: agent oblique case, Emph: emphatic, Excl: exclusive, Erg: ergative, Fut: future, Perf: perfect, Pers: person marker, Pl: plural, Pred: predicative marker, Pres: present, Pst: past, Rcpr: reciprocal, Rfl: reflexive, Sbjv: subjunctive.

[4]   The proper/common split permeates the entire case system, but I focus here on ergative and absolutive, since those are the most important cases in this paper.

[5]   For example, Dixon (1994:155) considers Samoan to be a pivotless language, following Mosel and Hovdhaugen (1992:704-17) who discuss the difficulties of assigning subjecthood in Samoan.

[6]   Biggs (1974) points out that the debate about subjects goes back a long way in Polynesian grammar with such linguists as Bataillon, Chapin, Churchward, Grézel, Hale, and Milner, taking agents as subjects, and others such as W.L Williams, H.W. Williams and Spencer Churchward not taking this position. See Biggs 1974 for references.

[7]   Since indirect arguments do not undergo fronting along with the VP in noun incorporation sentences, this analysis of noun incorporation necessitates a clause structure where they are outside of the minimal VP. As for adverbs, they appear between the fronted predicate and the A or S argument along with various clitics, as shown in (5). It is unclear if they are adjoined to vP, or if they are part of a clitic complex in INFL.

[8]   A case marker can appear within the incorporated noun phrase, as in (8) where the conjoined noun *ika* 'fish' is preceded by the case marker *e* 'Abs' (though this may better be analyzed as part of the conjunction *mo* 'and'). The prohibition is against a case marker on the maximal noun phrase *sipi mo e ika* 'chips and fish'.

[9]   I call this node "INFL" to align Niuean clause structure with that proposed for other languages. But INFL in Niuean does not correspond with either Tense or Agreement in other languages, since there is no agreement, and tense appears in a higher functional clause, perhaps CP. Perhaps the label "Pred" as in Bowers 1993 would be more appropriate than INFL, but I maintain here the more familiar label. (See Massam 2000b). The labels are important if we want to compare Niuean with other predicate initial languages, but they are nonetheless difficult to assign.

[10]   Another possible derivation is as follows. First, the subject merges in and receives ergative case, and its theta role. Then, the object DP moves out of VP and "tucks in" under the subject (Richards 1997) in order to check absolutive case. Since tucking in was developed for cases of multiple DPs checking one and the same feature, (and is ruled out for object shift by McGinnis (1998:58)), and since here the two DPs are checking different features, I will assume the derivation without tucking in, in order to derive the ergative-absolutive word order.

[11]   The intransitive light verb is not part of Chomsky 1995, but has been argued for by Alexiadou (1999), Harley & Noyer (1998), and Marantz (1997). It might be more properly labelled AgrO in the intransitive cases. Note here that I assume no unergative/unaccusative structural distinction for Niuean so that intransitive agents would also be base generated in the complement of V. But nothing hinges on this, so that intransitive agents could instead be seen as merging directly into the specifier of vP if an unergative/unaccusative distinction were to be maintained. I have not found any diagnostics for a structural distinction between intransitive verb types, and I follow Cummins (2000) in considering that, even in a language such as French, the claim that there are two intransitive verbs types which have different structures associated with them is incorrect.

[12]   See McGinnis 1998. Chomsky (1995:357) notes that the object could move to specifier of T, then the subject could undergo covert movement, thus satisfying the need for T to check nominative case, but he rules this derivation out on grounds of economy.

[13]   I assume the embedded clause in (13) is an indirect object, thus outside of the minimal VP, since it does not undergo predicate fronting along with the verb. There are other verbs in Niuean, such as *iloa* 'know' which take an ergative argument as well as a sentential argument. Here, the sentential argument checks absolutive case, consequently Raising to S or O is impossible with these verbs (Levin and Massam 1985).

[14] Unfortunately, data is not yet available regarding superiority effects in Wh-questions. Wh-words may appear in situ, or, as is more common with agent and patient Wh-words, they may appear as a predicate taking a headless relative as subject (see Seiter 1980).

[15] This was also argued to be the relevant distinction among nominals for the eastern Indonesian language Menó-Mené Sasak by Austin (2000).

[16] Seiter also mentions Relative Clause possessor, a grammatical rule whereby only the A or S of a relative clause can be optionally realized as a possessor of the head of the relative clause. I put this aside since it belongs, I think, to the nominal clause, which is accusatively organized (Seiter 1980, Massam 2000a) and hence must be discussed separately from the verbal clause.

[17] I have found no examples of O as a binder. This would be a crucial example, because it might isolate O from all other functions: A, S, Indirect Object and Oblique. This would show that O is a natural class on its own, which would be relevant, obviously. But what we can see from the available data is that with respect to the ability to be a binder, A, S do not pattern together as a natural class against all other functions.

[18] It should be noted, however, that McGinnis (1989) is assuming that the relation between the two elements is such that the higher specifier has moved past the lower specifier, not, as in Niuean, that the higher specifier is base-generated above the lower specifier, which has been moved.

[19] It is clear that precedence is not relevant, since there are examples such as (i), where the reflexively marked DP comes to precede its antecedent via clefting.

(i)   Ko ia   nî ne   fana e Mele.
           Pred   her   Rfl Pst   shoot Erg Mele
           'It was herself who Mele shot. (L85)

C-command could still be the relevant factor if binding relations are established on thematic positions (along lines suggested by Guilfoyle, Hung and Travis (1992), Travis (1998), Pearce (2000) and others). But then the violation of Lethal Ambiguity, as well as (26), would remain unexplained. Reinhart and Reuland (1993) attempt to put aside both c-command and thematic hierarchy conditions on binding in favour of conditions on chains. I will not resolve all the relevant issues here.

[20] I am putting aside equative and existential sentences that do not have an absolutive DP. See Seiter 1980 and Massam 2001 for a description of these clauses.

[21] Absolutive is thus the obligatory case, and ergative the transitive case, as in Bobaljik (1993) and Levin and Massam (1985).

WILLIAM D. DAVIES AND STANLEY DUBINSKY

FUNCTIONAL ARCHITECTURE AND THE DISTRIBUTION OF SUBJECT PROPERTIES*

It has long been assumed that subjects have special properties cross-linguistically. Depending on basic assumptions, these have been attributed to the property of "subjecthood" itself or to "certain epistemologically prior notions". But this assumption (underlying both positions) appears to be flawed. There is ample evidence, cross-linguistically, that no unified notion of subject exists. In this paper, we propose a syntactic account for the unified behavior of subjects in certain types of languages, showing why it is that subjects in certain other languages fail to display these properties. We will first show that languages such as English and French include a syntactic requirement that all subjects be DPs—importantly, this induces a DP node dominating non-NP subjects. However, this is not universal, as data from Bulgarian, Russian, and some V-initial languages show. This makes any semantic account of subject properties untenable. Instead, we suggest that this clustering of DP properties is attributable to the [D]-feature, as proposed in Chomsky 1995. English-type languages are 'D-feature prominent' while languages without this cluster of subject properties are 'V-feature prominent'. We further propose that this is correlated with clausal architecture—V prominent languages are those in which TP dominates all Agr projections while in D prominent languages an Agr projection dominates T.

1. NP PROPERTIES OF ENGLISH NON-NP SUBJECTS

English is a language in which subjects have an identifiable set of properties, and it turns out that all these properties can be reasonably classed as NP properties. In our discussion of English subject properties, we focus on the behavior of apparent non-NP subjects, as in (1), showing that they undergo obligatory raising (1.1), trigger subject agreement (1.2), host emphatic reflexives (1.3), and license plural adverbs (1.4).

(1)a.　　[$_{CP}$ that Shelby lost it] is true

　　b.　　[$_{PP}$ under the bed] is a good place to hide

William D. Davies and Stanley Dubinsky (eds.), Objects and other subjects: Grammatical functions, functional categories, and configurationality, 247—279.

    c.   [$_{AP}$ very tall] is just how he likes his bodyguards

1.1 Raising

Whether one adopts the GB or the Minimalist analysis of raising, it is clear in either account that NPs undergo raising precisely because they are NPs. That is, NPs raise because NPs (as opposed to other categories) need Case, or NPs raise because NPs have the capacity (not possessed by other categories) to check off a formal feature in T. Given this, the data in (2) are unexpected.[1]

    (2)a.   [$_{CP}$ that Shelby lost it]$_i$ appears [t$_i$ to be true]

       b.   [$_{PP}$ under the bed]$_i$ appears [t$_i$ to be a good place to hide]

       c.   [$_{AP}$ very tall]$_i$ appears [t$_i$ to be just how he likes his bodyguards]

In (2), the constituents that raise to matrix subject position are not NPs, but a CP, PP, and AP, respectively, and the theoretical perspectives that we have just reviewed do not account for this. Under either of the standard assumptions about NP-movement, the raising of non-NPs in (2) is mysterious. In a GB analysis, the non-NP subjects in (2) need not receive Case, thus precluding Case-motivation as a factor.[2] Thus, while a standard GB account does not explicitly rule these structures out, it can provide no coherent explanation for them. Under the Minimalist analysis the subjects in (2) lack D-features, and even though they are in spec-Agr$_S$, the D-features of the head of T should remain unchecked and the derivation should crash. The Minimalist position thus fares worse than the standard Case-motivated movement account in that it predicts that the sentences in (2) should be ill-formed.

    Moreover, not only must these accounts cope with their failure to motivate raising in (2), they must also contend with the fact that raising is obligatory. The non-NPs subjects of (2) **must** raise, as the data in (3) show.

    (3)a.   *it/there appears [[$_{CP}$ that Shelby lost it] to be true]

       b.   *it/there appears [[$_{PP}$ under the bed] to be a good place to hide]

       c.   *it/there appears [[$_{AP}$ very tall] to be just how he likes his bodyguards]

The fact is that standard GB assumptions wrongly predict that (3) should be the grammatical counterparts of (2), since the infinitival subjects should not need Case and the pleonastic subjects *it/there* should satisfy the 1982 formulation of the EPP. The Minimalist model makes similarly wrong predictions.

1.2 Subject agreement

Like NP subjects, CP, PP, and AP subjects can all trigger agreement on a tensed verb. In (2), the non-NP subjects trigger singular agreement on the tensed verb *appears*. Since in many languages third person singular agreement is a default, one might contend that the CP, PP, and AP actually play no role in determining the morphology on the verb in (2) and that they are indeed not even subjects (a frequent claim especially regarding CP subjects).[3] However, as pointed out in Levine 1989 with respect to PPs and in McCloskey 1991b with respect to CPs, conjoined non-NPs can (under certain circumstances) trigger plural agreement. This is illustrated in (4-6) for CPs, PPs, and APs.

(4)   [$_{CP}$ [$_{CP}$ that the march should go ahead] and [$_{CP}$ that it should be cancelled]] have been argued by the same people at different times (McCloskey 1991b:564)

(5)a.   Sandy talks a lot about her beach house and the family's Appalachian camping trips. As a result, [$_{PP}$ [$_{PP}$ along the coast] and [$_{PP}$ in the mountains]] remind me of Sandy's retirement fantasies

   b.   [$_{PP}$ [$_{PP}$ under the bed] and [$_{PP}$ in the fireplace]] are not the best (combination of) places to leave your toys(Levine 1989:1015)

(6)   [$_{AP}$ [$_{AP}$ very brawny] and [$_{AP}$ very studious]] are what Cindy aspires to be

The possibility of plural agreement in (4-6) provides evidence that the conjoined CPs, PPs, and APs are indeed NP subjects.

1.3 Emphatic reflexives

Another NP characteristic of non-NP subjects is the ability to license an emphatic reflexive. As illustrated in (7), definite NPs in any position can occur with an emphatic reflexive.[4]

(7)a.   The professor herself offered the student sage advice.

   b.   The zookeeper forced the monkey itself to clean up the cage.

   c.   I gave my x-rays to the doctor herself.

Like NPs, CPs and PPs when they are subjects, can license an emphatic reflexive as in (8) and (9).[5]

(8)a.   That Leslie arrived drunk itself put Kelly in a foul mood.

   b.   That there were 25 miles to go was itself enough to discourage Edwin.

(9)a.   You don't have to get the ball into the net. Right between the two red markers is itself sufficient to score.

   b.   Under the bed and in the closet are themselves reasonable places to stash the cash.

However, (10) and (11) show that outside of subject position, these same CPs and PPs cannot license emphatic reflexives.

(10)a.   Kelly was angry that Leslie arrived drunk (*itself).

    b.   Edwin hoped that there were less than 2 miles to go (*itself).

(11)a.   Sandy wants to retire in the mountains (*itself).

    b.   We stashed the cash under the bed and in the closet (*themselves).

Taken together with the pronominal facts, these data show that CPs and PPs can exhibit behavior characteristic of NPs, but crucially only when they are in subject position.[6]

1.4 Plural adverbs

One way of licensing the quantificational adverb *equally* in a sentence is via a plural NP or an NP with a mass noun as head.[7] As the data in (12) and (13) show, plural NPs in subject and complement positions are equally available as licensors.

(12)a.   The combatants were equally intransigent.

    b.   My rabbit and my hamster are equally annoying.

(13)a.   The professor distributed the As and Fs equally.

    b.   My grandmother was proud of the two children equally.

In the same way, conjoined CPs, PPs, and APs in subject position can license the presence of *equally*.

(14)a.   That he'll resign and that he'll stay in office seem at this point equally possible. (McCloskey 1991b:564)

b.   Under the bed and in the closet equally remind me of that game of hide-and-seek we played.

c.   Very tall and quaintly studious equally bring to mind my sixth grade science teacher.

However, nonsubject CPs, PPs, and APs cannot license *equally*.[8]

(15)a.   Dale thought that Dana left and that Terry wouldn't come (*equally).

b.   Leslie hid under the bed and in the closet (*equally).

c.   Ashley acts big and surly (*equally).

These data, together with the foregoing three paradigms, show that subject CPs, PPs, and APs display NP-like behavior (as opposed to nonsubject CPs, PPs, and APs). The table below summarizes our findings so far.

DP properties of non-NP subjects	English
agreement with coordinated non-NP subjects	YES
obligatory raising of non-NP subjects	YES
non-NP subjects host emphatic reflexives	YES
non-NP subjects license plural adverbs	YES

1.5 Non-NP subjects are DPs

As Chomsky (1995:55) suggests, the obligatory nature of the [spec,IP] position is "perhaps [due to] a morphological property of I ... the predicational character of VP". We might extrapolate from this and suggest that "subject properties" are also attributable either to properties of the functional complex or to semantic requirements imposed by the nature of the subject-predicate relation. That is, the apparent DP-hood of non-NP subjects might be a consequence of syntactic properties of English, or it might stem from semantic constraints on the possible denotations of subjects. Based on what we have seen above, both views are plausible. However, the choice between them is not free. If one assumes the former view, that the DP-like behavior of non-NP subjects is due to the functional structure and properties of English clauses, then we might reasonably expect to find cross-linguistic variation in this regard. That is to say, we might find languages with non-NP subjects which do not exhibit any of the behaviors illustrated above. Adopting the latter position entails a stronger claim. If DP-like behavior of non-NP subjects is a consequence of denotational limitations on subjects themselves, then all varieties of subjects in all languages should be expected to exhibit such behaviors. In sections 3 and 4, following, we will show both that non-NP subjects exhibit DP-like behavior in a variety of languages, and that these behaviors are not universal. In so doing, we hope to prove that the range of phenomena seen in this section have a syntactic, rather than a semantic explanation.

The syntactic explanation for what we have seen thus far is fairly straightforward. All subjects in English must be DPs (sometimes covertly so). This means that non-NP subjects have a DP-shell structure in English, and that the sentences in (1) actually have the structure given them in (16), in which the null head of DP carries the usual set of φ-features.[9]

(16)a. $[_{DP} [_{D} \varnothing] [_{CP} \text{ that Shelby lost it}]]$ is true

b. $[_{DP} [_{D} \varnothing] [_{PP} \text{ under the bed}]]$ is a good place to hide

c. $[_{DP} [_{D} \varnothing] [_{AP} \text{ very tall}]]$ is just how he likes his bodyguards

Under this view, these "subject" properties in English might be said to result from a requirement that the spec,Agr be filled by a DP (or, alternatively, the need to check a "strong" D-feature in T). We will have more to say about this in sections 4 and 5. In the meantime, we note the similarity of our analysis to proposals made for sentential arguments in earlier transformational frameworks. Lees (1960) and Rosenbaum (1967) both proposed an analysis of sentential subjects and objects in which an NP node immediately dominates an S. Our analysis of non-NP subjects is clearly quite similar to these, although we are only adopting it for sentential subjects.[10]

The analysis of PP and other non-NP subjects has received similar attention. Williams 1984 observes that "copular sentences [may have] ... non-NP subjects", as in (17).

(17)   (=Williams 1984, (55))
a.   From here to there is a long way.

b.   Under the bed is a nice place to hide.

c.   Relaxed is what Mary wants to be.

In attempting to account for this distribution and the fact that such subjects undergo raising and other NP-movement, he proposes the following exocentric phrase structure rule:

(18)   NP → X, for all X (= Williams 1984: (57))

However, Williams incorrectly claims that non-NP subjects are restricted to copular sentences,[11] and therefore supposes that his exocentric rule would have this limited application. On the exocentricity of his proposed rule, Williams defends this "fault" on the (mistaken) grounds that "verbal agreement is default third singular because the rule that introduces them is exocentric" (cf. section 1.2 above).

More recently, Bresnan (1994:103-111) considers the behavior of PPs in NP positions (as contrasted with inverted locative PPs).[12] On the basis of verb agreement, tag question formation, subject-aux inversion, and control of attributive VPs, Bresnan concludes that these PPs "behave like nominal phrases, not PPs." Accordingly, she proposes analyzing them as "place or time NPs whose missing nominal heads are contextually interpreted as instances of ellipsis", as shown in (19).

(19)a.   [$_{NP}$ (A PLACE) [$_{PP}$ under the bed]] is a good place to hide

b.   [$_{NP}$ (A TIME) [$_{PP}$ between six and seven]] suits her fine

She goes on to say that the analysis (of an understood/elided head) helps explain its distribution.   That is, one finds PLACE PPs where a locative is expected and TIME PPs where a temporal phrase is expected.

While sympathetic to the notion that the PPs in (19) are complements of a nominal category, we think that our DP analysis is preferable to one involving the ellipsis of a lexical noun. This is at least in part because an overt head noun is not always acceptable in these circumstances. Consider the following.

(20)a.   ??The location (of) under the bed is a good place to hide.

b.   *The time at 1 o'clock is when to arrive.

From (20), we see that Bresnan's analysis carries the additional burden of explaining why the head noun cannot be expressed in some instances. It therefore seems to us that under a DP analysis the job of being a phrase of a certain semantic category is always the job of the phrase and never the job of the head. This is just as true of NP complements of D as it is of CP, PP, and AP complements. DPs under our analysis just get their semantics from their complements.

2. DP PROPERTIES OF NON-NPS INSERTED INTO CANONICAL DP COMPLEMENT POSITIONS

This section will consider a set of analogous cases, in which non-NP complements inserted into canonical DP complement positions are found to exhibit DP properties. The DP-shell structure posited for English non-NP subjects is thus motivated for a separate set of cases, and is not limited to subject position (as Williams 1984 supposed). The data in (21) and (22) illustrate non-NP complements in canonical DP-complement positions.

(21)a.   they [$_{VP}$ discussed [$_{PP}$ after the holidays]] (=Jaworska 1986: (16a))

     b.   they [VP discussed [NP last year's office party]]

(22)a.   they [VP believe [CP that Grady quit the team]]

     b.   they [VP believe [NP the rumor that Grady quit]]

(21) and (22), with the verbs *discuss* and *believe*, contrast with cases in which only PPs or CPs (and not NPs) are allowed as complements.

(23)a.   they all [VP sat [PP in one corner of the room]]

     b.   *they all [VP sat [NP one corner of the room]]

(24)a.   they [VP hope [CP that Grady quit the team]]

     b.   *they [VP hope [NP the rumor that Grady quit]]

Crucially, these non-NP complements exhibit a range of DP properties, and some of these are the same as we find for English non-NP subjects. These non-NPs passivize (2.1), are islands for extraction (2.2), host emphatic reflexives (2.3), and license plural adverbs (2.4).

2.1 Passive

It has been noticed previously (Webelhuth 1992) that CP complements of verbs that can also take NP complements (such as *believe*) exhibit behaviors not available to CP complements of verbs that do not allow NP complements (such as *hope*). For instance, in (25), the CP complement of *believe*, but not that of *hope*, can passivize.

(25)a.   [CP that Grady will quit the team] is believed by everyone

     b.   *[CP that Grady will quit the team] is hoped by everyone

The same contrast can be seen in (26) with PP complements of *discuss* and *sit*.[13]

(26)a.   [PP after the holidays] was discussed by everone in the office for the entire month of January.

     b.   *[PP in that corner of the room] was sat by everyone in the seminar for the longest time.

This contrast is readily explained by assuming that the derived subjects in (25a) and (26a) both have a DP-shell structure, and that they are inserted into the structure as

DP complements of *believe* and *discuss*, respectively. The ungrammatical sentences (25b) and (26b) each involve verbs that do not allow DP complements.

2.2 Subjacency

When non-NPs are inserted into canonical DP-complement positions, they resist extraction in the manner of complex NP islands. This is clearly evident when the complement is an apparent PP.

(27)   Dale chose under the couch instead of behind the door.
         What did you choose under?   (with intended meaning)

(28)   Dale looked under the couch. What did you look under?

Similarly, we find that PP complements of Ps can also block extraction in the manner of DPs, as (29) and (30) illustrate.

(29)   We've been getting a lot of water damage lately. Pat is worried about behind the garage, the shed, and the retaining wall. *What are you worried about behind?

(30)a.   He lifted one end of the pole to above shoulder height.

    b.   What position did he lift one end of the pole to?

    c.   *What did he lift one end of the pole to above?

The ungrammaticality of the interrogative in (29) is predicted if we understand it to have the structure given in (31).[14]

(31)a.   *what$_1$ are [$_{IP}$ you worried [$_{PP}$ about [$_{DP}$ [$_{PP}$ behind t$_1$]]]]

    b.   what kind of handgun do you believe [that he bought]?

    c.   *what kind of handgun do you believe [$_{DP}$ the assertion [that he bought]]?

In (31a), the insertion of an extra DP node has the same effect on extractability as it does in the case of complex NP islands such as in (31c). Accordingly, the contrast between (27) and (28) is similar to the contrast seen in (31b) and (31c).

    The same prediction (and result) obtains for CP complements, although the argument is a bit more complicated. Clearly, extraction is possible from the CP complement of *believe*, as in (32).

(32)   who$_1$ do you believe [$_{CP}$ that Dale saw t$_1$]

However, it must be remembered that the complement of *believe* is only optionally a DP position (unlike the complement position of *choose*). In order to induce subjacency effect of the sort observed in (27), we must construct a sentence in which the CP complement of *believe* must be assigned a DP-shell structure. When this is done, we find that extraction out of CP is impossible. In this regard, we find that coordinated CP conjuncts of *believe* will resist across-the-board (ATB) extraction, if something in the clause triggers for them a DP-shell structure. Having shown, above, that the adverb *equally* indicates the presence of DP structure, we can test extraction out of the clausal complement of *believe* using this adverb. Compare (33a) and (33b).

(33)a.   Who do you believe that Dale saw and Dana heard?

   b.   ??Who did Dana believe equally that Dale would leave and that Terry wouldn't help?
           (from: 'Dana believed equally that Dale would leave John and that Terry wouldn't help him.')

In (33a), ATB extraction is possible out of the complements of *believe* (as we would expect for conjoined CP complements). However, in (33b), however, the presence of *equally* imposes a DP-shell structure on the complement clauses. In this instance, we see that across-the-board extraction is impossible.

2.3 Emphatic reflexives

Emphatic reflexives reveal a similar pattern. Section 1.3 demonstrated that subject PPs and CPs exhibit the nominal-like ability to host emphatic reflexives. While PP complements do not normally allow emphatic reflexives, it turns out that PPs occurring in positions canonically filled by DP complements can do so. Compare the data in (34).

(34)a.   I chose under the bed and in the closet themselves rather than under the sofa and behind the door.

   b.   *I hid my comics books under the bed and in the closet themselves, rather than under the sofa and behind the door.

The PPs in (34a) occur as complements of a verb *choose* that canonically takes DP complements, while those in (34b) are garden-variety locative PPs. As we might expect, only the PPs in the former can license an emphatic reflexive.

The same argument can be made for complement CPs, although the fact that they are in optional DP-positions, rather than canonical ones, seems to make the judgments less robust. Nevertheless, in the right context, we can contrast the complement of a verbs like *resent* which does allow DP complements, with that of *hope* which does not.

(35)a.　?I don't just resent that John used vile words in talking to me, but resent that he yelled at me in public itself.
(cf. It's not just that he swore at me. That John yelled at me in public itself made me want to quit my job.)

　　 b.　*I'm not just hoping that we have a Democratic majority on the school board again, but hoping that Carol won itself.
(cf. It's not just having a Democratic majority on the school board which is a good thing. That Carol won itself will start to produce positive changes.)

While the emphatic reflexive is in general not as good with complement CPs as with subject CPs, (35a) is still noticably more acceptable than (35b).

2.4 Plural adverbs

The fourth diagnostic used to establish the DP-like behavior of non-DP subjects was their ability to license the quantity adverb *equally*. Again we find plural PP in canonical DP positions have the ability to license *equally* (36a) while plural PPs in other non-subject positions cannot (36b).[15]

(36)a.　I worried about behind the garage and along the driveway equally.

　　 b.　Leslie hid under the bed and in the closet (*equally).

We also find that CP complements of verbs that also take DP complements (such as *believe*) can license *equally* in the same way, while those (such as *hope*) do not.

(37)a.　Dale resented equally that Dana wouldn't pay for gas and that she kept begging for rides.

　　 b.　??Dale hoped equally that Dana would start chipping in for gas and that she would stop asking for rides.

Thus, once more we find that non-DP complements exhibit DP-like behavior when occurring in potential DP-positions. The following table summarizes the results reported in this section.

Properties of non-NP complements in DP positions	English
passivization	YES
islands for subjacency	YES
non-NP subjects host emphatic reflexives	YES
non-NP subjects license plural adverbs	YES

3. NON-NP SUBJECTS IN FRENCH

The DP nature of non-NP subjects is not simply an artifact of English; there are a number of other languages which both have non-NP subjects and which show evidence of these subjects being DPs covertly. One of the languages that we have examined that falls into this category is French. Examples of non-NP subjects are illustrated in (38).

(38) Non-NP subjects in French (CPs, PPs, VPs):

a. [CP que tu me plaît] est evident
    'That you please me (I am attracted to you) is evident.'

b. [PP sous le lit] n'est pas un bon endroit pour se cacher
    'Under the bed is not a good place to hide oneself.'

c. [VP longer la côte] me parait une façon admirable pour connaître la vrai France
    'To go along the coast appears to me to be an admirable way to get to know the real France.'

3.1 Raising facts

As we found for English, non-NP subjects in French undergo raising in a manner similar to that of NPs, indicating (insofar as raising is case-motivated) that these constituents have a DP-shell structure.

Example (39) illustrates the facts. As the contrast between (39a) and (39b) shows, the subject PP must be raised from the complement clause to the matrix subject position when the complement clause is infinitival. Conversely, raising of the PP subject cannot occur if the embedded clause has a tensed verb, as seen in a comparison of (39c) and (39d).

(39)a. Il ne me semble pas que sous le lit soit/est un bon endroit pour se cacher.
        'It doesn't seem to me that under the bed is/were[subjunctive] a good place to hide oneself.'

b.   *Il ne me semble pas sous le lit être un bon endroit pour se cacher.
(It doesn't seem to me that under the bed to be a good place to hide oneself.)

c.   Sous le lit ne me semble pas être un bon endroit pour se cacher.
'Under the bed doesn't seem to me to be a good place to hide oneself.'

d.   *Sous le lit ne me semble pas que soit/est un bon endroit pour se cacher.
(Under the bed doesn't seem to me that is were a good place to hide oneself.)

When we examine the distribution of CPs, the paradigm is a little less complete, since the analog of (39a) with a CP subject is hard to get. This is because of a doubling violation that is created by the insertion of a *que* clause immediately following the complementizer *que*. Of course, the same CP subject cannot be inserted into an infinitival complement clause, even though there is no *que* complementizer to block it (see (40a)). In (40b), though, it is clear that the CP subject of the complement clause can only occupy the matrix subject position when the complement clause is infinitival.[16]

(40)a.   *Il me semble que Shelby l'a perdu être un fait.
(It seems to me [that Shelby lost it] to be a fact.)

b.   Que Shelby l'a perdu me semble être/*est un fait.
(That Shelby lost it seems to me to be/*is a fact.)

3.2 Agreement

In French as well, coordinated non-NP subjects can trigger plural agreement (under the right circumstances). Examples of these, involving CPs, infinitival phrases, and PPs, are given in (41).

(41)a.   Que le défilé continue ou qu'il soit annulé a/ont été discuté par les mêmes gens à différentes occasions.
'That the march should go ahead or that it should be cancelled has/have been argued by the same people at different times.'

b.   Qu'il démissionera ou qu'il restera toujours à son poste me semblent également possibles.
'That he'll resign and that he'll stay in office seem to me equally possible.'

    c.   Séjourner dans les montagnes et longer la côte me paraissent une façon admirable pour connaître la vrai France.
'Traveling through the mountains and going the coast appear to me an admirable way to get to know the real France.'

    d.   Sous le lit ou dans le placard ne sont pas de bons endroits pour se cacher.
'Under the bed and in the closet are not good places to hide oneself.'

The above data support the claim that non-NP subjects in French display NP-like properties with respect to subject-verb agreement.

3.3 Emphatic reflexives

French also has an emphatic reflexive whose distribution, like that of English, indicates that non-NP subjects are nominal. In French, though, *lui-même* 'himself' tends to be used only with persons. Abstract and non-sentient NPs normally have *lui-même* as the complement of an appropriate preposition, as example (42) shows.

    (42)a.   Le fait qu'il y avait 25 kilomètres à traverser était, par/de lui-même, assez pour décourager Edouard.
'The fact that there were 25 kilometers yet to go, by/of itself, was enough to discourage Edward.'

    b.   *Le fait qu'il y avait 25 kilomètres à traverser était, lui-même, assez pour décourager Edouard.
(The fact that there were 25 kilometers yet to go, itself, was enough to discourage Edward.)

In (42a), the emphatic reflexive associated with a 'the fact that ...' clause is preceded by the preposition *par* or *de*. In (43), we find that a bare CP subject licenses the same emphatic reflexives as do clausal subjects headed by *fait* 'fact'.

    (43)a.   Qu'il y avait 25 kilomètres à traverser était, par/de lui-même, assez pour décourager Edouard.
'That there were 25 kilometers to go was, by/of itself, was enough to discourage Edward.'

    b.   *Qu'il y avait 25 kilomètres à traverser était, lui-même, assez pour décourager Edouard.
(That there were 25 kilometers to go was, by/of itself, was enough to discourage Edward.)

Emphatic reflexives are also possible for PP subjects, and involve the preposition *en* 'in'. The data in (44) show that emphatic reflexives are available for PP subjects but not for PP complements, indicating once again the special nominal nature of the subject position.

(44)a. Sous le lit en lui-même n'est pas un bon endroit pour se cacher.
'Under the bed in itself is not a good place to hide oneself.'

b. *Shelby l'a perdu sous le lit en lui-même.
(Shelby lost it under the bed in itself/himself.)

When non-NP subjects are conjoined, we find that a bare emphatic reflexive is possible. (45a) and (45b) illustrate this for conjoined CPs and PPs, respectively.

(45)a. Qu'il démissionera et qu'il restera toujours à son poste me semblent maintenant eux-mêmes possibles.
'That he will resign and that he will remain in office seem to me at this point themselves possible.'

b. Séjourner dans les montagnes et longer la côte eux-mêmes me paraissent une façon admirable pour connaître la vrai France.
'Traveling in the mountains and going along the coast themselves appear to me an admirable way to get to know the real France.'

The appearance of *eux-mêmes* with the non-NP subjects in (45) supports the notion that they are in fact nominals covertly.

The facts above, taken together, present a convincing case for positing an obligatory DP structure for subjects in French and English. In the table below, we summarize the properties of non-NP subjects presented thus far.

Properties of non-NP subjects	English	French
obligatory raising of non-NP subjects	YES	YES
agreement with coordinated non-NP subjects	YES	YES
non-NP subjects host emphatic reflexives	YES	YES
non-NP subjects license plural adverbs	YES	(n.a.)

3.4 Subjacency and the relevance of subject islandhood

There is one additional diagnostic yet to be considered, that of subject islandhood. We have saved this for last because, under current P&P and Minimalist assumptions, the resistance to extraction of clauses in subject position is unconnected to their categorial status. This has not always been the case. In an attempt to provide a unified analysis for Ross' (1967) island effects, Chomsky (1973) adopted the Lees

(1960) and Rosenbaum (1967) NP-over-S analysis of sentential subjects, thereby providing a unified account for complex NP and subject islands (among others).

Chomsky (1986a) abandoned the theory of bounding nodes in an attempt to unify the subjacency account of subject and adjunct islands.

(46)a.　　*what$_1$ did [$_{IP}$ [$_{CP}$ t'$_1$ that John bought t$_1$] upset Jack]　　(subject island)

b.　　*what$_1$ did [$_{IP}$ Julia leave the party after [$_{CP}$ t'$_1$ Jack said t$_1$]]
　　　　　　　　　　　　　　　　　　　　　　　　　　　　　　　　　(adjunct island)

c.　　what$_1$ did [$_{IP}$ Julia think [$_{CP}$ t'$_1$ that Jack said t$_1$]]

In (46a) and (46b), extraction out of a CP in either subject or adjunct position creates a subjacency violation. These contrast with (46c), in which *wh*-movement is out of a CP complement of the verb *think*. This contrast is taken to result from the failure of subjects and adjuncts to be L-marked. That is, they are not (in Chomsky's terms) "directly θ-marked by a lexical category". Neither the subject CP in (46a) nor the adjunct CP in (46b) are L-marked. Both are therefore barriers. The IP that immediately dominates them is also a barrier (by inheritance). Thus, movement from t'_1 to $what_1$ crosses two barriers, violating subjacency. In (46c), by contrast, the CP object is L-marked and is not a barrier; extraction is therefore possible. Thus, in the *Barriers* model, sentential subjects are not islands for extraction due to any structural difference between them and sentential objects, but only due to differences in the way that they are θ-marked.

A closer look at the data shows that subjects and adjuncts are not quite as similar as Chomsky (and others) have supposed. It turns out that adjuncts, unlike subjects, are **not** always islands for extraction. (47) illustrates three varieties of adjuncts, while (48) illustrates the same phrases as subjects.

(47)a.　　*who$_1$ did [she go to Harvard [because she wanted to work with t$_1$]]

b.　　who$_1$ did [she go to Harvard [in order to work with t$_1$]]
　　　　　　　　　　　　　　　　　　　　　　　　　　　(Culicover 1997:253)

c.　　?what$_1$ did [he finish his thesis [without checking t$_1$]]

(48)a.　　*what$_1$ is [[that she wanted to learn t$_1$] unfortunate]

b.　　*what$_1$ is [[to learn t$_1$] very hard]

c.　　*what$_1$ is [[checking t$_1$] absolutely necessary before you turn in your thesis]

Here, we see that adjuncts are not always islands for extraction. In (47b) and (47c), extraction is possible out of an infinitival purpose clause and marginally out of a gerundive prepositional complement (in contrast with the tensed *because* adjunct in (47a)). Notice that the same phrases, in subject position, uniformly disallow *wh*-extraction. A *Barriers*-style account of subjacency applied to adjuncts wrongly predicts that (47b) and (47c) should be as ungrammatical as (47a), since neither is L-marked.

More recently, Uriagereka (1999) attributes subject islandhood to a left branch constraint on interpretation, and proposes that a system with multiple "spell-out" can predict certain islands. According to this account, if a category X is spelled-out, the system doesn't have access to its constituent parts, thus X becomes an island after its spell-out. By simplifying Kayne's (1994) LCA to its base step (iff A commands B, A precedes B), he ensures that right branches do not spell-out early, but left branches do. Since left-branches must spell-out early, if they are to be linearized by the LCA, left branching constituents such as subjects (in the languages we have examined) are predicted to be islands.

When we examine the facts of Bulgarian, we will have cause to question both of these current approaches to subject islandhood. However, we first want to establish that extraction from subject clauses is impossible for both languages under consideration. In French, as shown in (49) and (50), we find that extraction is impossible from both finite and infinitival subject clauses.

(49)a.   [que Marie a acheté une nouvelle auto], cela l'a énervé
          'That Mary bought a new car] made him angry.'

    b.   *quelle auto pensez-vous [que Marie a achetée] l'énervera
          (Which car do you think that Mary bought will make him angry?)

(50)a.   je pense [qu' acheter une nouvelle auto], l'énervera
          'I think that to buy a new car will make him angry.'

    b.   *que pensez-vous [qu'acheter] l'énervera
          (What do you think to buy will make him angry?)

From these and the preceding facts we can see that subjects are uniformly islands for extraction in both English and French. In the following table, these results are added to what we have already reported. Of course, if either the Barriers or the Minimalist accounts of subject islandhood are correct, then these facts are irrelevant to our current discussion of islandhood. However, note that both accounts make very strong claims regarding the universality of subject islandhood. Under the Barriers account, subject islandhood should be universal (since it is derived from the differences in how subjects and complements are assigned thematic roles). In the Uriagereka's Minimalist formulation, subjects should be islands whenever they are initial (i.e. occupy the left branch of a structure). In the following section, facts from Bulgarian will be seen to confound both accounts, and will lead us to propose that subject islandhood is connected with DP-hood of subjects, and that subjacency is best formulated in terms of bounding nodes (i.e., via reference to category labels).

Properties of non-NP subjects	English	French
obligatory raising of non-NP subjects	YES	YES
agreement with coordinated non-NP subjects	YES	YES
non-NP subjects host emphatic reflexives	YES	YES
non-NP subjects license plural adverbs	YES	(n.a.)
non-NP (clausal) subjects are extraction islands	YES	YES

4. THE CASE AGAINST A SEMANTIC ACCOUNT OF SUBJECT PROPERTIES

We made our initial observations about the constellation of properties characteristic of subjects and noted in particular that non-NP subjects and non-NPs in canonical NP complement positions displayed the full range of properties characteristic of DPs. Getting to this point, we were immediately hopeful of having discovered or come closer to discovering what the content of the EPP was. And if all languages exhibited these DP-properties, we'd have no reason to doubt that we were correct in our initial speculation. However, it did not take long to find that subjects do not exhibit this constellation of facts in all languages. For one thing, verb-initial languages routinely allow extraction from sentential subjects, a point we return to below. Of more immediate interest, however, is the case of Russian and Bulgarian, where we encounter languages in which non-NP subjects do not exhibit DP properties and not all subjects are islands. The Slavic data appear to support the position that subjects are islands when they are DPs and provide additional support for the notion that the islandhood of subjects can be reduced to the complex noun phrase constraint (CNPC). We will focus here on data from Bulgarian.

4.1 Bulgarian

Bulgarian has both "infinitival" IP subjects as in (51), and DP clausal subjects as in (52), that contain a clause headed by *tova* 'this' or *fakt* 'fact'. Infinitival subjects contrast with those in (52) in that they exhibit no DP properties (verb agreement, the ability to license emphatic reflexives, and islandhood).[17]

    (51)   [IP da zakəsnjavaš   na zasedanija] beše neprostimo
                        to be.late.2SG.IMP for meetings   was inexcusable
                    'To be late for meetings was inexcusable.'

    (52)a.   [DP tova/faktət če   Marija zabravi statijata] beše neprostimo
                    this/the.fact that Maria forgot   the.paper was inexcusable
                    '(The fact) that Maria forgot the paper was inexcusable.'

b.   [_DP_ zabravja-ne-to na knigata] beše neprostimo ot   strana na
        forget-ing-the of the.book was inexcusable from side   of
    Marija
    Maria
    'Maria's forgetting of the book was inexcusable.'

Bulgarian verbs agree with their subjects in person and number (and in gender with adjectival participles). As (53) shows, conjoined NPs obligatorily determine plural agreement on the copula with a predicate adjective.

(53)a.   Ivan i   Lili bjaxa nevnimatelni.
        Ivan and Lily were inattentive.PL
        'Ivan and Lily were inattentive.'

    b.   *Ivan i   Lili beše {nevnimatelna/nevnimatelen}.
        Ivan and Lily was {inattentive.FEM.SG/inattentive.MASC.SG}

While conjoined non-NP subjects in English and French can all trigger plural agreement on the verb, we find that plural agreement is not possible with conjoined infinitival subjects in Bulgarian. (54a) contrasts with (53) and (54b).

(54)a.   [_IP_ da zakəsnjavaš na zasedanija] i [_IP_ da zabravjaš knigite]
        to be.late   for meetings and to forget   the.books
        beše neprostimo / *bjaxa neprostimi
        was inexcusable.SG were inexcusable.PL
        'To be late for meetings and to forget the books was/*were inexcusable.'

    b.   [_DP_ tova če toj ne pozvəni] i   [_DP_ tova če ne se   izvini]
        this that he not called   and   this that not self apologized
        ?beše neprostimo / bjaxa neprostimi
        was inexcusable.SG were inexcusable.PL
        'That he didn't call and that he didn't apologize ?was/were inexcusable.'

We next examine the DP property of emphatic reflexives. Bulgarian NP subjects license emphatic reflexives, as in (55), where _profesorka_ licenses _samata_. As (56) shows, NP objects can also license the emphatic reflexive. (57) shows that nominalized -_ne_ clauses and _fakt če_ clauses also license emphatic reflexives.

(55)   Samata   profesorka proveri ispita   mi.
        the.herself professor   graded the.exam my
        'The professor herself graded my exam.'

(56)   (Az) vzex intervju   ot   samija   profesor.
          (I)   took interview from the.himself professor
          'I interviewed the professor himself.'

(57)a.   Samoto zabravjane na knigata beše neprostimo ot   strana na.
          the.itself forgetting of the.book was inexcusable from side   of
          Marija
          Maria
          'Maria's forgetting of the book itself was inexcusable.'

    b.   Samijat fakt če Marija zabravi knigata beše neprostim.
          the.self fact that Maria   forgot the.book was inexcusable
          'The fact that Maria forgot the book itself was inexcusable.'

Thus, emphatic reflexives can be licensed in Bulgarian by any type of NP in any
position, just as in English and French. However, unlike English, infinitival subjects
cannot license emphatic reflexives in Bulgarian. This is shown in (58), whose
ungrammaticality is due to the presence of the emphatic reflexive *samoto*.

(58)   *Samoto da zabraviš knigata beše neprostimo.
          the.self to forget   the.book was inexcusable
          (To forget the book was itself inexcusable.)

The ungrammaticality of (58) is evidence that non-nominal subjects in Bulgarian are
not open to the DP-shell analysis proposed above for English.
     We have established, in examining data from English and French, that non-NP
subjects have DP properties in these languages, and also that extraction from
sentential subjects is uniformly barred. If these two properties are correlated, as we
have shown above, then extraction from infinitival subjects in Bulgarian should be
possible. In fact, it is.

(59)   Kakvo beše neprostimo da zabraviš?
          what was inexcusable to forget
          'What to forget was inexcusable?'

(60)a.   Da publikuva roman beše celta   na nejnata kariera.
          to publish   novel was the.goal of the.hers career
          'To publish a novel was an important goal of her career.'

    b.   Kakvo da publikuva beše cel na nejnata kariera?
          what to publish   was goal of the.hers career
          'What to publish was an important goal of her career?'

(61)a. Mislja če za nego beše važno   da otide na kino.
        I.think that for him was important to go   to cinema
        'I think that it was important for him to go to the cinema.'

   b.   ?na kakvo$_1$ misliš   [če   beše važno   za nego [da otide t$_1$]]
        to what   you.think that was important for him   to go
        'To what do you think that it was important for him to go?'

   c.   na kakvo$_1$ misliš   [če [da otide t$_1$] beše važno   za nego]
        to what you.think that to go   was important for him
        'To what do you think that to go was important for him?'

(62)a. Tova če   toj šteše da otide na kino   beše važno   za nego.
        this that he would to go   to cinema was important for him
        'That he go to the cinema was important for him.'

   b.   Za nego beše važno   tova če   toj šteše da otide na kino.
        for him was important this that he   would to go   to cinema
        'It was important for him that he go to the cinema.'

   c.   *na kakvo$_1$ za nego beše važno   [tova če   toj šteše da otide t$_1$]
        to what for him was important this that he would to go
        (To what was it important for him that he go?)

In (59) and (60b), a *wh* element has been extracted from the infinitival subject of the matrix clause with grammatical results. In (61b) and (61c), a *wh* phrase extracted from the infinitival subject of the clausal complement of 'thinks' results in a well-formed constituent question. Notice in (62c), that extraction from a pronominally headed *tova če* clause is impossible (showing that, while extraction from subject clauses is possible, Bulgarian still has CNPC effects).

These data show unequivocally that extraction is possible from some subject clauses in Bulgarian (extraction which would be impossible in English and French). In fact, any explanation that does not appeal to a principled difference between Bulgarian infinitival subjects and their counterparts in English and French will fail. We would suggest that extraction out of Bulgarian clausal subjects is correlated with the language not requiring that all subjects be DPs. In contrast, extraction out of clausal subjects is impossible in English and French precisely because of the requirement that all subjects be DPs. With the DP node dominating the non-NP node, any extraction would necessarily cross two phrasal nodes and thus violate subjacency (under the more traditional node-based formulation), just as in a CNPC violation. In Bulgarian, when there is no DP node dominating a clausal subject, extraction does not entail a concomitant subjacency violation.[18]

The contrast between Bulgarian and the other languages examined above precludes the accounts of subject islandhood proposed in Chomsky 1986a and in Uriagereka 1999. Since not all subjects in all languages are islands, subject islandhood (where it is determined) cannot be a consequence of the manner in which subjects are assigned thematic roles. The non-universality of subject islands is further demonstrated in a number of V-initial languages (to be taken up in section 4.2). Accordingly, a thematically-based (i.e., semantic) explanation, such as that attempted in Chomsky 1986a, fails. An explanation based on some application of the Left Branch Condition (as Uriagereka (1999) suggests) fares even worse. Consider again the facts in (61). In (61c), the embedded infinitival subject occupies a left branch of the embedded clause whereas in (61b) the subject is postposed and occupies a right branch. Under Uriagereka's linearization-dependent account of islands, we would predict (61b) to be acceptable and (61c) to be ill-formed; however, native speakers report that (61c) is, in fact, preferable to (61b). This points once again to the conclusion that the difference rests in the category membership of the subjects in question, rather than their position. In other words, subject islands are simply another case of complex NP islands.

Given the distribution of properties summarized below, there is good evidence that Slavic non-NP subjects are not open to the DP-shell analysis we have proposed for English and French. This is especially important in that the Slavic data point away from a semantic explanation for the DP-like behavior of non-NP subjects in languages which do exhibit it, leading us to a syntactic account for the phenomena described in sections 1 and 3. This affirms our initial contention that the observed properties are due to the imposition of category membership (that is, a DP-shell structure). In the following section, we will consider the case of V-initial languages, and suggest that the ability of a language to impose DP-shell structure on subjects is at least to some extent configurationally dependent.

Properties of non-NP subjects	English/ French	Bulgarian/ Russian
obligatory raising of non-NP subjects	YES	(n.a.)[19]
agreement with coordinated non-NP subjects	YES	NO
non-NP subjects license emphatic reflexives	YES	NO
non-NP subjects license plural adverbs	YES	(n.a.)
non-NP (clausal) subjects are extraction islands	YES	NO

4.2 V-initial languages

This section examines V-initial languages with respect to obligatory DP-structure for subjects. We find that these languages fail to exhibit such properties, and propose that the reason for this is attributable to their structure. Specifically, we suggest that V-initial languages do not and cannot require their subjects to be DPs because of the manner in which VP constituents interact with the functional complex. In this regard, we follow Massam and Smallwood (1997) in their proposal for Niuean, wherein only the verb moves into the functional complex (and not the subject). By adopting their proposal as a general property of V-initial languages, we predict that such languages should (as a class) fail to have the subject properties found in English and French. Having argued, successfully we believe, that subject islandhood is a subcase of the CNPC, we will assume that it is another marker of obligatory DP-hood for subject position.

One immediately salient difference between languages, such as English and French, and V-initial languages is that raising (when attested) turns out not to be obligatory in V-initial languages. This is true at least for Irish (McCloskey 1985 and this volume), Malagasy (Travis, this volume), and Niuean (Seiter 1983). If V-initial languages do not require DP-hood of their subjects, then this is not surprising.

Malagasy, an Austronesian language of Madagascar, appears to provide some additional confirming evidence of our characterization of V-initial languages. Malagasy has a basic VOS structure, and there is evidence that non-NP subjects cannot be analyzed as NPs, thus making the DP-shell analysis untenable. NPs and CPs can appear as subjects, and can be conjoined; however, NPs and CPs take different coordinating conjunctions. The data in (63) illustrate conjoined CP subjects.[20]

(63)a.   mahasosotra an'i Soa [cp fa   nihira mafy i   Bozy
         annoy   ACC Soa   COMP PST.sing hard DET Bozy
         ary (*fa)   nitabataba   i   Be]
         and   COMP PST.make.noise DET Be
         'That Bozy sang loudly and that Be made a lot of noise annoys Soa.'

   b.   heveriko [cp fa   tsara tarehy i   Soa ary (*fa)   kinga saina i
         TT.think.me COMP good face   DET Soa and   COMP quick mind DET
         Rija]
         Rija
         'Soa is pretty and Rija is intelligent is thought by me.'

In (63a) and (63b) the conjoined sentences are subjects.[21] As (63) shows, *ary* is the coordinator for CP and IP constituents. In contrast, *sy* is the coordinator for NPs and smaller constituents, as seen below in (64) and (66). Thus, the first bit of evidence that the subjects in (63a) and (63b) are not NPs comes from the choice of coordinating conjunction. If the conjoined CP subjects in (63) were covert NPs (as might be expected if the EPP in this language involved a D-feature), then we might expect coordinated CP subjects to contrast with coordinated CP objects with respect to the coordinating conjunction that they selected.

The other piece of evidence for the non-DP-hood of CP subjects comes from the distribution of the quantificational adverb *samy* 'each'. When used preverbally, *samy* requires a plural subject; but crucially, only NPs can license this construction. (64) illustrates this with simple NPs.

(64)   Samy mamy ny   siramamy sy   ny   tantely.
        each sweet DET sugar   and DET honey
        'Both honey and sugar are sweet.'

When the conjoined subjects are CPs, this construction is illicit, as exemplified by
the ungrammaticality of the sentence in (65).

(65)   *Samy mahasosotra an'i Soa [CP fa   nihira   mafy i   Bozy
         each annoy   ACC Soa   COMP PST.sing hard DET Bozy
         ary (fa)   nitabataba   i   Be].
         and COMP PST.make.noise DET Be
         (Both that Bozy sang loudly and that Be made a lot of noise annoyed
         Soa.)

(65) is ungrammatical with or without the second complementizer. This contrasts
with conjoined nominalized clauses, which, as NPs take *sy* as a coordinator and can
license the occurrence of *samy*.

(66)   Samy mahasosotra an'i Soa i   Bozy nihira   mafy sy i   Be
         each annoy   ACC Soa DET Bozy PST.sing hard and DET Be
         nitabataba.
         PST.make.noise
         'Both Bozy singing loudly and Be making noise annoyed Soa.'

That the conjoined subjects in (66) are nominalized clauses is indicated by the word
order (the agent of the action here precedes rather than follows the verb).

Inasmuch as Malagasy clausal subjects do not display DP properties and thus are
not candidates for the DP-shell analysis, the fact that they are possible sites for
extraction is consistent with our proposal regarding subject islands. (67) illustrates
extraction from a clausal subject.

(67)   Oviano no nolazain-dRabe   fa   nanasa   lamba Rakoto?
         when   FOC PST.TT.say-GEN.Rabe COMP PST.wash cloth Rakoto
         'When was that Rakoto washed clothes said by Rabe?'

In this example, *oviano* 'when' crucially has scope over either the matrix or the
embedded predicate, and the resulting ambiguity reflects the possibility of extraction
from the CP subject.

As Chung (1982) points out, extraction is generally possible out of at least some
sentential subjects in V-initial languages. (68) provides an illustration from
Chamorro (from Chung 1982).

(68)   hafa₁ um-istoba hao [ni   maloago'-a . i   lhi-mu   t₁]?
         what UM-disturb you COMP want+NMLZ-his the son-your
         'What does that your son wants disturb you?'

Here, *hafa* 'what' has been extracted from the CP subject *ni maloago'-a i lhi-mu*
'that your son wants x'. Based on the evidence we have thus far and the

descriptions that we have available, we are led to the operative assumption that V-initial languages such as Chamorro, Malagasy, and Niuean do not require subjects to be DPs. Our analysis will follow on this assumption.

5. A TYPOLOGY OF SUBJECT-PROPERTIES AND
A THEORY OF SUBJECT POSITIONS

In this paper, we have tried to show that certain subject properties (when present) can be attributed to the language requiring that its subjects be DPs. The Bulgarian facts show that this property set is not universal, and is therefore unrelated to the semantic properties of subjects per se.

It is reasonable therefore to suggest that the requirement that all subjects be DPs (when a language imposes it) is due to the presence of some grammatical feature in a functional projection. In this regard, a D feature (Chomsky 1995) could be enlisted to do the job of explaining this requirement. Since an uninterpretable feature will force a derivation to crash if unchecked, the existence of a feature that is checked off by DPs might reasonably be expected to require that there be DPs to check. Thus, PP and CP subjects without DP shells would fail to check off the D-feature and would not yield licit derivations.

5.1 A typology

In comparing this state of affairs with that seen in V-initial languages, we might reasonably adopt Massam and Smallwood's (1997) account, which explains the language's V-initial (or predicate-initial) word order, the fact that "there are no [subject] expletives in the language" and that "grammatical subject ... is not associated with a unified position", and, by our predictions, the inability of Niuean and other V-initial languages to require subjects to be DPs. What emerges from this is a tentative typology of languages with respect to the requirement that their subjects be DPs. We have seen that SVO languages can , but do not always, impose a DP-subject requirement. For V-initial languages, the grammatical feature that produces V-initial (or predicate-initial) word order supplants the one that yields (in English) the DP-subject requirement, such that no V-initial language can require its subjects to be DPs This typology is expressed in the table here below.

	V-medial	V-initial
All subjects must be DP	English, French	—
Subjects need not be DP	Russian, Bulgarian	Chamorro, Irish, Malagasy, Niuean

From everything we have seen thus far, this typology appears to be correct. If it is not (that is, if there are V-initial languages whose non-NP subjects exhibit DP behavior), then Massam and Smallwood's account for V-initial order would need to be revisited. In what follows, we will propose an account in which Slavic languages share certain functional architecture of V-initial languages, even though their surface word order seems more like that of English and French.

5.2 A theory

Our proposal for the distribution of subject properties is as follows: Languages may be either V-prominent or D-prominent at the level of the clause. D-prominence correlates with the presence of a D-feature on T. V-prominence correlates with T being higher than Agr, and with the presence of a V-feature on T. Under this view, the EPP involves checking syntactic category features in T, which will be either D or V. In D-prominent languages, the EPP feature is checked by a DP in a spec position. In V-prominent languages, the EPP feature is checked by a verb moving into T.[22]

Given the mechanics of the EPP (or D-) feature under recent accounts such as Bobaljik & Jonas 1996 (B&J), the checking off of the D-feature of T will vary according to whether or not T projects a specifier position. Thus, for languages in which TP has no specifier (such as English), T (or the EPP feature itself) moves to Agr, and the D-feature of T is checked by an element in spec,AgrP. This is illustrated in (69). Now, as B&J have shown for Icelandic, some languages (optionally) have a spec,TP position in which the EPP D-feature can be checked. This results in transitive expletive constructions, such as (70) [=B&J:(27)]. The basic clausal architecture of Icelandic is given in in (71).

(69) $[_{AgrP}$ Spec $[_{Agr'}$ Agr $[_{TP}$ T ... $]]]$ English

(70) $[_{AgrSP}$ það $[_{Agr'}$ klaruðu$_2$ $[_{TP}$ margar mýs$_1$ $[_{T'}$ [alveg $[_{VP}$ t$_1$ t$_2$
          there   finished   many mice   completely
          ostinn] ...
          the.cheese

(71) $[_{AgrP}$ Spec $[_{Agr'}$ Agr $[_{TP}$ (Spec) $[_{T'}$ T ... $]]]$ Icelandic
                                          [+D]

In languages such as Icelandic, the D-feature of T can be checked from spec,TP (if it is present) or from spec,AgrP (assuming that the feature is passed up the tree when TP has no specifier position). According to Bobaljik 1995, the availability of a spec,TP correlates with the independence of tense and agreement morphology. In Bobaljik's terms "if tense morphology blocks agreement morphology, then that language does not license [spec,TP]." Icelandic contrasts with English in this regard, in having separable tense and agreement morphology. In this respect,

Bulgarian is similar to Icelandic. This is especially salient in the perfective verb
conjugation, given in (72).

(72)

	perfective	infinitival	aorist	future
1sg	kupja	da kupja	kupix	šte kupja
2sg	kupiš	da kupiš	kupi	šte kupiš
3sg	kupi	da kupi	kupi	šte kupi
1pl	kupim	da kupim	kupixme	šte kupim
2pl	kupite	da kupite	kupixte	šte kupite
3pl	kupjat	da kupjat	kupixa	šte kupjat

What is interesting about this verb conjugation is that the agreeing form cannot
normally be used as a main clause predicate without additional tense morphology, as
(73) shows. With added tense morphology, *kupya* can appear as a main or
embedded verb. This is shown in (74).

(73)   *(Az) kupja   pica.
            I   buy.1SG.PERF pizza
            (I (will) buy pizza.)

(74)a.   (Az) kupix   pica.
            I   bought.1SG   pizza
            'I bought a pizza.'

   b.   (Az) šte   kupja pica.
            I   will buy.1SG pizza
            'I will buy a pizza.'

   c.   (Az) iskam   da kupja   pica.
            I   want.1SG to buy.1SG pizza
            'I want to buy a pizza.'

The independence of Case/agreement from tense is further attested by the fact that
subjects of infinitival complements are nominative, when overt. This is seen in (32).
Thus, if Bobaljik's proposed correlation is accurate, Bulgarian should license (at
least optionally) a specifier of TP. We would propose that the special characteristics
of Bulgarian (and some other Slavic languages) arise from TP being superior to
AgrP, as in (75). In other words, Bulgarian is V-prominent.

(75)   (Az) iskam   tja da kupi   pica.
            I   want.1SG she to buy.3SG pizza
            'I want her to buy a pizza.'

(76)   [$_{TP}$ (Spec) [$_{T'}$ T [$_{AgrP}$ Spec [$_{Agr'}$ Agr ...]]]   Bulgarian
                     [+V]

Thus, unlike Icelandic (and English and French), Bulgarian has a V-feature in T, rather than a D-feature, and imposes no DP requirement on its subjects.

The structure proposed in (76) can explain other aspects of Bulgarian. If TP is higher than AgrP and if its specifier is optional, then we might expect to find clauses that are V-initial and which do not have any null pronominal preverbally. We do, in fact, find such structures and can show through definiteness restriction (DR) effects that they are truly V-initial, as Alexiadou and Anagnostopoulou 1998 (A&A) have done for Greek. Compare the English and Icelandic data in (77) [(34b)=A&A:(34)] with the Bulgarian example (78).

(77)a.   There arrived some students/*the students/*every student.   English

  b.   Lum nóttina   hafði [e] sokkið nokkrir bátar / *báturinn.   Icelandic
       in   the.night had   sunk   several boats   the.boat

(78)   Dojdoxa njakolko studenti / studentite / fsički studenti. Bulgarian
       came   some   students the.students all   students

As (77) shows, DR effects correlate with the presence of an expletive pronoun in subject position, whether overt or null. The lack of such effects in VS constructions can be argued to correlate with the absence of any such pronoun, and is consistent for Bulgarian with our proposal that the specifier of TP is optional. A partial derivation of (78) is given in (79).

(79)   [$_{TP}$ [$_T$ dojdoxa] [$_{AgrP}$ studentite [$_{Agr'}$ [$_{Agr}$] ...]]]

Notice that the inversion of TP and AgrP removes the need for an expletive to mediate the agreement of the verb with its following subject. In this account, *studentite* 'the students' does occupy spec,AgrP and has its agreement features and Case checked in the standard way.

Dative subject/nominative object experiencer verb constructions are another well-studied phenomenon that benefits under our account of Bulgarian clause structure. An example of this construction is given in (80). As is well known (Perlmutter 1978, Moore & Perlmutter 1997), the experiencer exhibits certain subject properties and the theme exhibits others. In particular, dative experiencers in Slavic are commonly found to precede the verb, as in (80), to antecede reflexives (in Russian, where the experiencer is a case-marked noun), and to control infinitival subjects as in (81). At the same time, the nominative theme controls verb agreement and carries nominative case. The structure of (80), in our account, is given in (82).

(80)   Na Marija i   xaresva   stolət.
         to Maria to.her is.pleasing the.chair.NOM
         'The chair is pleasing to Maria/Maria likes the chair'

(81)   Na Marija i   e neobxodimo da kupi knigata.
         to Maria to.her is necessary   to buy the.book
         'To Maria it is necessary to buy the book.'

(82) $[_{TP}$ na-Marija$_1$ $[_{T'}$ i-xaresva$_2$ $[_{AgrP}$ stolət$_3$ $[_{Agr'}$ t$'_2$ $[_{VP}$ t$_1$ t$_2$ t$_3$]]]

Here, we see that those subject properties best explained by command relations adhere to the dative argument in spec,TP, while the nominative/agreement properties are discharged in a lower AgrP. Coupled with the optionality of spec,TP and the absence of an EPP D-feature, this account can predict the possibility of V-initial order seen in (83), as well as the inversion of argument order, shown in (84).

(83)   Xaresva   i   stolət   na Marija.
         is.pleasing to.her the.chair.NOM to Maria

(84)   Stolət   i   xaresva   na Marija.
         the.chair.NOM to.her is.pleasing to Maria

In (83), we would assume that spec,TP is not instantiated, and in (84) we would suppose that the nominative theme moves through spec,AgrP to spec,TP and the dative experiencer remains in situ. As noted in Moore & Perlmutter, when the nominative theme occupies the higher position, it acquires additional subject properties, such as the ability to be a controlled PRO.

(85)a.   Marija$_1$ napravi fsičko vəzmožno ø$_1$ da mi   se   xaresa na men
         Maria   did   all   possible PRO to to.me self please to me
         'Maria did everything in order to please me.'

     b. *Marija$_1$ napravi fsičko vəzmožno na men da mi   se   xaresa ø$_{*1}$
         Maria   did   all   possible to me to to.me self please PRO

This is seen in (85). When the null pronominal is preverbal, it can be controlled by the subject of the matrix clause, and when the preverbal position is occupied by the dative experiencer phrase it cannot. Finally, if Bulgarian has the structure that we have proposed here and if V-initial languages also have TP as a highest functional projection (as in Massam & Smallwood), then the distinction between a language like Bulgarian and V-initial languages lies in the parametrization of spec,TP. According to our findings, Bulgarian is a fusion of Icelandic and Niuean properties.

ENDNOTES

[*]   We are extremely grateful to the following individuals for their questions, comments, and suggestions: Samuel Bayer, Si Belasco, Odutan Bode, Chris Culy, Alice Davison, Jila Ghomesi, Paula Kempchinsky, Gary Miller, Ileana Paul, Eric Potsdam, Nicholas Sobin, three anonymous reviewers for NLLT, participants at the 1999 LSA Institute Workshop on Grammatical Functions in Transformational Syntax, and audiences at ESCOL 1999 and WECOL 1999. Additionally, we are indebted to the following native speakers for extending their time and energy on behalf of our research: Hanaa Dornik, Elena Gavruseva, Denis Kopyl, Olga Petrova, Eric Roman, Elena Schmitt, and Mila Tasseva-Kurktchieva. Previous versions of parts of this paper have been presented and/or appeared as Davies & Dubinsky 1999a, b, and 2000b.

[1]   These observations are not novel. Stowell (1981) cites them in passing and Safir (1983) cites them as well, claiming that non-NPs in subject position are "honorary NPs" and for that reason must raise to receive case. We show below that actually the NP nature of all subjects is not "honorary" at all but is due to a much deeper facts about subjects, a fact which has ramifications beyond explaining the mysterious raising facts. Further, both Stowell (1981) and Safir (1983) claim that non-NP subjects are possible only with the copula *be*, a claim shown below to be incorrect.

[2]   Indeed, Stowell (1981) proposes that CPs should be prohibited from appearing in Case positions. His proposal follows from the widely accepted view first expounded in Emonds 1976 and Koster 1978, that sentential and prepositional subjects are not, in fact, subjects but in a topic position. Stowell's (1981) formalization of these claims is captured in his "Case Resistance Principle", which prohibits CPs, IPs, VPs, and PPs from appearing in Case-marked positions. In Davies and Dubinsky 2000c, we provide evidence that casts serious doubt on this view. We show that much of the data used to argue for this position are open to alternative (non-syntactic) explanations, or are simply not as unacceptable as previous authors have indicated (as measured by responses from a large number of speakers).

[3]   For independent reasons Sobin (1997) argues against the existence of default agreement in English.

[4]   As noted by Chris Culy (personal communication), there are cases in which an indefinite NP can host an emphatic reflexive pronoun.

> (i) Of course, that/a woman herself could decide to change her name.

Although a thorough account of the distribution of emphatic reflexives is outside the bounds of the current discussion, we observe that such exceptions necessarily involve 'possibility' modals such as *could, can, might*, or *may*. When the modal in (i) is absent, the emphatic reflexive is only possible with the definite NP, as (ii) shows.

> (ii) Of course, that/*a woman herself decided to change her name.

[5]   For reasons that are not entirely clear to us, emphatic reflexives with non-NP subjects are particularly perspicuous in *be enough to* locutions.

[6]   Since emphatic reflexives can only be used with phrases whose denotation is definite, AP subjects, which are properties, do not share this NP-like characteristic.

[7]   It is important to note that *equally* can also be licensed by conjoined predicates, as in (i). In (i), the subject is singular and the adverb *equally* is triggered by the two conjoined predicates.

> (i) Judy equally loved the candy and enjoyed the flowers.

For this reason, in testing the ability of APs to trigger *equally*, we are careful not to consider APs which are argument taking functions (i.e. predicates), but rather those which are arguments of a function (e.g. complements of a verb).

[8]   Chris Culy (personal communication) points out that the acceptability of *equally* with conjoined CP complements varies according to the choice of main verb. For instance, our example (15a) with *think* can be improved by use of the verb *believe*.

(i)   Dale believed equally that affirmative action is right and that he deserved to get the job.

In section 5, we will return to this issue, and demonstrate that the acceptability of (i) is dependent on the ability of *believe* (in contrast with *think*) to take a DP complement.

[9]   As stated above (note 2), our analysis precludes accounts of CP subjects that involve Case resistance (e.g., Stowell 1981), since "DP-covered" CP subjects occupy the normal subject position and behave as NPs. In Davies and Dubinsky 2000c, we show that finite clausal subjects are in fact not banned from inverted (and other relevant) contexts, as much of the literature has previously supposed.

     A further question arises as to the mechanism for licensing the null head of DP, which (appearing in spec,AgrP) occupies an ungoverned position. One possible mechanism for such licensing (as suggested by Liliane Haegeman, p.c.) would be to assume movement of the non-DP constituent to the spec,DP. The CP complement in (16a) would thus move as shown in (i).

(i)   [$_{DP}$ [$_{CP}$ that Shelby lost it]$_1$ [$_D$ ∅] t$_1$]

[10]   More recently, Webelhuth (1992) has proposed that external arguments must be nonverbal, i.e. [−V]. In his account, the distribution of CPs is constrained by their having to bind DP traces, rather than their being DPs themselves. We will return to this issue in section 5, which discusses the category type and distribution of verb complements.

[11]   Williams may have gotten this notion from Stowell 1981, in which it is claimed that subject PPs "appear to be strictly limited to copular constructions". However, counterevidence against this assertion is abundant (see, for example, Jaworska 1986).

[12]   Another recent paper, by Conway (1996), considers the status of certain PPs in subject and object positions. Based on similar evidence, Conway proposes an NP structure for these PPs, comparable to the one we have posited for non-NP subjects in general. However, her account suggests that these structures are limited to PPs and that their distribution is governed by semantic factors.

[13]   In his account of (25) and similar facts, Webelhuth proposes that "sentences can only bind DP traces". Under his analysis (25a) is grammatical because the trace following *believed* is a DP-trace (since *believe* allows a DP complement); (25b) is ill-formed because *hope* does not c-select DPs and the trace linked to the passivized subject cannot be a DP (as required). This account will not, however, explain the contrast in (26).

[14]   This analysis of the apparent island effect in (29) might lead one to wonder about the acceptability of sentences such as (i).

(i)   What rock did that creep crawl out from under?

We would suggest that the PP complements of *out* and of *from* are necessarily **not** DPs. This can be shown by trying to insert a DP in their place, as in (ii).

(ii)a.   *That creep crawled out it.

  b.   *That creep crawled out from it.

  c.   That creep crawled out from under it.

Examples (iia) and (iib) contrast with (iii).

(iii)   I'm worried about it.

[15] To say that plural or mass DPs license *equally* oversimplifies the situation. In fact, outside the case of conjoined predicates (cf. note 7), while a plural or mass DP is a necessary condition for licensing *equally* it is not a sufficient condition. It appears that there is some conditioning by verbal semantics as well. Thus, we find the following paradigm:

(i)a.   I believe Kerry and Kelsey equally.

b.   ??I believe Kerry and Kelsey equally well.

(ii)a.   I treat Kerry and Kelsey equally.

b.   I treat Kerry and Kelsey equally well.

(iii)a.   ?I know Kerry and Kelsey equally.

b.   I know Kerry and Kelsey equally well.

Important here is the fact that to the extent that (iiia) is acceptable, it is synonymous with (iiib). There is no such synonymy between (iia) and (iib), nor between (ia) and the unacceptable (ib). Thus, even though we have a plural DP in (iiia), *equally* is not licensed, a fact we attribute to the semantics of *know*.

[16] Of course, the PP and CP subjects can occur clause initially if the matrix clause has an impersonal subject **il** and the embedded clause contains a resumptive pronoun that is coindexed with it.

(i)   sous le lit$_1$, il ne me semble pas que ce$_1$ soit un bon endroit pour se cacher
        'Under the bed, it doesn't seem to me that it is a good place to hide oneself .'

(ii)   que Shelby l'a perdu$_1$, il me semble que ce$_1$ soit un fait
        'That Shelby lost it, it seems to me that it is a fact.'

[17] We focus here on infinitival subjects because they represent a class of elements that are unambiguously subjects and therefore allow us to make clear tests regarding the behavior of NP and non-NP subjects. While there are CP subjects and PP subjects which display the same properties as the infinitival subjects, there are at times confounding factors of analysis. CP subjects can be difficult to distinguish from complex NPs in certain environments, and because of this, it is difficult to state with certainty that a tensed exhibiting NP-like behavior is in fact a CP subject. PPs present an inverse case. The highly variable word order of the language makes it sometimes difficult to determine with certainty which clause-initial PPs are subjects and which ones are other left-dislocated phrases. Both locative inversion PPs and logical subject PPs of psychological predicates figure in this confusion. It can thus be difficult to ascertain whether the failure of a clause-initial PP to exhibit NP properties is due to the failure of subject position to induce such properties or to the mere fact that the PP in question is not a subject.

[18] Many have suggested to us that our DP-shell CNPC explanation for subject islands is challenged by the asymmetry in extraction from subject and object DPs, as exemplified in (i).

(i)a.   *who$_1$ were [$_{DP}$ these books about t$_1$] written by Ashley?

b.   who$_1$ did Ashley write [$_{DP}$ these books about t$_1$]?

In Davies & Dubinsky 2000a, we show: (1) that extractions such as in (ib) are quite limited in their distribution and normally involve activation of nominal argument structure, and (2) that extractions such as in (ia) are in fact licensed in Bulgarian.

(ii)   Za   kogo e knigata četena ot celija   klas
         about whom is book.the read   by whole.the class
         'About whom is the book being read by the class?'

This suggests to us that the contrast in (i), rather than being a problem for the analysis presented here, is instead a confirmation of it.

[19] The absence of raising constructions in Bulgarian and Russian turns out to be unsurprising if (as we show in section 5.2) their syntax is comparable to that of V-initial languages.

[20] We are indebted to Ileana Paul for the Malagasy data.

[21] In (25b) and (29), the verb is in the Theme Topic (TT) voice, one of the passive constructions in the language. In these sentences, the CP element is subject and the agent occurs in the genitive, suffixed to the verb.

[22] In the languages considered here, the choice of D or V as an EPP feature happens to correlate with the relative prominence of Agr and T. That is, the D-prominent languages English and French appear to have AgrP dominating TP, while the V-prominent languages (e.g. Bulgarian, Irish, and Niuean) have TP dominating AgrP. Goodall (in chapter 8) shows that Spanish has a D-feature in T (like English) but has TP dominating AgrP (as in Irish). He derives from this the behavior of pre- and post-verbal subjects. Proposals along these lines, in which a category oriented EPP feature is subject to parametric variation, have also been made in Massam and Smallwood 1997 and in Nash and Rouveret 1997 (although the particular implementation proposed is different in each case).

REFERENCES

Abney, Steven. 1987. *The English Noun Phrase in Its Sentential Aspect*, Doctoral dissertation, Massachusetts Institute of Technology.

Adger, David. 1996. 'Economy and Optionality: Interpretations of subjects in Italian' *Probus* 8, 117-136.

Adger, David. 1997. 'VSO Order and Weak Pronouns in Goidelic Celtic', *Canadian Journal of Linguistics* 42, 9-29.

Aissen, Judith. 1983. 'Indirect Object Advancement in Tzotzil' in David Perlmutter (ed.), *Studies in Relational Grammar 1*, University of Chicago Press, Chicago, pp. 272-302.

Aissen, Judith and David Perlmutter. 1976. 'Clause Reduction in Spanish', *Proceedings of the Annual Meeting of the Berkeley Linguistics Society* 2, 1-30. Revised version in David Perlmutter (ed.), 1983, *Studies in Relational Grammar*, University of Chicago Press, Chicago, pp. 360-403.

Alexiadou, Artemis. 1999. *On the Syntax of Nominalization and Possession: Remarks on patterns of Ergativity*, Doctoral dissertation, Universität Potsdam.

Alexiadou, Artemis and Elena Anagnostopoulou. 1998. 'Parametrizing AGR: Word order, V-movement and EPP-checking', *Natural Language and Linguistic Theory* 16, 491-539.

Allen, Barbara, Donald Frantz, Donna Gardiner, and David Perlmutter. 1990. 'Verb Agreement, Possessor Ascension, and Multistratal Representation in Southern Tiwa', in Paul Postal and Brian Joseph (eds.), *Studies in Relational Grammar 3*, University of Chicago Press, Chicago, pp. 321-383.

Alsina, Alex. 1992. 'On the Argument Structure of Causatives', *Linguistic Inquiry* 23, 517-555.

Alsina, Alex. 1993. *Predicate composition: A theory of syntactic function alternations*, Doctoral dissertation, Stanford University.

Alsina, Alex. 1996a. *The Role of Argument Structure in Grammar: Evidence from Romance*, CSLI Publications, Stanford.

Alsina, Alex. 1996b. 'Passive Types and the Theory of Object Asymmetries', *Natural Language and Linguistic Theory* 14, 673-723.

Alsina, Alex. 1999. 'Where's the Mirror Principle?', *The Linguistic Review* 16, 1-42.

Alsina, Alex. 2001. 'On the Nonsemantic Nature of Argument Structure', *Language Sciences* 23, 355-389.

Alsina, Alex and Sam Mchombo. 1993. 'Object Asymmetries and the Chichewa Applicative Construction', in Sam Mchombo (ed.), *Theoretical Aspects of Bantu Grammar*, CSLI Publications, Stanford, pp. 17-45.

Anderson, Stephen. 1976. 'On the notion of subject in ergative languages', in Charles Li (ed.), *Subject and Topic*, Academic Press, New York, pp. 1-24.

Austin, Peter. 2000. 'Arguments and Non-Arguments in Menó-Mené Sasak, Eastern Indonesia', Paper presented at the 7th Annual Meeting of the Austronesian Formal Linguistics Association, Vrije Universiteit, Amsterdam.

Baker, Mark. 1988a. *Incorporation: A Theory of Grammatical Function Changing*, University of Chicago Press, Chicago.

Baker, Mark. 1988b. 'Theta Theory and the Syntax of Applicatives in Chichewa', *Natural Language and Linguistic Theory* 6, 353-389.

Baker, Mark. 1991. 'On Some Subject/Object Non-Asymmetries in Mohawk', *Natural Language and Linguistic Theory* 9, 537-576.

Baker, Mark. 1993. 'Noun Incorporation and the Nature of Linguistic Representation', in William Foley (ed.), *The role of theory in language description*, Mouton de Gruyter, Berlin, pp. 13-44.

Baker, Mark. 1995. 'On the Absence of Certain Quantifiers in Mohawk', in Emmon Bach et al. (eds.), *Quantification in Natural Languages*, Kluwer, Dordrecht, pp. 21-58.

Baker, Mark. 1996a. 'On the Structural Position of Themes and Goals', in Johan Rooryck and Laurie Zaring (eds.), *Phrase Structure and the Lexicon*, Kluwer, Dordrecht, pp. 7-34.

Baker, Mark. 1996b. *The Polysynthesis Parameter*, Oxford University Press, Oxford.

Baker, Mark. 1996c. 'Unaccusativity and the Adjective/Verb Distinction: English and Mohawk Evidence', *Proceedings of the Eastern States Conference on Linguistics '96*, 12-35.

Baker, Mark. 1997. 'Thematic Roles and Syntactic Structure', in Liliane Haegeman (ed.), *Elements of Grammar: Handbook of Generative Syntax*, Kluwer, Dordrecht, pp. 73-137.

Baker, Mark. 2000. 'The Natures of Nonconfigurationality', in Mark Baltin and Chris Collins (eds.), *The Handbook of Contemporary Syntactic Theory*, Blackwell, Oxford.

Baker, Mark. to appear. *On Lexical Categories and Category Systems*, Cambridge University Press, Cambridge.

281

Baker, Mark, Kyle Johnson, and Ian Roberts. 1989. 'Passive Arguments Raised', *Linguistic Inquiry* 20, 219-252.

Baker, Mark and Osamuyimen Stewart. 1997. 'Unaccusativity and the Adjective/Verb Distinction: Edo Evidence', *Proceedings of the North Eastern Linguistic Society* 27, 33-48.

Baković, Eric. 1998. 'Optimality and Inversion in Spanish', in Pilar Barbosa et al. (eds.), *Is the Best Good Enough?*, MIT Press, Cambridge, MA.

Barbosa, Pilar. 1999. 'On Inversion in *Wh*-questions in Romance', unpublished manuscript, Universidade do Minho.

Barss, Andrew. 1986. *Chains and Anaphoric Dependence: On Reconstruction and Its Implications*, Doctoral dissertation, Massachusetts Institute of Technology.

Barss, Andrew and Howard Lasnik. 1986. 'A Note on Anaphora and Double Objects', *Linguistic Inquiry* 17, 347-354.

Bejar, Susana and Diane Massam. 1999. 'Multiple Case Checking', *Syntax* 2, 65-79.

Bell, Sarah. 1976. *Cebuano Subjects in Two Frameworks*, Doctoral dissertation, Massachusetts Institute of Technology.

Bell, Sarah. 1983. 'Advancements and Ascensions in Cebuano', in David Perlmutter (ed.), *Studies in Relational Grammar 1*, University of Chicago Press, Chicago, pp. 143-218.

Belletti, Adriana and Luigi Rizzi. 1988. 'Psych-Verbs and θ-Theory', *Natural Language and Linguistic Theory* 6, 291-352.

Biber, Douglas. 1989. 'A Typology of English Texts', *Linguistics* 27, 3-43.

Bickerton, Derek. 1990. *Language and species*, University of Chicago Press, Chicago.

Biggs, Bruce. 1974. 'Some Problems of Polynesian grammar', *Journal of the Polynesian Society* 83, 401-426.

Blake, Barry. 1990. *Relational Grammar*. Routledge, London.

Bittner, Maria. 1988. *Canonical and Non-Canonical Argument Positions*, Doctoral dissertation, University of Texas, Austin.

Bittner, Maria and Kenneth Hale. 1996. 'Ergativity: Towards a Theory of a Heterogeneous Class', *Linguistic Inquiry* 27, 531-604.

Bobaljik, Jonathan. 1992. 'Nominally Absolutive is Not Absolutely Nominative', *Proceedings of the West Coast Conference on Formal Linguistics* 11, 44-60.

Bobaljik, Jonathan. 1993. 'On Ergativity and Ergative Parameters', *MIT Working Papers in Linguistics* 19, 45-88.

Bobaljik, Jonathan. 1995. *Morphosyntax: the Syntax of Verbal Inflection*, Doctoral dissertation, Massachusetts Institute of Technology.

Bobaljik, Jonathan David and Dianne Jonas. 1996. 'Subject Positions and the Roles of TP', *Linguistic Inquiry* 27, 195-236.

Boeckz, Cedric. 2000. 'Quirky Agreement', *Studia Linguistica* 54, 354-380.

Bonet, Eulàlia. 1995. 'Feature Structure of Romance Clitics', *Natural Language and Linguistic Theory* 13, 607-647.

Borer, Hagit. 1980. 'Empty Subjects in Modern Hebrew and Constraints on Thematic Relations', *Proceedings of the North Eastern Linguistics Society* 10, 25-38.

Borer, Hagit. 1984. *Parametric Syntax: Case Studies in Semitic and Romance Languages*, Foris, Dordrecht.

Bošković, Željko. 1997. *The Syntax of Nonfinite Complementation: An Economy Approach*, MIT Press, Cambridge, MA.

Bowers, John. 1993. 'The Syntax of Predication', *Linguistic Inquiry* 24, 591-656.

Branigan, Philip. 1992. *Subjects and Complementizers*, Doctoral dissertation, Massachusetts Institute of Technology.

Branigan, Philip. 1996. 'Verb Second and the A-Bar Syntax of Subjects', *Studiea Linguistica* 50, 50-79.

Bresnan, Joan. 1972. *Theory of Complementation in English syntax*, Doctoral dissertation, Massachusetts Institute of Technology.

Bresnan, Joan. 1978. 'Realistic Transformational Grammar', in Morris Halle et al. (eds.), *Linguistic Theory and Psychological Reality*, MIT Press, Cambridge, MA.

Bresnan, Joan. 1980. 'Polyadicity: Part I of a Theory of Lexical Rules', in Teun Hoekstra et al.(eds.), *Lexical Grammar*, Foris, Dordrecht.

Bresnan, Joan. 1982a. 'Control and Complementation', in Joan Bresnan (ed.), *The Mental Representation of Grammatical Relations*, MIT Press, Cambridge, MA, pp. 282-390.

Bresnan, Joan (ed.). 1982b. *The Mental Representation of Grammatical Relations*, MIT Press, Cambridge, MA.

Bresnan, Joan. 1994. 'Locative Inversion and the Architecture of Universal Grammar', *Language* 70, 72-131.

Bresnan, Joan. 2000. *Lexical Functional Syntax*, Blackwell, Oxford.

Bresnan, Joan and Jonni Kanerva. 1989. 'Locative Inversion in Chichewa: A Case Study of Factorization in Grammar', *Linguistic Inquiry* 20, 1-50.

Bresnan, Joan and Lioba Moshi. 1990. 'Object Asymmetries in Comparative Bantu syntax', *Linguistic Inquiry* 21, 147-185.

Bresnan, Joan and Sam Mchombo. 1985. 'Agreement and Pronominal Incorporation in Chichewa', unpublished manuscript, Stanford University.

Bresnan, Joan and Sam Mchombo. 1987. 'Topic, Pronoun, and Agreement in Chichewa', *Language* 63, 741-782.

Burzio, Luigi. 1986. *Italian Syntax: A Government-Binding Approach*, Reidel, Dordrecht.

Campana, Mark. 1992. *A Movement Theory of Ergativity*, Doctoral dissertation, McGill University.

Campos, Héctor. 1997. 'On Subject Extraction and the Antiagreement Effect in Romance', *Linguistic Inquiry* 28, 92-119.

Cardinaletti, Anna. 1997. 'Subjects and Clause Structure', in Liliane Haegeman (ed.), *The New Comparative Syntax*, Addison, Wesley, Longman, London, pp. 33-63.

Carnie, Andrew. 1995. *Non-Verbal Predication and Head-Movement*, Doctoral dissertation, Massachusetts Institute of Technology.

Carnie, Andrew and Eithne Guilfoyle (eds.). 2000. *The Syntax of Verb Initial Languages*, Oxford University Press, Oxford.

Carnie, Andrew and Heidi Harley. 1998. 'Clausal architecture: the licensing of major constituents in a verb initial language', unpublished manuscript, University of Arizona.

Carstairs-McCarthy, Andrew. 1999. *The Origins of Complex Language: An Inquiry into the Evolutionary Beginnings of Sentences, Syllables, and Truth*, Oxford University Press, Oxford.

Casielles Suárez, Eugenia. 1997. 'On Topical Phrases in Spanish', Paper presented at 7° Congreso de Gramática Generativa, Universidad de Oviedo.

Chametsky, Robert. 2000. *Phrase Structure: From GB to Minimalism*, Blackwell, Oxford.

Chomsky, Noam. 1955. 'The Logical Structure of Linguistic Theory', unpublished manuscript, Harvard University and Massachusetts Institute of Technology. Revised 1956 version published in part by Plenum, New York (1975) and University of Chicago Press, Chicago (1985).

Chomsky, Noam. 1965. *Aspects of the Theory of Syntax*, MIT Press, Cambridge, MA.

Chomsky, Noam. 1973a. 'Conditions on Transformations', in Steven Anderson and Paul Kiparsky (eds.), *A Festschrift for Morris Halle*, Holt, Rinehart, and Winston, New York.

Chomsky, Noam. 1973b. 'Remarks on Nominalizations', in Steven Anderson and Paul Kiparsky (eds.), *A Festschrift for Morris Halle*, Holt, Rinehart, and Winston, New York.

Chomsky, Noam. 1981. *Lectures on Government and Binding. Studies in Generative Grammar 9*, Foris, Dordrecht.

Chomsky, Noam. 1982. *Some Concepts and Consequences of the Theory of Government and Binding*, MIT Press, Cambridge, MA.

Chomsky, Noam. 1986a. *Barriers*, MIT Press, Cambridge, MA.

Chomsky, Noam. 1986b. *Knowledge of Language: Its Nature, Origin, and Use*, Praeger, New York.

Chomsky, Noam. 1991. 'Some Notes on Economy of Derivation and Representation', in Robert Freidin (ed.), *Principles and Parameters in Comparative Grammar*, MIT Press, Cambridge, Mass, pp. 417-454. Reprinted (with minor revisions) in Noam Chomsky, 1993, *The Minimalist Program*, pp. 129-166.

Chomsky, Noam. 1993. 'A Minimalist Program for Linguistic Theory', in Kenneth Hale and Samuel Jay Keyser (eds.), *The View from Building 20: Essays in Linguistics in Honor of Sylvain Bromberger*, MIT Press, Cambridge, MA, pp. 1-52.

Chomsky, Noam. 1995. *The Minimalist Program*, MIT Press, Cambridge, MA.

Chomsky, Noam. 1998. 'Minimalist Inquiries: the Framework', *MIT Occasional Papers in Linguistics* 15, MIT Working Papers in Linguistics, Cambridge, MA. Reprinted in Roger Martin et al. (eds.), 2000, *Step by step: Essays on minimalist syntax in honor of Howard Lasnik*, MIT Press, Cambridge, MA, pp. 89-156.

Chomsky, Noam. 1999. 'Derivation by phase', *MIT Occasional Papers in Linguistics* 18. MIT Working Papers in Linguistics, Cambridge, MA. Reprinted in Michael Kenstowicz (ed.), 2001, *Ken Hale: A Life in Language,* MIT Press, Cambridge, MA, pp. 1-52.

Chung, Sandra. 1976. 'An Object Creating Rule in Bahasa Indonesia', *Linguistic Inquiry* 7, 41-87.

Chung, Sandra. 1978. *Case Marking and Grammatical Relations in Polynesian,* University of Texas Press, Austin.

Chung, Sandra. 1982. 'Unbounded Dependencies in Chamorro Grammar', *Linguistic Inquiry* 13, 39-77.

Chung, Sandra. 1983. 'An Object-Creating Rule in Bahasa Indonesia', in David Perlmutter (ed.), *Studies in Relational Grammar 1,* University of Chicago Press, Chicago, pp. 219-271.

Chung, Sandra. 1998. *The Design of Agreement,* University of Chicago Press, Chicago.

Chung, Sandra and James McCloskey. 1987. 'Government, Barriers and Small Clauses in Modern Irish', *Linguistic Inquiry* 18, 173-237.

Chung, Sandra and William Seiter. 1980. 'The History of Raising and Relativization in Polynesian', *Language* 56, 622-638.

Cinque, Gugliemo. 1990. 'Ergative Adjectives and the Lexicalist Hypothesis', *Natural Language and Linguistic Theory* 8, 1-40.

Cinque, Guglielmo. 1999. *Adverbs and Functional Heads: A Cross-Linguistic Perspective.* Oxford University Press, Oxford.

Clark, Eve. 1978. 'Locationals: Existential, Locative, and Possessive Constructions', in Joseph Greenberg et al. (eds.), *Universals of Human Language,* Vol. 4, Stanford University Press, Stanford, pp. 85-126.

Cole, Peter and Gabriella Hermon. 1981. 'Subjecthood and Islandhood: Evidence from Quechua', *Linguistic Inquiry* 12, 1-30.

Collins, Chris and Höskuldur Thráinsson. 1996. 'VP-Internal Structure and Object Shift in Icelandic', *Linguistic Inquiry* 27, 391-444.

Contreras, Heles. 1991. 'On the Position of Subjects', in Susan Rothstein (ed.), *Perspectives on Phrase Structure: Heads and Licensing, Syntax and Semantics* Vol. 25, Academic Press, New York.

Conway, Laura. 1996. 'NPs in Disguise', unpublished manuscript, University of Connecticut.

Cook, Kenneth. 1991. 'The Search for Subject in Samoan', in Robert Blust (ed.), *Currents in Pacific Linguistics,* Australian National University, Pacific Linguistics C-117, Canberra.

Croft, William. 1998. 'Event Structure in Argument Linking', in Miriam Butt and Wilhelm Geuder (eds.), *The Projection of Arguments: Lexical and Compositional Factors,* CSLI Publications, Stanford, pp. 21-63.

Culicover, Peter. 1997. *Principles and Parameters: An Introduction to Syntactic Theory,* Oxford University Press, Oxford.

Cummins, Sarah. 2000. 'Autopsie d'un diagnostic', *Proceedings of the Annual Meeting of the Canadian Linguistics Association.*

Dalrymple, Mary, Sam Mchombo, and Stanley Peters. 1994. 'Semantic Similarities and Syntactic Contrasts Between Chichewa and English Reciprocals', *Linguistic Inquiry* 25, 145-163.

Davies, William. 1984. 'Antipassive: Choctaw Evidence for a Universal Characterization', in David Perlmutter and Paul Postal (eds.), *Studies in Relational Grammar 2,* University of Chicago Press, Chicago, pp. 331-376.

Davies, William and Stanley Dubinsky. 1999a. 'Sentential Subjects as Complex NPs: New Reasons for an Old Account of Subjacency', *CLS 34: The Main Session,* 83-94.

Davies, William and Stanley Dubinsky. 1999b. 'The Syntax of Non-NP Subjects in an Exploration of Subject Properties', Paper presented at The Role of Grammatical Functions in Transformational Syntax Workshop, University of Illinois.

Davies, William and Stanley Dubinsky. 2000a. 'Bypassing Subjacency Effects: How Event Structure Amnesties Extraction out of Object NPs', Paper presented at North Eastern Linguistics Society 31, Georgetown University.

Davies, William and Stanley Dubinsky. 2000b. 'Functional Structure and a Parameterized Account of Subject Properties', *Proceedings of the Eastern States Conference on Linguistics '99,* 48-59.

Davies, William and Stanley Dubinsky. 2000c. 'Why Sentential Subjects Do So Exist (but are Nonetheless Kinda Weird)', Paper presented at South Eastern Conference on Linguistics, University of Mississippi.

Davies, William and Asunción Martínez-Arbelaiz. 1995. 'Mapping Basque Psych Verbs', in Clifford Burgess et al. (eds.), *Grammatical Relations: Theoretical Approaches to Empirical Questions,* CSLI Publications, Stanford, pp. 33-44.

Davies, William and Carol Rosen. 1988. 'Unions as Multi-predicate Clauses', *Language* 64, 52-88.
Davies, William and Luis Enrique Sam-Colop. 1990. 'K'iche' and the Structure of Antipassive', *Language* 66, 522-549.
de Hoop, Helen. 1992. *Case Configuration and Noun Phrase Interpretation*, Doctoral dissertation, University of Groningen.
Déchaine, Rose-Marie. 1993. *Predicates Across Categories: Towards a Category-Neutral Syntax*, Doctoral dissertation, University of Massachusetts.
Déchaine, Rose-Marie. 1994. 'Ellipsis and the Position of Subjects', *Proceedings of the North Eastern Linguistics Society* 24, 47-63.
DeGraff, Michel. 1997. 'Nominal Predication in Haitian and Irish', *Proceedings of the West Coast Conference on Formal Linguistics* 16, 113-128.
Demonte, Violeta. 1987. 'C-command, Prepositions, and Predication', *Linguistic Inquiry* 18, 147-157.
den Dikken, Marcel. 1995. 'Binding, Expletives, and Levels', *Linguistic Inquiry* 26, 347-354.
Diesing, Molly. 1990. 'Verb Movement and the Subject Position in Yiddish', *Natural Language and Linguistic Theory* 8, 41-80.
Diesing, Molly. 1992. *Indefinites*, MIT Press, Cambridge, MA.
Diesing, Molly. 1996. 'Semantic Variables and Object Shift', in Höskuldur Thráinsson et al. (eds.), *Studies in Comparative Germanic Syntax*, Vol. II, Kluwer, Dordrecht, pp. 66-84.
Dixon, R. M. W. 1968. *The Dyirbal Language of North Queensland*, Doctoral dissertation, University of London.
Dixon, R. M. W. 1979. 'Ergativity', *Language* 5, 59-138.
Dixon, R. M. W. 1994. *Ergativity*, Cambridge University Press, Cambridge.
Doherty, Cathal. 1996. 'Clausal Structure and the Modern Irish Copula', *Natural Language & Linguistic Theory* 14, 1-48.
Doherty, Cathal. 1997. 'Predicate Initial Constructions in Irish', *Proceedings of the West Coast Conference on Formal Linguistics* 15, 81-95.
Doron, Edit. 1991. 'V-Movement and VP Ellipsis', unpublished manuscript, The Hebrew University of Jerusalem.
Doron, Edit. 1999. 'V-Movement and VP ellipsis', in Shalom Lappin and Elabbas Benmamoun (eds.), *Fragments: Studies in Ellipsis and Gapping*, Oxford University Press, Oxford, pp. 124-140.
Dowty, David. 1979. *Word Meaning and Montague Grammar*, Reidel, Dordrecht.
Dowty, David. 1991. 'Thematic Proto-Roles and Argument Selection', *Language* 67, 547-619.
Dryer, Matthew. 1986. 'Primary Objects, Secondary Objects, and Antidative', *Language* 62, 808-845.
Duffield, Nigel. 1995. *Particles and Projections in Irish Syntax*, Kluwer, Dordrecht.
Dubinsky, Stanley. 1990. 'Japanese Direct Object to Indirect Object Demotion', in Paul Postal and Brian Joseph (eds.), *Studies in relational grammar 3*, University of Chicago Press, Chicago, pp. 49-86.
Dubinsky, Stanley. 1997. 'Predicate Union and the Syntax of Japanese Passives', *Journal of Linguistics* 33, 1-37.
Dukes, Michael. 1996. *On the Non-Existence of Anaphors and Pronominals in the Grammar of Tongan*, Doctoral dissertation, University of California, Los Angeles.
Dukes, Michael. 1998. 'Evidence for Grammatical Functions in Tongan', Paper presented at LFG98: International Lexical Functional Grammar Conference.
Dukes, Michael. 2000. 'Grammatical Properties of the Ergative Noun Phrase in Tongan', unpublished manuscript. Stanford University and University of Canterbury, New Zealand.
Eguren, Luis. 1999. 'Pronombres y Adverbios Demostrativos: las Relaciones Deícticas', in Ignacio Bosque and Violeta Demonte (eds.), *Gramática Descriptiva de la Lengua Española*, Vol. 1, Espasa Calpe, Madrid.
Emonds, Joseph. 1970. *Root and Structure-Preserving Transformations*, Doctoral dissertation, Massachusetts Institute of Technology.
Emonds, Joseph. 1976. *A Transformational Approach to English Syntax: Root, Structure-Preserving, and Local Transformations*, Academic Press, New York.
Epstein, Samuel. 1992. 'Derivational Constraints on A'-chain Formation', *Linguistic Inquiry* 23, 235-258.
Epstein, Samuel and Daniel Seely. 1999. 'Spec-ifying the GF 'Subject': Eliminating A-chains and the EPP within a Derivational Model', Paper presented at The Role of Grammatical Functions in Transformational Syntax Workshop, University of Illinois.
Fernández Soriano, Olga. 1999. 'Two Types of Impersonal Sentences in Spanish: Locative and Dative Subjects', *Syntax* 2, 101-140.

Fiengo, Robert and Robert May. 1994. *Indices and Identity*, MIT Press, Cambridge, MA.

Fillmore, Charles. 1968. 'The Case for Case', in Emmon Bach and Robert Harms (eds.), *Universals in Linguistic Theory*, Holt, Rinehart, and Winston, New York.

Finer, Daniel. 1997. 'Contrasting A'-Dependencies in Selayarese', *Natural Language and Linguistic Theory* 15, 677-728.

Fodor, Jerry. 1970. 'Three Reasons for Not Deriving 'Kill' from 'Cause to Die'', *Linguistic Inquiry* 1, 429-438.

Foley, William and Robert Van Valen Jr.. 1984. *Functional Syntax and Universal Grammar*, Cambridge University Press, Cambridge.

Franco, Jon. 1993. *On Object Agreement in Spanish*, Doctoral dissertation, University of Southern California.

Freeze, Ray. 1992. 'Existentials and Other Locatives', *Language* 68, 553-595.

Freidin, Robert. 1978. 'Cyclicity and the Theory of Grammar', *Linguistic Inquiry* 9, 519-550.

Fukui, Naoki and Margaret Speas. 1986. 'Specifiers and Projections' *MIT Working Papers in Linguistics* 8, 128-172.

Georgopoulos, Carol. 1985. 'Variables in Palauan Syntax', *Natural Language and Linguistic Theory* 3, 59-94.

Georgopoulos, Carol. 1991. *Syntactic Variables: Resumptive Pronouns and A-bar Binding in Palauan*, Kluwer, Dordrecht.

Gibson, Jeanne. 1980. *Clause Union in Chamorro and in Universal Grammar*, Doctoral dissertation, University of California, San Diego.

Gibson, Jeanne and Eduardo Raposo. 1986. 'Clause Union, the Stratal Uniqueness Law and the Chômeur Relation', *Natural Language and Linguistic Theory* 4, 295-331.

Goodall, Grant. 1992. 'On the Status of SPEC of IP', *Proceedings of the West Coast Conference on Formal Linguistics* 10, 175-182.

Goodall, Grant. 1993. 'SPEC of IP and SPEC of CP in Spanish *wh*-questions', in William Ashby et al. (eds.), *Linguistic Perspectives on the Romance Languages*, John Benjamins, Amsterdam, pp. 199-209.

Goodall, Grant 2001. 'On Preverbal Subjects in Spanish', in Diana Cresti et al. (eds.), *Current Issues in Linguistics Theory: Selected Papers from the 29th Linguistics Symposium on Romance Languages*, John Benjamins, Amsterdam, pp. 92-106.

Green, Georgia M. 1974. *Semantics and Syntactic Regularity*, Indiana University Press, Bloomington.

Grimshaw, Jane. 1979. 'Complement Selection and the Lexicon', *Linguistic Inquiry* 10, 279-326.

Grimshaw, Jane. 1982. 'On the Lexical Representation of Romance Reflexive Clitics', in Joan Bresnan (ed.), *The Mental Representation of Grammatical Relations*, MIT Press, Cambridge, MA, pp. 87-148.

Grimshaw, Jane. 1987. 'Psych Verbs and the Structure of Argument Structure', unpublished manuscript, Brandeis University.

Grimshaw, Jane. 1991. 'Extended Projection', unpublished manuscript, Rutgers University.

Grimshaw, Jane. 1997. 'Projections, Heads and Optimality', *Linguistic Inquiry* 28, 373-422.

Groos, Anneke and Reineke Bok-Bennema. 1986. 'The Structure of the Sentence in Spanish', in Ivonne Bordelois et al. (eds.), *Generative Studies in Spanish Syntax*, Foris, Dordrecht, pp. 67-80.

Gruber, Jeffrey. 1976. *Lexical Structures in Syntax and Semantics*. North-Holland, New York.

Guilfoyle, Eithne. 1990. *Functional Categories and Phrase Structure Parameters*, Doctoral dissertation, McGill University.

Guilfoyle, Eithne. 1994. 'VNP's, Finiteness and External Arguments', *Proceedings of the North Eastern Linguistics Society* 24, 141-155.

Guilfoyle, Eithne, Henrietta Hung, and Lisa deMena Travis. 1992. 'Spec of IP and Spec of VP: Two Subjects in Austronesian Languages', *Natural Language and Linguistic Theory* 10, 375-414.

Gutiérrez Rexach, Javier. 1996. 'The Scope of Universal Quantifiers in Spanish Interrogatives', in Karen Zagona (ed.), *Grammatical Theory and Romance Languages*, John Benjamins, Amsterdam.

Haeberli, Eric. 2000. 'Towards Deriving the EPP and Abstract Case', *Generative Grammar in Geneva (GG@G)* 1, 105-139.

Haegeman, Liliane. 1991. *Introduction to Government and Binding Theory*, Blackwell, Oxford.

Haegeman, Liliane. 1992. *Theory and Description in Generative Grammar: A Case Study in West Flemish*, Cambridge University Press, Cambridge.

Haegeman, Liliane. 1996. 'Verb Second, the Split CP, and Initial Null Subjects in Early Dutch finite Clauses', *GenGenP, Geneva Working Papers in Generative Linguistics*, 133-175.

Haegeman, Liliane (ed.) 1997. *Elements of Grammar: Handbook of Generative Syntax*, Kluwer, Dordrecht.

Hale, Kenneth. 1983. 'Warlpiri and the Grammar of Nonconfigurational Languages', *Natural Language and Linguistic Theory* 1, 5-49.

Hale, Kenneth and Samuel Jay Keyser. 1993. 'On Argument Structure and the Lexical Expression of Syntactic Relations', in Kenneth Hale and Samuel Jay Keyser (eds.), *The View from Building 20: Essays in Honor of Sylvain Bromberger*, MIT Press, Cambridge, MA, pp. 53-109.

Harley, Heidi. 1995. *Subjects, Events and Licensing*, Doctoral dissertation, Massachusetts Institute of Technology.

Harley, Heidi and Rolf Noyer. 1998. 'Mixed Nominalizations, Short Verb Movement and Object Shift in English', *Proceedings of the North Eastern Linguistic Society* 28.

Hawkins, John. 1994. *A Performance Theory of Order and Constituency*, Cambridge University Press, Cambridge.

Hernanz, M. Lluïsa. 1999. 'El Infinitivo', in Ignacio Bosque and Violeta Demonte (eds.), *Gramática Descriptiva de la Lengua Española*, Vol 2, Espasa Calpe, Madrid.

Hoekstra, Teun. 1984. *Transitivity: Grammatical Relations in Government-Binding Theory*, Foris, Dordrecht.

Hoekstra, Teun and René Mulder. 1990. 'Unergatives as Copula Verbs: Locational and Existential Predication', *The Linguistic Review* 7, 1-79.

Hoji, Hajime. 1985. *Logical Form Constraints and Configurational Sructures in Japanese*. Doctoral dissertation, University of Washington.

Hoji, Hajime. 1998. 'Null Objects and Sloppy Identity in Japanese', *Linguistic Inquiry* 28, 127-152.

Holmberg, Anders. 1986. *Word Order and Syntactic Features in the Scandinavian Languages and English*, Doctoral dissertation, University of Stockholm.

Holmberg, Anders. 1993. 'Two Subject Positions in IP in Mainland Scandinavian', *Working Papers in Scandinavian Syntax* 52, 29-41.

Holmberg, Anders and Urpo Nikanne. 1994. 'Expletives and Subject Positions in Finnish' *Proceedings of North Eastern Linguistics Society* 24, 173-187.

Holmberg, Anders and Christer Platzack. 1995. *The Role of Inflection in Scandinavian Syntax*, Oxford University Press, Oxford.

Hooper, Robin. 2000. 'Revisiting the Subject: Properties of Ergative and Absolutive Arguments in Tokelauan', *Leo Pasifika: Proceedings of the Fourth International Conference on Oceanic Linguistics*, 156-172.

Hornstein, Norbert. 1999. 'Minimalism and Quantifier Raising', in Samuel Epstein and Norbert Hornstein (eds.), *Working Minimalism*. MIT Press, Cambridge, MA.

Hung, Henrietta. 1988. 'Malagasy Field Notes', unpublished manuscript, McGill University.

Iatridou, Sabine. 1990. 'About Agr(P)', *Linguistic Inquiry* 21, 551-577.

Jackendoff, Ray. 1972. *Semantic Interpretation in Generative Grammar*, Cambridge University Press, Cambridge.

Jackendoff, Ray. 1990. 'On Larson's Treatment of the Double Object Construction', *Linguistic Inquiry* 21, 427-455.

Jackendoff, Ray. 1996. 'The Proper Treatment of Measuring Out, Telicity, and Perhaps Even Quantification in English', *Natural Language and Linguistic Theory* 14, 305-354.

Jackendoff, Ray. 1997. *The Architecture of the Language Faculty*, MIT Press, Cambridge, MA.

Jaeggli, Osvaldo. 1987. 'ECP Effects at LF in Spanish', in Jean-Pierre Montreuil (ed.), *Advances in Romance Linguistics*, Foris, Dordrecht.

Jaworska, Ewa. 1986. 'Prepositional Phrases as Subjects and Object', *Journal of Linguistics* 22, 355-74.

Jayaseelan, Karattuparambil. 1990. 'Incomplete VP Deletion and Gapping', *Linguistic Analysis* 20, 64-81.

Johnson, David and Paul Postal. 1980. *Arc Pair Grammar*, Princeton University Press, Princeton.

Johnson, Kyle. 1991. 'Object Positions', *Natural Language and Linguistic Theory* 9, 577-636.

Jonas, Dianne. 1996. Clause Structure, Expletives and Movement, in Werner Abraham et al. (eds.), *Minimal Ideas: Syntactic Studies in the Minimalist Framework*, John Benjamins, Amsterdam and Philadelphia, pp. 67-188.

Kayne, Richard. 1975. *French Syntax*, MIT Press, Cambridge, MA

Kayne, Richard. 1984. *Connectedness and Binary Branching*, Foris, Dordrecht.

Kayne, Richard. 1985. 'Principles of Particle Constructions', in Jacqueline Guéron et al. (eds.), *Grammatical Representation*, Foris, Dordrecht, pp. 101-140.

Kayne, Richard. 1989. 'Facets of Romance Past Participle Agreement', in Paola Benincà (ed.), *Dialect Variation and the Theory of Grammar*, Foris, Dordrecht.

Kayne, Richard. 1994. *The Antisymmetry of Syntax*, MIT Press, Cambridge, MA.

Kayne, Richard. 1998. 'Overt vs. Covert Movement', *Syntax* 1, 128-191.

Keenan, Edward. 1976a. 'Remarkable Subjects in Malagasy', in Charles Li (ed.), *Subject and Topic*. Academic Press, New York, pp. 249-301.

Keenan, Edward. 1976b. 'Towards a Universal Definition of "Subject"', in Charles Li (ed.), *Subject and Topic*, Academic Press, New York, pp. 303-333.

Keenan, Edward. 1999. 'Morphology is Structure: a Malagasy Test Case', in Ileana Paul et al. (eds.), *Formal Issues in Austronesian Linguistics*, Kluwer, Dordrecht, pp. 27-47.

Keenan, Edward and Bernard Comrie. 1977. 'Noun Phrase Accessibility and Universal Grammar', *Linguistic Inquiry* 8, 63-99.

Keenan, Edward and Baholisoa Ralalaoherivony. 1998. 'Raising from NP in Malagasy', *UCLA Working Papers in Linguistics*.

Kempchinsky, Paula. 2001. 'PP Preposing in Spanish and English: A Minimalist View' in Diana Cresti et al. (eds.), *Current Issues in Linguistics Theory: Selected Papers from the 29th Linguistics Symposium on Romance Languages*, John Benjamins, Amsterdam, pp. 140-153.

Kim, Jeong-Seok. 1997. *Syntactic Focus Movement and Ellipsis: A Minimalist Approach*. Doctoral dissertation, University of Connecticut.

Kiss, Katalin. 1996. 'Two Subject Positions in English', *The Linguistic Review* 13, 119-142.

Kitagawa, Yoshihisa. 1986. *Subjects in Japanese and English*, Doctoral dissertation, University of Massachusetts.

Koizumi, Masatoshi. 1993. 'Object Agreement Phrases and the Split VP Hypothesis', *Papers on Case and Agreement I, MIT Working Papers in Linguistics* 18, 99-148.

Koizumi, Masatoshi. 1995. *Phrase Structure in Minimalist Syntax*, Doctoral dissertation, Massachusetts Institute of Technology.

Koopman, Hilda and Dominique Sportiche. 1988. 'Subjects', unpublished manuscript, University of California, Los Angeles.

Koopman, Hilda and Dominique Sportiche. 1991. 'The Position of Subjects', *Lingua* 85, 211-258.

Koster, Jan. 1978. 'Why Subject Sentences Don't Exist', in Samuel Jay Keyser (ed.), *Recent Transformational Studies in European languages*, MIT Press, Cambridge, MA, pp. 53-64.

Kratzer, Angelika. 1994. 'The Event Argument and the Semantics of Voice', unpublished manuscript, University of Massachusetts.

Kratzer, Angelika. 1996. 'Severing the External Argument from Its Verb', in Johan Rooryck and Laurie Zaring (eds.), *Phrase Structure and the Lexicon*, Kluwer, Dordrecht, pp.109-138.

Kroeger, Paul. 1990. 'The Morphology of Affectedness in Kimaragang Dusun', unpublished manuscript, Stanford University.

Kroeger, Paul. 1992. *Phrase Structure and Grammatical Relations in Tagalog*. CSLI Publications, Stanford.

Kuroda, S. Y. 1988. 'Whether we Agree or Not: A Comparative Syntax of English and Japanese', *Lingvisticae Investigationes* 12, 1-47. Also appears in William Poser (ed.) *Papers from the Second International Workshop on Japanese Syntax*, CSLI Publications, Stanford University, pp. 103-143.

Lane, Chris. 1978. 'Niuean Field Notes', unpublished manuscript, Victoria University of Wellington.

Langacker, Ronald. 1969. 'On Pronominalization and the Chain of Command', in David Reibel and Sanford Schane (eds.), *Modern Studies in English*, Prentice-Hall, Englewood Cliffs, pp. 160-186.

Larson, Richard. 1988. 'On the Double Object Construction', *Linguistic Inquiry* 19, 335-391.

Larson, Richard. 1990. 'Double Objects Revisited: A Reply to Jackendoff', *Linguistic Inquiry* 21, 589-632.

Lasnik, Howard. 1976. 'Remarks on Coreference', *Linguistic Analysis* 2, 1-22. Reprinted, with minor revisions, in Howard Lasnik, 1989, *Essays on Anaphora*, Kluwer, Dordrecht..

Lasnik, Howard. 1989. *Essays on Anaphora*, Kluwer, Dordrecht.

Lasnik, Howard. 1995a. 'Case and Expletives Revisited', *Linguistic Inquiry* 26, 615-634.

Lasnik, Howard. 1995b. 'Last Resort', in Shosuke Haraguchi and Michio Funaki (eds.), *Minimalism and Linguistic Theory*, Hituzi Syobo, Tokyo, pp. 1-32. Reprinted with minor revisions, in Howard Lasnik, 1999, *Minimalist Analysis*, Blackwell, Oxford.

Lasnik, Howard. 1995c. 'Last Resort and Attract F', *Proceedings of the Formal Linguistics Society of Mid-America*, 6, 62-81.

Lasnik, Howard. 1995d. 'A note on Pseudogapping', *Papers on Minimalist Syntax, MIT Working Papers in Linguistics* 27, 143-163. Reprinted with minor revisions, in Howard Lasnik, 1999, *Minimalist Analysis*, Blackwell, Oxford.

Lasnik, Howard. 1997. 'Levels of Representation and the Elements of Anaphora', in Hans Bennis et al. (eds.), *Atomism and Binding*, Foris, Dordrecht, pp. 251-268. Reprinted, with minor revisions, Howard Lasnik, 1999, *Minimalist Analysis*, Blackwell, Oxford.

Lasnik, Howard. 1998a. 'On a Scope Reconstruction Paradox', unpublished manuscript, University of Connecticut, Posted on 'Chomsky Celebration' web page.

Lasnik, Howard. 1998b. 'Some Reconstruction Riddles', *University of Pennsylvania Working Papers in Linguistics* 5, 83-98.

Lasnik, Howard. 1999. 'Chains of Arguments', in Samuel Epstein and Norbert Hornstein (eds.), *Working Minimalism*, MIT Press, Cambridge, MA.

Lasnik, Howard. 2001. 'A Note on the EPP', *Linguistic Inquiry* 32, 356-362.

Lasnik, Howard. in press. 'Feature Movement or Agreement at a Distance?', in Artemis Alexiadou et al. (eds.), *Remnant Movement, F-Movement and the T-model*, John Benjamins, Amsterdam.

Lasnik, Howard and Mamoru Saito. 1991. 'On the Subject of Infinitives', *CLS 27: The General Session*, 324-343. Reprinted with minor revisions, in Howard Lasnik, 1999, *Minimalist Analysis*, Blackwell, Oxford.

Lasnik, Howard and Juan Uriagereka. 1988. *A Course in GB Syntax*, MIT Press, Cambridge, MA.

Lazard Gilbert and Louise Peltzer. 1991. 'Predicates in Tahitian', *Oceanic Linguistics* 30, 1-31.

Lee, Felicia. 2000. 'Remnant VP-movement and VSO in Quiavini Zapotec and Berber', in Andrew Carnie and Eithne Guilfoyle (eds.), *The Syntax of Verb Initial Languages*, Oxford University Press, Oxford. pp. 143-162.

Lees, Robert. 1960. *The Grammar of English Nominalizations*, Mouton, The Hague.

Legate, Julie. 1997. *Irish Predication: A Minimalist Analysis*, Masters thesis, University of Toronto.

Legate, Julie. 1998. 'Reconstruction and the Irish Nonverbal Predicate Construction', unpublished manuscript, Massachusetts Institute of Technology.

Levin, Beth and Malka Rappaport. 1986. 'The Formation of Adjectival Passives', *Linguistic Inquiry* 17, 623-661.

Levin, Beth and Malka Rappaport Hovav. 1995. *Unaccusativity: At the Syntax-Lexical Semantics Interface*, MIT Press, Cambridge, MA.

Levin, Juliette and Diane Massam. 1985. 'Surface Ergativity: Case/Theta Relations Reexamined', *Proceedings of the Northeast Linguistics Society* 15, 286-301.

Levin, Juliette and Diane Massam. 1986. 'Classification of Niuean Verbs: Notes on Case', *FOCAL 1: Papers from the International Conference on Austronesian Linguistics* 4, 231-244.

Levin, Juliette and Diane Massam. 1988. 'Raising and Binding in Niuean', in Richard McGinn (ed.), *Studies in Austronesian Linguistics*, Ohio University Monographs in International Studies, Southeast Asia Series No. 76, pp. 253-274.

Levin, Nancy. 1979. *Main Verb Ellipsis in Spoken English*, Doctoral dissertation, The Ohio State University Published 1986 by Garland, New York.

Levine, Robert. 1989. 'On Focus Inversion: Syntactic Valence and the Role of a SUBCAT list', *Linguistics* 17, 1013-55.

Li, Charles (ed.). 1976. *Subject and Topic*, Academic Press, New York

Li, Yen-Hui Audrey. 1990. *Order and Constituency in Mandarin Chinese*, Kluwer, Dordrecht.

Lightfoot, David. 1991. *How to Set Parameters: Arguments from Language Change*, MIT Press, Cambridge, MA.

Lipták, Anikó. 2000. 'On the Difference Between Focus Movement and Wh-Movement', Paper presented at GLOW Workshop on Focus, University of Deusto.

Lobeck, Ann. 1995. *Ellipsis*, Oxford University Press, Oxford.

Lynch, John. 1972. 'Passives and Statives in Tongan', *Journal of the Polynesian Society* 81, 5-18.

Lyons, John. 1967. 'A Note on Possessive, Existential, and Locative Sentences', *Foundations of Language* 3, 390-96.

Lyons, John. 1968. 'Existence, Location, Possession, and Transitivity', in B. van Rootselaar and T.F. Staal (eds.), *Logic, Methodology, and Philosophy of Science*, III, North-Holland, Amsterdam, pp. 495-509.

Maclachlan, Anna. 1996. *Aspects of Ergativity in Tagalog*, Doctoral dissertation, McGill University.

Maclachlan, Anna and Masanori Nakamura. 1997. 'Case Checking and Specificity in Tagalog', *The Linguistic Review* 14, 307-333.

Mahajan, Anoop. 2000. 'Eliminating Head Movement', Paper presented at GLOW Colloquium, Universidad del País Vasco/Euskal Herriko Unibertsitatea.

Manning, Christopher. 1996. *Ergativity: Argument Structure and Grammatical Relations*, CSLI Publications, Stanford.

Marantz, Alec. 1984. *On the Nature of Grammatical Relations*, MIT Press, Cambridge, MA.

Marantz, Alec. 1993. 'Implications of Asymmetries in Double Object Constructions', in Sam Mchombo (ed.), *Theoretical Aspects of Bantu Grammar*, CSLI Publications, Stanford, pp. 113-150.

Marantz, Alec. 1997. 'No Escape from Syntax: Don't Try a Morphological Analysis in the Privacy of Your Own Lexicon', unpublished manuscript, Massachusetts Institute of Technology.

Martin, Roger. 1999. 'Case, the Extended Projection Principle, and Minimalism', in Samuel Epstein and Norbert Hornstein (eds.), *Working Minimalism*, MIT Press, Cambridge, MA.

Massam, Diane. 1985. *Case Theory and the Projection Principle*, Doctoral dissertation, Massachusetts Institute of Technology.

Massam, Diane. 1991. 'The Syntax of Split Ergativity', Paper presented at North Eastern Linguistics Society 22, University of Delaware.

Massam, Diane. 1998. 'Niuean Noun Incorporation', Paper read at AFLA V, University of Hawaii.

Massam, Diane. 2000a. 'Niuean Nominalization', *Proceedings of AFLA 7*, 121-132.

Massam, Diane. 2000b. 'VSO and VOS: Aspects of Niuean Word Order', in Andrew Carnie and Eithne Guilfoyle (eds.), *The Syntax of V-Initial Languages*, Oxford University Press, Oxford, pp. 97-116.

Massam, Diane. 2001. 'Pseudo-Noun Incorporation in Niuean', *Natural Language and Linguistic Theory* 19, 153-197.

Massam, Diane and Carolyn Smallwood. 1997. 'Essential Features of Predication in English and Niuean', *Proceedings of the North Eastern Linguistics Society* 27, 263-272.

Masullo, Pascual José. 1992. *Incorporation and Case Theory in Spanish: A Cross-Linguistic Perspective*, Doctoral dissertation, University of Washington.

Matsuoka, Mikinari. 1999. 'Two Independent Positions for Dative Arguments', *Proceedings of the 1999 Annual Conference of the Canadian Linguistic Association, Cahiers Linguistiques d'Ottawa*, 201-212.

May, Robert. 1977. *The Grammar of Quantification*, Doctoral dissertation, Massachusetts Institute of Technology.

May, Robert. 1985. *Logical Form: Its Structure and Derivation*. MIT Press, Cambridge, MA.

McCawley, James. 1976. *Grammar and Meaning*, Academic Press, New York.

McCawley, James. 1988. 'Review article on "Knowledge of Language: Its Structure, Origin, and Use"', *Language* 64, 355-365.

McCloskey, James. 1980. 'Is there Raising in Modern Irish?', Ériu 31, 59-99.

McCloskey, James. 1983. 'A VP in a VSO language', in Gerald Gazdar et al. (eds.), *Order, Concord and Constituency*, Foris, Dordrecht, pp. 9-55.

McCloskey, James. 1984. 'Raising, Subcategorization, and Selection in Modern Irish', *Natural Language and Linguistic Theory* 1, 441-485.

McCloskey, James. 1985. 'Case, movement, and raising in Modern Irish. *Proceedings of the West Coast Conference on Formal Linguistics* 4, 190-205.

McCloskey, James. 1991a. 'Clause Structure, Ellipsis and Proper Government in Irish', *Lingua* 85, 259-302.

McCloskey, James. 1991b. *There, It*, and Agreement. *Linguistic Inquiry* 22, 563-67.

McCloskey, James. 1996a. 'On the Scope of Verb Raising in Irish', *Natural Language and Linguistic Theory* 14, 47-104.

McCloskey, James. 1996b. 'Subjects and Subject-Positions in Irish', in Robert Borsley and Ian Roberts (eds.), *The Syntax of the Celtic Languages: A Comparative Perspective*, Cambridge University Press, Cambridge, pp. 241-283.

McCloskey, James. 1997. 'Subjecthood and Subject Positions', in Liliane Haegeman (ed.), *Elements of Grammar: Handbook of Generative Syntax*, Kluwer, Dordrecht, pp. 197-235.

McCloskey, James. 1999. 'On the Right Edge in Irish', *Syntax* 2, 189-209.

McCloskey, James. 2000. 'Quantifier Float and Wh-Movement in an Irish English', *Linguistic Inquiry* 31, 57-84.

McCloskey, James. 2001. 'The Morphosyntax of Wh-Extraction in Irish', *Journal of Linguistics* 37, 67-100.

McCloskey, James and Peter Sells. 1988. 'Control and A-Chains in Modern Irish', *Natural Language and Linguistic Theory* 6, 143-189.

McEwen, J.M. 1970. *Niue Dictionary*. Dept. of Måori and Island Affairs, Wellington.

McGinnis, Martha Jo. 1998. *Locality in A-movement*, Doctoral dissertation, Massachusetts Institute of Technology.

Mchombo, Sam. 1992. 'Reciprocalization in Chichewa: A Lexical Account', *Linguistic Analysis* 21, 3-22.

Mchombo, Sam. 1993. 'On the Binding of the Reflexive and the Reciprocal in Chichewa', in Sam Mchombo (ed.), *Theoretical aspects of Bantu grammar*, CSLI Publications, Stanford, pp. 81-207.

Mejías-Bikandi, Errapel. 1990. 'Clause Union and Case Marking in Basque', in Katarzyna Dziwirek, et al. (eds.), *Grammatical Relations: A cross-theoretical Perspective*, CSLI Publications, Stanford, pp. 263-277.

Mohanan, K. P. 1982. 'Grammatical Relations and Clause Structure in Malayalam', in Joan Bresnan (ed.), *The Mental Representation of Grammatical Relations*, MIT Press, Cambridge, MA, pp. 504-589.

Mohanan, K.P. 1980. 'Grammatical Relations and Anaphora in Malayalam', unpublished manuscript, Massachusetts Institute of Technology.

Mohanan, K. P. and Tara Mohanan. 1998. 'Strong and Weak Projection: Lexical Reflexives and Reciprocals', in Miriam Butt and Wilhelm Geuder (eds.), *The Projection of Arguments: Lexical and Compositional Factors*, CSLI Publications, Stanford, pp. 165-194.

Montrul, Silvina. 1998. 'The L2 Acquisition of Dative Experiencer Subjects', *Second Language Research* 14, 27-61.

Moore, John and David Permutter. 2000. 'What does it take to be a Dative Subject?' *Natural Language and Linguistic Theory* 18, 373-416.

Moro, Andrea. 1989. '*There/Ci* as Raised Predicates', unpublished manuscript, Massachusetts Institute of Technology.

Moro, Andrea. 1997. *The Raising of Predicates*, Cambridge University Press, Cambridge.

Mosel, Ulrike and Even Hovdhaugen. 1992. *Samoan Reference Grammar*, Scandinavian University Press, Oslo.

Murasugi, Kumiko. 1992. *Cross and Nested Paths: NP Movement in Accusative and Ergative Languages*, Doctoral dissertation, Massachusetts Institute of Technology.

Nash, Léa and Alain Rouveret. 1997. 'Proxy Categories in Phrase Structure Theory', *Proceedings of the North Eastern Linguistic Society* 27, 287-304.

Neeleman, Ad. 1990. 'Scrambling as a D-Structure Phenomenon', in Norbert Corver and Henk van Riemsdijk (eds.), *Scrambling*, Mouton de Gruyter, Berlin.

Newmeyer, Frederick. 1998. *Language Form and Language Function*. MIT Press, Cambridge, MA.

Ngonyani, Deo. 1996. 'VP Ellipsis in Ndendeule and Swahili Applicatives', *Syntax at Sunset, UCLA Working Papers in Syntax and Semantics* 1, 109-128.

Noonan, Máire. 1992. *Case and Syntactic Geometry*, Doctoral dissertation, McGill University.

Noonan, Máire. 1994. 'VP Internal and VP External AgroP: Evidence from Irish', *Proceedings of the West Coast Conference on Formal Linguistics* 13, 318-333.

Noonan, Máire. 1997. 'Functional Architecture and Wh-Movement: Irish as a Case in Point', *Canadian Journal of Linguistics* 42, 111-139.

Ó Cadhlaigh, Cormac. 1940. *Gnás na Gaeilge*, Government Publications Office, Dublin.

Ó Curnáin, Brian. 1996. *Aspects of the Irish of Iorras Aithneach, County Galway*. Doctoral dissertation, University College Dublin.

Oehrle, Richard. 1976. *The Grammatical Status of the English Dative Alternation*. Doctoral dissertation, Massachusetts Institute of Technology.

Oehrle, Richard. 1977. 'Review of Semantics and Syntactic Regularity by G. Green', *Language* 53, 198-208.

Opdycke, John. 1965. *Harper's English Grammar*. Popular Library, New York.

Ordóñez, Francisco. 1997. *Word Order and Clause Structure in Spanish and Other Romance Languages*, Doctoral dissertation, City University of New York.

Ordóñez, Francisco and Esthela Treviño. 1999. 'Left Dislocated Subjects and the Pro-Drop Parameter: A Case Study of Spanish', *Lingua* 107, 39-68.

Otani, Kazuyo and John Whitman. 1991. 'V-raising and VP-ellipsis', *Linguistic Inquiry* 22, 345-358.

Parsons, Terence. 1990. *Events in the Semantics of English: a Study in Subatomic Semantics*, MIT Press, Cambridge, MA.

Paul, Ileana. 2000. *Malagasy Clause Structure*. Doctoral dissertation, McGill University.

Paul, Ileana. 2001. 'On Extraction Asymmetries', Paper read at AFLA VIII, Massachusetts Institute of Technology.

Paul, Ileana and Lucie Rabaovololona. 1998. 'Raising to Object in Malagasy', *UCLA Occasional Papers in Linguistics: The Structure of Malagasy II*, 50-64.

Pavón Lucero, M.ª Victoria. 1999. 'Clases de Partículas: Preposición, Conjunción y Adverbio', in Ignacio Bosque and Violeta Demonte (eds.), *Gramática Descriptiva de la Lengua Española*, Vol 1, Espasa Calpe, Madrid.

Pawley, Andrew. 1966. 'Polynesian Languages: a Subgrouping Based on Shared Innovations in Morphology', *Journal of the Polynesian Society* 75, 39-64.

Pawley, Andrew. 1967. 'The Relationships of Polynesian Outlier Languages', *Journal of the Polynesian Society* 76, 259-96.

Pearce, Elizabeth. 2000. 'Argument Positions and Anaphora in the Måori clause', *Proceedings of the Fourth International Conference on Oceanic Linguistics*, 313-325.

Pearson, Matthew. 1998. 'Event Structure and the Syntax of Themes and Instruments: the Case of the Malagasy Translative Voice (A-Passive)', Paper read at AFLA V, University of Hawaii.

Pearson, Matthew. 2001. *The Clause Structure of Malagasy: A Minimalist Approach*. Doctoral dissertation, University of California, Los Angeles.

Perlmutter, David. 1978. 'Evidence for Inversion in Russian, Japanese, and Kannada', unpublished manuscript, Massachusetts Institute of Technology.

Perlmutter, David. 1978. 'Impersonal Passives and the Unaccusative Hypothesis', *Proceedings of the Annual Meeting of the Berkeley Linguistics Society* 4, 157-189.

Perlmutter, David (ed.). 1983. *Studies in Relational Grammar 1*, University of Chicago Press, Chicago.

Perlmutter, David. 1984a. 'The Inadequacy of Some Monostratal Theories of Passive', in David Perlmutter and Carol Rosen (eds.), *Studies in Relational Grammar 2*, University of Chicago Press, Chicago, pp. 3-37.

Perlmutter, David. 1984b. 'Working 1s and Inversion in Italian, Japanese and Quechua', in David Perlmutter and Carol Rosen (eds.), *Studies in Relational Grammar 2*, University of Chicago Press, Chicago, pp. 292-330.

Perlmutter, David and Paul Postal. 1972. "The Relational Succession Law", unpublished manuscript, Massachusetts Institute of Technology. Revised version in David Perlmutter (ed.), 1983, *Studies in Relational Grammar 1*, University of Chicago Press, Chicago.

Perlmutter, David and Paul Postal. 1974. *Lectures on Relational Grammar*, LSA Linguistic Institute, University of Massachusetts, Amherst.

Perlmutter, David and Paul Postal. 1977. 'Toward a Universal Characterization of Passivization', *Proceedings of the Annual Meeting of the Berkeley Linguistics Society* 3, 394-417. Reprinted in David Perlmutter (ed.), 1983, *Studies in Relational Grammar 1*, University of Chicago Press, Chicago, pp. 3-29.

Perlmutter, David and Paul Postal. 1983a. 'The Relational Succession Law', in David Perlmutter (ed.), *Studies in Relational Grammar 1*, University of Chicago Press, Chicago, pp. 30-80.

Perlmutter, David and Paul Postal. 1983b. 'Some Proposed Laws of Basic Clause Structure', in David Perlmutter (ed.), *Studies in Relational Grammar 1*, University of Chicago Press, Chicago, pp. 81-128.

Perlmutter, David and Paul Postal. 1983c. 'Toward a Universal Characterization of Passivization', in David Perlmutter (ed.), *Studies in Relational Grammar 1*, University of Chicago Press, Chicago, pp. 3-29.

Perlmutter, David and Paul Postal. 1984. 'Impersonal Passives and Some Relational Laws', in David Perlmutter and Carol Rosen (eds.), *Studies in relational grammar 2*, University of Chicago Press, Chicago, pp. 126-170.

Pesetsky, David. 1982. *Paths and Categories*, Doctoral dissertation, Massachusetts Institute of Technology.

Pesetsky, David. 1989. 'The Earliness Principle', unpublished manuscript, Massachusetts Institute of Technology.

Pesetsky, David. 1995. *Zero Syntax: Experiencers and Cascades*, MIT Press, Cambridge, MA.

Pesetsky, David and Esther Torrego. 2001. 'T-to-C Movement: Causes and consequences', in Michael Kenstowicz (ed.), *Ken Hale: a Life in Language*, MIT Press, Cambridge, MA.

Pinto, M. 1994. 'Subjects in Italian: Distribution and Interpretation', in R. Bok-Bennema and C. Cremers (eds.), *Linguistics in the Netherlands*, John Benjamins, Amsterdam.

Poletto, Cecilia. 2000. 'Subject Positions', unpublished manuscript, Università di Padova.

Pollard, Carl and Ivan Sag. 1994. *Head-driven Phrase Structure Grammar*, University of Chicago Press, Chicago.

Pollock, Jean-Yves. 1989. 'Verb Movement, Universal Grammar, and the Structure of IP', *Linguistic Inquiry* 20, 365-424.

Pollock, Jean-Yves. 1997. 'Notes on Clause Structure', in Liliane Haegeman (ed.), *Elements of Grammar: Handbook of Generative Syntax*, Kluwer, Dordrecht, pp. 237-279.

Postal, Paul. 1974. *On Raising: One Rule of English Grammar and Its Theoretical Implications*, MIT Press, Cambridge, MA.

Postal, Paul. 1977. 'Antipassive in French', *Lingvisticae Investigationes* 1, 333-374.

Pullum, Geoffrey. 1996. 'Review of "The View from Building 20" by Kenneth Hale and Wayne O'Neil (Eds.)', *Journal of Linguistics* 32, 117-147.

Rackowski, Andrea. 1998. 'Malagasy Adverbs', in Ileana Paul (ed.), *The Structure of Malagasy, Volume II, UCLA Occasional Papers in Linguistics*, pp. 11-33.

Rackowski, Andrea and Lisa deMena Travis. 2000. 'V-Initial Languages: X or XP Movement and Adverbial Placement', in Andrew Carnie and Eithne Guilfoyle (eds.), *The Syntax of V-Initial Languages*, Oxford University Press, Oxford, pp. 117-41.

Radford, Andrew. 1997. *Syntactic Theory and the Structure of English: A Minimalist Approach*, Cambridge University Press, Cambridge.

Reinhart, Tanya. 1976. *The Syntactic Domain of Anaphora*, Doctoral dissertation, Massachusetts Institute of Technology.

Reinhart, Tanya. 1983. *Anaphora and Semantic Interpretation*, University of Chicago Press, Chicago.

Reinhart, Tanya and Eric Reuland. 1993. 'Reflexivity', *Linguistic Inquiry* 24, 657-720.

Richards, Norvin. 1997. *What Moves Where When in Which language?*, Doctoral dissertation, Massachusetts Institute of Technology.

Rigau, Gemma. 1988. 'Strong Pronouns', *Linguistic Inquiry* 19, 503-511.

Rizzi, Luigi. 1990. *Relativized Minimality*, MIT Press, Cambridge, MA.

Rizzi, Luigi. 1996. 'Residual Verb Second and the *Wh*-Criterion', in Adriana Belletti and Luigi Rizzi (eds.), *Parameters and Functional Heads: Essays in Comparative Syntax*, Oxford University Press, Oxford.

Rizzi, Luigi. 1997. 'The Fine Structure of the Left Periphery', in Liliane Haegeman (ed.), *Elements of Grammar: Handbook of Generative Syntax*, Kluwer, Dordrecht, pp. 281-337.

Roberge, Yves. 2000. 'Inner EPP Effects', unpublished manuscript, University of Toronto.

Rosen, Carol. 1983. 'Universals of Causative Union: A Co-proposal to the Gibson-Raposo Typology', *CLS 19: The Main Session*, 338-52.

Rosen, Carol. 1984. 'The Interface Between Semantic Roles and Initial Grammatical Relations', in David Perlmutter and Carol Rosen (eds.), *Studies in Relational Grammar 2*, University of Chicago Press, Chicago, pp. 38-77.

Rosenbaum, Peter. 1967. *The Grammar of English Predicate Complement Constructions*. MIT Press, Cambridge, MA.

Ross, John. 1967. *Constraint of Variables in Syntax*, Doctoral dissertation, Massachusetts Institute of Technology.

Ross, John. 1973. 'The Penthouse Principle and the Order of Constituents', in Claudia Corum et al. (eds.), *You Take the High Node and I'll take the Low Node*, Chicago Linguistic Society, Chicago, pp. 397-422.

Rothstein, Susan. 1983. *The Syntactic Forms of Predication*, Doctoral dissertation, Massachusetts Institute of Technology.

Rothstein, Susan. 1992. 'Case and NP Licensing', *Natural Language and Linguistic Theory* 10, 119-139.

Safir, Kenneth. 1983. 'On Small Clauses as Constituents', *Linguistic Inquiry* 14, 730-35.

Saito, Mamoru. 1985. *Some Asymmetries in Japanese and Their Theoretical Implications*, Doctoral dissertation, Massachusetts Institute of Technology.

Schachter, Paul. 1976. 'The Subject in Philippine Languages: Topic, Actor, Actor-Topic, or None of the Above?' in Charles Li (ed.), *Subject and Topic*, Academic Press, New York, pp. 491-518.

Schachter, Paul. 1996. 'The Subject in Tagalog: Still None of the Above', *UCLA Occasional Papers in Linguistics* 15, 1-61.

Seiter, William. 1980. *Studies in Niuean Syntax*, Garland, New York.

Seiter, William. 1983. 'Subject-Direct Object Raising in Niuean', in David Perlmutter (ed.) *Studies in Relational Grammar 1*, University of Chicago Press, Chicago, pp. 317-59.

Sells, Peter, Annie Zaenen, and Draga Zec. 1987. 'Reflexivization Variation: Relations between Syntax, Semantics, and Lexical Structure', in Masayo Iida et al. (eds.), *Working Papers in Grammatical Theory and Discourse Structure*, CSLI Publications, Stanford, pp. 169-238.

Sherman (Ussishkin), Adam. 1998. 'VP Ellipsis and Subject Positions in Modern Hebrew', *Proceedings of the Israel Association of Theoretical Linguistics* 13, 211-229.

Simpson, Jane. 1991. *Warlpiri Morpho-Syntax: a Lexicalist Approach*, Kluwer, Dordrecht.

Sobin, Nicholas. 1997. 'Agreement, Default Rules, and Grammatical Viruses', *Linguistic Inquiry* 28, 318-43.

Speas, Margaret. 1990. *Phrase Structure in Natural Language*, Kluwer, Dordrecht.

Sperlich, Wolfgang. 1994. 'A Theory of Verb Classes and Case Morphology in Niuean', *Proceedings of the International Conference on Austronesian Languages* 7, 22-27.

Sperlich, Wolfgang (ed.). 1997. *Tohi Vagahau Niue: Niue Language Dictionary*, Government of Niue and University of Hawai'i Press, Alofi and Honolulu.

Sportiche, Dominique. 1988. 'A Theory of Floating Quantifiers and Its Corollaries for Constituent Structure', *Linguistic Inquiry* 19, 425-449.

Sportiche, Dominique. 1990. 'Movement, Agreement, and Case', unpublished manuscript, University of California, Los Angeles.

Sportiche, Dominique. 1996. 'Clitic Constructions', in Johan Rooryck and Laurie Zaring (eds.), *Phrase Structure and the Lexicon*, Kluwer, Dordrecht.

Stechow, Arnim von. 1995. 'Lexical Decomposition in Syntax', in Urs Egli and Peter Pause (ed.), *Lexical Knowledge in the Organization of Language*, John Benjamins, Amsterdam, pp. 81-118.

Stenson, Nancy. 1981. *Studies in Irish Syntax*, Max Niemeyer Verlag, Tübingen.

Stowell, Timothy. 1981. *Elements of Phrase Structure*, Doctoral dissertation, Massachusetts Institute of Technology.

Stowell, Timothy. 1983. 'Subjects Across Categories', *The Linguistic Review* 2, 285-312.

Suñer, Margarita. 1988. 'The Role of Agreement in Clitic-Doubled Constructions', *Natural Language and Linguistic Theory* 6, 391-434.

Suñer, Margarita. 1994. 'V-movement and the Licensing of Argumental Wh-Phrases in Spanish', *Natural Language and Linguistic Theory* 12, 335-372.

Takahashi, Daiko. 1994. *Minimality of Movement*, Doctoral dissertation, University of Connecticut.

Tanaka, Hidekazu. 1999. 'Raised Objects and Superiority', *Linguistic Inquiry* 30, 317-325.

Thráinsson, Höskuldur. 1996. 'On the Non-Universality of Functional Categories', in Werner Abraham et al. (eds.), *Minimal Ideas: Syntactic Studies in the Minimalist Framework*, John Benjamins, Amsterdam, pp. 253-281.

Torrego, Esther. 1985. 'On Empty Categories in Nominals', unpublished manuscript, University of Massachusetts at Boston.

Travis, Lisa deMena. 1991. 'Derived Objects, Inner Aspect, and the Structure of VP', Paper presented at North Eastern Linguistics Society 22.

Travis, Lisa deMena. 1992. 'Inner Aspect and the Structure of VP'. *Cahiers Linguistique de l'UQAM* 1, 130-146.

Travis, Lisa deMena. 1998. 'Theta Positions and Binding in Balinese and Malagasy', *Canadian Journal of Linguistics* 43, 435-467.

Travis, Lisa deMena. 2000a. 'Eight Possible Paper Topics on Chamorro and Related Languages', *Oceanic Linguistics*. 39, 1-29.

Travis, Lisa deMena. 2000b. 'Event Structure in Syntax', in Carol Tenny and James Pustejovsky (eds.), *Events as Grammatical Objects*, CSLI Publications, Stanford, pp. 45-185.

Travis, Lisa deMena and Edwin Williams. 1983. 'Externalization of Arguments in Malayo-Polynesian Languages', *The Linguistic Review* 2, 57-78.

Ura, Hiroyuki. 1998. 'Ergativity and Checking Theory', unpublished manuscript, Osaka University.

Uriagereka, Juan. 1988. *On Government*, Doctoral dissertation, University of Connecticut.

Uriagereka, Juan. 1999. 'Minimal Restrictions on Basque Movements', *Natural Language and Linguistic Theory* 17, 403-444.

Uribe-Etxebarría, Myriam. 1995. 'On the Structure of SPEC/IP and its Relevance for Scope Asymmetries', in Jon Amastae et al. (eds.), *Contemporary Research in Romance Linguistics*, John Benjamins, Amsterdam, pp. 355-367.

Wasow, Thomas, 1976. 'McCawley on Generative Semantics', *Linguistic Analysis* 2, 279-301.

Webelhuth, Gert. 1992. *Principles and Parameters of Syntactic Saturation*, Oxford University Press, Oxford.

Wechsler, Stephen and Wayan Arka. 1998. 'Syntactic Ergativity in Balinese', *Natural Language and Linguistic Theory* 16, 387-441.

Williams, Edwin. 1980. 'Predication', *Linguistic Inquiry* 11, 203-238.

Williams, Edwin. 1981. 'Argument Structure and Morphology', *The Linguistic Review* 1, 81-114.

Williams, Edwin. 1984. 'Grammatical Relations', *Linguistic Inquiry* 15, 639-73.

Williams, Edwin. 1987. 'Implicit Arguments, the Binding Theory and Control', *Natural Language and Linguistic Theory* 5, 151-180.

Williams, Edwin. 1994. *Thematic Structure in Syntax*, MIT Press, Cambridge, MA.

Willis, David. 1996. *The Loss of Verb-Second in Welsh: A Study of Syntactic Change*, Doctoral dissertation, University of Oxford.

Woolford, Ellen. 1993. 'Symmetric and Asymmetric Passives', *Natural Language and Linguistic Theory* 11, 679-728.

Woolford, Ellen. 1997. 'Four-way Case Systems: Ergative, Nominative, Objective and Accusative', *Natural Language and Linguistic Theory* 15, 181-227.

Zubizarreta, Maria Luisa. 1982. *On the Relationship of the Lexicon to Syntax*, Doctoral dissertation, Massachusetts Institute of Technology.

Zubizarreta, María Luisa. 1998. *Prosody, Focus, and Word Order*, MIT Press, Cambridge, MA.

Zwart, Jan-Wouter. 1992. 'Dutch Expletives and Small Clause Predicate Raising', *Proceedings of the North Eastern Linguistics Society* 23, 477-491.

AUTHOR INDEX

Abney, S., 28

Adger, D., 189, 204

Aissen, J., 4, 93, 94, 100, 102

Alexiadou, A., 193-195, 216, 217, 219, 245, 274

Allen, B., 125

Alsina, A., 10, 78, 82, 83, 86, 90, 91, 99-102

Anagnostopoulou, E., 193-195, 216, 217, 219, 274

Anderson, S., 227

Austin, P., 229, 246

Baker, M., 3, 5, 10, 27, 30, 40, 47, 50, 53, 56-62, 64, 65, 67-72, 74, 75, 77, 79-81, 85, 87, 88, 90-92, 99, 101, 102, 124, 126, 127, 131, 133, 151, 153, 154, 163, 218, 223

Baković, E., 222, 223

Barbosa, P., 220, 222

Barss, A., 30, 75, 105

Bejar, S., 234

Bell, S., 8

Belletti, A., 84

Biber, D., 73

Bickerton, D., 74

Biggs, B., 227, 229, 237, 242, 245

Bittner, M., 19, 243

Bobaljik, J., 4, 7, 17, 128, 148-150, 152, 155, 158, 246, 272, 273

Bok-Bennema, R., 222

Bonet, E., 102

Borer, H., 55, 88

Bošković, Ž., 117, 118, 121

Bowers, J., 9, 245

Branigan, P., 8, 109, 110

Bresnan, J., 3, 24, 36, 78, 80, 82, 89, 90, 99, 100, 102, 113, 253

Burzio, L., 3, 47, 191

Campana, M., 19

Campos, H., 222

Cardinaletti, A., 8, 190, 197, 221

Carnie, A., 161, 167, 173, 179, 192, 229

Carstairs-McCarthy, A., 74

Chametsky, R., 74

Chomsky, N., 1-9, 18, 22, 23, 26-28, 30, 37, 38, 44-46, 50, 53-55, 59, 60, 63, 64, 74, 75, 87, 96, 101, 103-109, 112-114, 116, 119-121, 124, 125, 149, 159, 160, 166, 169, 177, 178, 188, 190, 191, 193, 201, 208, 213, 222, 225, 226, 232, 234, 239, 240, 245, 247, 251, 261, 262, 267, 271

Chung, S., 3, 125, 154, 167, 184, 189, 191, 211, 228, 270

Cinque, G., 47, 150

Clark, E., 168

Collins, C., 101

Comrie, B., 35

Contreras, H., 218

Conway, L., 277

Cook, K., 229, 244

Croft, W., 75

Culicover, P., 262

Cummins, S., 245

Dalrymple, M., 90

Davies, W., 13, 74, 75, 98, 101, 119, 152, 190, 207, 218, 227, 233, 244, 276-278

Déchaine, R., 191, 226

DeGraff, M., 167

Demonte, V., 84

den Dikken, M., 106

Diesing, M., 121, 148, 174, 176, 223

Dixon, R. M. W., 225-228, 237, 238, 243-245

Doherty, C., 167, 189

Doron, E., 162

Dowty, D., 46, 48, 60, 61, 65-67, 75

Dryer, M., 82, 100

Dubinsky, S., 13, 74, 75, 101, 119, 190, 207, 218, 219, 227, 233, 244, 276-278

Duffield, N., 161, 173, 179, 184, 189, 192

Dukes, M., 229, 240, 242

Eguren, L., 221, 222

Emonds, J., 55, 67, 276

Epstein, S., 195, 218

Fernández Soriano, O., 197
Fiengo, R., 162
Fillmore, C., 54, 55, 158
Finer, D., 211
Fodor, J., 64, 65, 70, 75
Foley, W., 225
Franco, J., 9
Freeze, R., 168
Freidin, R., 55
Fukui, N., 45, 123, 226
Georgopoulos, C., 211
Gibson, J., 4, 95
Goodall, G., 12, 15, 211, 219, 221-223, 279
Green, G., 63
Grimshaw, J., 11, 36, 63, 91, 192, 222
Groos, A., 222
Gruber, J., 54
Guilfoyle, E., 4, 7, 8, 123, 173, 184, 191, 226, 229, 237, 241, 246
Haegeman, L., 8, 19, 84, 190, 277
Hale, K., 30, 45, 46, 57-60, 62-64, 69, 177, 243, 245
Harley, H., 65, 74, 75, 161, 173, 178, 179, 225, 245
Hawkins, J., 73
Hernanz, M., 220
Hoekstra, T., 3, 168
Hoji, H., 30, 162
Holmberg, A., 79, 127, 128, 155, 158
Hooper, R., 229, 242, 244
Hornstein, N., 208, 209, 217, 222
Hovdhaugen, E., 245
Hung, H., 4, 7, 8, 123, 134, 135, 226, 229, 237, 241, 246
Iatridou, S., 9
Jackendoff, R., 30, 54, 55, 63, 70, 74, 75, 241
Jaeggli, O., 196
Jaworska, E., 253, 277
Jayaseelan, K., 107
Johnson, D., 33
Johnson, K., 75, 111, 112, 116, 121, 153

Jonas, D., 4, 7, 128, 158, 188, 190, 272
Kanerva, J., 78, 102
Kayne, R., 9, 71, 83, 111, 112, 195, 263
Keenan, E., 18, 35, 135, 137, 140, 153, 154, 225
Kempchinsky, P., 218, 219, 276
Keyser, S., 45, 46, 57-60, 62-64, 69, 177
Kim, J. S., 121
Kiss, K., 8
Kitagawa, Y., 4, 123, 226
Koizumi, M., 9, 14, 106, 153, 178
Koopman, H., 123, 178, 226
Koster, J, 276
Kratzer, A., 46, 159, 177, 178, 191
Kroeger, P., 131, 151, 153, 225, 226
Kuroda, S.-Y., 6, 123, 226
Lane, C., 244
Langacker, R., 109
Larson, R., 4, 5, 8, 9, 28, 30, 50, 60, 70, 71, 74, 121
Lasnik, H., 10, 14-16, 18, 19, 30, 39, 75, 101, 103, 104, 106, 107, 109, 110, 111, 113, 114, 119-121, 153, 195
Lazard, G., 229
Lee, F., 231
Lees, R., 252, 261
Legate, J., 167
Levin, B., 48, 62, 74, 239
Levin, J., 17, 228, 245, 246
Levin, N., 120
Levine, R., 249
Li, Y.-H., 205, 206, 221
Li, C., 229
Lightfoot, D., 74
Lipták, A., 220
Lynch, J., 229
Lyons, J., 168
Maclachlan, A., 148, 149
Mahajan, A., 222
Manning, C., 226, 237, 238, 241, 243
Marantz, A., 3, 27, 91, 102, 155, 177, 226, 242, 245

Martin, R., 109, 218
Martínez-Arbelaiz, A., 98
Massam, D., 10, 12, 14-17, 123, 136, 148, 227, 228, 230, 231, 233-235, 239, 242, 245, 246, 268, 271, 275, 279
Masullo, P., 218, 219, 222
Matsuoka, M., 147
May, R., 119, 162
McCawley, J., 63, 104
McCloskey, J., 4, 6, 7, 10, 12, 13, 15, 17, 161-163, 165-167, 169, 173, 179, 184, 185, 188-191, 193, 217, 221, 228, 244, 249, 250, 269
McEwen, J., 244
McGinnis, M., 240, 245, 246
Mchombo, S., 78, 82, 89, 90, 100, 102
Mejías-Bikandi, E., 98
Mohanan, K. P., 24, 29, 39, 98
Mohanan, T., 98
Montrul, S., 9
Moore, J., 192, 274, 275
Moro, A., 168
Mosel, U., 245
Mulder, R., 168
Murasugi, K., 19
Nakamura, M., 148, 149
Nash, L., 9, 279
Neeleman, A., 155
Newmeyer, F., 11, 73
Ngonyani, D., 162
Nikanne, U., 158
Noonan, M., 185, 191
Noyer, R., 245
Ó Cadhlaigh, C., 187
Ó Curnáin, B., 191
Oehrle, R., 63
Opdycke, J., 225
Ordóñez, F., 196, 197, 210, 215, 219, 222
Otani, K., 162
Parsons, T., 46
Paul, I., 146, 147, 153-155, 276, 279
Pavón Lucero, M.ª V., 206
Pawley, A., 225

Pearce, E., 244, 246
Pearson, M., 130, 143, 146, 147, 155
Peltzer, L., 229
Perlmutter, D., 1, 3, 4, 24-26, 78, 84, 100, 127, 134, 135, 192, 274, 275
Pesetsky, D., 5, 9, 63, 75, 153, 222
Peters, S., 90
Pinto, M., 204
Platzack, C., 79
Poletto, C., 218, 221
Pollard, C., 43
Pollock, J.-Y., 4, 5, 7, 9, 10, 158
Postal, P., 1, 3, 19, 25, 26, 33, 78, 100, 103, 104, 109, 116, 119, 120, 134, 135, 153
Pullum, G., 64
Rabaovololona, L., 154, 155
Rackowski, A., 15, 150, 151
Ralalaoherivony, B., 135, 137, 140, 154
Raposo, E., 4, 95
Rappaport Hovav, M., 47, 62, 74
Reinhart, T., 36, 37, 40, 154, 246
Reuland, E., 154, 246
Richards, N., 245
Rigau, G., 84
Rizzi, L., 84, 160, 190, 199, 200, 201, 202, 211, 215, 216, 219, 220, 223
Roberge, Y., 243
Roberts, I., 75
Rosen, C., 11
Rosenbaum, P., 70, 124, 252, 262
Ross, J., 73, 261
Rothstein, S., 63, 226
Rouveret, A., 9, 279
Safir, K., 276
Sag, I., 43
Saito, M., 19, 30, 103, 104, 106, 109, 113, 120
Schachter, P., 123, 225, 228, 229
Seely, D., 119, 120, 218
Seiter, W., 12, 228, 235-239, 241, 244, 246, 269
Sells, P., 91, 173, 184, 191
Sherman (Ussishkin), A., 162

Simpson, J., 24, 29, 50
Smallwood, C., 15, 123, 227, 233, 244, 268, 271, 275, 279
Sobin, N., 276
Speas, M., 26, 27, 31, 45, 123, 226
Sperlich, W., 229, 237, 242-244
Sportiche, D., 4, 6, 9, 123, 153, 178, 226
Stechow, A. von, 46
Stenson, N., 185
Stewart. O., 39, 154
Stowell, T., 28, 276, 277
Suñer, M., 84, 211
Takahashi, D., 110
Tanaka, H., 117, 118, 121
Thráinsson, H., 9, 101
Torrego, E., 202, 222, 223
Travis, L., 4, 7, 8, 10, 14, 15, 65, 123, 142, 151, 153, 154, 178, 226, 229, 237, 241, 246, 269
Ura, H., 231
Uriagereka, J., 108, 195, 263, 267
Uribe-Etxebarría, M., 195, 196, 208, 218
Wasow, T., 63
Wayan, A., 144
Webelhuth, G., 254, 277
Wechsler, S., 142, 144, 145, 237, 241
Whitman, J., 162
Williams, E., 45, 56, 75, 159, 177, 226, 229, 237, 241, 245, 252, 253, 277
Willis, D., 191
Woolford, E., 102, 231, 242
Zaenen, A., 91
Zec, D., 91
Zubizarreta, M., 112, 197, 204, 205, 222
Zwart, J., 158

SUBJECT INDEX

absolutive, 13, 16, 17, 19, 225, 228-235, 242-246

accusative, 8, 16, 17, 78, 79, 83-85, 87-90, 92, 95, 96, 98, 100-102, 119, 126, 153, 154, 158, 159, 165, 166, 181-185, 190, 191, 219, 228, 229, 234, 237-239, 242-244

advancements, 35, 102, 131, 133, 153

AgrP, 4, 5, 9, 10, 13-18, 103, 107, 110, 119, 121, 247, 252, 272-275, 277, 279

AgrIO, 9

AgrO, 5, 9, 14, 15-17, 19, 103, 105, 107-110, 119-121, 127, 128, 153, 179, 182, 245

AgrS, 5, 9, 10, 14-17, 19, 78, 103, 106-108, 110, 119, 127

INFL, 4, 7, 9, 33, 70, 72, 73, 226, 231, 233, 234, 245

alignment hypotheses, see:
Deep Alignment Hypothesis,
Uniformity of Theta Assignment Hypothesis,
Universal Alignment Hypothesis.

applicatives, 95, 102, 124-126, 131, 133, 141, 145, 146, 151, 153

bare nouns, 199, 200

binding, 10, 14, 28, 30, 41, 43, 50, 54, 71, 83, 86, 90-92, 96-98, 105-108, 110, 111, 116, 118, 120, 142-144, 154, 188, 189, 215, 216, 219, 225, 228, 237, 238, 239, 241-244, 246

binding conditions, see:
Condition A,
Condition B,
Condition C.

Binding Theory, 30, 50, 54, 239, 240

bound variable anaphora, 37, 39-41, 68

Case
abstract, 77-80, 82, 85, 86, 90, 97, 99, 100, 102
inherent, 10, 79-82, 84-89, 91-102

structural, 10, 77, 79-82, 84-86, 88-101

case, grammatical, 77, 79, 80, 82, 85, 86, 90, 92, 97-100, 126

Case Filter, 79, 82

Case Resistance Principle, 276, 277

causatives, 47, 57, 86, 87, 88, 90, 94, 98, 102, 138, 140, 141, 170

chômeur, 82, 100

clefting, 27-30, 153, 155, 168, 191, 235, 238, 246

cliticization, 29, 30, 116

clitics, 9, 29, 30, 75, 83, 87, 89-92, 102, 218, 219, 221, 235, 236, 239, 245

command
a-command, 36
c-command, 24, 28, 30, 36-38, 40-43, 47, 48, 50, 68, 70, 71, 73, 75, 104, 105, 119, 120, 189, 239-241, 243, 246
f-command, 36, 50
o-command, 43

complex NP islands, 255, 268

Condition A, 103, 105, 120, 240

Condition B, 39, 120, 239

Condition C, 37, 39, 41, 48, 50, 68, 71, 105, 109, 116, 117

constituency, 5, 10, 21, 22, 24-31, 36, 50, 161
constituency tests, 5, 10, 22, 24, 27-31, 36

control, 11, 25, 27, 29, 36, 75, 120, 154, 221, 225, 228, 237, 238, 241-244, 253, 274

c-structure, 30

dative subjects, 182-188, 192

Deep Alignment Hypothesis, 53, 60-68, 74, 75

double object constructions, 25, 30, 35, 50, 77, 79, 82, 83, 85, 86, 88, 90, 92, 94, 120, 124, 153

DP-shell, 252-254, 256, 258, 266, 268-271, 278

ECM (exceptional Case marking), see: raising, ECM

Empty Category Principle, 29, 57, 58, 74

EPP, 4, 6, 8, 12-18, 103, 107, 119, 120, 121, 153, 160-163, 165, 166, 168, 169, 176, 177, 181, 191, 193-197, 199, 203-209, 211, 212, 213-218, 225-228, 231-234, 236, 237, 243, 244, 248, 264, 269, 272, 275, 279

EPP-feature, 8, 12, 13, 15, 194-196, 199, 204, 213-215, 228, 272, 279

(EPP) D-feature, 12, 14, 15, 247, 252, 269, 271, 272, 274, 275, 279

(EPP) V-feature, 247, 272, 274

ergative, 16, 17, 19, 147, 227-229, 231-233, 235, 237, 242-246

existential constructionss, 106, 166-168, 175, 176, 191, 205, 246

expletives, 7, 106, 108, 159, 162, 168, 176, 193, 195, 204, 221, 237, 272, 274

Extended Standard Theory, 50

feature checking, 121, 231

feature movement, 120, 121

focus, 22, 34, 116, 117, 121, 150, 155, 168, 177, 190, 193, 196, 197, 202, 203, 209, 211, 214, 216, 218, 220-222, 245, 247, 264, 278

functional heads, 11, 15, 18, 29, 103, 105, 191, 232, 236

functional structure (f-structure), 10, 26, 32, 34, 191, 251

Generative Semantics, 46, 63, 64

Government and Binding theory, 1, 3, 4, 50, 54, 77-80, 101, 102, 123-126, 131, 157, 225, 226, 248

Government Transparency Corollary, 126, 127

Head Driven Phrase Structure Grammar, 17, 35, 43

incorporation, 3, 10, 16, 25, 30, 56-59, 74, 126, 127, 237, 238, 242, 243, 245

inflectional layer, 8, 9, 13, 15, 18, 160, 165, 177, 180, 188, 190, 193, 221

languages
Austronesian, 7, 8, 123, 229, 269
Balinese, 143-145, 151
Cebuano, 8, 25
Chamorro, 95, 154, 270, 271
Kalagan, 151, 152
Kimaragang Dusun, 131, 151, 152
Malagasy, 10, 14, 15, 123-125, 129-136, 142-145, 147-151, 153-155, 269-271, 279
Niuean, 12-17, 123, 225-246, 268, 269, 271, 275, 279
Tagalog, 7, 123, 148, 149, 153, 155, 228, 241
Tahitian, 229
Bantu, 89
Chichewa, 57, 77, 79-83, 85-102, 131, 133
Kichaga, 99
Kinyarwanda, 85, 131
Ndendeule, 162
Basque, 98
Chinese, 162, 205, 206, 221
Dravidian,
Kannada, 98
Malayalam, 24, 28, 29, 39, 98
Edo, 39
Germanic,
German, 84, 98, 148, 150
Icelandic, 7, 79, 127, 128, 148, 159, 176, 188, 190, 272, 274, 275
Greek, Classical, 166
Hebrew, Modern, 162
Hindi, 30
Irish, 6, 12-15, 17, 49, 157, 160-163, 165, 166, 168, 169, 172, 173, 175, 176, 179-181, 184, 185, 190, 191, 193, 217, 228, 229, 244, 269, 271, 279
Japanese, 6, 27, 30, 40, 85, 162
Korean, 162

Mohawk, 24, 30, 40, 50, 223
Navajo, 26, 31
Oneida, 126
Romance, 4, 19, 83, 89, 218, 221, 222
  Catalan, 77, 83-92, 95-98, 100, 102
  French, 6, 9, 13, 15, 19, 83, 91, 168, 245, 247, 258, 259-261, 263-269, 271, 272, 274, 279
  Italian, 84, 197, 204, 205, 220, 221
  Latin, 79, 98, 166, 218
  Spanish, 9, 12-15, 17, 84, 194, 195, 197, 199, 201-211, 213-223, 279
Slavic
  Bulgarian, 13, 15, 247, 263-268, 271, 273-275, 278, 279
  Russian, 192, 247, 264, 268, 271, 274, 279
Thai, 39
Turkish, 98
Tzotzil, 93-95
Warlpiri, 24, 29, 30, 50
Larsonian shells, 28, 29, 70, 71, 74
Left Branch Condition, 268
Lethal Ambiguity, 240, 241, 246
Lexical-Functional Grammar, 1, 3, 17, 21, 26, 27, 30, 34, 35, 78, 80, 100
lexical semantics, 11, 21, 46, 48, 50
light verb, 226, 231, 233, 236, 241, 243-245
minimal domain, 233, 234, 236
Minimalist Program, 1, 19, 50, 60, 61, 101, 123-127, 157, 231, 248, 261, 263
nominative, 11, 12, 15-17, 25, 78, 79, 82, 158, 159, 163, 165, 166, 169, 170, 212, 225, 234, 239, 242, 245, 273-275
null adverbials, 205, 206, 221
object shift, 103, 106, 108-110, 112, 114, 116-119, 124, 127, 147, 150, 155, 173, 174, 178, 188, 190, 231, 232, 234, 245
obliqueness hierarchy, 35
passives, 23, 25-27, 29, 35, 47, 54, 55, 67, 75, 80-82, 85-87, 92-94, 102, 114, 134, 142, 144, 147, 164, 169, 170, 176, 185, 242, 258, 279
predicate fronting, 151, 225, 228, 231, 233, 245
predicate, core, 225, 230, 232, 233, 244
predication, 56, 84, 170, 178, 225, 226, 228, 229, 231, 233, 237, 238, 244
Principles and Parameters, 50, 63, 64, 101, 157
Projection Principle, 4, 8, 16, 55, 56, 225
prominence
  D-prominence, 13-17, 247, 272, 279
  embedding prominence, 11, 36-39, 41-44, 46, 48-50, 59, 62, 67-75
  relational prominence, 10, 11, 36-39, 41-50, 59, 62, 67-69, 73-75
  V-prominence, 13-17, 228, 247, 272, 273, 279
pseudogapping, 107-110, 120, 121
Q-feature, 12, 212-216, 223
quantifier float, 6, 173, 236, 238
quantifier lowering, 114, 115
raising, 84, 124, 125, 130, 131, 141, 142, 144, 145, 147, 151, 153, 154
  agent phrase raising, 134-138, 140, 141
  ascensions, 35, 127
  ECM, 8, 84, 101, 103, 104, 106-108, 112-116, 118, 120, 121, 125, 126, 143, 153
    raising to object, 84, 124, 125, 130, 131, 141, 142, 144, 145, 147, 151, 153, 154
  possessor raising, 124-129, 131, 133-137, 141, 145, 147, 154
  pseudo-raising constructions, 138, 140

quantifier raising, 105, 106
raising to subject, 113, 114, 141
reciprocals, 37, 41, 68, 71, 90-92,
    102, 108, 186, 188, 189, 240, 244
reflexives, 7, 14, 23-25, 28, 29, 39,
    54, 83, 90-92, 142-145, 154, 155,
    238-240, 244, 246, 249, 256, 260,
    261, 265, 266, 274, 276
    emphatic reflexives, 247, 249-251,
        254, 256-258, 260, 261, 264,
        265, 266, 268, 276
Relational Grammar, 1, 2, 3, 5, 8, 17,
    21, 24-29, 31-33, 35, 38, 39, 47,
    49, 50, 78, 82, 100, 102, 124, 127,
    131, 133, 147, 225
relational hierarchy, 35, 36, 47
Relational Succession Law, 127, 154
sentential subjects, 13, 252, 262, 264,
    266, 270
small clauses, 28, 54, 56, 167, 180,
    183-186, 191
Specified Subject Condition, 3
Split VP Hypothesis, 179, 180, 182,
    190
Standard Theory, 3, 124
subjacency, 255, 261
subject condition, 109-111
subject islands, 261, 263, 267, 269,
    270, 278
subjecthood, 33, 153, 158, 163, 176,
    177, 180, 187, 190, 225-229, 237,
    245, 247
superiority, 10, 11, 13, 15, 38, 41, 42,
    48, 117, 118, 233, 234, 246
TAM (Tense/Aspect/Mood), 229,
    232
thematic layer, 9, 10, 15, 18
thematic roles, 10, 11, 31, 35, 45, 47,
    53, 54, 56, 58, 59, 61, 62, 67, 74,
    75, 79-81, 83, 84, 86-88, 90, 96-
    98, 102, 141, 232, 233, 237, 241-
    243, 245, 263, 268
    proto-roles, 60, 61, 65, 71, 75
theoretical frameworks, see:
    Extended Standard Theory,
    Generative Semantics,
    Government and Binding theory,
    Head Driven Phrase Structure
        Grammar,
    Lexical-Functional Grammar,
    Minimalist Program,
    Principles and Parameters,
    Relational Grammar,
    Standard Theory.
Theta Criterion, 55, 56, 62, 63, 67,
    74, 75
topic, 1, 5, 18, 22, 89, 102, 151, 153,
    180, 197-203, 209, 218-222, 276
TP, 7, 9, 10, 13, 107, 108, 158, 159,
    161-163, 168, 173, 181, 184, 186,
    188, 197, 201, 211-213, 247, 272-
    275, 279
transformational syntax, 1, 3, 4, 27,
    53
T-to-C movement, 209-211, 212,
    214-216, 222
unaccusative, 4, 11, 13, 16, 47, 62,
    64, 65, 108, 134, 137, 140, 154,
    163, 164, 169, 171, 173, 176, 178,
    221, 237, 245
unergative, 16, 176, 221, 245
Uniformity of Theta Assignment
    Hypothesis, 53, 56, 57, 59-63, 67,
    74, 75, 87
Universal Alignment Hypothesis, 75
Universal Grammar, 4, 9, 25, 55, 217
VoiceP, 46, 144, 159, 177, 178, 191
vP, 5, 9, 11, 14-16, 33, 45, 47, 49, 59,
    65, 70, 129, 173, 179, 191, 193,
    213, 226, 231-238, 242-245
VP-ellipsis, 162
VP-internal subject hypothesis, 4, 6,
    9, 45, 46, 177, 178, 226
VP-shells, see:
    Larsonian shells
wh-movement, 105, 106, 110, 112,
    117, 118, 155, 201, 202, 211, 215,
    220, 262
word order
    SVO, 130, 144, 151, 152, 163, 271
    VOS, 120, 129, 130, 151, 269
    VSO, 123, 160, 162, 163, 229, 230

Studies in Natural Language and Linguistic Theory

Managing Editors

Liliane Haegeman, *University of Geneva*
Joan Maling, *Brandeis University*
James McCloskey, *University of California, Santa Cruz*

Publications

1. L. Burzio: *Italian Syntax.* A Government-binding Approach. 1986.
   ISBN Hb 90-277-2014-2; Pb 90-277-2015-0
2. W.D. Davies: *Choctaw Verb Agreement and Universal Grammar.* 1986.
   ISBN Hb 90-277-2065-7; Pb 90-277-2142-4
3. K. É. Kiss: *Configurationality in Hungarian.* 1987. ISBN Hb 90-277-1907-1;
   Pb 90-277-2456-3
4. D. Pulleyblank: *Tone in Lexical Phonology.* 1986.   ISBN Hb 90-277-2123-8;
   Pb 90-277-2124-6
5. L. Hellan and K. K. Christensen: *Topics in Scandinavian Syntax.* 1986.
   ISBN Hb 90-277-2166-1; Pb 90-277-2167-X
6. K. P. Mohanan: *The Theory of Lexical Phonology.* 1986.
   ISBN Hb 90-277-2226-9;
   Pb 90-277-2227-7
7. J. L. Aissen: *Tzotzil Clause Structure.* 1987.   ISBN Hb 90-277-2365-6;
   Pb 90-277-2441-5
8. T. Gunji: *Japanese Phrase Structure Grammar.* A Unification-based Approach.
   1987.   ISBN 1-55608-020-4
9. W. U. Wurzel: *Inflectional Morphology and Naturalness.* 1989
   ISBN Hb 1-55608-025-5; Pb 1-55608-026-3
10. C. Neidle: *The Role of Case in Russian Syntax.* 1988   ISBN 1-55608-042-5
11. C. Lefebvre and P. Muysken: *Mixed Categories.* Nominalizations in Quechua.
    1988.   ISBN Hb 1-55608-050-6; Pb 1-55608-051-4
12. K. Michelson: *A Comparative Study of Lake-Iroquoian Accent.* 1988
    ISBN 1-55608-054-9
13. K. Zagona: *Verb Phrase Syntax.* A Parametric Study of English and Spanish.
    1988   ISBN Hb 1-55608-064-6; Pb 1-55608-065-4
14. R. Hendrick: *Anaphora in Celtic and Universal Grammar.* 1988
    ISBN 1-55608-066-2
15. O. Jaeggli and K.J. Safir (eds.): *The Null Subject Parameter.* 1989
    ISBN Hb 1-55608-086-7; Pb 1-55608-087-5
16. H. Lasnik: *Essays on Anaphora.* 1989   ISBN Hb 1-55608-090-5;
    Pb 1-55608-091-3
17. S. Steele: *Agreement and Anti-Agreement.* A Syntax of Luiseño. 1990
    ISBN 0-7923-0260-5
18. E. Pearce: *Parameters in Old French Syntax.* Infinitival Complements. 1990
    ISBN Hb 0-7923-0432-2; Pb 0-7923-0433-0

Studies in Natural Language and Linguistic Theory

19. Y.A. Li: *Order and Constituency in Mandarin Chinese*. 1990
ISBN 0-7923-0500-0
20. H. Lasnik: *Essays on Restrictiveness and Learnability*. 1990
ISBN 0-7923-0628-7;
Pb 0-7923-0629-5
21. M.J. Speas: *Phrase Structure in Natural Language*. 1990
ISBN 0-7923-0755-0;
Pb 0-7923-0866-2
22. H. Haider and K. Netter (eds.): *Representation and Derivation in the Theory of Grammar*. 1991 ISBN 0-7923-1150-7
23. J. Simpson: *Warlpiri Morpho-Syntax*. A Lexicalist Approach. 1991
ISBN 0-7923-1292-9
24. C. Georgopoulos: *Syntactic Variables*. Resumptive Pronouns and A' Binding in Palauan. 1991 ISBN 0-7923-1293-7
25. K. Leffel and D. Bouchard (eds.): *Views on Phrase Structure*. 1991
ISBN 0-7923-1295-3
26. C. Tellier: *Licensing Theory and French Parasitic Gaps*. 1991
ISBN 0-7923-1311-9; Pb 0-7923-1323-2
27. S.-Y. Kuroda: *Japanese Syntax and Semantics*. Collected Papers. 1992
ISBN 0-7923-1390-9; Pb 0-7923-1391-7
28. I. Roberts: *Verbs and Diachronic Syntax*. A Comparative History of English and French. 1992 ISBN 0-7923-1705-X
29. A. Fassi Fehri: *Issues in the Structure of Arabic Clauses and Words*. 1993
ISBN 0-7923-2082-4
30. M. Bittner: *Case, Scope, and Binding*. 1994 ISBN 0-7923-2649-0
31. H. Haider, S. Olsen and S. Vikner (eds.): *Studies in Comparative Germanic Syntax*. 1995 ISBN 0-7923-3280-6
32. N. Duffield: *Particles and Projections in Irish Syntax*. 1995
ISBN 0-7923-3550-3;
Pb 0-7923-3674-7
33. J. Rooryck and L. Zaring (eds.): *Phrase Structure and the Lexicon*. 1996
ISBN 0-7923-3745-X
34. J. Bayer: *Directionality and Logical Form*. On the Scope of Focusing Particles and Wh-in-situ. 1996 ISBN 0-7923-3752-2
35. R. Freidin (ed.): *Current Issues in Comparative Grammar*. 1996
ISBN 0-7923-3778-6; Pb 0-7923-3779-4
36. C.-T.J. Huang and Y.-H.A. Li (eds.): *New Horizons in Chinese Linguistics*. 1996 ISBN 0-7923-3867-7; Pb 0-7923-3868-5
37. A. Watanabe: *Case Absorption and WH-Agreement*. 1996
ISBN 0-7923-4203-8
38. H. Thráinsson, S.D. Epstein and S. Peter (eds.): *Studies in Comparative Germanic Syntax*. Volume II. 1996 ISBN 0-7923-4215-1
39. C.J.W. Zwart: *Morphosyntax of Verb Movement*. A Minimalist Approach to the Syntax of Dutch. 1997 ISBN 0-7923-4263-1; Pb 0-7923-4264-X

Studies in Natural Language and Linguistic Theory

40. T. Siloni: *Noun Phrases and Nominalizations*. The Syntax of DPs. 1997
ISBN 0-7923-4608-4
41. B.S. Vance: *Syntactic Change in Medieval French*. 1997 ISBN 0-7923-4669-6
42. G. Müller: *Incomplete Category Fronting*. A Derivational Approach to Remnant Movement in German. 1998 ISBN 0-7923-4837-0
43. A. Alexiadou, G. Horrocks and M. Stavrou (eds.): *Studies in Greek Syntax*. 1998 ISBN 0-7923-5290-4
44. R. Sybesma: *The Mandarin VP*. 1999 ISBN 0-7923-5462-1
45. K. Johnson and I. Roberts (eds.): *Beyond Principles and Parameters*. Essays in Memory of Osvaldo Jaeggli. 1999 ISBN 0-7923-5501-6
46. R.M. Bhatt: *Verb Movement and the Syntax of Kashmiri*. 1999
ISBN 0-7923-6033-8
47. A. Neeleman and F. Weerman: *Flexible Syntax*. A Theory of Case and Arguments. 1999 ISBN 0-7923-6058-3
48. C. Gerfen: *Phonology and Phonetics in Coatzospan Mixtec*. 1999
ISBN 0-7923-6034-6
49. I. Paul, V. Phillips and L. Travis (eds.): *Formal Issues in Austronesian Linguistics*. 2000 ISBN 0-7923-6068-0
50. M. Frascarelli: *The Syntax-Phonology Interface in Focus and Topic Constructions in Italian*. 2000 ISBN 0-7923-6240-3
51. I. Landau: *Elements of Control*. Structure and Meaning in Infinitival Constructions. 2000 ISBN 0-7923-6620-4
52. W.D. Davies and S. Dubinsky (eds.): *Objects and other Subjects*. Grammatical Functions, Functional Categories and Configurationality. 2001
ISBN 1-4020-0064-2; Pb 1-4020-0065-0

Kluwer Academic Publishers – Dordrecht / Boston / London